PROFILES IN JAZZ

SIDNEY BECHET

PROFILES IN JAZZ

From Sidney Bechet to John Coltrane

Raymond Horricks

Transaction Publishers
New Brunswick (U.S.A.) and London (U.K.)

Library of Congress Catalog Number: 91-9434
ISBN: 0-88738-432-3 (cloth)
Printed in the United States of America

Library of Congress Cataloging-in-Publication Data

Horricks, Raymond, 1933–
    Profiles in jazz : from Sidney Bechet to John Coltrane / Raymond
Horricks.
        p.   cm.
    Includes discography.
    ISBN 0-88738-432-3
    1. Jazz musicians—Biography. I. Title.
ML394.H67   1991
781.65′092′2—dc20
[B]   91-9434
                                                              CIP
                                                              MN

CONTENTS

BY WAY OF INTRODUCTION...

This is a personal book collecting my recent shorter writings about jazz music, but with as its central plank a year's studying different aspects of Duke Ellington for separate issues of *Crescendo International,* the musicians' magazine. Other big names are included: from Bechet and Tatum to Dizzy and Bird; from Miles and Gerry Mulligan to Ornette and John Coltrane. In addition though there are a lot of pieces about jazzmen I consider have been unjustly neglected; and I have wanted to do something to redress the balance. For I believe the only useful purpose of jazz writing is to be of service to the music and its players: to publicise and promote, to educate with biography and musical analysis, to encourage the uninitiated to listen. This is often overlooked by certain people who prefer to call themselves critics. ('Look, Hal, if you can't write   don't you learn to write criticism?': E. Hemingway in 'A Moveable Feast'). And yet without the music and its musicians these self-styled 'critics' would be out of existence. I prefer to say that I write *about* jazz.

I also adhere to a personal belief that the men who maketh the music are as important as human beings as the content of their music-making. It is their individuality and inner talent which creates the jazz; and more so with jazz than most other forms of music. So their lives and what they are like must be considered too. The notes follow the flesh and blood.

A majority of these writings have appeared in *Crescendo International;* and I have to thank that magazine's founder and managing editor, Dennis Matthews, for never interfering with my choice of musicians to write about. Although he, like myself, was surprised how long it took to get out all I wanted to say about the greatness of Duke Ellington! Nevertheless, he thought it important and went along with it over nine monthly issues. The pieces about Art Hodes, Al Haig and Gerry Mulligan first appeared in Eddie Cook's *Jazz Journal* and the Sidney Bechet biography was originally published in Laurie Wright's *Storyville.* The section in the Duke Ellington chapter on his concert of sacred music and the John Coltrane piece, 'A Love Supreme', were written as broadcasting scripts for BFBS, as programmes in that station's religious series, *Reflections;* both commissions for which I have to thank producer Ted King.

A final point, but one I find significant. While naturally American musicians predominate, there are pieces included about an Englishman, a Frenchman and an Australian. And these three are there on their merit. A sure sign that what originally grew out of Congo Square in New Orleans has now become a truly international musical language.

R.H.

CHAPTER ONE

SIDNEY BECHET

That note you hold, narrowing and rising, shakes
Like New Orleans reflected on the water

—Philip Larkin

What must it be like to be the second greatest soloist of the first, 'classic' period of jazz music and to be made to feel it? Frustrating? Perhaps even infuriating? Or is it simply a thing to shrug off because one also knows that what one is doing is good anyway?

For all of his working life, Sidney Bechet had to contend with the pre-eminence of Louis Armstrong. And not just in musical terms. Until the final few years and the god-like position he held with the French fans, the clarinettist/soprano-saxist had never enjoyed anything like financial security. Often in the 1930s his instruments were in hock. And once he had to go round to Mezz Mezzrow's flat and pull a knife before he got paid. It was the only money he received that week. But then Bechet didn't have Joe Glaser looking after his interests.

Glaser was one of the most extraordinary men I've ever met—which, when it happened, happened in his room at the Savoy Hotel, London, where I'd gone to discuss the possibility of recording Lionel Hampton. In the early minutes of any business-meeting he would do his damnedest to be 100% intimidating; his way, as he pointed out later, of 'softening up' the opposition. After this though, he became extremely efficient and even reasonably fair. 'There's gotta be somethin' in it for everyone, kid' he grunted, giving me a slap across the shoulders. 'C'mon, let's have a whisky now.'

Over his second large one he started reminiscing—quite sentimentally—about the 1920s and when he ran all the whorehouses on the South Side of Chicago for Al Capone. 'Yes, those were great days,' he recalled between slurps, 'better than the music business. Not so many pressures about then.' Not even from a Thompson sub-machine gun? I wondered!

However: the fact remains that Joe Glaser was second to none when it came to protecting and getting work for those jazz artists he had under management contracts. And at the top of his roster were Louis Armstrong and Jack Teagarden. (He was, incidentally, godfather to Big Tea's son.) Louis, of course, gained worldwide acceptance as the first true genius of jazz. Nevertheless, to begin with, Glaser made sure he was *heard* by the world and always properly presented; and then by shrewd business negotiations he turned the trumpeter into a millionaire.

1

Alas, for Bechet, there wasn't anyone in his life to effect this kind of push, and for years on end he was just scuffling.

But yet in terms of sheer emotion and actual dominance over his chosen instruments, Bechet's music-making was as finely developed as Armstrong's. The great trumpeter had revolutionised jazz phrasing; giving it fresh contours, adhesive form and a more variable set of dynamics. In addition he had wrenched the improvising player out of the typical New Orleans frontline and set him on the road to becoming a virtuoso soloist. Sidney, for his part, within the distinctive vibrato of his sound and the urgency and intensity of his melodic lines, introduced an element of *grand passion*, making him the best clarinettist to hail from New Orleans. While on soprano-saxophone he headed the field until his death in 1959—when the leader's jersey passed first to Steve Lacy and then to the totally radical John Coltrane.

I make no idle claims for him. I have no need to when there is the enormous authority of Duke Ellington to call upon. Duke always insisted that Bechet personified the Crescent City for him: ' . . . the foundation, the symbol of jazz, the greatest of all the originators. He always played the same way, the same way then as before he died.'

Eventually in France they named streets after him.

Sidney traced his ancestry back to a grandfather called Omar, who was a runaway slave and later died for his belief that man should be free. There is a marvellously moving chapter about him in 'Treat It Gentle,' the autobiography published in 1960: 'Omar . . . could do anything. He could sing, he danced, he was the leader. It was natural to him; and everyone followed him. Sundays when the slaves would meet—that was their free day—he beat out rhythms on the drums at the Square—Congo Square they called it—and they'd all be gathered there around him. They waited for him to start things: dances, shouts, moods even. He had a power. He was a strong man. No one had to explain notes or rhythm or feeling to him. It was all there inside him, something he was always sure of. All the things that was happening to him outside, they had to get there to be measured—there inside him where the music was.

'He made his own drums out of skins of a pig or a horse-hide. He knew horns. And when he wasn't working or hunting, he'd try them out.'

Sidney himself was born on May 14, 1897, and his earliest musical memories were also of the great square in New Orleans. 'Back in those days, like I said: Sundays were free for the Negroes. They'd be sleeping and they'd never know the time, but there was a clock for them in the dawn when it would come, and the dawn it woke them natural-like. All they felt, all that struggled to wake them up was there was work all day until night. Sometimes, if they dreamed, things would come to them out of Africa, things they'd heard about or had seen. And in all that recollecting, somehow there wasn't any of it that didn't have part of a music-form in it. Maybe they'd hear someone from one tribe signalling to another, beating the drums for a feast maybe. They'd sleep and it would come to them out of the bottom of that dream. They'd hear the drums of it, all sizes and kinds of drums. They'd hear the chants and the dance calls. And always they'd hear that voice from the other tribe, talking across the air from somewhere else.'

So, first there were the drums of Congo Square. And then there were the brass and reed bands . . . marching bands. The young boy was inspired! At six he borrowed his brother Leonard's clarinet, and within a few days found he could knock a tune out on it. After this there was no going back. Aged eight he became the *protégé* of George Bacquet, the famed clarinettist with John Robichaux's band, which was a kind of 'open Sesame' for him as regards New Orleans jazz. While still in his 'teens, he played with Freddie Keppard, Jack Carey, Bunk Johnson, Buddy Petit and the Eagle Band. From 1914 to 1916 he toured with Clarence Williams, then returned to the Crescent City to play with King Oliver's Olympia Band before moving north to Chicago and New York. In 1920 he visited Europe for the first time with Will Marion Cook's Southern Syncopated Orchestra and, while in Paris, attracted the attention of the great classical conductor Ernest Ansermet.

He stayed on in the French capital, working with Bennie Peyton, and it was also around this period that he began to play soprano-saxophone as well as the clarinet. He was obviously a very talented jazzman who would soon become a great one, but two years later when he returned to the U.S. he found work scarce. He made his first, and now justly celebrated, records with Clarence Williams' Blue Five; otherwise nobody seemed to know him—or even want to know him. He toured Europe again, firstly with Josephine Baker and the Black Revue (he had an affair with the beauty on the boat over) and again in 1928 with Noble Sissle's orchestra. But in 1929 he got into trouble in Paris and spent eleven months in jail. He'd been involved in a shooting incident with banjoist Gilbert 'Mike' McKendrick, although it was triggered off by another American, pianist Glover Compton. Sidney had had a tough upbringing, and like many of his fellow-musicians carried a licensed revolver for protection. Glover picked the fight, but unfortunately in the ensuing shoot-out a passing Frenchwoman was injured and Bechet took the rap.

Sidney did his time, and was then forced back to New York, his work permit having been revoked by the French authorities. He arrived in Manhattan just after the stock market crash. So he rejoined Noble Sissle and travelled to Berlin and then on to Russia, going as far south as Odessa. That was in 1931. The following year he led a six-piece band with trumpeter Tommy Ladnier at The Savoy in New York City. 'That was *the* band . . . the best band,' he recalled later. 'People liked it and we were all musicianers who understood what jazz really meant. We didn't have to make any arrangements . . . we just followed the old school and we all felt the same way.' After this he played with Lorenzo Tio at The Nest and he got to know another trumpeter, Roy Eldridge, who was working nearby at Small's Cabaret. But by now he was on the downward path as regards jobs. In 1938 he cut his first recordings as a leader. But by the end of that year both his clarinet and his soprano-sax were lying in a pawnshop window.

'Well, by then things were pretty bad, and for a while there Tommy(Ladnier) and I had a tailor shop up by St. Nicholas Avenue. It wasn't any shop for making suits—just a pressing and repairing place and we called it the Southern Tailor Shop. Tommy, he used to help out shining shoes. We were pretty easygoing with the money side of the business, but we got along. A lot of musicians who didn't have jobs, and some who did, used to come, and we'd have our sessions right there in the back of the shop!' When he had his instruments.

The 1940s were not much better. For a time he had a trio at Nick's in Greenwich Village, and he was particularly grateful to Eddie Condon who used him for Town Hall concerts. He had a spell in Chicago with Vic Dickenson and 'Big Sid' Catlett, but mostly his life remained uncomfortably close to the breadline. Until 1949 that is, when he returned to Paris and immediately created a sensation . . .

Which is ironic if one considers just how remarkable a jazz player Bechet had become by this time. Nat Hentoff has written of the tremendous impact Sidney made on him in the 1940s: 'The first jazz musician I remember seeing. I was twelve, and had evaded the bouncer's eye at a Boston night-club. I'd heard Bechet's throaty, swooping soprano-saxophone on recordings, but I wasn't prepared for the visual power of the man. Chunky, with a deceptively benign face and a soft Creole-drawl voice . . . he changed into a demonic top sergeant when he raised his long, straight soprano-sax, stomped out the beat, and hurled his band as if with his fist into the music.'

What he says is more than justified by the existing recordings. Fortunately there are a good number of these, and mostly they've remained available.

On clarinet there is *Blues In Thirds*, a jazz 'classic' by any standards. A 1940 trio recording for RCA Victor with pianist Earl Hines and Baby Dodds on drums (or traps, as he insisted on calling them), it is a superb example of what Max Harrison has referred to as Bechet's 'combination of violence and sensual beauty, a polarity met elsewhere in jazz, yet rarely in such strength. Violence . . . communicated through the intensity of his execution and the virtuoso athleticism of phrases whose emphasis still leaves the impression there is further power in reserve.' He agrees that, at his finest, Bechet conveys a passion, almost an ecstasy, that very few other jazz masters have paralleled, 'and which aptly mirrors his dominating personality and restless, wandering life.'

But the majority of Sidney's recordings feature his soprano-playing, and here any choice is bound to be arbitrary. I suppose the nearest thing to the emotional authority of *Blues In Thirds* is the 12-inch *Summertime* cut in 1939 for Blue Note with Meade Lux Lewis on piano and Sid Catlett on drums, which is remarkable both for its embellished solemnity and a deep, but controlled feeling. Other superior Blue Note titles include *Dear Old Southland* (1940), *Muskrat Ramble* and *Blue Horizon* (1944) and *Jackass Blues,* which, despite its opening imitation of the animal's braying, is otherwise a deeply serious and most dramatic performance.

Also quite remarkable (for their variety) are the eight Bechet-Spanier Big Four tracks cut for the Hot Record Society in 1940. With this, piano-less, group, which in some ways anticipates the Gerry Mulligan Quartet of the 1950s, Sidney's attack and technical command over the soprano are very much to the fore, while the quality of his counterpoint with cornetist Muggsy Spanier is a model for its empathy and poise. However, the performances still express the great jazzman's attitude to his music, of needing to give it spontaneity and, above all, an authentic ring. 'You take when a high note comes through,' he once said, 'lifting and going and then stopping because there's no place else for it to go. That's stepping music—it's got to rush itself right off your voice or your horn because it's so excited. You can feel it!'

Or again, 'All the music I play is from what was finding itself in my grandfather's time. Like water moving around a stone, all silent, waiting for the stone to wear away. Because of all the strains that went to make up the spirituals, they were still unformed, still waiting for the heart of ragtime to grab them up, mix in with them, bring them out of where only a few people could feel the music and need it, bring it out to where it could say what it had to say. It's like the Mississippi. It's got its own story. There's something it wants to tell. It's all those things and more, you could say, and some I don't know how to say. It's a way of living, a blood thing inside of you.'

Another 1940 performance I especially like is *Nobody Knows The Way I Feel This Morning* by Sidney's own New Orleans Feetwarmers, again made for Victor. Another majestic blues, he can be heard on clarinet in the opening chorus and then on soprano for the closing two.

Of course, there are plenty of good stompy solos as well; with Clarence Williams, the Red Onion Jazz Babies, Noble Sissle, Trixie Smith, Jelly-Roll Morton (including the tremendous *High Society*), Cliff Jackson, Joe Sullivan and the sessions with Mezz Mezzrow and Tommy Ladnier. On *High Society* Bechet had played the traditional fast and exciting duet with Albert Nicholas on clarinet and, in 1946, he had Nicholas back beside him for what I judge the best sides cut under his own name in the last years before he settled in France. Recorded for Blue Note, the titles are *Quincy Street Stomp* (now retitled *Blame It On*

The Blues), *Old Stack O'Lee Blues, Bechet's Fantasy* and *Weary Way Blues*, and the group is completed by Art Hodes, piano, Pops Foster, bass, and Danny Alvin on drums.

I must mention too a couple of untypical, but nevertheless thoroughly entertaining novelty items he cut in the 1940s. There is a hugely funny *Muskrat Ramble* issued as Professor Sidney Bechet with Doctor Henry Levine's Barefooted Dixieland Philharmonic and a multi-tracked *Sheik Of Araby* on which he plays all six instruments. 'I started out first with the piano, and then I got the drums and my soprano on. I meant to play all the rhythm instruments first, you know, but I got all mixed up and I grabbed hold of the bass and then I got the tenor. Oh, it was a great story for the newspaper men, and they raised so much hell that the union made the company pay me for six men and it was forbidden to do it again! But . . . oddly enough right after that I met Fats Waller going into the theatre; he was playing at The Polo. So he said to me, *Bechet, I'm telling you, boy, you certainly did make that one-man-band record!* And I said, *It would have been all right if we would have had a rehearsal before,* meaning the engineer and myself, you know. But Fats, he laughed and laughed and said, *Man, how the hell you going to have a rehearsal with yourself?*

Towards the end of 1948 Sidney missed the opportunity to play at the 'Festival of Europe' in Nice because he was under contract to Jazz Limited in Chicago, and so the young Bob Wilber went instead. But the following year, when Charles Delaunay invited him to go to the Paris Jazz Fair as a soloist, he determined that nothing, absolutely nothing, would stop him from going. He'd grown weary of the itinerant life, but at the same time felt that the jazz scene in the U.S. had little left for him. The traditional jazz he heard all around him had gone stale and there was a danger he'd get stale himself eventually. Also, the bottom had dropped out of his recording activities. He'd thought he was a partner/shareholder with Mezz Mezzrow in the King Jazz label, and had cut some fine titles with the likes of Hot Lips Page, Mezz himself, Sammy Price, Wellman Braud and Kaiser Marshall. Then he found there was no money left in the company and Mezzrow had done another of his disappearing acts. Suddenly, the prospect of being in France again appeared immensely attractive to him. It was 'nearer to Africa' too, and to what he knew of his family, in particular the inspiration of Omar.

There was still trouble over breaking with Jazz Limited. As he relates it in 'Treat It Gentle': 'I went over to the union, and I explained the whole fix and how I had an opportunity to do this jazz festival. They said, *You've got a contract, a musical contract,* and there it was.' Whereupon something snapped inside Bechet. '*I am very sorry,* I said, *I must take the full responsibility, but I'm going.'* And he did. In May of 1949 he boarded a plane in New York—together with Charlie Parker, Miles Davis, Lips Page, Tadd Dameron and others—and literally flew towards his years of fame.

Having been present as an impressionable late teenager at those riotous scenes in Paris whenever Sidney appeared, all I can say now, so many years later, is that they make me think of Woodstock and today's bigger 'pop' occasions, but brought about by an ageing smiling, slightly bewildered black American. And why hadn't America seen him in this light? He wasn't playing any differently. If anything, the musical settings and accompaniments were inferior to those available in the States. Nevertheless, the French fans went wild. They even threatened the lives of officials when, after nearly a dozen encores, the curtains finally came down; they mobbed him in the streets, and they begged him never to leave them. Between the Sunday and the Tuesday Bechet became a national hero.

When the Fair ended he did return to America, but only on a temporary basis. He accepted a number of gigs—at Jimmy Ryan's and then the Blue Note in Chicago—but these were just to tide him over while he made preparations to leave. 'Silence, exile and cunning,' James Joyce said of the period when he was removing himself from Dublin to Europe, and this was very much Sidney Bechet's attitude to the Stateside scene. It had failed the talent he knew he possessed, and he was more than ready to go. Following the adulation at and after the Paris Jazz Fair, Charles Delaunay had no trouble in arranging as much well-paid work in France as Sidney could handle; plus options to play in Holland, Belgium and Switzerland. And from 1953 French Vogue offered him a recording contract which, once signed, would last the rest of his life.

He arrived back in Paris in late September, 1949 to the sort of welcome only a (newly elected) President of the Republic or the nation's new favourite film-star might expect. He sniffed around the jazz clubs of St. Germain-des-Pres and decided he'd like to have Claude Luter's band back him. Then his second session for Vogue produced *Les Oignons,* the 'hit' single of that year in France.

The rest reads like a publicity hand-out. Apart from his appearances at the Vieux Colombier and different jazz clubs, he became almost as big a name in France's theatres as Edith Piaf and, much earlier Colette and Maurice Chevalier; while no festival was complete without Bechet, even as far afield as Algeria. With the francs pouring in, he bought a large, rambling, music-strewn house on the outskirts of the capital, right by the Seine where he could indulge his other passion, for fishing. And a request for French citizenship brought forth no mention of his earlier activities in the country from the authorities.

Then in 1951, at Juan-les-Pins, during Mardi Gras, he married a Frenchwoman. The excited crowds were the biggest seen on the Riveria since Aly Khan's marriage to Rita Hayworth.

As for the recordings of these final years, their sales continued to be enormous. In 1954 he celebrated the millionth sale with a free concert at The Olympia in Paris; and this was before the release of *Petite Fleur*, his most popular composition of all. He also composed a ballet, 'The Night Is A Witch', recorded under the direction of Jacques Bazire, and appeared in two films, 'Serie Noire' with Erich von Stroheim and 'Blues' with Viviane Romance.

There has been a critical tendency to either dismiss or damn with faint praise the French Vogue sessions—although nobody else has gone so far as the splenetic outburst of film-composer Michel Legrand: 'Bechet reminds me of a pig!' (I will refrain from comment on Monsieur Legrand's own vocal endeavours.) Again though, I think this is to do the player an injustice. Admittedly, there is nothing to equal the *Texas Moaner* of 1924, a *Blues In Thirds* or the exhilarating *Egyptian Fantasy* of 1941; but if there are no more jazz classics, there are still many solos which are a delight to the ear.

Forget the ones made with inferior French 'trad' accompaniments and concentrate instead on those he cut with American visitors or expatriates (now repackaged on two double albums by Vogue, with useful notes by Charles Fox). There are good tracks with Lil Armstrong and Zutty Singleton. Others team Sidney with Bill Coleman or Sammy Price's Texas Bluesicians, and there are six very powerful performances with Jonah Jones, the former Cab Calloway trumpet star. But best of the lot, in my opinion, are the fourteen tracks recorded with the Martial Solal Trio in March and June of 1957. Solal is an Algerian-born pianist, and also a modernist—deeply influenced by Bud Powell and Hampton Hawes as well as by Art Tatum. Still Sidney had heard him playing in the next studio and immediately wanted to record with him. At their first session they had Americans Lloyd Thompson and Al Levitt on bass and drums; for the second it was Pierre Michelot on bass and another expatriate, the great Kenny 'Klook' Clarke on drums. Practically everything was done in one 'take'. But the performances are a revelation with the soprano soaring and free and Solal never needing to compromise his own style in the backing. Who says the older jazzmen didn't or couldn't understand the music of the next generation . . .

This reference to age brings me to one other biographical detail I must mention. When Sidney died in 1959 he was sixty-two and actually passed away on his own birthday. He'd been feeling ill for some time, but far from seeking sympathy said, 'I'm an old man, I can't keep hanging on. I'm even wanting to go, waiting, longing to hear my peace.' Moreover, he didn't ask for the blues to be played at his funeral. He was mourned of course, and nowhere more than in France. But typically, his last thoughts were about jazz itself. Not his personal importance within it, which he knew was secure; but the music's durability and strength. 'I'd like to hear it all one more time,' he said. 'I'd like to sit in a box at some performance and see all I saw years ago and hear all I heard way back at the start. I want to sit there and you could come in and find me in that box and I'd have a smile on my face. What I'd be feeling is, THE MUSIC, IT HAS A HOME'.

1985

For much, much more about Bechet I recommend the reader to seek out John Chilton's full-length, definitive biography of 1987, published by Macmillan, 'Sidney Bechet, The Wizard Of Jazz'. Plus, naturally, the autobiography, 'Treat It Gentle'—perhaps the best book ever written by a jazz musician, or as Sidney would prefer to say, 'musicianer'.

CHAPTER TWO

ART HODES

Custodian Of The Blues

Sometimes, sitting and listening to this man play, if I close my eyes the colour contrasts begin to blur and then disappear. No more black and white. Instead certain silhouettes mentally pass in review: of Leroy Carr, of Jimmy Yancey in his more reflective moods and others important to the history of a particular form of music-making. All of them encapsulated in the style of a pianist who is very straight, very direct, as economic as Count Basie and who makes every note tell the truth, not just about how he himself feels, but also of the roots about which he is bedded and has been so thoroughly educated.

Of the three pianists I most respect who came from what can be called, but only for convenience, the white Chicagoan school of jazz, the late Joe Sullivan echoed—at least as it sounds to me—the rag and stride players he heard during his childhood. While Jess Stacy, great performances with Bud Freeman and George Wettling and accompanying Lee Whiley notwithstanding, was destined to build a lasting monument to himself within the best big band Benny Goodman ever led. Art Hodes, the present survivor of the three, speaks to us via his fingers about a lifetime's obsession with the Blues (I use the capital 'B' deliberately here) and because, or one suspects, he cannot prevent his outflow referring to them. After all, he has a most extensive knowledge of popular songs. But catch him improvising over the chords of *It Ain't Necessarily So* or *Someone To Watch Over Me*. The structural differences between 12 and 32 or 64 bars become unimportant. You will hear the blues: in feeling, in essence, in a beautiful simplicity. And they have been there, ingrained, ever since Louis Armstrong (personally) made sure that Art got to know their real meaning.

When I first met Art and his wife at the *Grande Parade du Jazz* at Cimiez in 1985, he gave me a small, folded-over business card: which gives his present address in Park Forest, Illinois, a township approximately 35 miles outside Chicago. On the front though it just states: *Did You Say Music?* Well, that is how he has passed a very long career; and even now he talks of the frustration during any period when he isn't used enough.

Undeterred by time and age he played some of the finest late-night sets I've heard over seven Summers covering the Nice Festival. Since when—I'm privileged to add—we have become friends.

However, profiles become better if one can worry out the actual beginnings. In the case of Arthur W. Hodes these originated in Russia; at Nikoliev to be precise, where the first day of his life was November 14, 1904. 'The name *Hodes* is what I inherited . . . and I've found others both here and in Europe with the same name. I believe from tales I heard around the house that my family left Russia because of, one, the military problems, two, trouble that my dad may have incurred, he could be very physical if accosted, and three, for a better life. My dad was a tinsmith both in Russia and in the States.' Both his father and uncle sang with their local church choir in Russia. But later on, in America his mother would be a stronger musical inspiration. For safety's sake his father wanted the boy to study civil engineering. But when he opted for music his mother urged him on—and made sure his lessons were all paid up.

The family emigrated to the United States when he was six months old. And found a cheap apartment in industrial Chicago, that amazing city which was, and has remained such a large chunk of Art's personal destiny. With work nearby his father called it 'home'.

Of Chicago itself Louis Sullivan, its most famous architect and the man who conceived the first skyscraper, once said, he saw the place as more than a city of things: in fact as a city of Man. While Studs Terkel, a longstanding comrade of Art's, has described its being 'like an old punch–drunk fighter, swinging wild roundhouse wallops to the laughter of the *Weisenheimers* at the ringside. But when it connects—oh, baby!' And *his* other close comrade, the late Nelson Algren then added: 'Chicago's rusty heart has room both for the hustler and the square'. Also crucial to our story, by the 1920s the city had developed into a capital for booze-running gangsters and the major staging post of jazz between New Orleans and New York.

The young Hodes, in his mid-teens, did most of his piano studying at Hull House, a noted 'settlement' house founded by the admirable Jane Addams. 'It was a course designed for poorer kids. But nothing wrong with the teaching'. Benny Goodman was another who studied there.

From Hull House Art turned the ignition-key on a professional career by playing at *barmitzvahs* and weddings. Anything he could get, in fact. Then, in 1925 he landed his first regular job as a soloist: at the Rainbow Gardens. 'It wasn't an easy gig,' he says. 'I had to play from 9 pm to 4 am. There was no such thing as a jukebox, of course. Plus the drinkers didn't like quiet. So I couldn't even go to the bathroom for more than a couple of minutes'. And he emphasises that he wasn't yet into jazz or the blues. 'No, I'd heard Butterbeans and Susie, and I was a rhythm man from the start. Nevertheless, my repertoire up to this date was based on popular songs of the day. Numbers like *I Wonder What Became Of Sally* and *Ain't She Sweet*'.

He was introduced to some of the authentic early jazz by bassist Earl Murphy. However, the real watershed came when Wingy Manone introduced him to Louis Armstrong. 'I'd gotten to know Wingy and later I roomed with him for a couple of years. Anway, he fixed the meeting with LA, and not only was I knocked out musically but Louis took to me as a person. Started taking me around with him. Into joints where there was all this black music I'd never known existed before. Jazz—and wow!—those great blues singers and guitarists and pianists. Louis made sure I completed my musical education!'

About the pianists, he says, 'They were quite different to those rolling left-hand or 'stride' men like Fats Waller or James P. Johnson. That was strictly the big New York scene—so that even Jelly Roll Morton was treated like a foreigner when he first went there. The Chicago players concentrated on the blues in a very direct way. On the feeling, the expression, the message. It was such things as these which grabbed me.

'I remember one day going to a record store to buy some Louis Armstrong Hot Fives. There was a loudspeaker outside in the street, and a crowd of black people listening. It was Leroy Carr's *That's Allright*. The best blues I ever heard in my life. Just simple, beautiful music. So I bought the record and afterwards the crowd just drifted away. Strangely, that disc has never been reissued. Later on I got to hear Leroy 'live', playing with Scrapper Blackwell'.

I asked him if he'd ever managed to play a date with Louis, his genius mentor?

'No. And for one very good reason. In Chicago black was black, especially in music and entertainment. It was taboo to mix black with white. In New York things were more liberal. But in Chicago the unwritten rules remained strict. Which is why the white boys, me, Wettling, all the rest who came to be known as the Chicagoans, started forming our own bands. On the other hand I had a good nine years of hanging out with black musicians. The only thing I didn't do was sleep with them!'

Once he'd evolved with a personal jazz style, and especially grasped the full meaning of the blues and their musical cousin, boogie-woogie, Art felt confident enough to branch out. In 1926 he had toured, briefly and as an experiment with The Wolverines (Bix Beiderbecke was out of the group by then). Now he began to flex his fingers with all his leading contemporaries of the white Chicagoan school. With Gene Krupa, Frank Teschemacher, Bud Freeman, Floyd O'Brien and Muggsy Spanier. He got to know Dave Tough. And he played with various combos at the Liberty Inn, or Derby and Harry's New York Bar. Also he cemented the relationship with Wingy Manone. He even for a time played in a big band fronted by Wingy.

Meanwhile too he had been paid an absolute compliment by Omer Simeon. The great clarinettist said Hodes reminded him of Jelly Roll

Morton. At which point I should add that much of Art's subsequent career has involved him with outstanding clarinettists. With Teschemacher, Albert Nicholas, Rod Cless, Pee Wee Russell, Barney Bigard, Edmond Hall, Joe Marsala and Kenny Davern. Surprisingly not Irving Fazola. But best of all, in the 1940s Sidney Bechet. (However, more of this latter collaboration later.)

Finally: of this first, lengthy Chicago period I questioned Art about associations with the gangsters and bootleggers. 'Well,' he responded, 'I confess to drinking quite a lot myself in those days. And there was never *any* trouble getting the stuff. But I don't recall problems with the gangsters. Mezz Mezzrow fantasised too much in that book ("Really The Blues") about gangsters. Mostly they liked jazz and its musicians. Also they could be very generous, if they'd enjoyed your playing. It was only towards their rivals or the law that they turned dangerous. I played for Capone and his buddies. Although the gangster I remember most clearly was named Mangano. He had two brothers in the Musicians Union and himself played banjo, tuned guitar-style and sang dirty songs. Anyhow, he hired me for a club he had some financial interest in. One night in this club he left $100 for the band. The manager gave us $5 only—and Mangano found out. The guy never worked again and was scared shitless. Appropriately he finished up as a toilet attendant . . .'

He stayed on in Chicago until 1938. Which was long after all the other main jazzmen had departed. Even then he didn't want to go. 'Well, it's my hometown. It's not perfect, but I love the place. Always have.'

I promptly quoted Studs Terkel again: 'And Chicago is a city of working people, who came to earn their daily bread in heavy industries—steel, packing, railroads, farm equipment. They came seeking more than bread though. There has always been, in this city, this cockeyed wonder of a town, a quest for beauty.'

'Well, yes,' Art said, 'I fully agree. And incidentally, I've been pals with Studs over many years. I took part in that TV biography of him. But after Prohibition the music declined. By '38 only accordian-players were working. The need for pianists and jazz had dried up. Pee Wee was gone, Muggsy, Wettling. Even Earl Hines hit the road.'

So, albeit reluctantly, he headed for New York City. Where the next decade became the most feverish, most varied and certainly influential of his entire working life. At first though he couldn't know this. There was the immediate problem of getting a Union card.

'For three months I didn't work steady. Single engagements only. Joe Marsala hired me for his band at The Hickory House. The Union stopped it. Bunny Berigan had wanted me too.

'After the card came through I spent some time in New Jersey accompanying Frankie Laine. I actually taught him *My Desire,* the song that became his first big hit. Meanwhile an agent approached by me said, *There isn't anything in the world I wouldn't do for you.* He did nothing!'

But following getting his card he did work 'steady'. And a lot. With George Brunies, Rod Cless, and at Jimmy Ryans with his own trio *et al.* In addition he was to become a kind of house pianist for Alfred Lion's newly-formed Blue Note Records; also the only white player on Don Qualey's Solo Arts label.

In 1940 he accompanied Edmond Hall for Blue Note—and of course later took part in the classic Sidney Bechet sessions.

Suddenly he laughed, At Ryan's he'd been told: 'Don't have any pictures taken with the band. And above all don't rehearse. Otherwise you'll get your notice!' Afterwards he gravitated towards a more satisfactory situation at The Village Vanguard, where he had alongside him Wild Bill Davison and on drums Freddie Moore. Later Max Kaminsky replaced Wild Bill on trumpet.

'Also we had great singers there. Pearl Bailey sang off the floor. And there were a lot of good blues. In particular by Big Bill Broonzy, who always had a fifth of Scotch with him. He used to gargle with the stuff! Moreover it was due to Big Bill that I got to meet Leadbelly (Huddie Ledbetter). He stopped by the club one night, and Bill sang and I played *Happy Birthday* to him . . .'

Art's working stint in New York lasted with hardly a pause until 1950. During these years he recorded his own favourite solo, *K.M.H. Drag,* partly based on *Tin Roof Blues* (for Blue Note); as well as introducing what is perhaps his best-known composition, *Selection From The Gutter.* Plus making the aforementioned Sidney Bechet sessions. These date from 1944 to 1946. Sidney had re-emerged from his tailor's shop and was playing with undiminished passion and vigour. *Blue Horizon* is one of his very greatest clarinet solos; and there are good stompy items such as *Muskrat Ramble* and *Salty Dog.* Art plays underrecorded, but otherwise highly sensitive and appropriate accompaniment to Bechet's continuously unfolding *Horizon* solo. And shines on many other tracks—not least during the three numbers, *Blame It On The Blues, Weary Way Blues* and *Old Stack O' Lee Blues,* where Bechet (on soprano as well as clarinet) duets with clarinettist Albert Nicholas, recreating their old partnership from the *High Society* days with Jelly Roll Morton.

Additional notable Hodes recorded performances from this period include *Jack Dailey Blues* (with Oliver Mesheux), *Feelin' At Ease* with Albert Nicholas and Baby Dodds and a variety of titles with Mama Yancey singing: *Good Package Blues, Get Him Out Of Your System* (Art playing authentic boogie) and *Grandpa's Spells.*

But piano-playing wasn't his only jazz activity through the 1940s. For over a year he had his own radio show on WNYC, taking over from Ralph Berton, Vic's brother. 'I played records, and interviewed many musicians. 'Cow Cow' Davenport, James P. Johnson, many others. We were reaching a million listeners . . . in Connecticut, all over.

'After this I decided to organise jam sessions in Greenwich Village. I got hold of Sidney (Bechet) and we became co-leaders. Others joined in, 'Pops' Foster and so on. Sidney was tremendous then, *the* force. Yet one time I heard a 'hip' cat say to another, *Wasn't he great!*—who replied, *Yes, but he can't read.* That's one of our troubles today. There are a lot of terrific new musicians, but they don't all have that same street feeling . . .'

Also, too, there was his much-respected magazine, *The Jazz Record.*

'Around this time Jess Stacy had recommended me to Benny Goodman. But I knew I wasn't right for that job. And in my case there was too much going on in NY. Including the magazine. The *Record* ran for 5 years and went to 60 issues. From February, 1943 to November, 1947. My whole idea was to have musicians talking about other musicians—and as a result it became something of an insider, cult publication. I'd be playing nights, editing during the day. And I was lucky to have a good printer in Dale Curran. He operated a small press on 10th Street in Greenwich Village.

Copies of this magazine have been scarce of late; and consequently much sought after. But a book comprising its most interesting pieces is now available, 'Selections From The Gutter.'

'Therefore, with this much going for you, why quit New York at all? And so suddenly?'

Art gave me a sharp look, Then, 'I didn't quit, I was forced out,' he answered definitively. 'And because of the Jazz War!'

'War? You mean the traditional versus modern jazz arguments?'

'Exactly. And the chief culprit for stirring them up was Leonard Feather. Aided and abetted by Barry Ulanov. Before they came along we all used to hang out together: be-boppers, mainstreamers, traditionalists. We respected each other. And we had plenty of things in common.' [As a footnote confirming this, in my biography of Dizzy Gillespie there is a photograph of a late '40s jam session at Eddie Condon's. Apart from Dizzy and Condon himself, the players involved include Jo Jones, Milt Hinton, Gerry Mulligan, Pee Wee Russell, Bobby Hackett and Milton Jackson: *RH*]

'As regards Feather,' Art continued, 'England's export was her gain and our loss. He drove the wedge in, promoted and sensationalised a division. You have to realise the tremendous power he had accumulated by the end of the 'forties. When he arrived from London, he hustled— and before long he was the dominant broadcasting voice and magazine writer, for *Metronome, Esquire, Down Beat.* He began to organise those popularity polls. And he acted as if Jelly Roll Morton had once kicked him in the arse.

'So a lot of us got hurt. Although, note, he avoided attacking Duke Ellington—because it's now known he was working as one of the Duke's press agents. Anyway . . . he first slammed me personally via *Metronome.*

Said he could play me under the table with one hand.' [An ironic as well as a cruel remark, since Feather has no rating as a pianist with any other jazz musicians I've met: *RH*]

'After this, it got so bad that if I played *Ballin' The Jack* as a 2-beat it emptied the house. Also it cost me the album I was just about to make with Lester Young. Prez had wanted to do this, an all-blues collection. After Feather's *Metronome* attack on me the record company cancelled the date.'

Soon there was no employment at all. And he had five children. So he returned to Chicago—and near-obscurity. With the jazz and blues scene all-but dead there the 1950s represent the nadir of his professional life.

'It was bad for others too. I even heard Big Bill Broonzy get booed by his own people!'

He worked with or led various New Orleans-style groups, now dubbed as 'Dixieland', and he appeared intermittently at Rupneck's. There was never any publicity. At one stage he managed to organise a band intended as support for the Louis Armstrong All-Stars bill. It featured Pee Wee Russell, Brunies, Wild Bill, 'Pops' Foster, Zutty Singleton—and Bechet (temporarily back from France) agreed to guest. It lasted just eleven weeks. 'Temperament and booze finished that band. And I got so low and depressed, in the end I drank along with the rest of them.' He made one record: with Floyd O'Brien (for Mercury). And finally he began to teach piano—an occupation he has never since ceased to do, in between public engagements; and which would lead, eventually, after his first wife's death, to a second happy marriage. But he landed no regular solo job until 1961 when Bob Scobey visited Chicago and requested that Art be booked opposite him.

From here on things began to pick up. And then to snowball. So much so that I will have difficulty listing everything he did through the 1960s. Leonard Feather was no longer a power in the land, and Art Hodes and others he had castigated came to be revalued.

When the season with Bob Scobey ended there were invitations to tour. To visit Toronto, Denver, St. Louis, Detroit. His club dates became much more regularised. He played lots of colleges. And in 1967 he had a group of his own at Disneyland. Also there was a revival of his being used by the communications media. This included a lecture-concert programme on jazz history which appeared over Chicago's educational TV channel; a regular column, *Jazz Junction,* for the newspaper, *The Reporter;* and pieces in *Down Beat* under the headline *Sittin' In.* As regards records, there were two sets under his own name, 'Cats On The Keys' (on Con-Disc) and 'Summit Meeting' (Jazzology), plus a reunion one with Albert Nicholas (Delmark).

As a pendant to the 1960s, but perhaps not surprisingly, in 1968 he was voted Citizen of the Year by Park Forest where he'd now made a permanent home . . .

On into the 1970s and he had a call from Columbia Artists. Would he put together an all-star band for a nationwide tour? 'I was just back from playing in Denmark. But I managed to put together Wild Bill, Barney Bigard and I persuaded Condon to join us as well. The money was remarkable for those years. $250 a week for the guys, double for me. In the end it worked out that we kept going for a full year—after which, almost immediately I was off on tour again, this time with Jimmy McPartland. Seventeen weeks playing spirituals, blues and of course 'classic' traditional jazz. This last tour ended in 1973, and records of it were issued by Jazzology. After which he continued to work the festival circuit and lead his own combo. He wrote for *Esquire: Jazz, The Sweet, Slow Comeback*. He received an Emmy award in Chicago for a half-hour TV special recital. And he hosted on six national education TV shows. He made another Delmark LP, 'Bucket's Got A Hole In It' with Barney Bigard; plus a recital set, 'The Art Of Hodes' for Euphonic.

But the most memorable single 'gig' he remembers of this period occurred towards the end of the decade when he played at the birthday party Paul Newman threw for his wife Joanne Woodward. 'Again it was a call coming right of the blue, although I knew they'd heard me before this in clubs. Anyway, Paul flew me 850 miles just for the one night. I got paid, but otherwise was treated as another guest who happened to be able to entertain at the piano. And at the end Joanne said she was my No. 1 groupie!'

Which leads us into the 1980s, bringing my profile almost full-circle with out meetings at the Nice Jazz Festival.

This has been a period of at least one significant residency, several solo records and not least, the new marriage. The latter even draws an interesting parallel with the great 'cellist Pablo Casals, who also in later years married one of his pupils. Art's first wife had died. Jan (now Hodes) is a classical pianist who came to him for some jazz tuition—with the additional result. Now, at concerts, they feature two or three attractive duets, including *After Hours* and one based on Art's *Salute To 'Cow Cow' Davenport*. Jan insists Art must go on playing; and quips that she will keep him alive until he reaches his ton! (Well, Eubie Blake made it. And Art certainly doesn't look his years.)

The important residency lasted through 1981 at Hanratty's in New York and represented something other than rehabilitation. More like a jazz knighthood. 'It was publicised as, *Art Hodes returns to Hanratty's after 31 years*. And the opening night was a complete sell-out. All the big guns were there: Ertegun, Hammond, Avakian, Gabler. It was almost as if I'd never left New York!'

One LP is available of his 'live' performances at Hanratty's, 'Someone To Watch Over Me' (Muse MR 5252). It includes excellent renderings of *Grandpa's Spells,* Hoagy Carmichael's *Georgia On My Mind,* Art's own *Plain Ol' Blues,* a thoughtful *St. Louis Blues* and a naturally livelier *Struttin' With Some Barbecue,* plus a marvellously evocative revival of *Selection From The Gutter.* When originally I reviewed this set, and with no idea I'd be bumping into Art at Nice, I wrote: 'What I like most of all about this album is that Hodes, despite devotion to his early 'hot' heroes and bluesmen . . . has in no way allowed his own playing to become mummified. He plays with an obvious feeling and, on the quicker numbers, a youthful enthusiasm—qualities which give the collection both sincerity and freshness.' Other recent recordings soon to reach our shops are a solo recital taped in Canada, "South Side Memories" (Sackville 3022); a blues collaboration suggesting many delights with trumpeter Doc Cheatham and Carrie Smith on Concord; and further sets with Milt Hinton (Muse) and Kenny Davern (Monmouth).

George Wein had booked Art once before for Nice, in 1975. During his return in 1985 he played one truly exciting set with a fellow veteran, saxist Benny Waters (83 years young); backed by the crisp drumming of Bobby Rosengarden. But for me his best moments were still to be heard at late-night recitals in the main area. Surrounded by Roman arches, tall cypresses like standing sentinels and with JVC's big balloon hovering above, a splash of red against the pale Provençal sky, then we heard Hodes as the real custodian of the blues. Reflective, but based on deep knowledge, quiet because of his delicate gradation of touch, and, thinking back on it, acutely sensitive to the entire history of blues feeling. It doesn't come to you much better than the way he expressed himself on these open-aired occasions.

Most days we'd meet up, just to talk. One morning I expressed my admiration for the late Charles Edward Smith, the American writer about jazz who can still make musicians live for me with his words: about Big Tea, Pee Wee and Billie Holiday especially. Art smiled. 'Yes, Charlie used to hang around with us all the time. And, you know, he grew with his book! Began to mouth at too great a length. So the always laid-back Eddie Condon decided to take him in hand. Said we were going somewhere where if you didn't actually play they'd shoot you! Charles Edward became human again. But really, what a lovely guy he was . . .'

More importantly, I asked him about other pianists *he* admired. I knew about Leroy Carr, Jelly Roll, Hines and, naturally, Art Tatum ('A little piece of God sat here').

But others?

'Well, I love Jay McShann—that heavy blues-style he has. Also Bud Powell, Horace Silver, Bill Evans (a beautifully delicate player) and I've been listening to the keyboard-player here with the Airto & Flora band this year, Kei Akagi. Very talented. But I stop after McCoy Tyner, another fine player. If it gets too way out then my attention starts to wander. Much as I admire good schooling, the message is more important.

'I haven't stopped listening,' he concluded. 'And I'll never stop playing. Okay, Jan insists I go on playing. Really though, it's not difficult to convince me. I feel music and the blues deep inside me still. It isn't a dead issue.'

1985

Selections From The Gutter
Portraits from *The Jazz Record*
edited by Art Hodes and Chadwick Hansen. University of California Press, Berkeley.

'This magazine speaks for the music and its musicians,' Art Hodes wrote of *The Jazz Record* in 1945. 'To set down those things a horn itself cannot express, to bring alive the personalities on your record labels, and to encourage the musicians and those who like their work to keep playing the real and authentic jazz.' This book is a rich anthology drawn from the magazine's pages; and very well illustrated, including reproductions of many of the original covers.

Even the most articulate of jazzmen rarely find time to talk about their art. Still less to find a suitable outlet. Hodes made them make time and provided the outlet. Lots of these musicians are now gone from us forever: and this is the only book where we can find these people talking about each other. Of all the white Chicagoans Hodes was probably the closest to black roots; and to the original Blues: which the collection reflects. There are marvellous insights on Louis Armstrong by Wingy Manone and Art himself. Together with cryptic gems by Cow Cow Davenport and Montana Taylor. Big Bill Broonzy gives us a several-page autobiography. While drummer Kaiser Marshall remembers when Satchmo first hit New York, and another drummer, Fred Moore, details the troubles which beset King Oliver's last tour.

There is a great spirit of place. Together with a very full coverage of the multiple problems which accompany the jazz life. There are too portraits of underrated players such as Rod Cless and Joe Darensbourg. Plus the big names: Gene Sedric is good on Waller and I particularly like the long profile of Muggsy Spanier by Alma Hubner.

All in all as enthralling to read as 'Hear Me Talkin' To Ya'; with the care and concern of Hodes coming at you from every page.

1986

CHAPTER THREE

BUDD JOHNSON

Workhorse Into Thoroughbred

Pity the deputy leader of a band. Not for him the triumph at the end of the night when the audience yells the name of the man standing out in front. Nor the kudos that attaches to a good press review. Not even a share in the royalties—unless the boss is feeling in generous mood.

On the other hand, and for not much more salary than the rest of the players he is usually expected to put the band together, drill it, discipline it, take it through the new scores, boost the morale of the younger members, sort things out when the coach is late or the road manager's had two too many—*and still be outstanding on his own instrument.*

Marshall Royal, an obvious example, spent something like two-and-a-half decades doing it with the Count Basie band—and has lived to tell the tale. But then 'it wasn't all that difficult,' he told me: 'Because Base himself trusted me and liked me to get on with things. With other leaders, sure, the job can be a nightmare.'

I was once privileged to be present when he rehearsed the Basie saxophone section (with which he played lead alto), and it was one of the most absorbing attendances I've ever experienced in music. The respect received by Marshall from gifted soloists such as the Franks Foster and Wess and the veteran baritone-saxist, the late Charlie Fowlkes was truly amazing. With an economy of words but a wealth of practical demonstration he first of all *showed* the way and then led them through it. 'Whether you're hard or easy with the guys at any specific moment is largely a matter of intuition, and I suppose experience,' he said afterwards. 'However, it's no good hiring talented players and then demanding of them things you can't do yourself. Base has always had great soloists, but the crown of the band is still the absolute togetherness of the ensemble . . .'

Budd Johnson has probably put together more bands than anyone in the history of jazz. For Earl Hines and Benny Goodman and Gil Evans, to name only three of the most distinguished. While his organisational duties have resulted in his touring with nearly every modern leader of consequence: from Cab Calloway, Billy Eckstine and Dizzy Gillespie to Woody Herman, the revived Tommy Dorsey band of 1966 under Urbie Green, Earl Hines again, Quincy Jones, Basie, Sy Oliver and not least the Louis Armstrong 'tribute' group which toured Russia in 1975.

Over the years it almost became a standard cry to 'send for Johnson' whenever the band had a particularly tricky schedule to get through. And the man himself seemed not only capable but actually to enjoy the responsibility heaped on his shoulders. He became a regular workhorse who was also thoroughly liked by both leaders and sidemen for his consistently unselfish approach to their day-to-day problems and the general demands of music-making. In addition to which he proved a marvellous utility man to have in a band because he plays all the saxophones, even soprano, plus good clarinet, is a brilliant rehearser and has a very sound knowledge of composition and orchestration.

The only snag was that all of this valuable and long-standing service to the big band business tended to obscure just how fine he can be as a tenor-saxophone soloist. There are odd choruses and half-choruses of his improvisation scattered about on innumerable records going back to Earl Hines' 'Grand Terrace Swing' sessions of 1939/40 (which featured several of Budd's most exciting arrangements as well). But items like *Father Steps In* and *Tantalizing A Cuban* are truly tantalising on account of their being mere moments of revelation by a man who until recently has been an overlooked 'classic' tenor-player. For let's make no mistake about this: Budd Johnson merits mention in the same breath as Coleman Hawkins, Ben Webster and Don Byas on the one hand, and Lester Young and even as far as John Coltrane on the other. A soloist of great ideas and invention, with a superb technique and, above all, the natural curiosity to keep him mentally young. He has worked his playing through every major school of jazz tenor and is still in 1983 able to play alongside the youngsters—a voice of authority whose big, booting tone is in no way compromised by his likelihood to slip in some very modern running of the chord changes.

Fortunately, since the early 1970s we have been treated to rather more of him. He'd once said: 'In the music business you're there to work and to make money,' but at last he cut out the big band work and the one-nighters. He took up golf, started going to the Museum of Modern Art and now spends a lot more time with his family. He began to work more selectively in the context of smaller groups or often with just a rhythm section—and obviously developed an increased taste for it, because this is how he continues to work, dividing up his time with lecturing and composing. He's much in demand for jazz festivals; and both with these and on disc has recently revealed a previously unsuspected, and therefore unexploited, ability to improvise truly along solos in a 'jam session' format which offer vitality, abundant facility over the tenor and a rich flow of the imagination, whether the theme is Charlie Parker's *Confirmation* or an Earl Hines' type mainstream number.

It's especially true of his staggeringly energetic and yet well-thought-out blues solos—with often twenty choruses ripping forth before he takes the instrument from his mouth. But then he has a somewhat different and certainly refreshing attitude towards the blues. Although as a youngster he'd first absorbed them from singers, he doesn't believe they should continue to be associated exclusively with race or even with their traditional twelve-bar form. He points to the white players he specially likes playing the blues—Zoot Sims and Pee Wee Russell, for instance. And as he explained to Graham Colombe in an interview of 1974: 'People always thinks of the blues as being just one way, but there's all different kinds of blues. Everybody plays twelve-bar blues but you can play blue on any song. And that's part of my style—to play blue. I like the blue notes. Then there's a happy feeling—create a little happiness—but I like to interject a little blues in there because . . . it sort of identifies me in a way.' Which is a fairly modest way of describing some of the most intense and impassioned blues blowing of recent years.

Budd is actually a Texan, born at Dallas in 1910, and he first studied music with the daughter of Booker T(aliaferro) Washington, the Negro educationalist and writer. His baptised Christian name is *Albert*, and to add to the contradictions of his earlier career he toured as a drummer for at least two years before taking up the saxophones. Which he found came to him naturally. (So much so that he was later to give the formidable Ben Webster *his* first lessons on them.) He then went North. Initially to Kansas City, where he got to know Walter Page's Blue Devils and had a job with the George E. Lee band. One week when he was broke he had free meals in a restaurant run by Jimmy Rushing's father.

Afterwards he moved on to Chicago where he played with both Teddy Wilson and Louis Armstrong before joining Earl Hines at the Grand Terrace Club in September, 1934. Al Capone owned a quarter of it and his hoods were regular patrons. But there was nothing wrong with the music and Budd stayed on until 1942. When the long years with the other big bands began . . .

One can also date his reverting to small group jazz by cross-reference to the friendship and association with Hines. He worked with the pianist's quartet from 1965 to '69, travelling in Eastern Europe and South America as well as all over the United States. After which he formed his own JPJ Quartet with Bill Pemberton and Oliver Jackson. Apart from club appearances they played seminars to a total of more than 300,000 students.

There have been lots of records too (and at last a number of longer solos). Over the years since first playing in the Grand Terrace band Budd has been on sessions with Sarah Vaughan, Dizzy Gillespie, Bennie Green, Coleman Hawkins (an accolade in itself, being accepted by the pioneer of jazz tenor), Booker Pittman, Milt Hinton, Roy Eldridge and Red Richards.

Some of the best and most exciting of his solos on record though have been those made with the Hines Quartet. Their 1967 sessions with

Jimmy Rushing were particularly rewarding ones—especially for Budd's tribute to Sidney Bechet, a dazzling and dramatic soprano solo version of *Summertime*, originally prepared for the Newport Jazz Festival of that year. Also for four flying choruses on Earl's *Changing The Blues*.

However, I want to conclude by drawing the reader's attention to the *La Nevada* track on Gil Evans' 'Out Of The Cool' album (Impulse A-4). Because as clearly as any performance I know by him it illustrates how his music-making has progressed over the years: all of its emotionalism and verve becoming reconciled and integrated with a further exploration of technique and an acute awareness of the new directions John Coltrane had set up. That the tenorman was working with the most progressive jazz composer and bandleader apart from Duke Ellington suddenly made many things possible for him.

Budd, as usual, had been very active in the organisation of this particular Evans band, which made its debut at New York's Jazz Gallery in 1960. It featured a remarkable collection of sidemen. Johnny Coles and Phil Sunkel (trumpets), Jimmy Knepper, Keg Johnson and Tony Studd (trombones), Bill Barber (tuba), Eddie Caine, Budd and Bob Tricarico (saxes and woodwind, including a bassoon), Gil on piano, Ray Crawford (electric guitar), Ron Carter (bass), and two drummers: Elvin Jones and Charlie Persip. They recorded under the aegis of Creed Taylor and the fifteen-and-a-half minutes of *La Nevada* constitute a jazz masterpiece, with brilliant ensemble passages (developed in action) encapsulating several of the most emotive individual improvisations of their decade.

The actual composition is short and had been recorded previously under the title *Theme*. It reflects Gil's long-standing interest in Spanish music and is exactly four bars in structure. But its moving back and forth from G minor seventh to G major gives it a memorable melodic quality while allowing for a remarkable degree of freedom in the solos. There's a gradual build-up of the rhythm section—Elvin Jones playing kit and cymbals and Charlie Persip fleshing it out on maraccas—before the theme is introduced via the three trombones. It's then taken up by the full band and the solos follow—but with different players or groups of players embellishing the lines in an entirely unplanned and consequently marvellously stimulating way. Behind Budd's solo, for instance, there are some groovy prop-chords by Gil, then a variation by the trumpets (muted), and at a one point the woodwind combine with the trumpets to urge him on.

Anyway, the tenorman contributes a suitably varied and inventive solo: starting out with a few deliberately easy phrases in the G minor but soon introducing more notes per bar and abruptly raising the temperature with his attack. He also complicates the chord changes very excitingly, examining them this way and that before returning them to their original formation, and near the end he unleashes a spectacular burst of Coltraneish harmonics. (The end itself is defused by a single phrase of slap-tonguing!) Overall, what he is saying impresses one as being balanced, imaginative, unhesitating and deeply-felt—in other words, it has the hallmarks of a great jazz solo stamped upon it.

As for the reference to 'Trane, Budd says: 'I always liked him.' And about this attitude to modernism in general he states: 'You don't just keep beating a dead horse—you jump on another train. When Parker and Gillespie got together they made a wonderful team; so naturally you have to like it. I liked it—I like that style of music even today. It's more difficult to play than *avant garde* because you have to run *all* the changes correctly, and that's a bit difficult because you must develop outstanding technique, and you must have this technique in order to play what you feel inside and let whatever it is—come out.' He adds: 'And I'll tell you something—what they call free style—ever since I can remember jazz has always been freedom.'

In order to feel free, though, you have to be a jazz master. Otherwise the lack of invention and technical ability lead not to liberty but to frustration. They are the twin-millstones around the necks of the second-rate. Budd Johnson, naturally, belongs with the chosen.

1983

Budd died on October 20, 1984, just two months before his 74th birthday. Just hours before he'd played a gig with his old friend Jay McShann—in Kansas City, where he'd made his recording debut fifty-five years before. Also just before the release of one more album. And a superb one: 'The Old Dude And The Fundance Kid', with wonderful duets by Budd with his so talented junior, altoist Phil Woods. The album includes BJ's final composition too, Confusion: *very modernistic, with much contrapuntal interplay and ¾ figures, but still (in the words of sleeve-note writer Dan Morgenstern) 'in essence bluesy. Budd does some fine preaching.'*

CHAPTER FOUR

CHARLIE SHAVERS

Firecracker

Since the early 1970s the pursuit of exactitude by the more dedicated discographers of jazz has taken these generally unpaid enthusiasts to the borders of nightmare. It wasn't easy before then, gathering the information that fans and collectors expect. Labels as important as those started by Norman Granz, for their mysterious reasons stubbornly withheld vital session details. And even a company as prestigious as Blue Note neglected to put recording dates on its album-covers.

But from the beginning of the 'seventies the situation has become far more complex. Long-standing contracts between American mothers and their European and other licencees have run out, catalogues have changed hands and so the repackagings proliferate. Often these are make-up jobs, and some not very intelligent at that—with tracks drawn from two, three, perhaps as many as a dozen different LPs. Then there is the problem of bootleg issues, and of those copyrights which have simply run out altogether and so are up for grabs. Sympathise with the poor discographer, therefore, and his task of sifting and identifying it all; every matrix number, date and change of personnel. With the critical claws out for him if he gets it wrong.

Just one example of the sort of thing that gives him a hard time is sitting on my desk at this moment. Or rather its sleeve is. The disc is steaming away merrily on the B & O. It is deep mid-Winter as I write. Gulls, driven inland by the cold, wheel and scream between the blocks and all the boats in the river marina are icebound. But the music coming from the record-player is hot: the Tommy Dorsey band at its best. While the trumpet soloist who bursts through every so often is hotter still—the irrepressible Charlie Shavers. So, I cup my hands around the coffee-cup again and listen. I am enjoying the jazz even if the discographical bit is proving troublesome.

The LP ('Tommy Dorsey And Company' on First Heard Records FH24) is a genuine curio—and fascinating even in its off moments. For one thing it's in a limited edition of 3,000 copies. And Side 1 consists entirely of air-shots from 1943—in other words, from those particular Dark Ages when an arrogant Caesar Petrillo of the American Federation of Musicians imposed a ban on his members making studio recordings. (It hurt the bands and the fans equally. The big companies merely turned to other forms of popular music. And by the end of two years so had lots of the fans.) Anyway, the tracks all come from what were originally programmes sponsored by the Raleigh Tobacco Company. Their recording quality is not bad for the time; the Dorsey guys play really well, and one keeps getting little added excitements and surprises—rather like biting on corianders and other such spices in a Thai curry.

For instance, on Side 1, band 4 arranger Sy Oliver pops up beside Jo Stafford to help out with the vocal of *Yes, Indeed!* And two tracks later we hear Private Ziggy Elman back with the band to play *And The Angels Sing.* It sounds more *Hava Nagila* than ever, but who cares—at least the nostalgia's still there. Meanwhile there are occasional passages with eight violins and four violas added, plus harp, and Larry Stewart is the cure for all insomniacs during his 'refrain' on *Night And Day.*

Everything on the album appears to have been broadcast from a station in Hollywood, and Side 2 (dating from 1945) teams Paulette Goddard with the band for some alleged 'comedy sketches.' Miss Goddard, apart from being beautiful and a delightful actress, is one of the film world's notably intelligent ladies; as her marriages might suggest: to Chaplin, Burgess Meredith and Erich Maria Remarque, author of 'All Quiet On The Western Front'. Even she though has a tough time with the gags. Sample. She had just finished filming 'Kitty' with Ray Milland and Cecil Kellaway for Paramount. So, Tommy: 'Kitty, eh. Would that be any of the cats we know?' Later on Paulette shows she has a remarkably fine French accent. The gags stay uniformly bad.

However, pity the poor discographer once again. The First Heard people have done their best, but the personnels remain mere suggestions. One can identify bits and pieces of solo work here and there: Buddy De Franco, Vido Musso. Al Porcino and Chuck Peterson were evidently sharing most of the trumpet leads. Nelson Riddle sometimes led on trombone and there are suspicions of Jess Stacy on piano (*Tico Tico*). Only two men appear to me beyond dispute. Drummer Buddy Rich thundering the band along in the first full flush of his maturity. And, of course, the aforementioned Charlie Shavers on trumpet. One could hardly fail to recognise them. They both sound so good; both so individualistic! (On *Well, Git It!* the trumpet star even takes over TD's famous trombone bridge. One wonders . . . where was Tommy?)

I must admit, what I now find myself compelled to write down about Charlie Shavers is tinged with guilt. He was not an underrated player. He was never overlooked. *It's just that he was so good a lot of us kind of took him for granted.* The 'Tommy Dorsey And Company' LP is an attractive, albeit deliberately commercial setting. A setting within which nobody actually plays badly. But whenever Charlie—the firecracker—steps out from the ensemble to solo, the whole thing is given an immediate lift. On *Dinah, Song Of India, Well, Git It, 42nd Street, Chloe, Alexander's Ragtime Band* and the inevitable *Tico Tico* he clearly demonstrates that he was, well, what we should all have remembered him to be: one of the fiercest, most explosive and daring big blowers in jazz.

By way of making posthumous amends I must put Mr Shavers into some sort of historical perspective. Certainly for myself. Hopefully as well for those others who, like myself, have admired his work but still take him for granted.

He put his talents about quite a bit. On a superficial level he has a niche in popular music as the composer of *Undecided*. This has now become a standard (and he has several other, lesser-known, but still attractive themes to his credit, notably *Pastel Blue*). But to the real *aficionados* of jazz he is probably best-known for his solos and arranging with the John Kirby Sextet of 1937 to 1944. To followers of the big bands his name is inevitably linked to the great Dorsey years: 1943 and onwards for the next decade, with occasional 'guest'-spot reappearances even after 1956 when Tommy died and the band began to be fronted by Sam Donahue. He was also something of a globetrotter—with Benny Goodman, Budd Johnson or groups led by himself. While the more showy and—often—humorous side of his playing kept him in almost continuous demand for jazz stage-spectaculars. He was an obvious success at Gene Norman's Just Jazz concert of June 23, 1947, joining the King Cole Trio, Louie Bellson, Willie Smith, Stan Getz *et al*. And he worked a lot, later on, with Norman Granz' Jazz At The Philharmonic. (It was the latter which led to his inclusion—and an outstanding contribution from him—on the famous *Funky Blues* date featuring for once and all time the world's then three greatest altoists, Johnny Hodges, Charlie Parker and Benny Carter).

At the same time though, this seems to be a piecemeal presentation. I would much rather state what is overall and—I believe—clear-cut. That if Louis Armstrong and Bix Beiderbecke were the 'key' trumpet-players of the first period of jazz, and Dizzy Gillespie and Miles Davis of the third, then Roy Eldridge and Charlie Shavers must be regarded as the most important trumpeters of the second, middle or Swing period. In addition to which, in several respects—although not the most *vital* one—Shavers had the edge on Roy.

Charlie was a native New Yorker, born in August 1917—and a cousin to Dizzy Gillespie, who he initially influenced when they played together, briefly, in the Frank Fairfax band in Philadelphia. (Dizzy played the musical obituary at Charlie's funeral in 1971). His first instrument was, of all things, the banjo, but he quickly discovered where his true talents lay. After leaving Fairfax in 1935 he played in New York City bands: Tiny Bradshaw's, and more significantly Lucky Millinder's, where he met John Kirby, Buster Bailey and Billy Kyle, the nucleus of the future Kirby Sextet. By this time musicians were starting to recognise that in Charlie jazz had a new and very powerful soloist;

although as it transpired power was not to be the reason for his success with the Kirby Sextet. His ability to 'lift the full weight' would only really come into its own when he joined Tommy Dorsey.

When John Kirby formed his sextet and opened at the Onyx Club in NYC he had Frankie Newton on trumpet and Pete Brown on alto. But somehow it wasn't working out, and, after a violent disagreement with Newton, the leader turned to his old friends in the Millinder band. The justly-celebrated JK Sextet was then formed with Charlie Shavers on trumpet, Russell Procope (alto-saxophone), Buster Bailey (clarinet), Billy Kyle (piano), Kirby (bass) and O'Neil Spencer (drums). It's success was almost instantaneous.

Oddly enough, Charlie's most important contribution to the group was as its arranger; and such was his style of arranging that he had to keep the most extrovert qualities in his trumpet-playing severely under control, featuring instead a smaller open tone or using a variety of mutes. On the other hand, there was no mistaking the style he gave the group. It was light, breezy, tastefully swinging, clean-sounding and always illuminated by a considerable musical polish and *finesse*. It caught on with everyone, not just the jazz fans, and into the 1940s was probably the most popular small group in America. It was certainly taken up by the 'smart' set; and this enabled it to do a number of things normally taboo to Negro musicians then. They played at the Waldorf-Astoria, for instance, at that time the most 'in' place in New York if you had the money and wanted to dine and dance. Also, in 1940, there was a network radio series, *Flow Gently, Sweet Rhythm,* co-starring Maxine Sullivan, who had become Kirby's wife. Charlie wrote his *Undecided* which was an immediate best-seller. And he penned some very popular adaptations of classics into swingtime: Greig's *Anitra's Dance,* Dvorak's *Humoresque* and Tchaikovsky's *Sugar Plum Fairy* from 'The Nutcracker Suite'.

The group's success slalomed on until 1944, when Kyle had been conscripted and Charlie joined Tommy Dorsey on a permanent basis.

He had been guesting with the band for over a year, and it wasn't just a question of bigger pay cheques. It had allowed him to start blowing really hard again and it excited him—as well as exciting the Dorsey fans. Also Dorsey was fiercely protective about his new solo 'star' in matters appertaining to the colour bar. Although an irascible man (especially when his own brother was around) he proved a good boss. Moreover, he had the national popularity to ensure that Charlie was treated as the whites in the band were treated. (He suffered none of the indignities which poor Roy Eldridge faced when he went on the road with Gene Krupa.) The trumpeter much appreciated this. Mr TD was in his book always the perfect gentleman. And, of course, as a soloist he was given his head. Dorsey didn't just want another good trumpeter; he had a fine section anyway. He wanted exactly what Charlie Shavers had to give: the aura of being a larger-than-life player. A man who could dazzle the audience within eight bars of take-off.

So, Sy Oliver was set to work to provide frames and Charlie to take advantage of them. With Dorsey he didn't so much play the trumpet: *he erupted through it!* There you would have the whole brass section playing the theme double-*forte*—and sounding pretty hairy. Then Charlie Shavers launched out upon one of his solos and suddenly the whole top of the volcano went up . . .

As I've said, he stayed with TD a long time and guested with the band for a long time after that. He occasionally sang with the band too. He was a short, rotund man, in his photographs a little bulgy-eyed and babyfaced and with his hair gleaming with oil in the best Hollywood Don Ameche style. He had a quickly realisable sense of humour and this often spilled over into his playing. But within the boundaries of taste; i.e. it was fun, but it stayed firmly musical.

Through until his death (which Phil Payne of Time-Life Records tells me was premature even possibly a medical botch-up) he continued to make a lot of records as well as playing international tours. He recorded with Georgie Auld, Charlie Ventura, Lionel Hampton, a string group (under his own name) for Bethlehem, Teddy Wilson, Billie Holiday, Charlie Barnet, Coleman Hawkins, Louie Bellson, Benny Goodman, Tadd Dameron and, again under this own name, at The Crazy Horse in Paris. Not a bad tally. Also there was an LP for Capitol whose title describes him equally as well as Firecracker: "Excitement Unlimited."

To conclude though I must say something to qualify the opinion I expressed before about Charlie Shavers being second only to Roy Eldridge in the Swing era's hierarchy of trumpeters. Because in the departments of technique, range and valve-facility allied with lip and tonguing Charlie was Roy's superior. He could do without worrying about it all that Roy had to reach out and strive for. In fact, Charlie could do most things easily. He had a fine flood of improvised ideas. And if it was a question of generated heat, and swing, then he could do a bellows'-job on an audience from virtually any concert platform.

But he wasn't so original in his ideas as Roy. The latter in growing up had listened mainly to saxophone players and set out to imitate their lines on the trumpet; so developing a method of phrasing which was revolutionary in itself and led on towards Dizzy Gillespie, Fats Navarro, Kenny Dorham and, in a way, Clifford Brown. Charlie's own ideas began as a volatile distillation descended from Louis Armstrong. (Although once he realised what Eldridge had done, he incorporated the best of it and used it as skilfully as if he'd been the inventor!)

Eldridge and Shavers. Both big blowers. Both amazing jazz trumpeters to listen to. And if Roy was one notch up for originality, it also has to be said that they were so far ahead of the pack that rivalry didn't come into it. The other two Swing trumpeters of importance—Buck

Clayton and Harry Edison—only made it by going around the woods on the other side.

1983

My longtime associate, friend and discographer Tony Middleton doubts that all the CS solos listed with Dorsey are by him; also the presence of Buddy Rich. In both cases on account of U.S. Army duties. I can only argue with him that to me the 'presences' sound like Shavers and Rich.

CHAPTER 5

ART TATUM/BEN WEBSTER

This man was the greatest jazz instrumentalist of all time . . . bar none. I mean simply that Art Tatum played more piano than anyone else played any other instrument.

—Red Callender

Although almost totally blind, Tatum possessed by nature the technical abilities which most pianists strive for throughout their lives and never obtain. Admired by the young Horowitz (and also by Rachmaninov), he might have become a classical master himself. But an original harmonic sense and matching talents for improvisation drew him towards jazz. Perhaps the enjoyment of competition as well. For the 1930s was *the* period for instrumental duels between jazzmen, usually after hours in small clubs and especially in New York, where Tatum arrived as Adelaide Hall's accompanist in 1932. Like Minerva from Jupiter's headache, he appeared to spring upon the scene completely formed. Suddenly the rags and blues of James P. Johnson were dated, boogie-woogie shown as the scarecrow it truly was and any pianist who took up battle-stations swiftly routed. Earl Hines, originally an influence on Art, kept his distance (and, as a result, his dignity). Fats Waller, the other early influence, complained to a friend: 'I play piano, but tonight God is in the house,' and promptly left the piano in the New York club where he was playing. 'We'd turn him loose . . . and it was goodbye to all the others' (Roy Eldridge).

My favourite early Art Tatum solo is *Sweet Lorraine,* cut in February, 1940, several years after his initial impact had been felt in New York. It is an unaccompanied solo, but since the pianist plays like a self-contained orchestra this is no drawback. His left-hand comes through full-sounding, steady and swinging as any rhythm section. All the other features of his remarkable style are on display. The melodic variations (so ornate, yet in the sharp, symmetrical way Gothic castles are ornate) fitting and filled out by his advanced sense of harmony. The lightning runs which both break and bridge the passages of straight rhythm. The force and depth of his left-hand work contrasted with a light, delicate, 'singing' quality from his right. And the whole of it presented with so much ease. 'Ease—no apparent effort at all' (Everett Barksdale, the guitarist who would later work with Tatum).

Certain critics (even including several Tatum admirers) had said that his one weakness was an inability to merge his talent with those of other musicians. I just can't agree. On *Lonesome Graveyard Blues* (recorded in

1941) he accompanies blues-shouter Joe Turner with extreme sensitivity and no dilution of his characteristic powers. While for the last twelve years of his life (he died in 1956, aged only 46) he chose to work with a trio (Tiny Grimes was his first guitarist, Everett Barksdale his second and Slam Stewart his bassist) rather than pursue the loneliness of solo concert performances. The real problem, I believe, lay in finding men who would complement his own extraordinary musical strengths. But from 1954 until his death, the impresario/record producer Norman Granz teamed Art with a series of his peers (Buddy De Franco, Benny Carter, Roy Eldridge, Lionel Hampton, Harry Edison and—finest of all—Ben Webster) which brought an Indian Summer to his recording career. There would be also a superb trio set with Red Callender (bass) and Jo Jones (drums): the two rhythm men coping with everything the pianist threw at them as regards time-signatures and tempo changes. 'The greatest compliment of my life was to be picked to play with Art' (Red Callender).

Tatum's heir (technically, and to a certain extent in style) is Oscar Peterson, the Canadian pianist of big-handed chords, glittering attack and magnificent, biting swing. However, Art had existed—so Oscar comes to us as less of a surprise.

But to go back to those carping critics. They complained that Tatum's harmonic abstractions and fast right-hand runs tended to break up the beat, and consequently the rhythmic flow of his solos; and so made it doubly difficult for other musicians, no matter how good, to keep up with his mental processes in the course of an improvisation. This was totally disproved from 1954 when he signed with Granz. Admittedly, his first session was a day-long, marathon solo performance. But then came the recordings with the other musicians.

The results of which I, personally, became aware of with the release of the 10-inch LP featuring Art with Red Callender and the ex-Basieite drummer, Jo Jones. The opening track, based on Cole Porter's *Just One Of Those Things* (from the show 'Jubilee' of 1935) is one of the fastest piano solos I have ever heard. Not that speed in itself is necessarily a musical merit. But Tatum pianistically is absolutely himself—with no stylistic differences—and Callender and Jo Jones (using wire-brushes) pacing every bar of the way. It is a true trio recording. As Callender, in interview, put it later: 'To play with Art Tatum? Well, it was a ball, of course. I suppose I felt as any musician did about playing with Art— the mere fact that he asked for me, expressly—what a great honour.'

'He was a meticulous, unbending perfectionist. He liked playing alone . . . and he also liked playing with other people—but the others had to keep up with him. With Art there was very little margin for error. Nothing annoyed him more than a note or a change that wasn't just right. You might say that as a jazz artist he was overpowering to anyone playing with him. You never thought of taking a solo, for instance, because—let's face it, what *could* you play? Not that Art would deliberately cut you, but what he played was just so naturally brilliant there was nothing left to say . . .

'He was a meticulous artist, as I've said. We would have a conference just before starting to play and that's when the decisions would be made regarding what notes and changes we'd play. It was like a guide, though, not an absolute blueprint. So what followed once we started to play was what you might call planned improvisation.'

And he added: 'Jo Jones played the drums that day as though he'd invented them.'

However, Callender himself then went on to play on what must be regarded as the finest Tatum teaming of all, *and incidentally his last*: the Los Angeles sessions of September, 1956 with tenor-saxist Ben Webster. When the drummer was Bill Douglass.

Webster (b.1909) was very much a product of the long-blowing, gutsy and imaginative Kansas City tenor-saxophone school of the 1930s. In fact, he took part in the most famous Kaycee cutting contest of all time, when Coleman Hawkins, the pioneer of the tenor in jazz and then the nationwide star with Fletcher Henderson's orchestra, decided to stay over and take on the local 'boys', who happened to include Lester Young and Herschel Evans. It was Ben who tapped on pianist Mary Lou Williams' window at 4 am in the morning and said, 'Get up, pussy-cat, we're jammin' and all the pianists are tired out now. Hawkins has got his shirt off and is still blowing. You got to come down.'

Hawk never did manage to win that one—although he blew through to breakfast-time. (He later burnt out his new Cadillac trying to catch up on the next job with the Henderson crew in St. Louis.) But Lester Young and Herschel and Ben had outgunned him. 'Yes, Hawkins was king until he met those crazy Kansas City tenormen': Mary Lou.

She also had a number of interesting comments to make about Tatum. 'Art had a radio programme, also a job at a dicky private club, but preferred wailing after hours. It was this place every night then. Whenever I wasn't listening to Tatum, I was playing—Art inspired me so much. Chords he was throwing in then, the boppers are using now. And his mind was the quickest.

'Art usually drank a bottle of beer while the other pianists took over, and didn't miss a thing. For instance, there was a run that Buck Washington showed me. (Buck, of the Buck and Bubbles team, played a lotta piano, especially when out jamming. Everything he did was unusual.) Now Art heard me play this run, which consisted of F, E-flat, D-flat, C; (octave up) C, B-flat, A-flat, G; and so on all the way to the top of the keyboard. When he sat down, he played it right off. Other pianists had heard and tried, but taken time to pick it up.' ('Hear Me Talkin' To Ya').

Ben Webster went on to achieve his own particular fame, still as a hard–blower, with Duke Ellington's band of the early 1940s; with such invigorating solos as *Cotton Tail, Ko-Ko* and, of course, *Perdido.* But by the time he recorded with Tatum he had also become one of the most sensuous interpreters of ballads. Breathy, subtle and a master of the sustainted note.

Tatum himself was not an original composer (except within his improvisations). Everything he played was created upon the melodies and chords of the best of popular, standard songs; plus the occasional blues. And thus the two men came together.

On September 11, 1956, two months before Tatum's death, they recorded seven titles. Six were released as an LP called 'The Art Tatum—Ben Webster Quartet': *My One And Only Love, My Ideal, Gone With The Wind, Have You Met Miss Jones?, Night And Day* and *Where Or When.* Within themselves they made a magnificent collection. Ben surpassed himself and he never played better than on this session. Tatum too was unusually inspired (no doubt, not least by the company) and added to his legacy of genius. But it was the first track recorded that day, based on Jerome Kern's *All The Things You Are,* and which was issued separately as part of a Tatum sampler LP, together with tracks by Art with Buddy De Franco, Benny Carter *et al.* It has to be regarded as a jazz 'classic'. Perhaps a finer and more beautiful and clever popular song than *All The Things You Are* has never been written. What results when these two jazz masters turn it into its profundities is almost beyond belief; except that their performance still exists to be heard. It was, apparently, completed in one straight take with no edits; despite Tatum's blindness and the consequent problem of communication. Ben eases himself into a tenor solo which says everything for the marvellous nature of the song, and is vocal without words. Tatum plays as the pianist who, certainly technically, and perhaps also imaginatively, has never had an equal in jazz—but who, on this occasion, was also for some reason, extremely, personally moved, and, as a result, gives out to the listener, in addition to his display of mighty natural powers, a most genuine warmth and understanding for the attributes of the song. I have no hesitation in describing it as one of the dozen greatest jazz performances I have heard in four decades of listening.

1988

CHAPTER SIX

FREDDIE GREEN

Mister Rhythm

When I first met Freddie Green in London in 1957, he told me: 'I'm a quiet guy. Not shy, mind you. Just quiet. I liked to be there on the sidelines, but *near* the big action. To observe it, to know what's going on.' He also liked Jaguars, golf, good food and he stood fairly tall and handsome, with no physical ravages to indicate the number of years given up to the touring life. (In 1982 he still looked a miracle of self-disciplined preservation.)

He words might be taken as indicative of his attitude towards the array of jazz giants he's accompanied since his earliest days with the Basie band. Buck Clayton and Harry Edison, Joe Newman and Thad Jones, Dicky Wells, Henry Coker and Benny Powell, Lester Young and Herschel Evans, Eddie 'Lockjaw' Davis, the Franks Foster and Wess and, of course, the singers: Jimmy Rushing ('Mister Five-By-Five'), Helen Humes and Joe Williams; also too 'Lady Day' (Billie Holiday) who, it's been said, wanted to marry him. He's been a member of two of the finest rhythm sections the jazz world has known: the pre-'49 one with Walter Page on bass and Jo Jones ('The Wind') on drums and the 1950s one when Eddie Jones took over on bass and Gus Johnson was the drummer.

The words understate his own importance though. Freddie Green has been the most quietly *effective* guitarist in jazz, the outstanding *acoustic* 'rhythm' one and a player without whom the ongoing Basie beat could hardly have survived. He is both the core of its swing and guardian of the band's cohesiveness.

Also, one mustn't mistake the quiet of the man for any lack of resolution. In addition to being the long-term protector of his rhythm, he often serves as Basie's musical conscience. 'From time to time, we'll see Freddie Green lecturing him (The Count) off to one side—never the other way around', a veteran of the band told Nat Hentoff. And after the departure of Gus Johnson from Basie in December, 1954, the guitarist took to travelling a stick—rather like a short snooker cue—which he used for poking in the ribs any subsequent drummer who rushed the tempo or indulged in exhibitionism to the detriment of the band's swing.

Another thing to note is how he avoids playing improvised solos. But not for any reasons of incapacity. There are a few solo passages on an album he made with Basie and singer Joe Williams called

'Memories Ad Lib' on the Roulette label; and he can be heard playing some very delicate, almost Django Reinhardt-like accompaniment to Brother John Sellers on a Vanguard session from the 1950s (the *Boll Weevil Song*). Again, there are some guitar intros and codas on Joe Newman's RCA Victor LP 'All I Wanna Do Is Swing'. But these are untypical of him: not his way at all. He did them because he was asked to do them, not because he wanted a place in the sun. What matters to Freddie Green is *the rhythm*. This is the central house of his music, and with his great concentration, careful strumming and natural swing is what he does so superbly well. He doesn't use (or need) an amplifier. Nor does he particularly attack the strings. But listen to whichever Basie record you care to pick out, and the sound of the guitar is always there—clear, incisive, impeccably accenting the famous 1-2-3-4 beat and never leaving the rhythm section in doubt about the toe-tapping tempo and basic feel. There are certain Basie-inspired examples of his sustaining a tempo for as long as twenty minutes at a time (I'm thinking of the Buck Clayton Jam Sessions on CBS). He never falters though, and throughout the swing has that essential relaxation typifying the jazz which began in Kansas City.

This last characteristic might seem slightly odd to those looking into his biographical details, because he was not a partner in the original Kansas City, free-blowing, all-through-the-night jam sessions there. Before joining Basie in New York City he had little knowledge of the jazz going on in the South-West and quite definitely hadn't heard Basie's most important forerunners: Walter Page's Blue Devils and the big band of Bennie Moten. However, once into the Basie group he immediately sounded exactly right and what drummer Jo Jones has called 'the bouncing ball' effect of its beat was complete. 'Freddie joined us when we were working at The Roseland,' the Count remembered. 'John Hammond came by one Sunday afternoon and said he had a guitarist he wanted me to hear. It seemed strange to audition a guitarist, but we went down to the dressing-room. He was on the bus the next day when we went to Pittsburgh, and he's been with us ever since. Freddie is Mister Hold-togetherer!'

Freddie was born in the old South, at Charleston (the Carolinas on March 31, 1911). To begin with he was largely self-taught as a musician. But he had a friend in Charleston, Lonnie Simmons, who played the tenor-saxophone and who got him his first professional job with a group called The Nighthawks. The father of another friend, a trumpeter called Sam Walker, taught him to read music—as well as encouraging him to add to his first-choice instrument, a banjo, the six-string acoustic guitar of European, classical construction.

This Mr Walker Snr. held a position at the local orphanage, helping to organise what became widely-known as Jenkins Orphanage Band, and, although not an orphan himself, Freddie went on tour with them.

(Cat Anderson, the trumpeter who later made his name with Duke Ellington, also played in the group). Eventually they got as far North as Maine, and this persuaded the young musician to go on and try his luck in New York. That was in 1930. For a time he stayed with an aunt who was much into the 'rent parties' scene, and whose house frequently reverberated to the sounds of the great stride piano-players, Fats Waller, James P. Johnson and so on. Freddie got work as a furniture upholsterer, plus a job in the evenings at a club called the Yeah Man. It was here he finally decided to dump his banjo and concentrate fully on the guitar.

He then moved to the Exclusive Club, working with the pianist Willie Gant and having to learn lots of chord changes in order to accompany the many guest singers. There was no drummer, but people in the club still liked to dance, and so Freddie came to appreciate the value of a steady swing and tempo.

When John Hammond heard him for the first time he had a job at The Black Cat in Greenwich Village, earning eleven dollars a week and playing with Lonnie Simmons (tenor), Fat Atkins (piano), Frank Speakman (bass) and the ubiquitous Kenny Clarke on drums. Since that time, of course, he has become a favourite rhythm guitarist with many musicians and singers and their predilection has led to his being included on hundreds of different recording sessions spanning five decades. But the association with the Basie band remains uninterrupted. (He even worked with the otherwise modern jazz Septet of 1950, when economic circumstances forced Basie to disband his full group).

As for the distinctive Basie beat which he is such an important part of, this had a normal growth in the late 1920s jazz of the American South-West (mainly Missouri), was developed to a stage of grand excitement at the early 1930s impromptu sessions in Kansas City and then had its parallel quality of a streamlined relaxation added in New York when the leader put together his definitive team of Freddie Green, Walter Page on bass and Jo Jones, drums. In the South-West a guitarist called Ruben Lynch had shown the way with Page's Blue Devils—playing advanced chords for that period, but very evenly, four to the bar. And when Basie arrived in New York this was more or less how the guitarist he used on his first recording session for Decca, Claude Williams, played. In between though there had been the marathon Kaycee 'jams', giving that city the reputation for having the most dazzling new jazz soloists in the entire United States. The real 'stars' of the jamming, players like Lester Young and Herschel Evans, were now members of the Basie band and required extra-perceptive accompaniment. Also the band's ensemble style, based on short riff-phrases and the blues, demanded a very special form of rhythmic support—something tightly together but musically open, superficially propulsive while inside needing to be flexible, even laidback.

Freddie Green's recruitment, added to the big, rich sound of Walter Page's bass and Jo Jones' fresh approach to drumming, brought about the ultimate refinement of what we currently identify as Basie's beat—aided and abetted by the leader's own piano style. Jo Jones, or 'The Wind' as his admirer Don Lamond describes him, lessened the force of his bass-drum beats, then delivered a series of regulated stick-shots on his hi-hat cymbal, creating a permanently shimmering effect, and with this more fluid beat he swept the band along with comparative ease. Page introduced a new mobility with his bass-playing, and the guitar was used to reaffirm the sure and steady 4/4 time by equally accenting the first, second, third and fourth beats of the bar—in other words, like 'a bouncing ball', to re-quote Jo Jones.

The outcome of it all proved to be as refreshing as it was stimulating. Not only did the Basie band swing and play with enormous flair and attack, but its soloists felt they had an underlying safety net and could therefore take off to play a whole series of adventurous things. Lester Young in particular, a musician of extraordinary imagination, at last felt free to improvise back and forth across the bar-lines in a surging, extended way, the equal of which jazz had never known before. Lester was a genuine revolutionary with what he said through his instrument, but even revolutions require a large measure of surrounding support . . .

So Basie has described Freddie Green as the man who holds the band together, adding that this is based on the invariably reliable nature of his swing. The guitarist himself views his principal function rather differently. 'A performance has what I call a rhythmic wave,' he has said. 'And the rhythm guitar can help to keep that wave smooth and accurate. I have to concentrate on the beat, listening to how smooth it is. If the band is moving smoothly, then I can play whatever comes to mind.'

Others have been in a position to extol his musical virtues much more highly though. Especially the band's leading arrangers—men such as Neal Hefti, Ernie Wilkins and Quincy Jones. As the latter put it: 'That man Freddie Green is a sort of spirit. He doesn't talk loud and he doesn't play loud. But man!—you sure know he's there. The brass and reeds can be up there shouting away, but there's Freddie, coming right through it all, steady as a rock and clear as a bell. He's something special. What he represents is the only one of its kind in existence.'

This reference by Quincy to one's being always aware of the guitarist with Basie, even when the band is at full ensemble and playing double-*forte,* touches upon the other important feature of his contributions to the thousands of appearances and hundreds of recordings over the years. In addition to his knowledgeable guarding of the band's rhythmic style and feeling, there is a unique quality of sound. When moving his fingertips over the strings, the effect he produces is deceptively light and airy. It's also unusually clean, with no nail-scrapings. But at the same time the sound is very true, and it does have a cutting edge to it—which comes through against any odds once his strumming has hit that vital beat. There isn't much rise or fall in the actual level of the sound—although obviously it tends to become more exposed when there is just an improvised solo on the go. Mainly it is the fine finish and the controlled incisiveness of the string tone which make him so easy to recognise. Listening to him on, say, the tremendous 'Jazz Giants 56' LP (recorded for Norman Granz) with Lester Young, Roy Eldridge, Teddy Wilson and, appropriately, Jo Jones, one realises that the strength of his sound is exactly balanced by its purity. The guitar is an audible constant for every bar of the way: lightly touched, ringing without being unduly echoey, but above all *clear-cut,* a reminder of where the section is gaining its cohesion and lift.

Before the Basie band's first-ever tour of Britain in 1957 there were a number of significant personnel changes from the one I'd listened to earlier in France. Sonny Payne had replaced Gus Johnson, Bill Graham was playing second alto instead of Ernie Wilkins and Bill Hughes had just joined on trombone. Added to which there was the new and considerable impact of singer Joe Williams. Understandably, therefore, the leader appeared nervous during the hours between arrival and the opening date (a concert at the Royal Festival Hall with as its special VIP Princess Margaret). Having been kept out of the country for so long, due to a Musicians Union ban, it was terribly important to him that the band made a good showing.

In fact, he needn't have worried. The jazz-starved fans gave the players a fantastic reception anyway. But while the first half of the concert was very good indeed, the Count's somewhat apprehensive attitude resulted in its being played ever so slightly 'safe'. The ensemble work was quite magnificent—with just a touch of restraint. The solos were skilful and imaginative, but never completely uninhibited.

In the interval backstage between the halves I was then a witness to one of Freddie Green's celebrated asides to Basie. As always it was delivered in gentlemanly fashion, but the gist of it came across plainly. 'Look,' he said, 'we've got to let it all swing out more this second time. Those people out there, they can take it. That's what they came for. They know our music already from records. They're on our side, but they expect us to swing *the most*—so that's the way it's gonna have to be.' His leader didn't say a word; just nodded in agreement, and Freddie moved along to have a word with drummer Sonny Payne.

With the wraps truly off, that next half proved a sensation. From the leader's opening piano introduction—economic, as usual—to the final shouting, swinging climax and with a full hour in between the British jazz scene had heard nothing to compare with it. The solos by Joe Newman, Thad Jones, Henry Coker and the two Franks were stunning. And at the end the people in the audience were still stunned—

for at least six seconds, until they broke out into a gigantic ovation (standing, of course!). At which point my eyes happened to be on 'Mister Rhythm' as he put his guitar down. He in turn was looking across at Basie. The latter was preparing to take his first bow; but before he did so I noticed that brief, satisfied smiles of understanding passed between the two men.

1982

Freddie Green died in 1987 after a short illness. Until a few weeks before his death he had remained with the continuing Basie band, led in turn by Thad Jones and since then by Frank Foster.

CHAPTER SEVEN

THE COURAGE OF ARNETT COBB

At Nice '82 I nicknamed him 'General Cobb'. Partly because of the way, during the all-night jam sessions at Valentino's, he would use authoritative hand-signals to bring the protracted proceedings of each number to a close. Partly though on account of the great respect shown to him by all the other participants, be they youthful-thinking veterans like Frank Foster and Paul Jeffrey, or the truly youthful and gifted Wynton Marsalis.

However, there was something else I noticed about Arnett at Nice '82. He has charisma—and consequently crowd-pull. As everyone who has ever visited the Nice-Cimiez Festival knows, there are three actual arenas: the big, old Roman one; then the so-called 'Dance Stage' and finally, down below and between the olive-trees, a garden arena. Now Arnett, officially, was only booked to appear as featured soloist with the Lionel Hampton band. But in addition he contrived to get in on every other possible set that was going. And when he did, and the word got around, it was noticeable how many people left whatever else they'd been listening to and moved towards whichever stand he was blowing from. It was uncanny—and yet, with no disrespect to any of the other great soloists at that Nice (which, for me, was the best I've been to), people just seemed to want to catch as much of General Cobb as they could. As if he had for them exactly the right blend of fireworks and sensitivity.

It used to be much the same afterwards at Valentino's. After a very hot evening up at Cimiez—yes, it was also the hottest weather in the Festival's history!—I would dash for the bus, weighed down by a JVC recorder and two cameras, shower at the hotel, down two mouthfuls of duty-free and then hare along the street to grab a ringside seat at what had become by common consent *the* jammers paradise of the Festival. Even players who didn't join in would be there drinking and listening: Percy Heath, Louis Hayes—in fact, a host of big names. But something strange always came over the place when the General arrived. Something electric; a definite lift, an air of expectancy.

Normally Valentine's is a dark, comfortable, seafront bar with a grand piano situated strategically between the bar proper and a long, narrow eating area. It has a resident girl singer/pianist ('Muriel'), and often my friend Jack Hobbs would take over as the transitional player as the various jazzmen began to pile in from the Festival. Sometimes the entire

41

Clark College band from Atlanta would turn up (including a very good drummer called Chas Thomason). And most nights would have Frank Foster, still an avid jammer, stunning everyone with thirty or forty choruses on any theme that was picked. Plus a marvellous new pianist from the Jazz Messengers by the name of Johnny O'Neal—formerly with Milt Jackson and definitely a soloist with a future.

Usually Arnett would come along later. After he'd changed from the Festival and had a meal. But then his arrival would cause its usual stir, and immediately the other musicians would clear a prominent space for him—right in front of the piano. Following which, it wasn't as if he sought to dominate what was going on; and he certainly wasn't selfish in the length of time he played; but when he did play, one could rely on something special coming out—that certain little *extra* which is the hallmark of a jazz master. Also, every night he would treat us to one of his lovely ballad performances: *The Nearness Of You* or *I Got It Bad And That Ain't Good.* I never tired of hearing these, even though he might have played the same one up at Cimiez a few hours before.

Moreover he was invariably the last man to pack his horn away— and often by this time it could be around seven o'clock, with most of us thinking in terms of a French breakfast (with the coffee suitably laced!). The only nights I marked him absent, I discovered he had recording sessions the next day and therefore considered it prudent to be in bed early (comparatively).

On another occasion at Cimiez, while he waited to go on, I remarked on the tremendous stamina, as well as the guts, he'd shown by playing so many sets. 'Well, I refuse to be beaten,' he said. 'And I've reached the age when I like to get in as much music as I can. Especially when there are all these wonderful guys here in one place to blow alongside.' I then added that, if anything, his own blowing is now better than ever. 'I hope you're right,' he replied. 'In which case you've made an old man very happy . . .'

A quick potted biography of the General tells us he was born Arnett Cleophus Cobb in Houston, Texas on August 10, 1918. Also that he studied piano (with his grandmother), violin, trumpet and C-melody-sax before settling for the tenor-saxophone. He made his public debut in 1933 with a band led by one Frank Davis, a drummer; then he played with Chester Boone (1934-6) and Milt. Larkin ('36-'42). But his real break into the *big time* came when he replaced Illinois Jacquet with the Lionel Hampton band. As anyone who remembers that particular Hampton band of the 1940s or has since collected its records will testify, the musical policy was based on feverish excitement, even at times amounting to pandemonium. Illinois Jacquet as featured tenor had pioneered the high, harmonic 'shriek' note to fit into such a policy; so naturally in choosing his successor Hamp wanted someone who would play more of the same. Arnett duly joined, stayed for five years and proved a great success: at one point being billed as 'The World's Wildest Tenor Man!'

However, what the above does not say is just how much of an all-rounder he is with the tenor. Those years with Hamp are only part of the story. True, he can do all the gutsy stuff, making a big, booting sound, running the changes and shrieking on high whenever the occasion demands. He was also, post-Hampton, to go touring on the Rhythm-and-Blues circuit. But this should not be confused with those other occasions when he is allowed to be a different self and play with more natural warmth, the best of taste and, above all, a very interesting flow of ideas. At Nice he was just as happy blowing alongside Clark Terry, say, or Benny Bailey or Jay McShann as he was with Hamp. And wherever he moved he was welcomed.

I noticed especially the keen attention he paid to construction in his solos. He would take a given theme and then build it up very gradually, piling the ideas one upon the other until there was a real sense of achievement about it. No theme was ever treated to a *cliché*. He would take it, examine it this way and that, and in the end always worry something valuable out of it. Meanwhile adding feeling and drama as he went along.

As for his ballads, they were so beautiful to the ear! More often than not he would keep them deliberately simple, but giving them tenderness and heart and just a general expressiveness which reminded me so much of the late Ben Webster. It was for precisely this reason, I think, that he could play *The Nearness Of You* so many times and yet never bore people with it. A case of total dedication to the task in hand.

To go back in time again though, because this involves the courage factor, the General left Hamp as a regular player in 1947 to start his own band. Having become a highly-regarded name, not least at the box-office, the future looked unusually bright. And so it turned out to be for the next year. His group (a six-piecer) recorded for Apollo, and although certain items like *Go, Red, Go* and *Big League Blues* generated a similar overt fury to his famous *Flying Home, No. 2* with Hampton, nevertheless with other items he clearly demonstrated his abilities as an accomplished all-rounder. (Incidentally, these Apollo sessions are now on LP, but to the best of my knowledge only available in France).

Disaster first struck Arnett in 1948. Recurring back trouble necessitated an operation which would keep him off the scene for two years. Undeterred, he then reformed—it was another excellent group—and became a big influence upon the rapidly-expanding Rhythm-and-Blues scene.

This time he kept going as a bandleader for six years, until 1956, when disaster really *did* strike. There was a terrible automobile crash. Afterwards Arnett was pulled out of the wreckage barely alive, and so badly mangled it had to seem the end. The lower part of his spine was completely shattered, which, in turn, brought paralysis to the legs. The doctors did a splendid job, but there are some things you just can't put back together . . .

It was—I believe—one of those crucial points when a vast majority of us would have broken down psychologically as well and accepted a bathchair and dressing-gown. Not so the General. There was a long convalescence, of course: but that was merely the preliminary skirmish in his battle, not only to be able to move around, but an absolute determination to play in front of the public again. Returning to his native Houston by the end of the 1950s he was fronting a sixteen-piece band at one of the city's nightclubs—and eventually he became the manager there as well.

Eventually too it became that he could stand once more to play—although he has to wear special footwear and can only walk with the aid of crutches. Never mind. He'd won the battle—and fortunately his stomach, lungs, mouth and brain emerged completely healed from the course of it.

One other battle now remained. To regain the position in jazz he had lost due to the crash. He'd not been written off together with the car—but he still had to make the world aware of the fact.

Not surprisingly it proved hard going at first. How do you persuade a tough club owner to let you go on on crutches? But since then there has been a steady progress leading towards the kind of adulation he received at Nice. When he got his first booking at Ronnie Scott's, for example, he was the supporting act; with Ernestine Anderson topping. And to those who didn't know his background and his courage and his abilities his opening appearance came as a strange sight. At the end of the first night though there was a standing ovation. He blew and he blew and he blew: sometimes hard, sometimes with just a deep natural beauty—until even the social drinkers at the club's long bar paused, put down their glasses and joined in the applause. Afterwards Pete King was wreathed in smiles. Yes—he'd booked another winner!

'I didn't mind being booked as the supporting act,' Arnett told me afterwards. 'I just want to play. I wouldn't want to live without playing.' And there was humility to go with the courage. 'Ernestine's great anyway,' he added. 'Why should I feel put out?'

He has also been active again on the recording scene. Albums for Prestige with Eddie 'Lockjaw' Davis and Wild Bill Davison ('Blow, Arnett, Blow'), Coleman Hawkins and Buddy Tate ('Very Saxy'), Ray Bryant ('Party Time') and Red Garland ('Sizzlin'), plus a marvellous collection of his ballads, including *Blue And Sentimental* and *P.S. I Love You*. Also 'Arnett Is Back' on Progressive with Derek Smith, George Mraz and Billy Hart. Another one not to be overlooked (on JRC) comes from a NYC Town Hall concert of 1973, featuring him with Milt

Buckner, Panama Francis and, for good measure, the man Arnett replaced with Hampton in '42—Illinois Jacquet. Next—and soon, I hope—there will be the Nice sessions on release.

Which brings me to one further point I'd like to make about *mon ami* the General. In order to want so much to overcome his disability and play on, then the level of his jazz inspiration must have been singularly high in the first place. Anyway, in the year 2000 those of us still around are bound to be paying tribute to this great tenorman. And—knowing Arnett as I now do—he'll want to be on hand to join in the fun and, of course, do a little blowing for us.

1983

CHAPTER EIGHT

ASPECTS OF GEORGE GERSHWIN

From as far back as I care to remember I've placed Jerome Kern, George Gershwin and Cole Porter at the top of the popular songwriting tree. With just a few other names (Harold Arlen, Hoagy Carmichael, Richard Rodgers/Lorenz Hart, Vincent Youmans, Frank Loesser, then more recently Lerner and Loewe and Stephen Sondheim) perched on the branches nearest them.

But, with the exception of Carmichael and possibly Harold Arlen, these composers could never have visualised how important their works would become to later generations of improvising jazz musicians. Because in the main they were writing essentially for Broadway musicals—or for the moguls of Tin Pan Alley to 'fix' with the biggest name singers of the day. Nevertheless, they fashioned fine, pliable melodic lines over sophisticated sequences of chords, and these were to become—together with the twelve-bar blues—the chief souce of inspiration for most of the jazz and dance music that followed. Even a large proportion of jazz originals would be based upon these composers' chords. As just one example, Dizzy Gillespie's well-known *Anthropology* is an entirely new melody superimposed on the harmonies of George Gershwin's *I Got Rhythm*.

There has been much re-focussing upon Gershwin this year, which is the fiftieth since his death. Though why we should celebrate a death has never been very clear to me. Surely an artistic creator's birth is the more important. Or, in the case of a musical composer, the dates when his 'key' works first became public. But this is a different discussion altogether. Suffice it to say that two interesting Gershwin collections issued by ASV have just reached me—both worthy releases, although for quite separate reasons. And together they do trigger off further reminders of Gershwin's great talent.

At the age of fifteen George (his real name Gershowitz) got a job as a staff pianist and song-plugger with the Remick Music Corporation—for which he was paid $15 per week. He supplemented his income by making piano-rolls for the Perfection and then the Aeolian labels. And he submitted his own first composition to these several employers, only to be told: 'We hired you as a pianist, not a writer.' George perservered though—and eventually got his first song published by one Harry Von Tilzer in 1916. It was called *When You Want 'Em, You Can't Get 'Em (When You Got 'Em, You Don't Want 'Em)*. I've never managed to hear this song, so I can't be sure what *'Em* means! But it did bring Gershwin to the attention of Max Dreyfus, the powerful head of Harms Music, who then commissioned George to write the score for his first revue, 'Half Past Eight', which both opened and closed before reaching New York. Gershwin's first real hit was *Swanee,* which he had pressed upon Al Jolson at a Manhattan party, and as a result the singer included it in his 'Winter Garden' show and recorded it. *Swanee* sold two million records and one million sheet music copies. Success on Broadway then followed in 1919 with 'La La Lucille', which played for a hundred and four performances and 'Scandals' (no less than five productions between 1920 and 1924).

Where these initial successes subsequently led (quite apart from 'Rhapsody In Blue', 'An American In Paris' and the piano concerto) has been most carefully, and, one is tempted to add, lovingly, documented by Kevin Daly on 'The Song Is . . . Gershwin' (ASV Living Era AJA 5048). This compilation consists of seventeen 'deep history of Gershwin' tracks, many from Daly's own collection, all systematically filtered and cleansed in the process of transfer to tape and mastering for LP.

Ethel Merman made her debut in 'Girl Crazy' with the legendary song by Gershwin *I Got Rhythm.* (Before going on to 'Gypsy' and the classic mother-in-law of 'A Mad, Mad, Mad, Mad World'.) *Newsweek* magazine stated that 'Miss Merman made history by holding one note of *I Got Rhythm* for the full second chorus in defiance of the law of thermo-dynamics, i.e. all forces must eventually come to rest'. But Kevin Daly has found a Fats Waller version of the song for this LP, recorded in 1935, which is no less entertaining. We then proceed to *The Man I Love* sung by Elizabeth Welch in London in 1936 and backed by Benny Carter (who plays a stirring trumpet solo on the track). A great song, it had a doubtful start in life. Introduced by Adele Astaire, it had such a poor reception that it was dropped from the show 'Lady Be Good' after the opening night in Philadelphia on November 17, 1924. But Lady Mountbatten, visiting the USA, liked the song so much she took a copy back to England and soon had every bank in London playing it.

We stay with the show 'Lady Be Good' for *The Half Of It, Dearie, Blues* sung by Fred Astaire, with Gershwin himself at the piano, and *Oh Lady Be Good/Little Jazz Band* played by Jack Hylton with a vocal by no less than Chappie D'Amato. Then there is *Do What You Do* from 'Show Girl', sung by Zelma O'Neal, and *Funny Face* and *My One And Only,* also from 'Funny Face', the former directed by Carroll Gibbons, the latter an instrumental with Gershwin back at the piano.

So far all these selections have lyrics by George's brother Ira, who lived for much longer and whose wife lived long enough to take a 'Porgy And Bess' troupe to Russia in 1956 (giving rise to Truman Capote's hilarious book, 'The Muses Are Heard'—*When the cannons are silent the*

Muses are heard: USSR Minister of Culture). But George did work with other lyricists; thus *I Found A Four Leaf Clover* for George White's 'Scandals Of 1922', a Gershwin-Da Silva co-authorship, and *Nashville Nightingale* with words by Irving Caesar and played by Fred Waring's Pennsylvanians.

For all the remaining songs on the album though Gershwin was back with Ira: *Sweet And Low/That Certain Feeling* (recorded by 'One Take' Selvin in 1926); *Liza* (Al Jolson, 1929); *When Do We Dance* (Gershwin himself again, London, 1926); *Someone To Watch Over Me* (Gertrude Lawrence, 1927); *S'Wonderful* (written for Adele Astaire and recorded by Marius B. Winter's Hotel Cecil Dance Band in 1929); *Fascinating Rhythm* (Cliff Edwards, ukelele, Adrian Rollini, bass-sax, 1924); *I'll Build A Stairway To Paradise* (Paul Whiteman, 1922); and finally, *I Got Plenty O' Nuttin'* from 'Porgy And Bess' sung by the famous international tenor Lawrence Tibbett in 1935 with orchestra conducted by Alexander Smallens. All in all, for collectors of rare items, a nostalgic feast . . .

'Gershwin Gold' (ASV Digital RPO-8008) is a recent recording by the Royal Philharmonic Orchestra with Andrew Litton as conductor and also taking the piano solos. Litton, ex-Juilliard and La Scala, Milan, was the 1982 winner (the youngest-ever) of the BBC/Rupert Foundation Institute's Conductor Competition. Since when he has fronted most of the great orchestras in the West. He is distinguished by a lively style and is a very fine pianist.

Gershwin was told by a schoolmate, the future violin soloist Max Rosen, that he would never make it in music. Fortunately, he did persevere. And, as well as forging an important breakthrough with his songs, still hankered after composing on a grander scale. Which eventually led to his masterpiece, the opera 'Porgy And Bess'. But before settling down to write this later work he had been commissioned by the popular bandleader Paul Whiteman to furnish him with an extended orchestral piece. Gershwin was busy with yet another Broadway musical and dragged his feet; then got in a panic when he read about his non-existent composition in a newspaper. He buckled down—but left the orchestration to Whiteman's own arranger, Ferde Grofé. Who scored *Rhapsody In Blue* for piano, jazz band (saxes, brass, string-bass, bass doubling tuba, drums) and eight violins. Grofé was so pleased with the result that he next arranged it for a full symphony orchestra—the arrangement most often used today. Now, having heard the earlier version, I've no doubt in my own mind that it is much more exciting. And it seems to suit the piano parts better. It makes the later symphonic score sound languid. Litton excels with his keyboard rendition.

The album proceeds via the first four items from 'The George Gershwin Songbook' (comprising his own songs George most enjoyed entertaining with at Manhattan socialite parties, cigar clamped in mouth): *Swanee, Nobody But You, Do It Again* and *Clap Your Hands (Yo' Hands)*.

And is then completed by the remaining 'Songbook' numbers. Which I find the most intriguing of all. Because they are grouped under the title 'Who Cares?' and, following upon Gershwin's original piano solos, have been fully orchestrated by Hershy Kay. (I've felt indebted to Mister Kay for years, ever since his brilliant conducting of the Eddie Sauter string arrangements on the Stan Getz 'Focus' LP.)

The story as I can piece it together is as follows. Kay was working with the famed Russian choreographer George Balanchine, another Gershwin admirer, who one day was playing through the 'Gershwin Songbook' and decided he 'had to do a ballet based upon these themes'. Kay was 'phoned immediately. 'Who Cares?', the result, had its first performance with the New York City Ballet on February 5, 1970. Afterwards Balanchine wrote: 'George's music is so natural for dancing, so easy to work with . . . I remember he spoke often to me about wanting to write for the ballet. So I like to think this is George's ballet: this is the ballet we have done for him.'

Just to tidy up the statistics. Balanchine and Kay used sixteen Gershwin songs in the ballet, but only fourteen from the original 'Songbook': *Strike Up The Band, Sweet And Low Down, Somebody Loves Me, S'Wonderful, That Certain Feeling, Do Do Do/Lady Be Good, I'll Build A Stairway To Paradise, Fascinating Rhythm, Who Cares?, My One And Only, Liza, The Man I Love* and *I Got Rhythm*. The two they added were *Bidin' My Time* and *Embraceable You*. The four they left out are the same now collected by Andrew Litton as piano solos.

I have found both LPs fascinating—as much so as George Gershwin's rhythms!

1987

CHAPTER NINE

MEL POWELL

A Jazz Conundrum

The reputation of Melvin 'Mel' Powell is a somewhat strange one. As a piano-player he is known to *aficionados* of most schools of jazz music; and as both pianist and composer/arranger he is well-known to the followers of the big commercial Swing bands. Yet hardly anything—aside from single-sentence references—is ever written about him. There appears to have been something elusive, almost Ariel-like about his career. Also, I have heard him being put down as 'too eclectic.'

Well, the latter seems to me a gross oversimplification of the case. Are we right to wage punitive criticism against versatility, against the musician who cannot be pigeon-holed, against the man who is restless and spends all of his life probing? Because I believe Mel Powell emerges as just such a person. So, for that matter, does Gil Evans. And what the two men have in common—within their otherwise very different music-making—is a healthy fear of the *cliché*.

Another interesting point about Mel Powell is his date of birth (December 2, 1923). For it enabled him to grow up, and then to grow *through* the traditional streams of jazz before the major changes of the 1940s. I can remember the late, great trumpet-player Clifford Brown complaining that *his* birthdate (1930) meant he grew up aware of and inspired by modern jazz—and then had to go back and dig to learn about Louis Armstrong and Sidney Bechet. For Powell though there were no such problems. As a teenager he was fully aware of everything Earl Hines had done to transform early jazz piano-playing. In his late 'teens he played with white Chicagoan groups and also with one or two New Orleans masters. He then moved into Swing groups, made a name with the big bands in their heyday, experimented with Be-bop (briefly) and participated in the Mainstream revival of the 1950s. Moreover since World War II he has quietly consolidated an equally important position within classical music; and at the time of writing is deeply into electronic forms.

Clearly none of this extraordinary diversification could have been achieved without two things. First, his already-mentioned, ever-enquiring mind. And secondly a (naturally) gifted pianistic technique. He can perform easily at the keyboard what other creative players sometimes find difficult . . .

Anyway, to look at his *curriculum vitae* in more detail now. Mel was born a New Yorker and from his first few piano lessons came to be regarded as a musical prodigy. By the age of twelve he was already leading his own Dixieland-style sextet in Nyack, New York. He graduated from high school at fourteen and then worked with various combo leaders: Bobby Hackett, the tailgate trombonist George Brunies, drummer Zutty Singleton and Muggsy Spanier. But he made a 'key' move in 1941 when he joined the Benny Goodman band.

There was a touch of comedy about the way he entered the Goodman ranks, and George T. Simon, veteran *Metronome* editor, tells the story well. 'The hiring of Powell,' he recalls, 'serves as a classic example of how unintentionally exasperating Goodman could be. Knowing that Benny was looking for a new pianist, I told him about Powell, who was playing with a Dixieland group at Nick's. Benny suggested I bring him over to the MCA rehearsal room the next afternoon. At the audition he seemed quite impressed. Benny that is, but after Mel had left he kept asking me, *Is there anyone better around?* and I kept answering *No, no, no!* So that night Mel sat in at The Garden (Madison Square) and reportedly did very well. But sure enough, the next day, Benny, after telling me how well Mel had performed, popped the same question, *Is there anyone better around?* and I kept answering *no,* with a couple of *for Chris' sakes!* Benny said *O.K. I guess I'll take him.*'

Powell immediately became a 'star' attraction with Goodman. Apart from his solo work he composed and arranged *The Earl* (dedicated to Hines), a highly successful recording in spite of its being made without a drummer. Dave Tough had collapsed again. Benny booked Jo Jones for the session but the Musicians' Union wouldn't let Jo play. No matter. Mel was capable of swinging the band all on his own! His other scores for Goodman included *Jersey Bounce, Clarinade, Darktown Strutters Ball* and also *Mission To Moscow,* the last side the band cut before James Caesar Petrillo's disastrous union recording ban of 1942.

In 1943 the draft took Mel into the AAF band fronted by Major Glenn Miller, for whom the pianist soloed on the big hit, *String Of Pearls.* And as Sergeant Powell he headed the band's jazz group. In 1945 he won Esquire's Armed Forces New Star Award.

By this time though Mel was growing dissatisfied with the big band scene. Upon discharge he flirted with the idea of a career arranging for films. He did a little work in Hollywood—where he met and married actress Martha Scott. But then he changed tack entirely, enrolling as a student of musical composition at Yale University, which led on to a close association with Paul Hindemith, to further piano studies with Nadia Reisenberg and finally to his appointment as Professor of Music Theory at Queens College. By when, it seemed, he was well and truly lost from jazz.

Until the mid-1950s that is, when there was a sudden freak-out, rush of blood, yearning: call it what you will. At any rate, he played a whole string of club-dates with Goodman; did some staff work at the ABC

Studios; and cut two superb albums for Vanguard, containing his finest jazz solos on disc.

Just as on his famous *The Earl* recording with Goodman Mel was able to function perfectly well without a drummer, so for the Vanguards he elected to do without a bass-player. However, so strong is his own left-hand, also his developed harmonic sense, that the listener is never made to feel that anything is really lacking. He uses the same drummer throughout (the articulate Bobby Donaldson, who at the time of recording was working with Buck Clayton). And he has one frontline soloist on each album. For the first, originally titled "Borderline", there is the Lester Young-inspired tenorman Paul Quinichette, while on the second, called "Thigamagig", he has a trumpeter, the ubiquitous, rollicking Ruby Braff. But Mel himself is very much the authoritative leader and the star, despite his support of and attractive 'conversation'-pieces with the other musicians. There are moments when his earlier enthusiasms and influences break through. The flash and glitter of Earl Hines' right-hand; a Tatumesque run placed against a harmonic abstration; a deep, rolling figure so typical of Fats Waller; the order and form of a Teddy Wilson phrase. But essentially this is the mature and individual Mel Powell at his best. A strikingly two-handed player, a brilliant improviser, the master of his instrument and possessed of a gradation of touch to rival Bill Evans'. One notes too the later classical influences: the frequently fugal developments and some Debussy-like chromatics in passages of the ballads. Even so, the jazzman still comes out on top—playing with verve and excitement and above all *joy*. To attempt to sum up Mel Powell in a phrase: he is one of those comparatively rare intellectuals of music who always manages to sound happy.

1980

CHAPTER TEN

JIMMY BLANTON

A Short Life

To die at the age of twenty-one strikes us as a particular human tragedy; especially if it was a gifted guy. But an early death doesn't necessarily mean that the creative importance remains unfulfilled. Alexander the Great had an Empire larger than Europe while still in his 'twenties. Rimbaud died at thirty-six, but had written all of his revolutionary poetry before his eighteenth birthday—when he deserted the art to become a trader in the Levant and Ethiopia. Jimmy Blanton died at twenty-one, in July, 1942, with only a handful of records to his name. By which time he had revolutionised jazz bass-playing so that it could never return to its earlier, purely rhythmic style.

The remainder of his biography can be cobbled together in one paragraph. He worked with the Jeter-Pillars Orchestra in St. Louis, and then he boated up and down the Mississippi in a group led by caliopist Fate Marable. Next Duke Ellington heard and hired him. That was in 1939. Two years later Duke sent him to a sanatorium in California—when it proved to be too late. Tuberculosis took its final ghastly toll.

While underlining the Ellington band (arguably at this period at its greatest, with Cootie Williams, Johnny Hodges, Ben Webster, Lawrence Brown, Harry Carney and Ray Nance as it's featured soloists), Jimmy Blanton mesmerised everyone in jazz with the things he began to play on a previously sometimes trundling and rhythmically straightforward instrument. It also coincided with the unveiling of some of the very best of Duke's compositions: *Ko-Ko, Concerto For Cootie, Cotton Tail, Bojangles, A Portrait Of Bert Williams, Blue Goose,* and *Harlem Air-Shaft,* plus Billy Strayhorn's *Take The 'A' Train,* destined to become the Ellington signature tune. All of which employed the bass as no one had thought of doing before.

However, what really shook up the jazz rhythm section for all time were four daring bass-and-piano duets which Blanton recorded with Duke as his partner. The date was October 1, 1940, the place was Chicago and the titles were *Pitter Panther Patter, Sophisticated Lady, Body And Soul* and *Mr J. B. Blues* (released on RCA Victor). In addition, Jimmy played on a couple of sessions issued under trumpeter Rex Stewart's name and one led by Johnny Hodges. But the pleasure of listening to these items, *Poor Bubber, Menelik-The Lion Of Judah* and so on, should not be confused with the importance to jazz bass-playing of the four Blanton-Ellington duets.

Until this point in time the double bass (borrowed by jazz from the symphony orchestra) had merely replaced the oompah-sounding tuba of the New Orleans marching bands. Certain players before Blanton (notably 'Pops' Foster and then Wellman Braud, who also worked with Ellington) had performed their rhythmic roles superbly well: featuring a solid beat, evenness of fingering and a decent tone. But they remained essentially a crutch for the rest of the soloists to lean on. Nor did Blanton seek to pull this crutch away. If anything, his work stressed that the bass was and always will be the pivot of the jazz rhythm section. But what he showed as well, or at least pointed the way to, is just how agile and imaginative a bass can become under the hands of a skilled practitioner. Nobody before him had ever considered the instrument as a latent source of melody or harmonic sophistication. And certainly nobody had realised it could be flown alongside the horns and used for extended improvised solos. Until his arrival on the scene, jazz bass was thought of in the terms of quarter-notes. Then suddenly here was a man playing eight and sixteenth-note runs on it! And yet still playing with immense drive, definition, timing and, above all, a wonderfully pure tone.

His impact on other players and students was naturally enormous. And we have to remember that it all happened forty odd years ago. Since then jazz has been serviced by a magnificent crop of emancipated bass players. Oscar Pettiford, Ray Brown, Nelson Boyd, Red Callender, Scott LaFaro, Ron Carter, Richard Davis and Jaco Pastorius, to name just a few of the standouts. It's even debatable, had he lived, whether Blanton could have held his own with some of them (although I tend to think so). But this is no longer important. What is important is that he started it all.

A short life, yes, but a very productive one.

1983

CHAPTER ELEVEN

CLASSIC ELLINGTON

1. THE MUSIC ... THE MEN

As I grow older, so a goodly proportion of one's magazine and/or book readership registers the intake of new blood, i.e. *Youth*. I'm also aware that many new readers are already extremely talented in music; and likely to go far. But at the same time are faced with a dilemma. As they themselves move forward, so they are forced to look backwards into musical history as well. Where jazz is concerned, I can remember the late Clifford Brown saying that, as a youngster, he grew into the form being aware of Dizzy Gillespie, Fats Navarro, Kenny Dorham *et al*, but then had to go back and listen to what Louis Armstrong and Roy Eldridge had been doing in order to get a true perspective. No harm in this though. The symphonic student has to go back many centuries into musical history.

Every so often I like to point to the landfalls of earlier jazz. To items which have withstood the pulls of time; and as a result are worth bringing to the attention of younger readers. But to endeavour to do this with Duke Ellington, the music's greatest composer so far, can be a daunting task. I'm immediately reminded of John Cowper Powys in his 'Visions And Revisions' on the subject of Rabelais: 'There are certain great writers who make their critics feel even as children, who picking up stray wreckage and broken shells from the edge of the sea waves, return home to show their companions *what the sea is like.*'

Well, I feel somewhat similar about Duke Ellington. The huge suggestiveness and tremendous spirit in his music is not easy to communicate in the space of any single chapter. Also Duke lived a long life and his output was both furiously fast and, in the end, enormous. Nevertheless, I will try to describe *something* of what the sea is like. Ostensibly by picking out, here, and in a series of short following essays, certain important events in his remarkable career. Beginning with *Creole Rhapsody*, cut in 1931 for the old Brunswick label; then touching upon other, later shores.

Creole Rhapsody was issued on two sides of a ten-inch 78 rpm disc and featured a band already containing such 'stars' as Cootie Williams, Joe 'Tricky Sam' Nanton, Juan Tizol, Barney Bigard, Johnny Hodges and Harry Carney. More importantly though, it was the first success by any musician to write jazz in extended form. It even broke with a jazz tradition of writing in four-bar phrases. (The trombone chorus halfway through has a pattern of five, five, four and two bars.) But most important of all: it confirmed that in Edward Kennedy 'Duke' Ellington the music at last had a composer of genius. A man as significant to composed and arranged jazz as Louis Armstrong was to the improvised solo.

Ellington was born in Washington D.C. in 1899 and his family were modestly prosperous. He started in music as a ragtime pianist 'with flashy hands', but began to lead a band from 1918. Some of the men who came into this band during the '20s were markedly individual jazz soloists. Players like trumpeter Bubber Miley and trombonist Joe 'Tricky Sam' Nanton, both adept with mutes and plungers (Duke's 'jungle' effects), and the burly Harry Carney, the first man to play jazz on the baritone-saxophone. These men prompted Duke's longstanding method of writing for the sounds and styles of the musicians who would actually have to play his creations. Even so, by the time of *Creole Rhapsody* and its recording, the Ellington band was firmly dominated by its leader's abilities as a composer/arranger. And it would remain so ever afterwards; even after his death. Changes of personnel as late as the 1970s became additional colours to be mixed on his intensely personal and original palette.

Not that Duke restricted the art of improvisation in jazz. On the contrary, some of the finest solos on record have been created by members of his band. But he has imposed form on the duration of these solos and texture on the surrounds to them—as well as providing the thematic materials which inspire them. In other words, he makes the improvisation appear a logical extension of the main composition. And in the final analysis of *Creole Rhapsody,* or any other Ellington work, it is this dramatic, yet natural–sounding fusion of the written and the free in jazz which gives his music its perfect moments.

Turning to the composed parts themselves: it is a straight fact that Ellington has written more jazz themes of lasting value than anyone else—by about two hundred and fifty. Many of these (with lyrics added) have found their way into the musical heritage of popular song. Pieces like *Mood Indigo, Sophisticated Lady* and *I Got It Bad And That Ain't Good.* The majority though, after Duke's initial and even secondary recordings, have been fully absorbed into jazz as a continuing source of inspiration for musicians of all schools and ages. So strong are their melodies, chords and rhythmic patterns that it comes as no surprise to hear Art Tatum improvising on *A-Settin' And A-Rockin',* Buck Clayton and J. J. Johnson playing *In A Mellotone* or Charles Mingus recasting *Main Stem.*

Ellington the melodist is alternately romantic or groovy. He could write long, beautiful and instantly hummable lines which never tripped over the edge into oily sentimentality *(Prelude To A Kiss, Solitude, Warm Valley* and *Something To Live For)* or short, jumping and equally hummable 'riff'-type figures like *C Jam Blues, Perdido* and *Cotton Tail.* As a harmonist and textural writer he reveals an almost continuous curiosity—and in the variety of his findings has been to jazz what Debussy and Ravel were to earlier 20th century French music. His harmonies and subsequent development of them are strong, but remarkably flexible—while his tone colours reveal as sophisticated a knowledge of the jazz orchestra's potential as Delius had of the large modern symphony orchestra. His instrumental shadings are often exquisite, many of them impressions of Negro life in all its myriad forms around the United States. And he reinforces this through his use of rhythm. No one could argue that the 'hip' swing of *Harlem Air-Shaft* doesn't emphasise the picture he has created of 'teeming life' with the melody and texture. Or that the whole clanking, grinding underneath to *Happy-Go-Lucky-Local* isn't the chug-chugging of a decrepit old train meandering its way through the Deep South . . .

Next I turn to the highlights of Ellington's 1940/41 band. 'Ellington plays the piano, but his real instrument is his band' (Billy Strayhorn).

I have said that when Duke composed and orchestrated he made a full use of the players currently in his band. It is important, therefore, that we listen very closely to several of these: the individuals who have coloured the sound and style of his music.

I would choose for such a purpose the band Ellington led in 1940 and '41. Most musicians and writers now agree it was the best he ever fronted for the variety and character of its soloists. (I think the early 1950s one and the mid-'50s group of 'Such Sweet Thunder' come nearest to rivalling it). And it coincided with some of the leader's finest shorter pieces: *Ko Ko/Concerto For Cootie/Conga Brava/Cotton Tail/Bojangles/Portrait Of Bert Williams/Blue Goose/Harlem Air-Shaft* and *Sepia Panorama*. Plus Billy Strayhorn's *Take The 'A' Train,* the band's future signature tune. To America over this period Hitler's war in Europe seemed a million miles away.

The following are thumb-nail sketches of the principal men involved, and the Duke's themes they helped make famous.

COOTIE WILLIAMS, trumpet. A glowing, broad-toned stylist who on *Concerto For Cootie* proceeds to defy any thought of a fixed mood, murmuring mutedly, growling in anger, cutting in acidly, mellowing into humour and finally standing up and really shouting through his instrument in the style of his first idol, Louis Armstrong. (Later André Hodeir described Duke's use of the concerto-formula as a pure masterpiece and its theme, of course, became a popular song, *Do Nothin' Till You Hear From Me.*)

REX STEWART, trumpet (or cornet). Again originally a Louis Armstrong disciple; for Ellington though he makes much play with a squeezed tone via the half-valve effects he has developed. (Heard in a vital character part during *Portrait Of Bert Williams,* a whimsical study of the old vaudeville 'patter man'.)

WALLACE JONES, trumpet. The powerful lead and real workhorse of the trumpet section. (Important on every performance.)

RAY NANCE, trumpet and violin. Joined the band in 1941, replacing Cootie; makes an immediate impact on *Take The 'A' Train,* playing in a strong, but rather romantic style—with some humour and violin antics just around the corner.

LAWRENCE BROWN, trombone. Another romantic, but with a languid, more sophisticated sound. (Heard to advantage on the easy-paced *Blue Goose.*)

JOE 'TRICKY SAM' NANTON, trombone. The No. 1 expert in playing Duke's 'jungle' effects, using either rubber plunger or wa-wa mutes; also capable of sounding remarkably like the human voice in downcast blues numbers. (Tremendously important on *Ko Ko:* one of Ellington's most daring experiments with the 12-bar form, which he subjects to unusual modulations, instrumental timbres and emotive drama.)

JUAN TIZOL, valve-trombone. A Puerto Rican, with a smooth sound but an exotic style of phrasing. (States the theme of, and helped Ellington compose the Latin-American *Conga Brava.* Also *Perdido* and *Caravan.*)

BARNEY BIGARD, clarinet. Once a New Orleans player, with Ellington's band he has turned to longer, more florid lines and a whole display-cabinet of technical effects. (At his best and most useful on *Harlem Air-Shaft,* which Duke said attempted to contain the full essence of this district. 'You hear fights, you smell dinner, you hear people making love. You hear intimate gossip floating down. You hear the radio. An air-shaft is one great big loudspeaker.')

JOHNNY HODGES, alto-saxophone. More deeply romantic-sounding than any other soloist in jazz, with a sleek tone, wonderful sustained notes and an exquisite turn of phrase. (Best-known of all the Ellington soloists, he also plays some soprano-saxophone on *Blue Goose,* but is heard to greater advantage on slow, sensuous features like *Warm Valley.*)

BEN WEBSTER, tenor-saxophone. A mean-sounding, pugnacious player, of the Coleman Hawkins school but via all the hard jamming in Kansas City; he takes the first real solos on this instrument in an Ellington setting. (The jumping *Cotton Tail* is Ben's exciting showcase, and he plays well on *Bojangles,* a jazz portrait of the great tap-dancer Bill Robinson.)

HARRY CARNEY, baritone-saxophone. The massive-toned, decisive anchorman of every Ellington reed section and the pioneer soloist on this heavy instrument. (Two short, but typically enriched solos during *Sepia Panorama,* an altogether quieter sketch of Harlem life.)

JIMMY BLANTON, bass. Quite simply the most important

pioneering bass-player in jazz history. (Solos with the full Ellington band include: *Jack The Bear, Ko Ko, Bojangles, Sepia Panorama.*)

SONNY GREER, drums. Hardly a great rhythmic drummer (Duke would have to wait for Louie Bellson and Sam Woodyard before that); but the band makes good use of his showy fill-ins, together with the kit he has enlarged to include tympani, gong and tubular bells.

BILLY STRAYHORN, deputy pianist, composer, arranger. The Duke's *protégé* and amanuensis (frequently) from 1939 onwards. It is sometimes difficult to tell where one creator leaves off and the other begins. (Billy, nicknamed 'Swee' Pea' by Duke, is best-known for his gentle, impressionist pieces like *Lush Life, Chelsea Bridge, Day Dream* and *Passion Flower.* But a more swinging side to him is revealed by *'A' Train* and *Johnny Come Lately.*)

'By letting his men play naturally and relaxed, Ellington is able to probe the intimate recesses of their minds and find things that not even the musicians thought were there.' (Strayhorn)

Finally, or rather as a prelude to continuation, I will touch upon the undoubted masterpieces of 1950.

In 1947 Duke Ellington introduced a whole new series of contrasting compositions, including *Lady Of The Lavender Mist, New York City Blues, On A Turquoise Cloud, Hy'a Sue, Golden Cress* and Billy Strayhorn's *Progressive Gavotte.* Together with *The Liberian Suite.* But in 1948 there was an AFM (Musicians' Union) ban on recording as a result of a dispute with the major record companies. And this, coupled with Ellington's seldom going into the studios during 1949 and '50, started several critical enquiries as to whether Duke was now 'over the hill'. Ignoring *Creole Rhapsody,* others had been carping for years that the leading composer of jazz was a gifted miniaturist and no more: even pointing to the short movements of *Black, Brown And Beige* and *The Liberian Suite,* although in fact the length of these had been mainly determined by their being on 78 rpm records.

Near the end of 1950, however, Duke made a recording which indicated he was alive and well and writing very well in New York City. (When he wasn't writing on tour with the band.) Also he took advantage of electro-magnetic tape and the advent of the long-playing record to dispel, once and for all, the myth concerning his so-called 'inability' to compose and arrange in extended form.

The 'Masterpieces' LP of December 18/19, 1950 (on Columbia) consists of four concert-length scores. Three are of earlier Ellington compositions: *Mood Indigo* of 1931, *Sophisticated Lady* of 1933 and *Solitude* of 1934. And it becomes clear after listening to them that Duke's original thematic materials, far from weakening in the course of extended arrangement, have all the musical attributes necessary to make their further exploration both possible and logical. Duke is as firmly in control of shape and structure, of development and climax, as within any of his three-minute scores. Meanwhile the textures he weaves have all the freshness and colour of a good Spring. Nor has any pretentiousness crept in. The music remains naturally jazz music, with the players relaxed and Duke still letting their individual sounds affect the overall sound.

The Tattooed Bride has an added importance, being a composition written specifically for the recording and with some evidence that the processes of composition and arrangement were allowed to grow up simultaneously. (Probably at rehearsals, once Duke had his main motifs and skeletal routine.) It also tells a story. That of a young man who marries, only to discover on the wedding-night that his bride has been tatooed. (I presume Jimmy Hamilton's final high-note on clarinet represents the shock of discovery.) Anyway, the work has point, delightful themes and engrossing changes of atmosphere and tempi, from a moody contemplation to the wildly erotic: all expressed vividly by the scoring and by the voices of the Ellington soloists.

I believe that *The Bride* is not just a landfall for Ellington himself and for jazz, but can stand beside the works of our major European straight composers as a valuable addition to 20th century music. Basically, I suppose, because it collects so many of the Duke's great qualities into one work. Also because these qualities are in no way derivative. Duke once listed his own favourite composers as George Gershwin, Stravinsky, Debussy and Respighi. But in fact he owes these men very little. His music remains very much himself. Which is qualfication enough.

Other extended works followed, the most notable perhaps being 'A Tone Parallel To Harlem' (1951), 'A Drum Is A Woman' (1956), 'Such Sweet Thunder' (1956/57) and 'In The Beginning God' (1965).

2. THE YEARS OF TRANSITION

I had intended moving on next to Duke's great band of the early 1950s: the Louie Bellson—Britt Woodman—Willie Smith—Clark Terry band. Plus Paul Gonsalves. And with veterans Ray Nance, Jimmy Hamilton, Russell Procope and Harry Carney still there. But then a bout of personal musical conscience intervened. For two reasons. First, there has recently landed on my desk an impressive boxed-set, four LPs in all, containing the very best of Ellington's 1940-43 band. Not to review this package would be a serious omission. Secondly, although the later 1940s were somewhat patchy in the furtherance of Ellingtonia (largely due to circumstances beyond the leader's control), they were by no means barren years. Between the ending of the earlier AFM ban on recording—on December 1, 1944—and the "Masterpieces" album of late 1950 (already discussed), my small mountain of historical notes point to frequent, intermittent bursts of medium to high creativity which require recognition.

Hailed as 'the reissue of the year', the boxed-set of 1940-43 items is on RCA and is in a limited edition which comes with a sixteen-page booklet and a good selection of original black-and-white pictures. All the tracks have been digitally remastered. Also the box is aptly headlined 'Duke Ellington. The Blanton-Webster Years' after the band's two most revolutionary new players over this timescale. Jimmy Blanton was singlemindedly transforming the double-bass from being a simple rhythmic prop into a potent solo force. While Ben Webster, a product of the Kansas City hard-jamming school, was Duke's first great tenor-saxophone soloist. The leader would not later find an adequate replacement for him until the advent of Paul Gonsalves.

Another important feature of the package is that, as well as acknowledged masterworks such as *Jack The Bear, Ko Ko, Concerto For Cootie, Cotton Tail, Bojangles* and *A Portrait Of Bert Williams,* it mops up a whole host of 'second division' titles which nevertheless contain brilliant Ellington touches. The opening track, for instance, *You, You Darlin',* is a trite Tin Pan Alley song which the Duke had been persuaded to record as a commercial vehicle for singer Herb Jeffries. But then the leader supplies the central, vocal area with a curling countermelody for the reeds, following a good opening solo by Webster, which he turns into a hymnal sound behind Lawrence Brown's trombone conclusion and suddenly we are back in the presence of genius. A pause, and next we are into the overt genius of *Jack The Bear.* A showcase mainly for Jimmy Blanton, no other jazz composer at this time would have dared implement such a revolutionary structure around the pioneering bass-player. Blanton enters with much drama after a brief fanfare from trombones and reeds. And what a player he turns out to be! After first improvising melodic lines, he then proceeds to 'walk' with guitarist Fred Guy and drummer Sonny Greer, and to double a syncopated saxophone line in a three-times-repeated transition before reappearing towards the end with more improvisation and a chromatic cadenza leading into the final chord. Ellington's orchestral plan for all of this combines a *ritornello* (the bass-and-saxophone line), 32-bar song form and five choruses of a 12-bar blues. Which, against apparent odds, works in a mesmeric fashion.

The package bulges with these typically Ellington dares. As well as his writing for the men behind each instrument as human individuals, exploiting their separate sounds and styles to the utmost. By the final track on Side Eight (*Sherman Shuffle,* recorded on July 28, 1942), one realises just how far the Duke has progressed as a composer and leader since the primitivism and 'jungle'-based effects of his 1920s Cotton Club days. He comes across as very sophisticated, rich in melodic, harmonic and rhythmic invention and, above all, the most questing spirit in modern American music . . .

So let us now turn to the later 1940s. During the protracted wrangle between the AFM and the major record companies, Duke had cut only a handful of V–Discs, sanctioned as part of the American war effort and which included Rex Stewart's cornet extravaganza, *Boy Meets Horn.* And perhaps it was with a gentle irony, therefore, that when the ban was lifted, for his first 'official' session Duke decided to call a delightful new song he'd written: *I'm Beginning To See The Light.* By this time too there were some fresh faces in the band. The reeds were fairly settled with Hodges, Otto Hardwick, Al Sears, Jimmy Hamilton (clarinet and second tenor) and Carney, of course, the root-like baritone. But the brass had regrouped with trombonist Claude Jones replacing Tizol and in the trumpet section the volatile Taft Jordan, the 'impossible' high-note specialist Cat Anderson (always 'my phenomenon' to the Duke) and Shelton Hemphill replacing Rex Stewart and longtime lead Wallace Jones. Joya Sherrill and the blind Al Hibbler were singing with the band.

It was a period of several important Ellington songs, including *Prelude To A Kiss, I Let A Song Go Out Of My Heart* and his dedication to a schoolmistress, *Sophisticated Lady,* together with the recording of two more concert works, 'New World A-Comin' (written around Duke's own piano playing) and another collaboration with Billy Strayhorn entitled 'The Perfume Suite', a work describing 'the transitory character of Woman behind her aromatic facade.'

In four movements, the latter opens with *Strange Feelings,* said to represent violent love. Al Hibbler sings of the physical sensations immediately preceding love, his acrid voice at times finding it difficult to manipulate the melodic line due to its angular bends. But then it is left to Cat Anderson to create an instrumental impression of such sensations and he is heard prowling restlessly against the remainder of the ensemble, a hemmed-in, dangerous creature, playing tightly-muted, growling phrases from his throat, stabbing others hotly, even deliberately stuttering some phrases to heighten the tension. It is an alternative trumpeter to Cat, however, this time the amiable Ray Nance, who plays the broad-toned introduction to *Balcony Serenade,* set to define a more dignified method of love-making as typified by the under-the-balcony wooing by the male partner. Ellington's series of imposing block chords at the piano (executed with a concert-like flourish) eventually make way for the most delightful melody of the entire work, which flows out from the reed section with appropriate deployment against only semi-active brass. The third movement, *Dancers In Love,* representing the naive stage of courtship, resolves itself into a brief, happy romp played by Ellington himself with the support of only Junior Raglan's singing bass—and it provides a *scherzo*-like relief within the construction of the suite. *Coloratura,* the conclusion, meant to portray the woman who includes maturity and sophistication in her love-making, becomes another Cat Anderson *tour de force,* and his stratospheric powers are brought out to the full here. Cat, whose top C is merely the prelude to higher things, blows a series of melodic variations in true *aria* fashion over the main body of the orchestra and produces, as he soars towards his climax, the most extrovert music of this transitional work.

Leaving aside now 'The Deep South Suite' of 1946/47 and the 'Liberian Suite' of 1947 as suitable lead-ins to an analysis of later concert works, I will conclude this section with the more important shorter items of the remaining 1940s.

Duke continued to record V–Discs for broadcasting use even when World War II hostilities had ceased—ostensibly as a workshop measure whereby he could introduce themes of dubious commercial appeal and estimate the public reaction to them. The more successful ones he would then re-orchestrate and record commercially at a slightly later date. *Unbooted Character* and Strayhorn's *Esquire Swank* took their bow in this way.

The extension to the Duke's RCA Victor contract terminated in 1946. In July, August and September of that same year, in Hollywood, the band recorded its last batch of titles for the label. Taft Jordan did everything but burst a blood vessel with *Suddenly It Jumped.* Kay Davis, a legitimate soprano voice, fused herself wordlessly with the instrumental grouping written by the Duke on *Transbluency,* the first of her experiments in the Adelaide Hall style with the band. Jimmy Hamilton led off an organised ensemble score of *Royal Garden Blues* and Al Hibbler put into words more of Duke's thoughts about the feminine *mysterioso* with *Pretty Woman.*

A destroying illness took 'Tricky Sam' Nanton as these last Victor sessions were being held. Duke replaced him with Tyree Glenn, the former Cab Calloway trombonist who doubled on vibes.

In the closing months of 1946 the band recorded for the new Musicraft label. Ray Nance frisked vocally and instrumentally through the light-hearted *Tulip Or Turnip.* Hodges lazed with the melody of *Sultry Sunset.* Jimmy Hamilton displayed his dexterity again throughout *Flippant Flurry.* And Strayhorn wrote his two-part *Overture To A Jam Session,* while Ellington himself introduced his *Beautiful Indians* impressions and Mary Lou Williams wrote a dashing arrangement of *Blue Skies* with high-powered brass, calling it *Trumpet No End.*

Then from August, 1947 the Duke began to record for Columbia, later to become CBS. These were the *Lady Of A Lavender Mist* sessions. Add to them Jimmy Hamilton's immaculate, concerto-like clarinet performance during *Air-Conditioned Jungle,* paced by Oscar Pettiford on bass, plus Harold Baker's throbbing trumpet on *Three Cent Stomp,* and you have the best of the Ellington output up until the second AFM ban of 1948/49.

It was at Manchester in the Summer of 1948 that I was taken to see my first 'live' Ellington performance (my father's arm having been twisted), but this was but a capsule distillation—because he came to England without his band. The Duke was touring Europe as a variety act, his piano playing augmented by Kay Davis and the multiple talents of Ray Nance. After an urbane medley of the better-known Ellington songs, it was then left to 'Floorshow' Nance to *break it up!*—which he proceeded to do with alacrity, via trumpet mimics, violin skits, pre-Sammy Davis Jr-style singing and post-Bojangles-style tap dancing. It was another *tour de force*. His culminating sequence, high-kicking and doing the splits, brought the audience cheering into the aisles.

Musically though the decade did not end well for the Duke. A Wall Street relapse was playing havoc with the entertainment business, and particularly the big bands with their heavy overheads. The Ellington concert tours often needed subsidies from the royalty fund he accrued as a composer.

And as 1949 drew to a close, all was not well within the band's ranks. Al Killian, the new high lead trumpeter, was having lip trouble; so the leader kept another, similar specialist, Ernie Royal, within hailing distance. Hodges, Hamilton, Procope and Carney remained with the reeds, but the band had no real tenor-saxophone soloist of note. Drummer Sonny Greer was suffering from ill-health. So Butch Ballard travelled with the band as his deputy. However, the major problem concerned the trombones, with the announced departure of Tyree Glenn. Rumours of a European tour with the full band in 1950 had triggered this. Tyree had visited Europe in 1946 with Don Redman, and in Paris there had been a friendship with a French girl. The trombonist's wife made it clear there would be no more overseas tours for him. Though remaining a nominal member of the band, and actually making some of the 1950 record dates, Glenn's tenure was nearly through. Which added to 1949 being a year of insecurity in every way for the Duke.

3. THE NEW MEN OF THE 'FIFTIES

As the United States of America turned into the 1950s an embattled President Harry S. Truman ('the captain with a mighty heart': Dean Acheson), the man who had saved Western Europe economically after World War II with his authorisation of the Marshall Plan, blunted Stalin by instituting the Berlin Airlift and had recently turned the tide against Far East Communism in the Korean War, found his two greatest enemies were his own fellow-countrymen, the dreadful Macs: the arrogant General MacArthur in Tokyo (Truman stripped him of his commands in 1951) and the sinister Joseph McCarthy, Senator for Wisconsin, whose ambitions had turned him into a political, anti-left, witch-hunter in the Robespierre category (one Richard Milhaus Nixon, another aspiring politician, served on his staff). By the time Truman left office in January,

1953 he had set in motion the necessary national conscience to pull the rug out from under McCarthy as well. But I recount these facts merely as an illustration of how a crisis of self-confidence had hit the American public at this time. We now know that MacArthur's overweening vanity had turned his youthful talents into a Japanese-lantern of a general. And McCarthy was as low as only a politician can be. The then-criticised Truman is currently realised to have been one of the best American Presidents.

Unfortunately though, these events, economically, and with the crisis of self-confidence, hit the band business particularly hard. Woody Herman was forced to break up. Count Basie had to tour for a year with just a seven-piece (albeit one which included Clark Terry, Charlie Rouse, Freddie Green, of course, and Buddy Rich). Duke Ellington leaned even more heavily upon his composer's royalties to subsidise the continuation of his orchestra. But other than the 'Masterworks' LP there is something lacklustre about the remaining recordings of 1950 and into 1951. They suggest a decided loss of morale . . .

Three events only illuminate this dreary year in Ellingtonia. One: recruiting of tenor-saxist Paul Gonsalves from the defunct Dizzy Gillespie big band (another victim of the recession). Secondly, Duke cut a solo, *New Piano Roll Blues,* using a piano fitted with a 'mandolin' attachment, but more importantly urged on by the relentless drumming of Max Roach. The leader crashes out some hard, angular, percussive phrases which reveal he has been listening to Thelonious Monk. At last, belatedly, be-bop was beginning to enter his soul. Finally, behind the scenes, Ellington had been working away steadily on his long, beautifully-integrated piece, *A Tone Parallel To Harlem.*

On January 21, 1951 the Harlem piece was premiered at the Metropolitan Opera House in New York during a concert in aid of the National Association for the Advancement of Coloured People, together with a variety of Ellington standards such as *The Mooche* (featuring Russell Procope and Jimmy Hamilton on clarinets, Quentin Jackson, trombone, and Ray Nance), *Frustration* (Carney), *Take The 'A' Train* (Gonsalves) and *Violet Blue* (Hodges). Also the Duke added Joe Benjamin on bass and Bill Clark on drums to play in unison with Wendell Marshall (perhaps his best bass-player since Blanton) and Sonny Greer. Mike Levin reviewed it as one of 'the finest concerts in years'; but nevertheless added: 'Something important and vital is missing from the Ellington band. Exactly what, it's hard to say.'

In fact, this time it wasn't just a question of morale. It was an actual *plot.* Within weeks of the NAAC charity concert Duke received the veritable body blow. Hodges, Lawrence Brown and Sonny Greer gave notice, *en bloc.* They would be forming a new band with tenor-saxist Al Sears and fronted by Hodges. They'd even been measured for band uniforms in preparation for an opening at Chicago's Blue Note on March

9, '51. And behind Duke's back Hodges had signed an exclusive recording contract with Norman Granz.

If all of this came as a shock to Ellington, to the world jazz audience it was the equivalent of nuclear fission. After all, Hodges had been *the* Ellington soloist for twenty years. And a sublime soloist at that. Okay, he was a very prickly fellow. Okay, he had evidenced jealousy of his leader. Nevertheless, his lovely, silken tone and romantic phrasing on alto-saxophone had become almost an extension of the Duke's own thinking. Many shook their heads; his band without The Rabbit was, well, unthinkable.

But Ellington had some steel in his soul as well as creativity and beliefs. He found a temporary replacement for Greer in Bill Clark, while the Kansas City tenorman Tommy Douglas agreed to switch to alto as a substitute for Hodges. And the tide began to turn when Duke gained a permanent replacement for Lawrence Brown in Britt Woodman. Woodman, a boyhood friend of Charles Mingus had been playing with the latter in a Los Angeles group called The Stars Of Swing (in effect, the very first Mingus Workshop). He is a trombonist of enormous range, including symphonic experience and one of the most original stylists of modern jazz.

When the Duke telephoned him he accepted the job on condition he was given two weeks alongside Lawrence Brown to learn the book. The reputation of the Ellington band parts (dog-eared at best, some mere scraps of paper) had made him wary. At the end of his first night in Las Vegas—sitting beside Brown—he said: 'Thank God I've got another two weeks.' 'The Hell with that', Lawrence retorted, 'I'm leaving tonight!'

Left to his own devices, the next night Woodman reverted to his natural style. Forget Lawrence, he told himself. *He would lead the trombones his way!* At the end of the show Duke sent for him. *Well, this is it,* the trombonist thought. *Obviously I don't fit.* Instead of which he found himself being lavishly praised. 'You're certainly different,' Ellington said, 'but I like what I hear. Go on leading the' bones exactly as you're doing. And I'm going to write some new pieces for you. I've got your sound coming into my head now.' All of which led on eventually to the famous *Hank Cinq* and later still *Princess Blue*.

Meanwhile, the trumpet section had been strengthened by the intake of Clark Terry, originally a St. Louis man who had worked with Count Basie. An irrepressible, extrovert soloist, like Woodman he too thoroughly understood the Be-bop Revolution. (He later played on Thelonious Monk's 'Brilliant Corners' LP). With Gonsalves, Woodman and Terry the New Guard now had a firm power base inside the band.

But these three were only half the transformation. Because Ellington was about to stage the most outrageous *coup* of his entire bandleading career. At least in purely human terms. He quite deliberately 'poached' lead alto Willie Smith and drummer Louie Bellson from the Harry James band; and, as if for good measure, re-recruited valve-trombonist Juan Tizol from the same band. It became known as 'the Great James Raid'— and afterwards Harry wouldn't speak to Ellington for a long, long time . . .

In Willie Smith the Duke gained not just a brilliant soloist (in the vertical style of Benny Carter rather than the linear one of Hodges), but also a lead alto and a rehearser of saxophone sections second to none. For a decade (until 1941) he had been the power at the helm of the Jimmy Lunceford saxes: the most admired in the United States for precision and togetherness. And he now applied his talents to Ellington's wayward section. Though wayward only due to years of neglect. Out of his supreme selfishness and personal brilliance Hodges hadn't bothered to rehearse the saxes at all. They relied on record dates under Duke's or Strayhorn's direction to get into collective practice. Suddenly everything was changed. Smith drilled them and drilled them and drilled them. As well as showing them musical possibilities they'd never even imagined existed. And they responded. Within the timescale of two months Duke had the best saxophones *as a section* he'd ever known. Crisp, precise and swinging together as if with a single voice.

Alongside which, in the trombones the situation was as follows: Britt Woodman, lead and the more modernist solos, Quentin Jackson, the earlier muted and 'jungle' solos, and Juan Tizol, the other exotica— not least when Ellington dusted off and rearranged their previous collabortions, *Perdido, Caravan, Bakiff* and *Conga Brava.*

The trumpets were Clark Terry and Harold 'Shorty' Baker, Cat Anderson (back as the high-note specialist) and Ray Nance (good medium-range trumpet solos; gutsy violin; zany comedy).

And behind all of these there was placed a whirlwind called Louie Bellson.

The Duke had never encountered such a drummer before. Sonny Greer, with the band since 1919, had been a flashy player with an elaborate display of kit. But his technique was limited; and his swing variable, often subject to the tyrannies of the gin bottle. In contrast the younger Bellson was an extraordinary technician who could drive a big band with full fury. From Rock Falls, Illinois, before the age of eighteen he had won various contests run by Gene Krupa. Since when he had played with Benny Goodman and Tommy Dorsey ahead of joining Harry James. But although a powerhouse drummer, when the occasion demanded he was also an extremely articulate one, with a control over dynamics which put him into the Buddy Rich class. Add to this his concept of featuring twinned bass-drums, plus his ability to think percussively as an arranger and he couldn't fail to have a major impact on any band he played with. Now, with a good bass-player beside him (Wendell Marshall), he took over the engine-room of Duke's.

Ellington was both pleased with and excited by his new band. 'Take

Britt Woodman,' he said. 'He came to us out of a left field. From Los Angeles, to be exact. He's phenomenal. He plays notes that are two octaves off the horn! Naturally he's got to demand respect. Then take Willie Smith. He's not only a helluva soloist but a really wonderful section man. And Juan is back with us again. You know nobody has a sound like him. And Louie Bellson. He breaks it up everywhere—even in the coldest places we work. You know, when a guy hears applause like that it makes him say, *I was right* and he feels good. But Bellson's not only a great soloist; he has a helluva drive and he's a helluva arranger.'

So, these were the new men of the early '50s. They would help constitute one of the two greatest bands Ellington ever led and they were all in position now. In the next segment I will try to tell something about what they did. Also what the Duke did with them . . .

4. A STARRY-EYED, SATISFYING TIME

The Duke's first recording with his new men was a small-group date for the independent Mercer label, in which the leader himself had a financial stake and which was named after and run by his own son. On April 17, 1951, they recorded *Cat Walk,* a Bellson/Ellington theme and featuring Cat Anderson for once playing in a growled-out middle register; Juan Tizol's *Moonlight Fiesta* with a good solo by Willie Smith; *She* by Cat Anderson again; and *The Happening* (based on the chord sequence of *Get Happy*), a sweeping Paul Gonsalves solo urged on by Louie Bellson's driving drums.

Then on May 18 Duke was encouraged to set up another small group session for Mercer. This time featuring Willie Smith more prominently *(Indian Summer)* backed by the band's three trombones. And with a solo from Britt Woodman *(Sultry Serenade)* and a Woodman-Quentin Jackson duet *(Britt And Butter Blues).*

In between though, there had been one very lively big band session for Columbia (now CBS) on May 10. It proved a spirited occasion indeed, with Duke the composer back in full spate *(Fancy Dan, V.I.P.'s Boogie* and *Jam With Sam,* plus his humorous monologue-with-music, *Pretty And The Wolf).* But the best-known item to emerge from the session—and which gave Ellington a medium-sized hit single—was Louie Bellson's original composition and arrangement, *The Hawk Talks.* If anything it was nearer to the Woody Herman mid-1940s sounds of *Wild Root* and *Apple Honey* than to Previous Ellington. On the other hand Bellson had taken full advantage of the Duke's smartened-up musicianship and his own belting swing to give the piece a real cutting edge.

Duke himself became positively starry-eyed. 'The guys call their own rehearsals,' he reported with amazement. 'Now you know that hasn't happened for years in our band. Another thing, there's no rudeness on the stand. When the guys stay together too long, they're apt to get tired of looking at each other. Not this crew!'

In May, 1951 the band scored a notable public success at Birdland. And on June 20 an even bigger one when they played a charity concert in aid of the Damon Runyon Cancer Fund at Lewissohn Stadium. The first half of the concert featured *Fancy Dan, The Hawk Talks, Controversial, Coloratura, Take The 'A' Train* and *Monologue-Duet-Threesome*. Then after the interval the band was joined by sixty members of the NBC Symphony Orchestra for Luther Henderson's arrangement of Duke's *New World A-Comin'* and Duke's own score of *A Tone Parallel*. Followed by Louie Bellson's *Skin Deep* and the inevitable *pot-pourri* of early Ellington songs (the interminable medley which Duke misguidedly foisted upon his audiences for the next two decades). This medley was supposed to end the concert—but the audience demanded more and better. When according to *Down Beat*: 'Duke repaired a serious oversight—he brought forth Willie Smith, who hitherto had not played a single note, to blow an unrehearsed *Tea For Two*. With Duke, Louie and Wendell Marshall, Willie wove his delicate way through a chorus or two; then the reed-men started to lay down a light background; the brass joined in; and finally the longhairs leaped in, the bass men plucking frenziedly, the violinists sawing with vigour!' (Britt Woodman told me recently that much as Duke admired what Willie Smith had done in turning around the saxophone section, nevertheless he still fretted over the loss of Hodges as a soloist.)

In March, 1952 a similar concert took place in Seattle, a recording of which was released in England by HMV. But the more significant events of this year were the addition of Willie Cook, another be-bop specialist, to the trumpets; and then on August 10 the definitive, studio recording of Bellson's *Skin Deep*.

This last gave the Duke his first really big hit record in years. Issued as a double-sided single, after the opening brass fanfares, its whole central *raison d'être* is a drum extravaganza, a solo of great length, daring and, above all, imagination. Louie Bellson's technique is formidable, his inserted ideas seemingly limitless. And the whole as articulate as it is dynamic. Truly one of the finest kit performances. (A personal anecdote here—not without its touch of humour. When *Skin Deep* entered the US charts I was working on the staff of English Decca, whose management in its infinite wisdom decided we ought to do a cover version. One of our leading drummer/percussionists was called in to listen to the Ellington disc. About a minute into Bellson's drum solo he broke into a sweat. Then he shook his head. 'Not me,' he said. 'Definitely not me!')

Louie Bellson left the band in January, 1953. He had recently married the singer/entertainer Pearl Bailey, and wanted to tour with her. Duke replaced him briefly with Ed Shaughnessy, a one-time pupil of Dave Tough and—following Bellson—a user of twinned bass-drums. Eventually though, after several deputies, the leader gave the drum-stool to Butch Ballard on a regular basis. Willie Smith had left several weeks before Bellson: to go back to Harry James. Duke replaced him with ex-Cab Calloway lead alto Hilton Jefferson, who shared Smith's approach to rehearsing the saxophones.

Also in 1953 Ellington signed a new recording contract, with Capitol—and at the band's very first session (on April 6, in Hollywood) cut what would become one of his best-known shorter works: *Satin Doll*. Many more titles, mostly standards like *Stormy Weather* and *Three Little Words* were recorded on April 7 and 9. And over April 13/14 the leader cut a 10-inch piano album backed by Wendell Marshall and Butch Ballard. Of this last album, my friend Alun Morgan wrote at the time: 'The Duke has never made a feature of his own playing, preferring to speak with the voice and authority of his full orchestra. I have always regretted this reticence on his part, for when the veil has been lifted for a brief moment it has revealed a most interesting and unique approach to piano jazz. He seems capable of producing always the most enchanting little passages to insert into his orchestral compositions; the piano towards the end of *Fancy Dan* is a good example. As a technician he has been criticised both by uncomprehending outsiders and, more modestly, by himself. Technique is a valuable attribute, but there are several jazzmen whose value exceeds their musicianship. To play these eight titles through is more than an interesting experience. It is a penetrating insight into the mind of a remarkable man.'

Still with Capitol, later in 1953 Ellington recorded a number of arrangements featuring vocalist Jimmy Grissom (*Nothin', Nothin' Baby, Ballin' The Blues*) and over the next year began to lay down the titles eventually issued as the LP 'Ellington '55'. Critic Nat Hentoff called this last collection 'disappointing', not from the band but because he thought the arrangements 'retrogressive'. However, and again to refer to Alun Morgan, not even Ellington could produce another 'Black, Brown And Beige' or 'Harlem' at the drop of a hat. His arrangements for 'Ellington '55' suited the excitements of the bands and its music. While the Duke himself argued his own satisfaction with their setting in his sleeve-notes (a great rarity for him to write any . . .) 'They're the most accurate impressions of the Ellington orchestra ever made,' he insisted. 'Not only from the technical—the recording—viewpoint, but because the musicians were on an inspired emotional level . . . a level that's just *never* achieved during ordinary sessions. You can hear it.' He was right. "Ellington '55" is an exciting foot-tapper from beginning to end.

But in contrast to the *level* of "Ellington '55", the Duke did record a number of absolute 'dogs' during his Capitol years; most notoriously *Bunny Hop Mambo,* Charlie Chaplin's *Smile* in a gluey score, *If I Give My Heart To You* and *Twelfth Street Rag.* Not even the fine musicianship could salvage these particular items.

Through the Summer of 1955 the band appeared in Elliot Murphy's *Aquacade* show at Flushing Meadows, Long Island. But the Duke had to drop (temporarily) Rick Henderson (alto), Gonsalves, Woodman, Willie Cook and drummer Dave Black because they weren't union members of Local 802. Nor did Ellington think much of having the show foist another pianist, two girl harpists and a string section upon him . . .

In 1956 there were further significant personnel changes. The most important one being the return of Johnny Hodges, following the failure of his own group. Hodges was playing as well as ever; but his reappearance caused some bad blood between the band's Old Guard (who regrouped around The Rabbit) and the newer, more modern jazz-orientated soloists. However, there were no problems about the new drummer, Sam Woodyard ('The best drummer I've had since Louie Bellson': DE). Woodyard and bass-player Jimmy Woode would now remain with Ellington for quite a few years.

The Capitol contract fizzled out dismally with such trivia as *La Virgen De La Macarena, Clarinet Melodrama* and *Theme For Trambean.* Whereupon Duke promptly made two albums for Bethlehem: "Historically Speaking—The Duke", which traced his own history through the years with a selection of his best-known tunes, and "Duke Ellington Presents". There is much good Hodges, Carney, Terry, Gonsalves and Woodman scattered over these two releases; while the Woodyard-Woode rhythmic partnership was already a force to be reckoned with.

Then Ellington decided to re-sign with Columbia (CBS). His first new recording for the label featured singer Rosemary Clooney. The only all-instrumental track on this particular LP is a reworking of *Passion Flower,* a Johnny Hodges solo. And in March '56 The Rabbit went on to cut four of his own compositions with the band: *Hi Ya, Texas Blues, Duke's Jam* and *You Got It Coming.* At the same sessions Cat Anderson recorded two of *his* own compositions, *The Happy One* and *Night Walk.* Lawrence Brown rejoined the band for these. But not Sonny Greer. Sam Woodyard was too satisfactory to be dropped.

Towards the end of 1956 Duke was quietly working away on another longer work, the suite "A Drum Is A Woman". But in the October he still found time to supervise a batch of small group titles for Columbia. The themes were his own *Duke's In Bed, Just Squeeze Me* and *Black And Tan Fantasy* (originally co-authored with trumpeter Bubber Miley), Strayhorn's *Ballade For Very Sad, Very Tired Lotus Eaters* and *Take The 'A' Train,* Hodges' *Meet Mr. Rabbit, Confab With Rab* and *Ah Oodie Oobie,* plus the standard *It Had To Be You.* The musicians involved were Terry,

Nance, Jackson, Hamilton, Hodges, Carney, Strayhorn on piano, Woode and Woodyard.

And also towards the end of the year Duke had a go at those 'cocooned' critics of his current band. 'I don't think it's fair to talk about something today and compare it to something some time ago,' he told *Down Beat.* 'What is happening in my work today is a result of an investment in time and money that is *of the present.* The only reason we're still in it is mainly artistic interest. We're not one of those people who stay in the business only so long as business is good. We stay in it fifty-two weeks a year. And the most important thing we do, I think, is to present people we like ourselves. To compare the band of the present with the band of another period involves, for one thing, trying to recall another audience to which that older band was playing. And that band also was playing from another perspective. I don't see the basis of comparison. The audiences are different, and we're different in a way. And it really boils down to an ugly thing like—do you have better taste than I do? After all, if these men who perform the music now didn't believe in it, they wouldn't do it.'

The truth was that Duke would never be caged by his traditionalist admirers—by those who argued that he had peaked in his early career with *Creole Love Call* and *East St. Louis Toodle-oo* and had never been as good since. In reality he was already light years ahead of these people. And his mind was still fresh and questing. Genius may from time to time make mistakes, but it does not respond well to chains . . .

5. THAT SPECIAL FESTIVAL

Before his death in 1974, Duke played many festivals all around the world. But *the* special jazz festival, for his many friends and long-time Ellington watchers, was at Newport, Rhode Island, on July 7, 1956. Principally for one long performance of *Diminuendo And Crescendo In Blue* which blazed into life on that fine Summer's night. Issued on record by Columbia (CBS), it became, together with *Skin Deep* and the composition *Satin Doll* the third of his most popular successes of the decade.

1956 was the year of the third Newport Jazz Festival—an event first of all sponsored by a non-profit-making organisation led by Louis Lorillard and his wife. In later years, after the Newport Rebels (Mingus, Roy Eldridge, Eric Dolphy, Jo Jones *et al*) had camped out in a separate compound and played their protests at the way things were being run, the official Newport degenerated into an event of teenagers being drunk on *concessionaire* beer by midday and eventually riots, which the Lorillards resigned from in disgust and the Police Department decided to close the festival down. But in 1956 the Newport Festival was still young—

and at its best.

Just to bring readers up-to-date—once contracts were signed, the band Duke took to this most agreeable New England setting consisted of Cat Anderson, Clark Terry, Ray Nance and Willie Cook (trumpets), Britt Woodman, Quentin Jackson and John Sanders (trombones—Sanders the bass-trombone), Johnny Hodges and Russell Procope (altos), Paul Gonsalves (tenor), Jimmy Hamilton (tenor, clarinet), Harry Carney (baritone), Ellington and/or Billy Strayhorn (piano), Jimmy Woode (bass) and Sam Woodyard on drums.

The weather was especially good that Summer in this, the smallest of all the states of the Union. The setting seemed ideal and the crowds were large. Also Ellington himself was fit and well, very much looking forward to the occasion.

On the evening before, July 6, there had been a particularly exciting set by trumpeter Buck Clayton's All-Stars. His group was completed by J. J. Johnson on trombone (proving that as the leading trombone of be-bop he still knew what the Swing era was all about), Coleman Hawkins (who double-handedly had taken the tenor-saxophone from vaudeville into jazz music for all time), Dick Katz, piano, Benny Moten, bass (but no relation to the old Kansas City bandleader) and Gus Johnson on drums. After a marvellous *You Can Depend On Me,* wherein The Hawk had a 'go' at his longstanding rival Lester Young, Buck closed the set with a tribute to Ellington and a suggestion of what *might* happen the following night by playing *In A Mellotone,* the Duke's 1940 counter-melody to *Rose Room.*

When Columbia issued their records from the Newport Festival, they made the Clayton set Side 2 of an album prefaced by various Ellington items played the following night. Items designed to cool down the audience after the excitements of *Diminuendo And Crescendo In Blue.* Thus, although the album opens with Strayhorn's *Take The 'A' Train,* which in fact opened the concert, it then continues with 'the coolers': *Sophisticated Lady* (featuring Harry Carney, who plays the verse as well as the celebrated chorus); *I Got It Bad And That Ain't Good* (a Hodges solo); and finally *Skin Deep.* Sam Woodyard has the great good sense not to try to emulate Louie Bellson's 'hit' solo. (Only Buddy Rich arguably could have done this.) Instead Sam 'The Man' plays his own thing, based entirely on his kit knowledge and swing, and as a result scores a personal triumph . . .

But now we must turn to the other Ellington Newport LP, the one which encapsulates *Diminuendo And Crescendo In Blue,* and which was released first.

By the beginning of the evening of July 7, the audience at Newport was made up of disparate groupings: of many Ellington admirers, some elderly, others new; then the other *young,* most genuinely learning about jazz, and just a few clutching cans; plus, of course, the Lorillards; Nat

Hentoff, who reported it all; George Wein (the booker, always conspicuous by his presence); a heavy contingent of Manhattan denizens; and, apparently, a smaller contingent of local residents—who had sidled in to discover what-the-hell was going on. By the end of the Ellington set, all of them, from d-j'd NY socialites to drummer Jo Jones (who played his own part in the proceedings) were agog, left reeling by one particular performance by the Ellington band. But really all revolving about one tenor-saxist, offstage a shy and retiring man, and with many personal problems, but who played with something approximating genius that night.

Paul Gonsalves (b. Boston, 1920) had started out on guitar and then played tenor with Count Basie and Dizzy Gillespie before joining Ellington. On ballads he tended to play in a rhapsodic style drived from Coleman Hawkins: with a gruff, vibrato-laden tone and sinuous melodic phrasing. But given the chance to play up-tempo his experiences with be-bop also tended to come through. Also, when improvising he was a long–distance runner. And he could swing at the drop of a hat. On the night of July 7, 1956 with *D & C In Blue* he was destined to make jazz history.

Moreover, it went against expectations. Ellington and Billy Strayhorn had readied a new three-part work, which, following the band's booking, they titled 'Newport Jazz Festival Suite and which was expected to be the highlight of the occasion. The opening movement, *Festival Junction* has solos by Jimmy Hamilton (a cadenza and then stating the theme), Ellington himself, Willie Cook, Gonsalves (still under wraps), Britt Woodman (very good), Harry Carney (good), Quentin Jackson (predictable, but immaculate), Russell Procope (very good) and Cat Anderson (predictably high). This part of the work is medium-paced. The second movement, *Blues To Be There* is a tempo release, deliberately slow and with solos by the Duke, Russell Procope (good again) and Ray Nance (earthy). The melody of this movement is a strong one; and had Ellington not been so busy over these years might have been progressed towards a song. (But Duke did not gain a suitable lyric-writer over the 1950s.) Part Three of the suite, *Newport Up* is the most surprising though. Never, anywhere else in the whole published *corpus* of Ellington's work, have I come across such an overt and explicit example of composed and orchestrated be-bop. The closing sequence stems directly from the 1940s experimental sessions at Minton's Playhouse and the musical brain-chambers of Dizzy Gillespie and Charlie Parker. Solos follow from Jimmy Hamilton, Clark Terry, Sam Woodyard and Paul Gonsalves; then there are bar-swapping exchanges between Terry, Gonsalves and Hamilton. Terry is the outstanding soloist during this part of the festival programme—although it begins to sound as if Gonsalves is limbering up! The final phrasing of the ensemble is pure Yardbird.

Between the Ellington/Strayhorn 'Festival Suite' and the *Diminuendo And Crescendo* there occurs a beautiful alto-saxophone spot by Johnny Hodges. He had been given no solo space within the 'Suite': perhaps for purely psychological reasons—Duke realising the tension which had arisen between Hodges, the returned, but also the disappointed 'star' and the New Guard: Terry, Woodman, Woode, Woodyard; even Hamilton, with whom The Rabbit didn't exactly hit it off.

But there can be no denying the quality of the solo Hodges plays on *Jeep's Blues.* As saxophone playing goes it is pure, inspirational magic. The man was at his best. Tonally, slow-rhythmically and with that particular kind of languid phrasing which only he possessed. Sam Woodyard plays a double-tempo beat against the opening part of the solo, but Johnny sounds so smooth, it's as if he is walking down Savile Row.

And, in its own way, it's this sheer smoothness which makes what erupts next sound so remarkable.

Diminuendo And Crescendo In Blue is not in itself one of the Duke's most distinguished compositions. It dates from 1937 (he mistakenly announces it at Newport as being of 1938 vintage). But it contains a potent blues riff—and suddenly Paul Gonsalves was unleashed. The performance opens with four choruses of characteristic piano by the Duke himself, followed by a series of brass and saxophone exchanges (in all taking up about three-and-a-half minutes). By this time too Woode and Woodyard had got the beat really rocking. Fast, but not racing. In effect, an ideal swing. After the ensemble passages the Duke returned for two more choruses. But then came the bridge. *The bridge.*

Paul Gonsalves improvised the solo of his life *for twenty-seven straight choruses.* He was urged on by two drummers. Sam Woodyard from the Ellington rhythm section. But also ex-Basie drummer Jo Jones, who had played an earlier set with pianist Teddy Wilson, got excited all over again and urged on Gonsalves by beating on the edge of the stage with a rolled-up copy of the *Christian Science Monitor.* The other saxes began shouting back at Jo—even including Hodges—and then it all broke loose.

Gonsalves began to dig in. During his seventh thundering chorus, a tall, statuesque blonde girl in a black dress began dancing in one of the boxes (not the usual Lorillard Newport decorum). Moments later the aisles were filled with dancers!

And Gonsalves stormed on. With Jo Jones still beating the *CSM* on the stage-edge, and Jimmy Woode and Sam Woodyard playing as much to him as they were grooving behind the tenor solo.

When eventually Paul let the tension go, of the seven thousand audience, *it had become,* according to George Avakian, *an enormous single living organism, reacting in waves like huge ripples to the music played before it.*

'But the management and the police, unable to sense the true atmosphere of that crowd as it felt from the stage, grew more apprehensive with every chorus.' (After Paul had let go, Cat Anderson was driving the brass into a climax-fury.) Fearful of a serious injury in the milling crowd, which by now had pressed forward down the aisles (the open area between the boxes and the elevated stage was already jammed with leaping fans), booker-producer George Wein and one of the officers tried to signal Duke to stop. Duke, sensing that to stop now might cause a riot, chose instead to sooth the crowd down with a couple of quiet numbers.

Thus ended the most famous of all the Newport Jazz Festivals.

Diminuendo And Crescendo In Blue is not universally accepted. In his edited biography of Duke Ellington, my friend and a much respected writer, Peter Gammond describes Gonsalves' choruses as 'animalistic'. But I can't go along with him here. The two greatest qualities jazz music has for me are improvised excitement and improvised invention. *D & C* has all I expect of the former; and Gonsalves in twenty-seven choruses never improvises a *cliché*.

6. THE ORCHESTRAL SUITES

Such modern concert works as Ravel's 'Daphnis And Chloe', Debussy's 'La Mer' and 'Afternoon Of A Faun', Delius' 'In A Summer Garden' and Holst's 'The Planets' were most cherished by the eminently nocturnal Duke Ellington, a single-minded creator whose own work progressed steadily behind a multiplicity of personality masks: as dandy, sensualist, gourmet and not least hypochondriac. That these other composers appealed to the professional painter's eye of the Duke there can be no doubt; although he admired them chiefly for their inherent beauty, not from any presumptuous motive.

On the other hand, the continually enquiring mind of Ellington, operating via its chosen medium, does bring about comparison between his exertions and those of a Ravel, if only because it sought to extend the imaginative boundaries of the musical form on which it subsisted. He could be a relentless pursuer when seeking to exploit the glimmerings of some new personal idea. Often he'd attempt something, miss it, attempt it again, miss it again, attempt it three, four or five times without fully succeeding; but he'd grasp hold of it in the end. Nowhere is this better demonstrated than in his series of orchestral suites, beginning with 'Black, Brown And Beige' in 1943.

Irritated perhaps by the *petit maitre* tag, orginally attached to his work by Constant Lambert in "Music Ho!" and critically limiting his abilities to the sculpting of exquisite miniatures, Ellington also gave every indication of having been frustrated by the limits (until the 1950s, and the advent of tape and LP) of the three-minute 78 rpm disc: allowing him sufficient room only for an opening chorus, perhaps two choruses of accompanied improvisation and then a reprise. He had attempted to overcome this in 1931 with *Creole Rhapsody* and in 1935 with *Reminiscing In Tempo* (another double-sided single). But when he began 'Black, Brown And Beige' he was still limited by pre-microgroove records to writing short movements. He was bursting with the raw materials for telling longer stories in jazz. Also with technical advances (e.g. the seven-part fugue which opens the *Come Sunday* movement of 'Black, Brown And Beige'). However, it would not be until 'A Tone Parallel To Harlem' that he finally escaped the suites of short, swift sketches towards some truly extended writing.

'Black, Brown And Beige', which Ellington banged on the head of Jim Crow, had its first performance at Town Hall, New York on January 23, 1943—although it was not recorded until December '44, when RCA spent two full days collecting its four movements on to master wax. The composition surveys the history of the Negro in North America—depicting first his importation as a slave and later his life in the aftermath to the Civil War. It is outspoken about the colour bar, sometimes aggressively so.

Work Song, the opening, pictures the Negro in chains, and Harry Carney's baritone solo is a vehicle for despair. The movement does end, however, on a note of growing rebelliousness expressed by the rubbery, quasi-vocal trombone of 'Tricky Sam' Nanton playing over a series of brooding ensemble punctuations, and by the calculated coda played by Johnny Hodges. *Come Sunday,* the first scene change, shows the black workers congregating in their small, primitive churches, and the mood of the spiritual is poignantly present. Ray Nance's violin—played with both bow and finger—is used to expose the main melodic line, after which Johnny Hodges takes over with an alto prayer, soaring to great heights in its appeal, his tone full and sensuous, while Ellington places an orchestral sound reminding one of a church organ behind him.

The third movement is *The Blues,* sung by Joya Sherrill; and with some rugged tenor-sax by Al Sears. The blues can express many diverse feelings, but there is no doubt about the composer's intentions here when Joya sings 'the blues ain't nothin' but a cold, grey day'.

The concluding movement, heralding brighter days, consists of three short and lively dances: *West Indian Dance,* with its fiery rhythm and dedicated to the valour of seven hundred free Haitian soldiers of the Fontages Legion who came to the Americans' aid during the siege of Savannah in the Revolutionary War; *Emancipation Celebration* (featuring Taft Jordan's sparkling trumpet describing the joy of the young and the incredulity of the old upon the abolition of slavery; and finally *Sugar Hill Penthouse,* dominated by Duke's own piano-playing and representing 'the unique atmosphere in an apartment house in the liberated Negro district of Harlem'.

Altogether different, the four movements of 'The Perfume Suite (earlier discussed) described, via overt impressionism,' the sexual character that a woman might assume under the influence of each of four American perfumes'. It was recorded on July 24 and 30, 1945.

The 'Deep South Suite', premiered during an Ellington concert at New York's Carnegie Hall on November 25, 1946, but only ever issued on record as a wartime V-Disc, is again full of pictorialism—and again tinged with Duke's racial feelings.

Magnolias Dripping With Molasses portrays the South as the Dixie Chamber of Commerce and a number of state senators would 'dream' paint it: as an ideal place to be. Trombonist Lawrence Brown in a lengthy improvisation quotes from the nostalgic melodies of Stephen Foster. But with *Hearsay,* the subsequent movement, we are brought back to reality with an ugly thud. Brooding orchestration and Harold Baker's spiky trumpet, backed by Sonny Greer's marching tom-tom drums remind us of slavery, segregation and innocent black bodies hanging from trees; and not scented magnolia trees. *When Nobody Was Looking,* another Ellington piano solo, portrays the contentedness which could exist if only white would stop trying to run black.

Then to conclude, Ellington sketches that unique piece of mechanical transport, the *Happy-Go-Lucky Local,* a lazy old train that grinds and clanks its way through the South, stopping at all those places no outsiders have ever heard of. It features Jimmy Hamilton humming tunes on his clarinet, Cat Anderson playing squealing brakes and jerking the string of the steam-whistle, all done over Oscar Pettiford's thudding bass. It was destined to become a popular part of the band's regular repertoire.

The 'Liberian Suite' was commissioned by President Tubman in 1947 to celebrate that nation's centenary. A small republic in West Africa, some 46,000 square miles in area, it had been originally founded for freed American slaves to work out their own destinies. The suite consists of five lively and varied dances, prefaced by another Al Hibbler vocal, *I Like The Sunrise.* The dances incorporate good solos by Ray Nance, Jimmy Hamilton, Harry Carney, Johnny Hodges and the high-note specialist replacement for Cat Anderson, Al Killian. Plus something new to the Ellington band when incoming trombonist Tyree Glen laid down his horn and played vibraphone.

Lastly here we come to Ellington's seventeen-minute 'A Tone Parallel To Harlem', recorded on December 7, 1951 after the reshuffle of personnel had brought in Willie Smith, Britt Woodman, Clark Terry and Louie Bellson to replace Hodges, Brown and Greer. In one continuous progression Duke surveys the district of Harlem, again using his painter's eye. Throughout the work he hinges much upon Wendell Marshall's bass: as the footsteps of a man exploring the streets and crowds, past tenement blocks, dazzling niteries, theatres and a serene church (Harlem was not so rundown or as dangerous then). Sometimes the man breaks into a trot and on occasions he runs.

As the work opens there is a two-note phrase stabbed out by Ray Nance's trumpet—a phrase chosen by Ellington because it symbolised for him the two-syllable name 'Harlem'. This is taken up quickly by the full ensemble as a mighty tonal impulse, suggesting a vast body stirring, awakening and stretching, and then denoting the commencement of another day as its intensity is increased. Then the district comes to life. The picture survey begins, with the bass wending its way down street after street, the composer's gaze as it wanders suggested by Jimmy Hamilton's clarinet. The ensemble sketches in tenements, saloons, eating houses. Carney blows a line between weaving reeds—through crowds of people. Paul Gonsalves' tenor slinks in with a sustained note, furtively, as though an evil character on the sidewalk. Mighty percussion against trombones, then full brass: more buildings, radios blaring. A Latin-American rhythm—Harlem is the new home of many Puerto Ricans and of the rhumba. Louie Bellson relaxes into a lightly swinging 4/4 time—a modern dance-hall. Unison trombones dictate. Change to counterpoint between reeds and brass—shops, with dealers and customers bargaining. A high octave fanfare by the trumpets; the rhythm at a standstill; another mood is heralded. Hamilton's blue clarinet leads us down the aisle of a church, overawed, it seems, by the rich organ harmonies from the saxophones, leading into an ensemble choir topped by more powerful brass. Carney's clarinet weaves another preconceived line, while in the background a solitary trombone (Woodman) introduces a spiritual theme, an element of Negro song, used as Dvořák implied in his 'New World Symphony'. A clarinet and other instruments take up the theme and Hal Baker's trumpet heightens and then concludes this solemnity. Next, as the ensemble remoulds the spiritual melody the music is already gayer . . . a change to the theatres and nightclubs. The orchestra blazes the theme in a rising unison figure over Bellson's sustained drum-roll. As the conclusion nears, so the power of attack increases. The coda is magnificence in brass—a testimony to the overall might of this city within a city.

7. SOME LATER ORCHESTRAL SUITES

My personal preferences among the Duke's various and varied suites are for 'Black, Brown And Beige', 'A Tone Parallel To Harlem', 'Such Sweet Thunder' and the train-movement, *Happy-Go-Lucky Local* from the 'Deep South Suite' (all of which I have now written about), together with the 'New Orleans Suite', which will be the subject of my conclusion.

However, I do not allow my preferences (believing all musical appreciation to be personal) to blindfold recognition that there is much of value, and much that makes for enjoyable listening in the other works which qualify for the title 'suite'.

I have listened again to 'The Queen's Suite' of 1959, also the 'Far East Suite' of 1966 and the 'Latin-American Suite' of 1968, and have come away from them without any sensing that they are major works. The first has a certain impressive stateliness; the other two a number of exciting happenings rhythmically. But the themes themselves have not lodged in my memory-bank in the way that so many other Ellington compositions have.

Much better, I think, is 'And His Mother Called Him Bill' of August 28, 1967—although the Duke didn't label it as a suite officially. It is his warm and loving tribute to his long-term collaborator, Billy Strayhorn, recently passed away following a drawn-out and painful illness. Ellington here has orchestrated a favourite collection of Strayhorn originals with meticulous attention to detail, and in so doing captures more than enough of the rich imagery, languour and exotica, plus the alternative swing, which were so uniquely 'Swee' Pea'. He has left out *'A' Train, Lush Life* and *Chelsea Bridge,* presumably because these are already so well-represented on disc, but includes *Boo-Dah, U.M.M.G. (Upper Manhattan Medical Group), Blood Count, Smada, Raincheck, Rock Skippin' At The Blue Note, My Little Brown Rock* and finally a quartet of piano solos: *Lotus Blossom, Snibor, After All* and *All Day Long.* Overall, it provides a fitting testament to the gifts of the little giant.

Another fine record is a fleshing-out of two movements from 'Black, Brown And Beige' which Duke cut for CBS during February, 1958. The half-suite is presented in six parts: *Work Song* is Part 1 and is combined with *Come Sunday* to make up Part 3. All the other parts are concerned with or have grown from *Come Sunday.*

Ellington has pointed out that, 'When the Negro got shipped over here from Africa, he thought he was going to be eaten. Think how relieved he must have been when he found out all he had to do was work . . .' Which might account for the optimistic mood he gives to this later recording. Sam Woodyard's drums thunder out the insistent rhythm, introducing the ensemble and the subsequent solos by Harry Carney (a variation on his earlier solo), Harold Baker, trumpet and Quentin Jackson, trombone.

Part 2, the first exposition of *Come Sunday* is again all-instrumental and features solos by John Sanders, valve-trombone, Ray Nance, violin, the Duke himself, Carney and Baker. In Part 3 then, when the two themes come together, the solos are by Baker, Cat Anderson (using a plunger mute) and Britt Woodman, trombone.

Part 4 is magnificent—even by Ellington standards. The composer had spent two years of persuading America's greatest gospel singer, Mahalia Jackson to make her first record with a jazz orchestra. Over this period he called her a dozen times from a dozen different cities before he overcame her worries. In the event, she became so inspired by his backing that, after singing the written lyrics, she hummed an extra chorus—as if, after realising the power of her performance, she felt reluctant to let the music go.

Part 5 is a reprise of *Come Sunday* played by Ray Nance on violin. In reality it is a mere bridge leading towards Mahalia's triumphant return.

Ellington was appearing at a Hollywood club when the gospel mistress arrived at Union Station in Los Angeles clutching her music for *Come Sunday,* to which the lyrics had only just been added. During the week which followed they rehearsed every afternoon. And for the last afternoon Duke asked her to bring her Bible with her. He opened it at random on the Twenty-Third Psalm. He played a few chords and asked Mahalia to sing. Thus was born an amazing, beautiful and completely spontaneous Ellington orchestration which serves as a finale to the record. With the singer, on her own home ground, if anything even more inspiring. (Ellington considered her the finest singer in America—and the best cook . . .)

Two other suites, one recorded before, the other after this later 'Black, Brown And Beige' also deserve close inspection.

'A Drum Is A Woman' dates from the Autumn of 1956; 'The Nutcracker Suite' from mid-1960. Both are fusion of Ellington's composing and orchestration talents with those of Strayhorn.

After another soaring alto introduction by Johnny Hodges, every section of 'A Drum Is A Woman' includes a vocal of one kind or another; as well as much spoken commentary by the Duke in his best penthouse style. The vocals (by Margaret Tynes, Joya Sherrill and Ozzie Bailey) are more distinguished than the lyrics and the slender story-line: Caribee Joe, a contented jungle musician, able to communicate with the animals, is both desired and lured North by a sophisticated witch, Madam Zajj, who is able to turn herself into a drum at will. The action moves between Africa, Barbados, New York, then to Mardi Gras in New Orleans (where Madame Zajj turns up, in drum form, of course, as Queen to a King of the Zulus, the legendary trumpeter Buddy Bolden). It ends, vaguely, in more jungle not far from Congo Square.

The idea of telling the story of jazz in terms of Ellington's music was first mooted by Orson Welles in 1941. But it remained no more than an outline and twenty-eight bars of trumpet solo until the mid-'fifties, when Duke was playing a series of one-nighters in the South and West, and began writing the music in hotel rooms or in the back of Harry Carney's car. By the end of the tour his pockets as usual were bulging with written-over paper: scraps of staved manuscript, restaurant menus, pages of bus and train timetables. Then later, at a dance in Camden, New Jersey, Ellington startled a large attendance of dancers by testing out the *Congo Square* part on them. In such ways the work was gradually progressed towards its final shape.

Ambitious claims have been made for it. Not least by CBS, who describe it as 'a musical fantasy paralleling the history of the origins . . . based upon Ellington's own definition of jazz and expressed in his personal, highly original language'. Peter Gammond, in his book 'Duke Ellington, His Life & Music', while lamenting some aspects of the lyrics, nevertheless goes on to marvel at 'the wonderful balance of the piece as an entity, its dramatic rightness of sequence, and its subtle changes of pace and mood. Starting as a flag-waver, with all its richest melodies at the beginning, rather in the manner of "La Traviata", it takes on a tighter, more dramatic form as it progresses, and concentrates on building some abstract characters.'

In reality though, given the benefit of hindsight after thirty years, the sung and spoken parts now sound decidedly dated as well as slight. One must go directly to the instrumental interludes and backings to find the gems. Including, not unnaturally, an unfolding panorama of drums and percussion by Sam Woodyard, Candido and Terry Snyder. (Duke also uses a harpist: Betty Glamman.)

Part 1 of 'A Drum' (after Hodges' intro) is a vocal by Margaret Tynes over a moody Ellington ensemble and continues with a more spirited *Rhythm Rum Te Dum* for chorus and orchestra. It ends with a calypso, *What Else Can You Do With A Drum?* sung by Ozzie Bailey. Despite the banal lyrics, still I agree with Peter Gammond here: that 'In the exquisitely simple backing . . . the way the instruments are blended and the incredibly delicate playing are quite breathtaking. Tantalisingly brief, this must be one of the moments of greatest beauty that Ellington has achieved'.

Part 2 opens with *New Orleans,* a further commentary by Ellington, introduced by Russell Procope on sub-tone clarinet. This is the beginning of Mardi Gras and Madame Zajj's *leitmotiv* is punched out by Britt Woodman's trombone. Then follows a superb interlude by Clark Terry, representing *Hey, Buddy Bolden* (elected King of the Zulus for a year) calling his flock. Presumably this is a rewrite of the mere twenty-eight bars of trumpet solo Ellington got down on paper for Orson Welles— after receiving an advance of 12,500 dollars. Joya Sherrill sings the *Bolden* lyrics and those of the subsequent movement, *Caribee Joe*—leaving Ellington then to describe *Congo Square,* together with some very good Paul Gonsalves and more Procope.

Side Two of the album, and Part 3 of 'A Drum' brings back Margaret Tynes and features a more aggressive Johnny Hodges. We move on. After Ozzie Bailey's song *You Better Know It* (his best contribution, backed by Gonsalves' tenor), to a longer *Madam Zajj* sequence (with more Clark Terry); and then into another dimension via a *Ballet Of The Flying Saucers,* returning Hodges to us and some vital drumming by Woodyard. It concludes to the sound of chimes.

Lastly, Part 4 begins with *Madame Zajj's Dream* involving Cat Anderson and Ray Nance around the Sherrill vocal. Which also paves the way towards *Rhumbop.* This latter, new theme is meant to portray Madam Zajj luring Caribee Joe to the neon lights of New York—especially along 52nd Street. In Duke's description: 'When Joe is exposed to the city, his own primitive music takes on aspects of modern jazz. For . . . you can take the boy out of the city, but you can't take the city out of the boy.' No matter—because this idea has become the excuse for a delightfully overt piece of big band be-bop.

Afterwards Ellington proceeds to wrap things up with more of *Caribee Joe* and a blazing finale.

In contrast, 'The Nutcracker Suite' is completely a musical fun-making machine—and like nothing else within Ellington's essential canon. Both he and Strayhorn are never less than playful here; and at times quite irreverent in their interpretation of Tchaikovsky's famous ballet. But it remains the best kind of fun—boisterous, very swinging, with an obvious manifestation of enjoyment. Never in bad taste.

Duke and Swee' Pea worked on 'The Nutcracker' in Las Vegas while the Ellington band was setting new attendance records at the Riviera Hotel. The suite begins, naturally enough, with Peter Ilyich's own *Overture,* done as a medium swinger with solos by Paul Gonsalves (the most lengthily-featured individual soloist on the album), Booty Wood in the plunger trombone role of 'Tricky Sam' Nanton and later Quentin Jackson, and Ray Nance, who plays some excellent broad-toned trumpet. *Toot Toot Tootie Toot (Dance Of The Reed Pipes)* follows, featuring reed duets by Jimmy Hamilton with Russell Procope and Gonsalves with Carney—in the words of producer Irving Townsend, 'a toy pipe foursome'. *Peanut Brittle Brigade* (Tchaikovsky's famous *March*) comes next and is immediately transformed from its normally rigid 'squareness' into another uninhibited swinger. Solos by Nance and Hamilton are followed by one from the Duke himself: a rare one within the album, because, as he confessed later, with this particular work he had so much extra to do with the band. The ensemble following his solo features a five-octave sax figure from the bottom of Carney's baritone up through the section to Hamilton's clarinet on top. Rounded off by a Gonsalves cadenza of intricate elaboration. *Sugar Rhum Cherry (Dance Of The Sugar Plum Fairy),* perhaps the cheekiest interpretation from the ballet, begins and ends with Carney and Gonsalves duets, with Nance, Willie Cook and Booty Wood wailing in the background. The real cheekiness though lies with Sam Woodyard, whose clever drumming turns the peaches-and-cream European ballerina into a West Indian beauty disappearing into the cane fields! *Ent'racte* is actually a reprise of the opening theme, with solos by Hodges (very chirpy), Carney/Gonsalves again, Lawrence Brown, trombone (a bit choppy) and Hamilton playing up high.

The second half opens with *The Volga Vouty (Russian Dance),* heralded by a brass fanfare before Sam Woodyard lays down another of his fine medium tempos. Nance solos briefly, the main soloist is Hodges at his most poised; then there is some more plunger work from Booty Wood. Gonsalves returns to the forefront for *Chinoiserie (Chinese Dance)*, this time playing an ultra-quiet duet with Jimmy Hamilton over just a touch of trombones and Woodyard using bass-drum and finger cymbals. Tenor and clarinet reverse their respective roles for the final chorus—with Duke on piano having the last chords.

Dance Of The Floreadores (Waltz Of The Flowers) is the grooviest swing of the suite. Both from the ensemble and the soloists set against it: Carney, Hamilton, Booty Wood, Nance, Brown—and then, an added excitement, Booty slogging it out with Britt Woodman. Finally, *Arabesque Cookie (Arabian Dance)*. Russell Procope had been practising for months on a bamboo whistle before making his debut on record with it here. The man who always wrote for the man behind the instrument simply jumps in and utilises him. Juan Tizol, seemingly an expert on tambourine, helps make up the Arabian flavour in conjunction with Woodyard's drums. Carney switches to bass-clarinet. Willie Cook is voiced with the reeds over all of this. Until the moment when the rhythm changes from Middle East to 4/4 and some of the most elegant Hodges soloing of his last years.

'The Nutcracker' is unlike any other Ellingtonia on account of its basis. And yet it's still unmistakeably Duke. If you already own it, or decide to go out and buy it, then I urge you to treat the disc as he treated the work: in a spirit of being high without any artificial stimulants.

INTERLUDE

Duke Ellington: Great Original Performances, 1927-1934 (BBC Records)
Jubilee Stomp/The Blues With A Feelin'/Hop Head/What Can A Poor Fellow Do?/Chicago Stompdown/Black Beauty/Hot And Bothered/Misty Morning/The Mooche/Paducah/East St. Louis Toodle-oo/Creole Love Call/Fast And Furious/Solitude/Stompy Jones/Live And Love Tonight.
Personnel includes: Duke Ellington (piano), Louis Bacon, Frederick Douglas, 'Freddie' Jenkins, Louis Metcalf, James Wesley, Bubber Miley, Jabbo Smith, Artie Whetsol, Cootie Williams (trumpets), Lawrence Brown, Joe 'Tricky Sam' Nanton, Juan Tizol (trombones), Barney Bigard, Otto Hardwick, Johnny Hodges, Rudy Jackson, Harry Carney (clarinets, saxophones), Fred Guy, Lonnie Johnson (banjo, guitar), Wellman Braud, Henry Edwards (bass), Sonny Greer (drums), Baby Cox, Adelaide Hall (vocals).

Ironically, this record reaches me for review just as I am completing a year's contributions to *Crescendo International* about the momumental career of Duke Ellington, the greatest single figure in this history of American music. I write 'ironically' because my essays, which began with the idea of just two and then became a compulsion covering the next ten months, have been—in the main—devoted to the final two-thirds of the Duke's career, as my way of trying to show how he remained creative right through to the end of his days. As a kind of answer, if you like, to the frequently-pushed views of those critics who have and still do believe that almost all of his most important work was completed before the 1940s. And now, suddenly, I am being invited to comment upon that earlier work!

Well, first I want to say that this latest BBC Enterprises release is, in my opinion, the finest transfer I have yet heard by Robert Parker from early 78s to digital stereo. His filtering processes have been criticised by those who seem to prefer authentic scratches to the quality of the music. What rubbish! I want to hear *more* of the music. And to give the reader just two examples: Duke's own piano-playing on *Fast And Furious* and the very soft, delicate reed accompaniments during *Solitude.* These are now minor miracles of clarity. So, let us stand by Mister Parker's achievements . . .

The second thing I want to say about this album, in a way, I hope, redresses the balance in my series about Ellington. I did not write the series with any prejudice against the great man's earliest work. It was simply that I have wanted to rescue some of the best of his middle and later years of composing and bandleading from an unjustified neglect. But there can be no taking away from the value of his early masterpieces, all but one of which *(Black And Tan Fantasy)* are gathered together here. *The Mooch, East St. Louis Toodle-oo, Creole Love Call* and *B & T Fantasy:* these four short scores changed orchestral jazz for good as regards texture and atmosphere, and must be regarded as *the* masterpieces of the Duke's 'jungle' period, which also involved the 'vocalised' instrumental contributions of Bubber Miley and Joe 'Tricky Sam' Nanton. Meanwhile, with 'Hot And Bothered' the leader was injecting a new kind of urgency into big band jazz, and with *Solitude* was laying the foundations for his parallel career as a jazz songwriter. Finally, with *Black Beauty* he began experimenting his way towards the first of his orchestral suites. All these items (no, gems!) have been collected and treated with love by Parker. With some simpler numbers like *Stompy Jones* and *Hop Head* put in for good measure.

8. A QUESTION OF BELIEF

As well as writing and presenting many music programmes for BFBS (British Forces Broadcasting Service) over the years, I do occasionally contribute to *Reflections,* the station's weekly religious programme. Now, before any readers abruptly turn the page, let me hasten to add that I do not wear a dog-collar and, quite apart from being without the necessary qualifications, have never expressed any wish to preach or sermonise. My programmes have been entirely concerned with the history of religion. It began when Ted King, the producer of *Reflections,* picked up on my enthusiasm for Pierre Teilhard de Chardin, the French Jesuit geographer/geologist and author of 'The Phenomenon Of Man'. He suggested I tackled him as a radio subject. By the end of which I had enjoyed it so much I promptly plunged into a long exploration of Blaise Pascal, his 'Pensées' and the whole Jansenist reform at Port Royal during the reign of Louis XIV. Several months went by. I then suggested to Ted we devote a third programme to Duke Ellington's Concert of Sacred Music dating from 1965.

Because I consider his religious beliefs and composing vital to the Ellington story, I have, therefore, obtained permission from BFBS to reproduce the script as part of my on-going series about this towering musician: my admiration for Aaron Copland notwithstanding, still *the* great composer in American music thus far.

I reproduce the script exactly as presented . . .

REFLECTIONS: *Duke Ellington's Concert of Sacred Music (RCA 7811SF) Written and Presented for BFBS by Raymond Horricks Music in: Come Sunday from 'Black, Brown And Beige'; Mahalia Jackson (vocal) CBS 84406 Side 2, Band 1; Fade after 1 min. 25 secs.*

To Alistair Cooke, the doyen of living broadcasters, I owe the valuable intelligence that the Episcopal Cathedral of St. John the Divine on the Upper West Side in New York City is arguably the largest cathedral in the world. And, upon foundations laid in 1892, its building is still going on. It holds ten thousand people.

However, I doubt whether it has witnessed anything quite so remarkable as the ceremony which took place there on Monday the 27th of May, 1974. Every pew was filled, the aisles were choked and several thousand more people were listening to loudspeakers strategically placed out in the street. And the people were of all shades of colour, from deep purple black to the most pallid white. The occasion was to mourn the passing of a man who had grown supreme in a musical art that began in the brothels of New Orleans and ended on the concert platform of the Metropolitan Opera House and with his receiving the Presidential Medal of Freedom. His real name was Edward Kennedy Ellington. He is known to us simply as 'The Duke': the greatest composer in American music thus far.

But if we associate the Duke only with *Mood Indigo, Sophisticated Lady,* the swing and excitement of *Perdido* or *Cotton Tail* and the more than five hundred other compositions he and his band have presented us with over the years, then we have sadly missed out on the other important part of his music-making, which became increasingly overt as he and his players grew older: namely, the strongly intuitive ties so often existing between his deeply-held religious beliefs and his musical expression. We can point to the same thing in Bach, in Handel, Berlioz, Verdi, Elgar and many more European composers who lived secular lives but used their talents to build a number of monuments to God. Duke Ellington belongs with this *élite*.

I date his first public presentation via music of his personal religious beliefs from 1943 at Carnegie Hall and sections of the 'Black, Brown And Beige' suite. You heard a little of this from a later recording with the great gospel singer Mahalia Jackson at the beginning the programme. And the presentations were to be continued, intermittently, and introducing various new works right up to his death. Including one concert at Westminster Abbey, London.

For our programme though I will concentrate on the Concert of Sacred Music he presented at New York's Fifth Avenue Presbyterian Church on December 26th, 1965. As well as 'Black, Brown And Beige', 'New World A-Comin'' and Duke's special setting of *The Lord's Prayer,* it also included *David Danced Before The Lord With All His Might,* featuring tap-dancer Bunny Briggs, and the highly original piece I want to play excerpts from now: called simply *In The Beginning God* after the first four words of Genesis.

Now it's not my purpose to speak of the ecumenical movement—its desirability or otherwise. But what is for certain is that Ellington has managed to pull off a most remarkable religious synthesis within his composing. A synthesis of Western Christianity—after all, Ellington himself, born in Washington D.C., came from a modestly well-to-do family—with African roots and Pantheism, gospel singing, the chronicles of the Bible, the aspirations of the New Testament and, not least, the extra problems faced by mankind in our modern society.

First though, Africa meets the West as Ellington's piano introduces the elemental awe and soul searching personified by Harry Carney's baritone-saxophone:

Play: In The Beginning God—Side 1, Band 1; Cut at 2.30 mins.

We move on. Via the human voice of the famous actor/singer Brock Peters. Ellington wonders at the unimaginable, when there was no Heaven, no Earth.

Play: In The Beginning God (vocal at tempo): Cut at 2.55 mins.

However: God has filled the void and created Man. Against Paul Gonsalves' swirling tenor-saxophone the choir chants his development with the titles of the books of the Old Testament.

Play: In The Beginning God (after applause); Cut at 2.15 mins.

One final excerpt, although not quite the end of the work. Cat Anderson's trumpet goes up into orbit, speaking of Man's aspirations towards God. As Duke himself adds, 'That's as high as we go . . .' In the beginning, God.

Play: In The Beginning God (from orchestral chords); Cut at 1.35 mins.

I will add now just a few words by the Rev. Bryant M. Kirkland D.D.: Minister of the Fifth Avenue Presbyterian Church at the time of the concert. 'It provoked', he says, 'deep discussions of what constitutes sacred music. While each will answer on the basis of his own needs and tastes, many discovered a new spiritual exaltation in the modern idiom. There was a sense of joy and gratitude to God as well as personal involvement in the Creator's work, which moved the audience beyond routine existence to a fresh relatedness to the Almighty. Some felt for the first time that there are other religious emotions besides fear, guilt and dread. There is also wonder, love and praise.'

Duke himself commented at the time: 'Wisdom is something that Man partially enjoys—One and only One has *all* the wisdom. God has total understanding. There are some people who speak one language and some who speak many languages. Every man prays in his own language, and there is no language that God does not understand. It has been said that there was once a man who accompanied his worship by juggling. He was not the world's greatest juggler, but it was the thing he did best. And so it was accepted by God.

9. INSIDE CRESCENT CITY

So: Ellingtonia. And still I have only managed to make forays into it. The Duke's recorded legacy is massive. He had a long life, and persisted in composing and leading a band in public until just weeks before his death in 1974. He played many more concerts of sacred music—and increasingly at American universities, where he received several honorary doctorates. Meanwhile a host of younger talents passed through the ranks of the Ellington orchestra. Son Mercer Ellington returned to the trumpets, together with Herbie Jones, Johnny Coles, Harold Johnson and Barry Lee Hall. The trombone section gained Buster Cooper and Chuck Connors (the latter on bass-trombone). Into the saxes came Harold Ashby, Norris Turney and Harold Minerve. With the rhythm section employing Joe Benjamin (bass) or Aaron Bell, and in turn Rufus Jones, Sam Woodyard (again) and Rocky White on drums.

Interestingly too, Duke's last three orchestral LPs were all made in England: 'The English Concert' (a double album) at Birmingham in October, 1971; his 'Third Sacred Concert' in London during October, 1973; and the 'Eastbourne Performance' there in December, 1973—the latter including *The Piano Player, Creole Love Call, New York, New York, Pitter Panther Patter, Meditation* and *How High The Moon.*

I apologise to readers for what has been left out. But there is only so much room and other musicians will claim me. And so I have decided to bring the Ellington sequence full circle by saying something about the marvellous 'New Orleans Suite' of April and May, 1970. For while in a long life, and in his own individualistic way, Duke never ceased to progress the raw materials of jazz into new and satisfactory musical areas, at the same time he never, ever distanced his output from its natural roots. New Orleans jazz had been his first inspiration and he did nothing to disguise this fact.

The suite is also important for a dramatic human event. Between the first and second sessions there occurred the sudden death of Johnny Hodges, for so long an integral part of the Ellington sound. Deeply shocked and, of course, saddened, the Duke did not seek a replacement alto for the second session.

But to return to New Orleans, the Crescent City. Before he left Washington for New York in the 'Twenties, Ellington had heard the one New Orleans musician he would always afterwards refer to as 'the foundation', 'the symbol of jazz' and 'the greatest of all the originators': Sidney Bechet. 'He always played the same way,' he recalled of the great soprano-sax/clarinettist. 'The same then as just before he died. I remember hearing him play *I'm Coming, Virginia* in 1921—the greatest thing I ever heard in my life. I'd never heard anything like it. It knocked me out.'

A few years later Duke and his Washingtonians were 'knocked out' a second time—by the other main virtuoso soloist of New Orleans jazz, Louis Armstrong. And not long after this the composer took two prominent New Orleans musicians into his band. Barney Bigard, clarinet, had been taught by Lorenzo Tio Jr in New Orleans before joining King Oliver's band in Chicago. He played with Ellington from 1928 until 1942. But his influence remained longer. So much so that up to his own death Duke demanded that all of his saxophone-players doubled on clarinet. Wellman Braud, bass, instructed his fellow-Ellingtonians in the culinary delights of New Orleans, as well as supplying a big, full tone and rock-steady beat benath the ensemble. He was Duke's finest bass-player before the coming of the instrument's first revolutionary genius, Jimmy Blanton.

One other big New Orleans influence within the band was the laying on of hands on Johnny Hodges. Although he hailed from Cambridge, Massachusetts, Johnny as a youngster had idolised Sidney Bechet from records. Then, when he actually met Bechet in Boston, the New Orleans pioneer not only took a liking to him, he gave The Rabbit one of his personal sopranos, together with a dozen or so lessons. Herein, therefore, lies another of the human internal tragedies of the 'New Orleans Suite'.

Duke wrote the suite for the New Orleans festival of 1970. Before which he took an engagement at Al Hirt's Bourbon Street club and, as usual, composed there until the last minute, rehearsing the entire work in the club the night before its Festival premiere. Whereupon a drunken gent, who had made repeated requests for *Sophisticated Lady,* left Hirt's club shouting indignantly 'I don't believe you *know* how to play *Sophisticated Lady!*' This last anecdote from Stanley Dance.

Anyway—the premiere was a triumph. So let me now turn to the music itself. It was recorded out of its final running-order; and Hodges was missing from all the movements bearing the title *Portrait*.

Blues For New Orleans, the opening and longest track, is a slow–medium twelve-bar and the last blues and the last recording made by Hodges. The performance was stimulated by the presence of Wild Bill Davis on organ—and by the Duke himself, who abandoned the control-box so that he 'could conduct, routine, clap his hands and mime his requirements as the arrangements unfolded'. (Dance) Hodges is dazzling. This most prickly of men could, when his ego was flattered and the ambience correct, play like an angel. Which is exactly what he does here. Poised, his satiny-sounding tone at the point of perfection, he improvises deliberately few notes, and many of these sustained. But each of these is placed exactly right—and no one could doubt his feeling for the blues. I am left feeling it is my favourtie solo of any he ever recorded. As with Ellington, all I can add is: *What a loss!*

The second movement, *Bourbon Street Jingling Jollies* is, in Duke's own words 'a rhythmic tone parallel to the excruciating ecstasies one finds oneself suspended in when one is in the throes of the rhythmic jollies of Bourbon Street'. Norris Turney, the first flautist to play with the band, dominates this section, recalling 'the overall pastel enchantment of New Orleans'—backed by three trombones, three flugelhorns (a Clark Terry legacy to the band) and Harry Carney on bass-clarinet.

This is followed by *Portrait Of Louis Armstrong,* featuring Cootie Williams, back with the band on an intermittent guest basis. Williams first heard Satchmo over the radio playing with Fletcher Henderson at the Roseland Ballroom in New York, and later, living with Wellman Braud, got to know Louis personally. He remained an unashamed admirer; like Ellington he referred to the trumpet pioneer as 'an American standard'. The performance is medium tempo, but 'hot'.

Thanks For The Beautiful Land Of The Delta stresses the religious element in New Orleans life via a passionate tenor-saxophone solo by Harold Ashby, the ensemble giving out lively religious responses behind him.

Portrait Of Wellman Braud closes Side One, with modernist Joe Benjamin (ex-Sarah Vaughan Trio) taking the Braud role. Braud stayed with Duke from 1926 until 1935. He was also the senior musician in the band, who kept the younger cats disciplined. And he made sure his bass was always prominently recorded. Benjamin understudies the part well. Solos by Carney (bass-clarinet), Cootie Williams and Russell Procope.

Second Line is dedicated to followers of the New Orleans marching bands. Their high spiritis are catalogued by Booty Wood and Julian Priester, trombones, indulging in a cutting contest. Then by Russell

Procope's longer solo over a wild ensemble—and Cootie Williams' chorus, making its way down Canal Street.

Two evenings before *Portrait Of Sidney Bechet* was recorded (on May 13, 1970), Duke, at dinner, was mulling over how best to persuade Johnny Hodges to dust off his soprano-sax and play the part. Then the news was telephoned through that The Rabbit was no more. As a result, the composer decided to feature Paul Gonsalves on tenor-sax instead. Which resulted in another great performance. If Gonsalves is best-known for his exciting *Diminuendo And Crescendo In Blue,* then this 'Bechet' profile has to be regarded as his most sensitive slower solo with Ellington. Although playing a different instrument, he reaches for Bechet's vibrato and intensity, and so comes close to the man himself in a wonderful evocation. Poor Paul, with all his personal problems—but what a great player!

The suite is now nearing its end. *Aristocracy A La Jean Lafitte* is in memory of a pirate whose aristocratic behaviour once helped the city. This piece is in waltz time; but Harry Carney is no pirate, nor is Canadian Fred Stone on flugelhorn.

To conclude, we have the moving *Portrait Of Mahalia Jackson:* with solos by Norris Turney (flute), Cottie Williams, Gonsalves and Julian Priester. Which reminds us that the source of so much New Orleans music was not only African or early jazz, but equally the Church.

It also concludes this section. Fortunately though, there is never any end to Ellingtonia. He is with us on record for as long as there is civilisation. A massive output, left there for our betterment and the understanding and education of all future generations.

1987/88

CHAPTER TWELVE

1956

A Jazz *Annus Mirabilis*

There are certain 'key' years in jazz which have altered the course and/or the style of the music in an obviously radical way. 1917, for instance, when the US Secretary for the Navy closed down all the brothels in the Storyville district of New Orleans and caused a general exodus of musicians up the Mississippi to a new headquarters in Chicago. Then 1924, with the virtuoso soloist Louis Armstrong taking his hotness and daring away from King Oliver in Chicago and into the larger context of Fletcher Henderson's band in New York City. Several years in the late 1930s and early '40s were important to the development of be-bop. While 1948/49 saw a further revolution in modern jazz with Miles Davis and 'The Birth Of The Cool'.

However, not all years before or since have witnessed another stage in jazz evolution or the startling emergence of an Ornette Coleman or an Eric Dolphy. Some years have been largely ones of consolidation. Others have simply encapsulated much mature work by artists whose pioneering days were thought to be over, but who continued to be searching and creative.

1956 clearly belongs with the latter—and I take this opportunity to write of the several recordings which have made it a favourite year for me.

The early '50s had seen the release of Louis Armstrong's best album in many years ('Louis Armstrong Plays W.C. Handy'), Stan Kenton's 'New Concepts Of Artistry In Rhythm' (in fact, the *older* concept, meaning a strong propulsion), Charlie Parker's dazzling remake of *Now's The Time*, the first Count Basie 'Dance Session' with scores by Neal Hefti and Ernie Wilkins and the first LPs by several important new groups: the Gerry Mulligan Quartet, the Modern Jazz Quartet, the Chico Hamilton Quintet, Art Blakey's Jazz Messengers and the Jimmy Giuffre Trio. Also they had included the short, tragic career of Clifford Brown; and not least the Vic Dickenson Vanguards (with Ruby Braff, Edmond Hall *et al*) and the magnificent 'A Buck Clayton Jam Session' of December 16, 1953 (with the side-long *Robbins Nest*). Stanley Dance appropriately dubbed these last recordings 'Mainstream' and the name has stuck, meaning a style involving the heat and timbre of early jazz up-dated with the musical devices and rhythmic sweep of Swing.

In contrast my *Annus Mirabilis* offers no new groups, new virtuosi, no rebellions, no revivalism. Just a display of wealth.

It began on January 21, the afternoon/evening when Norman Granz taped the 'Jazz Giants '56' album. Had this particular recording been Granz' sole contribution to jazz then his name would still deserve a commemorative plaque. Titles: *Gigantic Blues, This Year's Kisses, You Can Depend On Me, I Guess I'll Have To Change My Plan* and *I Didn't Know What Time It Was.* Again the springboard was three-quarters of a Basie rhythm section; on guitar Freddie Green (with Basie's band from 1937), on bass Gene Ramey (originally taught by Walter Page, then in the band 1952-53) and on drums 'The Wind', Jo Jones (with Basie 1936-48). Passing over them are heard four outstanding soloists, of whom Lester Young, Roy Eldridge and Vic Dickenson had never recorded all together before and Lester and Roy had not recorded with pianist Teddy Wilson for almost twenty years.

No matter. The resultant solos show off all the qualities of greatness. Everyone started to inspire everyone else. Teddy Wilson, such a calm and quiet player with Benny Goodman, began biting emotionally in a way never thought possible of him. And Vic Dickenson took his cue from this, varying his attack considerably and allowing a free rein to his sense of humour, the best-developed of any musician in jazz. It also sounds like Dickenson verbally encouraging Roy Eldridge and Lester Young during *This Year's Kisses.* Clearly Roy was in no mood to worry about the occasional fluff at the session—and consequently achieves what seems to be a personal best on record. Growling, stabbing, strutting along, reaching for and getting one or two almost impossibly difficult high notes, sometimes attacking like a madman, then a minute later playing with muted discretion: for creativity and feeling he breaks every previously-known bond around his talent.

Though of necessity less fierce-sounding than Roy's, Lester Young's contributions are just as surprising. For several years prior to Granz' session he had appeared a tired and rather dispirited soloist. In fact, he was only recently out of hospital when the date took place. Nevertheless he plays with all the glory of bygone days reinvested. The subtly insistent swing, the loping and oblique invention, the heart and the grasp of form. Everything is back as strongly as it was on the great Basie records. He even re-assesses his famous *You Can Depend On Me* solo, with some freshly gratifying conclusions. Perhaps it was his rest in hospital, and switching from hard liquor to wine; perhaps the uplifting effect of his companions. But by the end of the session Lester had played his last outstanding solos on record.

Next, Erroll Garner's 'Concert By The Sea'. Titles: *I'll Remember April, Teach Me Tonight, Mambo Carmel, Autumn Leaves, It's All Right With Me, Red Top, April In Paris, They Can't Take That Away From Me, How Could You Do A Thing Like That To Me?* and *Where Or When.* Garner (piano), Eddie Calhoun (bass) and Denzil Best (drums). Recorded by CBS. As proof that there is still a place in jazz for a keyboard virtuoso in the

Art Tatum tradition, we have the proof of this public and recorded success at Carmel, California—now Clint Eastwoodville.

In 1947 Erroll played (by accident) on the famous Charlie Parker *Cool Blues* session for Dial. But apart from this he recorded only solo or with his own trio. Partly because he didn't read music, relying on a fabulous ear and his vivid imagination. Essentially though on account of his being so like an orchestra, complete in all he played. He was less adroit technically than Tatum and a less sophisticated musician, but he extracted a bigger sound from the piano and at his best could be more emotionally explosive. *Identifying features*: bursts of spread, vibrating two-handed chords developed, via modernism, from James P. Johnson, Fats Waller and the earlier Harlem players. At faster tempi a delayed-action right hand, single-note style, over a proud, trotting left. Tremendous swing. On balance a florid *mélange* of romantic, extrovert impressions.

The year then continued with Dizzy Gillespie's 'World Statesman' LP for Clef. Titles: *Dizzy's Business, Jessica's Day, Tour De Force, I Can't Get Started, Doodlin', Night In Tunisia, Stella By Starlight, The Champ, My Reverie* and *Dizzy's Blues*. Arrangers: Quincy Jones, Ernie Wilkins, Melba Liston, A. K. Salim and Gillespie himself (*Tour De Force*).

After the desperate corn associated with his band in 1949 (including *You Stole My Wife, You Horse Thief*) had failed to stave off the ignominy of a break-up in 1950, Dizzy returned to playing with small groups. Economic conditions were very much against the big bands at the time—with even Basie in trouble.

On the other hand, he remained a magnificent soloist, and in 1956 he did lead a big band again: just briefly, and the result of an unexpected politial decision. He was invited by the State Department to take a band on 'goodwill' tours of the Middle East and South America. (Actually the first time *any* United States government had officially recognised jazz, let alone promoted it as a cultural export!) Both tours proved wildly successful. For Dizzy personally, and for the band. 'Diz was always with cobras or camels or something for publicity purposes, but really I think he enjoyed every minute of it.' (Quincy Jones) On stage, he appeared the perfect leader: witty, effusive and giving the other musicians lots of encouragement. 'As well as playing a storm on trumpet.' (Jones)

The recordings were taped at one marathon session immediately after the band returned from the Middle East. There were no retakes and the balance is far from perfect. But there is no disguising the excitement of the occasion, the dynamics of the ensemble and the fireworks from the soloists, plus Dizzy in abundance.

Much more calculated was Thelonious Monk's great album of the year and his third for the Riversdale label, 'Brilliant Corners'. Titles: *Brilliant Corners, Ba-lue Bolivar Ba-lues-are, Pannonica, I Surrender, Dear* and *Bemsha Swing*. With Monk (piano and celeste), Clark Terry (trumpet),

Ernie Henry (alto-sax), Sonny Rollins (tenor), Oscar Pettiford or Paul Chambers (bass) and Max Roach (drums and tympani).

If another pianist/composer, Tadd Dameron, had suffered neglect in the late 1940s and early '50s (until his 'A Study In Dameronia' of 1953), it was nothing to what Monk was made to suffer. Apart from being pushed into obscurity, this important figure of early modern jazz had been reviled—frequently—by people who failed or had no wish to understand his music. 'He has written a few attractive tunes, but his lack of technique and continuity prevented him accomplishing much as a pianist.' (Leonard Feather)

As the 1950s unfolded though there were signs of an important change in this position. First, with a revival of critical interest. Later as a result of his signing a long–term contract with Riverside and being produced by Orrin Keepnews. At last Monk had a creative shop-window: for his piano-playing, his newer compositions and for re-arrangements of his previous ones. A widespread recognition followed, so that he was able to tour at the head of his own group. And through the 'sixties and 'seventies, what was once considered controversial in his jazz came to be thought of as the sound planning of a revered Elder Statesman.

Thelonious the pianist and innovator at Minton's Playhouse was a natural musician, a genuine original—and such people always go their own way. He was largely self-taught and knew few classical works. Consequently, he remained free from any inhibitions a knowledge of them might have imposed. He was able to conceive sounds and shapes and shadows in jazz utterly different from any other group thinker. And he would tread where they had many fears. On to a ground of dischords and abstractions where curious contours of melody, harmony and rhythm lurked. But—and this was where originality was illuminated by talent—what he found there and brought back to show us, then appeared perfectly logical. At least, after careful examination.

Nor did Monk allow for compromises. It had to be the whole truth as he saw it. The complex harmonic progressions, over which hard, angular melodies are forced to climb; the strange, emotive tensions within the pieces, sometimes erupting into wit but just as soon into anger; the responsive dischords, more effective when voiced than written down. These things are immediately identifiable with Monk and no one else. At times those who played with him were made to sweat. Listen to *Brilliant Corners* itself, for instance, with its uneven metre and stipulated tempo changes. Thelonious has the two saxophones vary their sound strengths appreciably in the theme statements, and even blow unison vibrato explosions. While the soloists are made to observe every tempo variation as they improvise over the chords. When the musicians first saw the arrangement on the recording date they shook their heads. 'Hard?' Sonny Rollins exclaimed: 'No, it's impossible!' However, they persevered—and afterwards agreed it had been a most rewarding experience. Even Monk himself, another perfectionist, was almost satisfied . . .

Finally: Duke Ellington's 'Such Sweet Thunder', an LP started in 1956 and completed early in 1957. Titles: *Such Sweet Thunder, Sonnet For Caesar, Sonnet For Hank Cinq, Lady Mac, Sonnet In Search Of A Moor, The Telecasters, Up And Down, Up And Down (I Will Lead Them Up And Down), Sonnet For Sisters Kate, The Star-crosses Lovers, Madness In Great Ones, Half The Fun* and *Circle Of Fourths.* Recorded for CBS.

'I like to hear the sound of the band,' Ellington often remarked. And so, as with Basie and in spite of his own increasing age, the Duke persisted in leading an orchestra. His had never been so personally disciplined a band as Basie's; but since he was the greatest composer in the history of jazz and always wrote for the man behind the solo, his groups are all always interesting. At their best they can make an inspiring impact. As obviously they did on the Duke as much as anyone.

A significant upheaval of personnel occurred in 1951. Johnny Hodges, Lawrence Brown and Sonny Greer left *en bloc* to form a little band of their own. Ellington brought in Britt Woodman on lead trombone, a phenomenal technician and a childhood friend of Charles Mingus. 'I was given one night to learn a book Lawrence Brown had built up over twenty years!' (Woodman) Duke also acquired Willie Smith, lead alto, Louie Bellson, drums, and re-acquired Juan Tizol (all from Harry James' band). Paul Gonsalves, ex-Dizzy Gillespie, joined on tenor, and Clark Terry (at home with every kind of jazz) on trumpet. Later Hodges rejoined, which caused some internal dissent between the old and the *avant garde*.

But Ellington himself was satisfied with the changes, and afterwards continued to employ modern jazz soloists. If 'employed' is the right word; perhaps *absorbed* would be a better one.

Meanwhile, as a composer and now possibly after the frustration of twenty years of being confined to three-minute recordings, the Duke showed an ever-increasing interest in writing longer works (e.g. 'A Tone Parallel To Harlem') or jazz suites, like the delightful and humour-filled reinterpretation of Tchaikovsky's 'Nutcracker'. Best of all though, I find, is 'Such Sweet Thunder', based on Shakespearean characters and dedicated to the Shakespeare Festival at Stratford, Ontario. It was the first attempt by any jazz composer to interpret a set of well-known literary figures through the playing styles of well-known jazz soloists. Also I think it is Ellington's finest collaboration with co-composer Billy Strayhorn.

The sketches and portraits are extremely varied. Beginning with a swinging overture, inspired by, according to the Duke: 'The sweet and swinging, very convincing story Othello told Desdemona'—before Iago put in his appearance. Then we hear Britt Woodman's incredibly rangy *Hank Cinq* solo, at two different speeds to denote 'the changes of the map as a result of wars'. (Woodman: 'I used to miss the final high note at one concert in four!') *Lady Mac* features Russell Procope on alto and Clark Terry in 3/4 time. 'Though a lady of noble birth, we suspect there was a little ragtime in her soul.' (Ellington) But the ominous last chords suggest she had something extra in her soul! *The Telecasters* features trombones (the three witches) and Harry Carney (Iago) 'They all had somehing to say.' (Ellington) Afterwards there is Clark Terry again with his half-valve effects *á la* Rex Stewart and even a couple of Dizzy Gillespie-like phrases. He is Puck in *Up And Down*: making mischief about the other 'Midsummer Night's Dream' characters and shaping with clever accents the famous line 'Lord, what fools these mortals be.

Next to appear on the stage are a tender Johnny Hodges (Juliet) with a warmly passionate Paul Gonsalves (Romeo) as *The Star-crossed Lovers*: a typically Ellington melody. But we encounter a far different Hodges (as Cleopatra) in *Half The Fun*. He is much more exotic here, languidly reclining over the stick-figures (barge-oars?) of drummer Sam Woodyard. Then Cat Anderson goes off the stage; or rather, his high trumpet notes disappear as if into the stratosphere. Actually this track (*Madness In Great Ones*) is intended to parallel Hamlet's blowing his top; however, as Duke commented: 'In those days crazy didn't mean the same thing it means today.' To conclude, Gonsalves takes a stormy solo which progresses by the interval of a fourth through every musical key. *Circle Of Fourths*, this finale, was, according to Duke, inspired by Shakespeare himself and the four major parts of his artistic contribution: tragedy, comedy, history and the sonnets. (It could also describe how four hundred years later, the genius of an English playwright had come to be interpreted by a surprising, but wholly worthy new Actor/manager, himself a genius too.)

Unfortunately, Ellington's later 'New Orleans Suite' falls outside my time-scale. But it reveals an undoubted vigour and invention from a man well into his seventies.

Of course, if one is prepared to make the year 1956 a little flexible (in other words, to cheat), then just around the corner into 1957 there are other riches. Mingus Workshops, the mature Sonny Rollins, the Miles Davis/Gil Evans 'Miles Ahead', Stan Getz and J. J. Johnson 'At The Opera House', George Russell's Smalltet and not least the first LP by Wes Montgomery, 'The Montgomery Borthers and Five Others' (which includes a seventeen-year-old Freddie Hubbard). However, these deserve their own essay. To paraphrase the popular song, it was another very good year.

1987

CHAPTER THIRTEEN

BIRTHDAYS

1. GIL EVANS

As an English writer about jazz I feel privileged, and I hope on all our readers' behalf in this country, that the ongoing musical magician agreed to celebrate his 75th Birthday in London with a magnificent concert by his NY 'Monday Night' Orchestra at the still-smoking Odeon, Hammersmith on May 13—after which he was justly lionised. I use the word 'justly' because this man, who carries his years lightly, remains the most dazzling and adventurous orchestrator of our music outside the legacy of Duke Ellington. And his adventures do not end. When you attend a Gil Evans performance don't anticipate *anything* except a continuous striving towards excellence and the likelihood of some surprises. On this occasion there were musical surprises, plus some surprise guests.

The concert was set up by Serious Promotions, followed by others in Nottingham, Newcastle and Edinburgh before Gil journeyed to the Continent with his team of players—the sounds of British applause still ringing in his ears. He was heading for Germany, Paris, Norway, France again, Geneva and with the last appearance in Cologne.

Of late, Gil has been contributing to the soundtracks of certain feature films—I believe 'Absolute Beginners' and 'The Colour Of Money'—as well as being in discussion with the pop group Sting. But his programme at Hammersmith still had room for an early Charlie Parker composition, another by Jimi Hendrix and his own ritualistic *Priestess*. Plus new writing by fellow-members of the Orchestra. Most notably (for me, at least) Delmar Brown's *Sometimes*, with its beautiful beginning based on church organ harmonies richly synthesized and then a build into his towering falsetto singing. But the real point about all of these items within Gil's programme is that they are never completely 'set' arrangements. They are always under review, *in action,* and as a result have to be regarded as collective improvisation in the truest sense.

Meanwhile, the current musicianship does everything expected of it and more. Once, many years back, I described Gil Evans as a great picker of men. Well, the real difference today is that the best of men are only too anxious to be picked—afterwards proceeding to shine via the exciting tapestry of his music.

At the Odeon, Britain was well represented in the saxophone section with John Surman, Don Weller and also the underrated Chris Hunter (who now lives near Gil in New York City). The latter has most confidently and with his own individuality taken over the Dave Sanborn role on alto. Then there is veteran George Adams, who once he gets going is like a full saxophone section all by himself. And Gil places his French horn-player John Clarke right in the middle of the saxes.

All of the frontline players got a share of the solo space. Beginning with Steve Lacy on soprano, who turned up as a special guest. Among the trumpets, Lew Soloff has shouldered the Ernie Royal lead parts as well as a heavy solo quota, while Gil's own son Miles is maturing fast and Palle Mikkelborg provides a fleet contrast while playing with electrification. A new face and sound with an impressive technique is lead trombonist Dave Bargerone. Clearly a man we will be hearing more from.

Gil himself continues to avoid a soloist's mould as he concentrates on feeding chords of inspiration to the other players. The more overt keyboard work was deliberately left in the capable hands of Delmar Browne, whose deep roots in gospel music and the blues seem perfectly reconciled with his more progressive ideas. But the most 'active' stage showing was taken up by guitarist Hiram Bullock—*literally*. By keeping his electric-guitar on remote control he is forever on the move in and around the band while he plays. However, close your eyes to this considerable visual aspect and the playing still sounds good.

Other guest spots were filled by Van Morrison (just a single song) and then by a most amazing tambourine solo from Airto Moreira.

All in all, it was a most memorable occasion; and the band ended on a sonorous *Happy Birthday To You* as balloons deluged down. Gil rightly was given a long and sincere standing ovation.

2. DIZZY GILLESPIE

Hot on the heels of Gil Evans' 75th birthday celebrations on May 13 came Dizzy Gillespie's 70th at the non-smoking Royal Festival Hall on July 2—together with his new big band, the best he's fronted, be it for a single festival or a tour, since his 'World Statesman', Quincy Jones-organised crew of 1956/57. The hall, I'm pleased to report, was appropriately packed; and the High Priest of Be-bop did not disappoint anyone. He remains the master of his particular instrumental craft, matured over four-and-a-half decades, and although he paces himself these days ('Dizzy like a fox'), he gave generously of himself in the solo spaces, including the more famous and familiar pyrotechnics as well as a number of new phrasings.

He also kept up the carefully balanced mixture of the expected Dizzy clowning (not least the tree-bell dance at the start of Act II) with the obviously serious approach to more recently completed writing: an extended version of John Lewis' 1946 *'Round Midnight* arrangement (by

I don't know who), a newly commissioned Jimmy Heath original and, as an encore, a fresh composition of his own dedicated to his continuing membership of the Bahai Faith—for which he elicited audience participation. Before which he had ended the concert proper with a devastating workout (*sweatout* might be a more appropriate description!) of Quincy Jones' 1956 score of *The Champ*. Although, for me at least, the finest single item of an overall great concert had been another extended arrangement, of a Gillespie theme from the 1940s, *Manteca*, with Daniel Ponce taking over the co-authors, Chano Pozo's, role on congas and Jon Faddis dominating the middle of the performance with a series of out-of-tempo, stratospheric trumpet breaks which appeared to please Dizzy as much as they astounded the audience. This man *is* the world's No. 1 jazz trumpet technician, despite the greater publicity recently accorded to Wynton Marsalis. (A Buddy Rich of his instrument would not be an outsize analogy.)

Mention of Faddis, over many years a Gillespie protege and now the leading New York session trumpeter, brings me back to the band itself. With a standard of ensemble playing so good I can only hope Dizzy keeps it going for longer than the present year of international festivals and touring gigs. Faddis is serving as musical director, as well as taking responsibility for the auditorium sound mixes; with Dizzy coming in to put the finishing touches (and/or necessary morale boosts) at rehearsals. Also, too, JF is the main featured trumpet soloist after the leader, but all of the other trumpets—Glenn Drewes, Earl Gardner and Virgil Jones—got solo space at the concert.

Which brings me to grouse about the trombones. Because the band has two of the best trombonists in the world today sitting there, Britt Woodman and Steve Turre, but apart from short segments in *'Round Midnight* they were given no features. They make the section sound magnificent; but what a waste! However, the band is young in its timescale and no doubt the book will not neglect them for too long. Meanwhile Steve Turre amazed even this hardened concert reviewer with what was the first-ever jazz improvisation I've heard on a set of conch-shells . . .

Bob Stewart (formerly with Gil Evans) represented a new Gillespie addition on tuba, while the saxes mixed veterans Sam Rivers, Howard Johnson and Jerry Dodgion—a last-minute replacement for Arnie Lawrence—with two younger players, Ralph Moor and Jauppo Perjo. But Rivers too suffered from a lack of solo space for someone of his status. Anyway, again one hopes a future extension of the band's book will rectify this.

No such problems though for pianist James Williams, ex-Art Blakey Messengers and now a solo album-maker in his own right; with two trio recitals available on Concord—and he tells me he has a new LP ready backed by Ray Brown and the Blakey man himself. James was given ample opportunity to shine within the band's programme and proceeded to do so. Backed by a very good rhythm section: Ed Cherry, guitar, John Lee, bass and a dynamic drummer, Ignacio Berroa, from Cuba. Of the latter, Dizzy quips that he swam through shark-infested waters all the way to Florida to join the band.

Finally, back to the High Priest himself—and may I on behalf of all our readers wish him many more playing-birthdays.

You know, the man really does respond to his audiences. I met him backstage, less than an hour before the concert, sipping a cup of tea, grey with travel and fatigue. Came the opening, and the roar of the fans, and he literally bounced on to the stage, to all intents and purposes the same enthusiastic go-getter who as a much younger man changed jazz music forever at Minton's Playhouse.

1987

CHAPTER FOURTEEN

CLINT EASTWOOD AND BIRD!

The Movie

In 1949, when I was a student in Paris, I both heard and met the legendary Charlie Parker, 'Yardbird'. Musically and socially these events changed my life. First call upon my careful and precious hoarding of francs at the Jazz Fair of that year had been Sidney Bechet—and I had not been disappointed. But then came Parker (together with Kenny Dorham, trumpet, Al Haig, piano, Tommy Potter, bass and Max Roach, drums). And I believe my mouth literally fell open. I was totally unprepared for a saxophone-player who could impose chord changes upon a melodic line with the speed and imagination which now assailed me. Within the time-scale of a single concert the course of all future listening was set. I also passed a most agreeable day-and-a-half in his company (as his devotee, but also as a fellow-devotee of Edward Fitzgerald's translation of 'Omar Khayyam'), when, although there were hints of his interior chaos, he was clearly enjoying being lionised.

When Bird died in 1955 at the age of thirty-four his co-founder of the Be-bop Revolution, the otherwise resilient Dizzy Gillespie, broke down and cried. The rest of the jazz world knew how he felt. Someone of the utmost importance had been taken from us. A natural genius whose personal life had become a familiar artistic tragedy. Modern jazz had, in him, experienced its Marlowe, its Chatterton, its Rimbaud and, in another sense, its Oscar Wilde. The stranger-doctor who examined Parker's body after the fatal heart attack thought he was a man in his late 'fifties.

Given so much brilliance musically and such a difficult, drug-haunted, alcohol underpinned, rubbish-fed (a dozen hamburgers at a time) and generally incoherent life, Parker was always set to become the subject of a major film—and now, at last, it seems evident that we have one. Facts can nearly always outstrip fiction in the putting together of a story, and no less a Hollywood personage than Clint Eastwood has clearly grasped the significance of this. His forthcoming "Bird" must be looked forward to as a major movie.

Megastar Eastwood, who is also now the Mayor of Carmel, California, has likewise been a Charlie Parker buff from way back. He plays some jazz piano himself, and since gaining control over his own film destiny has always paid sharp attention to music soundtracks. More importantly in this context though, in recent years he has turned himself into an extremely accomplished director. Which is not so common as one might think. Ever since the towering example of Orson Welles and 'Citizen Kane', it's sad fact that the majority of actors who are credited with being their own directors as well have, in actuality, left most of the workload to their fellow-actors, their scriptwriter, but most of all, the cameraman. However, in the directional department Clint Eastwood is the genuine article. He has studied the work carefully and properly and come up with some outstanding results. 'Bird' is his thirteenth film as a director, and only the second in which he himself has not starred ('Breezy' with William Holden and Kay Lenz, made in 1973, was the other).

One other important contribution by Clint Eastwood to 'Bird' has been in the additional role as producer, and, in fact, getting the project off the ground in the first place. Joel Oliansky had written a screenplay for the film as far back as 1982, as an assignment for Columbia Pictures. But then for various reasons it got overlooked. Upon learning about it, Eastwood determined the project would gather dust no longer. He is known for many things in the film industry: not least his organisational abilities and his popularity with fellow-actors and unit technicians. In addition though, on account of his name-value, he also carries enormous clout. Before very long 'Bird' was a Malpaso Production and signed for a Warner Bros. release. The traffic-lights were on green . . .

The film opens with a vignette of Parker as he was aged sixteen. That was in 1936 in Kansas City, and he was just about to take part in his first public jam session. He is gawky and unseasoned, but when he begins to blow there are glimmerings of the displays of musical genius which will come later. An outburst of genius which, together with Dizzy Gillespie, Thelonious Monk, Kenny Clarke and a handful of other pioneers, would be destined soon to change the face of jazz for all time.

Apparently this vignette is typical of Clint Eastwood's methods throughout the film, with flashes back and forth and making very clever use of time-scales. Gradually he is building up a compassionate portrait of the man and musician, reflecting his era and art, via visual techniques which parallel Bird's own amazing rush of invented phrases and startling tone. On the one hand we have the power and originality of Parker the player, but with on the other the continual chaos and pitfalls of his life off-stage and which propelled him with a terrible relentlessness towards his premature death. He was calmed, and only then at times, by the woman he loved and made his second wife, Chan, and by their two children (until tragedy intervened even here). The relationship with Chan was unconventional, but at least provided a thread of continuity. Probably the only one outside his music Charlie ever knew.

There is a glimpse of the young alto-saxist battling it out with a veteran player, 'Buster'—presumably the well-known Kansas City reedman Buster Smith, whom Bird admitted to be his own forerunner and single important influence. And this is intercut with flashes of the mature Parker opening the big club named after him in New York City, Birdland. This was in 1945, when his revolution with Dizzy Gillespie and others, known as Be-bop, had become an established phenomenon. Also by this time his reputation as the leading alto soloist of jazz had become supreme. But off the stand he was living a drug-haunted existence. With many financial and legal hangups. There were attempts at rehabilitation, with Chan forever seeking to stabilise his affairs. In the end though even her Herculean efforts failed and heroin took its final ghastly toll. John Lewis once told me that often, on the road, Bird's entire earnings were being consumed by his addiction.

The film covers the 1930s, '40s and '50s with Joel Oliansky's script balancing the successes against the struggles. It was shot on location in Los Angeles and in the Sacramento delta region near Stockton, California. There were also specially prepared sets at the Burbank Studios, where Oscar-winning production designer Edward Carfagno recreated various 'key' New York streets of the Be-bop era.

Clearly, for overall producer Eastwood 'Bird' has been a labour of love from first to last. And at the very beginning of the project he secured the agreement and co-operation of Chan Parker, flying her from Paris to Los Angeles to advise actress Diane Venora, who plays her in the film. And of course he took his usual care in the selection of musicians. As his soundtrack co-ordinator he chose ex-Kenton altoist Lennie Niehaus, now an arranger of over forty TV and feature films with music supervisor Jerry Fielding.

As well as supervising the music for 'Bird', Niehaus was also extensively employed in preparing actor Forest Whitaker (who plays Parker) so that he could suitably duplicate Parker's physical presence while actual Parker tapes were being used. He then went on with great care to remix these tapes, previously unreleased until brought to light by Chan, who had been holding them at her Paris apartment. Thus we now will have some tunes Bird never otherwise put out on commercial discs: *All Of Me, I Can't Believe That You're In Love With Me* and *Lester Leaps In*, plus a 'live' performance of *Laura*. This done, Niehaus finally had to teach Forest Whitaker, Damon Whitaker, Keith David, Sam Wright and Michael Zelniker (actors all cast as musicians in the film) how to play scales and simple tunes on their instruments so that his sound dubbing would appear credible.

Meanwhile, and in consultation with Niehaus, Clint Eastwood was lining up a considerable roster of real jazz musicians for the film: including Ray Brown, Ron Carter and Chuck Berghoffer (bass), Walter Davis, Monty Alexander and Barry Harris (piano), Johnny Guerin (drums), Charles McPherson, Bob Cooper, Gary Foster and Pete Christlieb (saxophones); also Red Rodney, to understudy himself and Jon Faddis to understudy Dizzy Gillespie on trumpets.

Evidently, Eastwood has been equally careful in his choice of acting talent. Certainly from the stills and clips I have seen. Forest Whitaker, who plays Bird, possesses a quite remarkable facial likeness to his subject. This is his first feature film in a leading role, although he has appeared in many smaller parts, notably in 'Bloodsport', 'Platoon', 'The Colour Of Money' and 'Fast Times At Ridgemont High', as well as many TV films, and before that stage work ranging from 'Hamlet' to 'Jesus Christ, Superstar'. The greatest problems which must have faced him in 'creating' this role of Bird on film would be to reconcile the man's periods of inspiration with his deep love for Chan and their children and then set these against the times of almost total irresponsibility. How exactly he has brought this off is one of the features of the film I am looking forward to most keenly.

Diane Venora, who plays Chan Parker, has a very different form of human character to interpret. Chan was born in Westchester, but as the daughter of a night-club producer grew up in New York City. She became a dancer and extremely knowledgeable about modern jazz before meeting Bird. Later she would re-marry, to another tremendously gifted alto-player and a Parker disciple, Phil Woods. She is strong-minded, independent and singularly lacking in pretensions. First drawn to Bird by his music, she then devoted herself to the difficult endeavours of making him feel peaceful, looked-after— *and loved.*

Venora attests to the help she received from Chan in portraying the latter's essential contribution to the Parker lifelines—which frequently meant trying to throw him one. A much-experienced actress, especially in classical roles, she can claim to have been one of the few women ever to play Hamlet (in the New York Shakespeare Festival), together with other important stage parts in Chekhov's 'The Seagull', Ibsen's 'Peer Gynt', Chekhov's 'Uncle Vanya' and Strindberg's 'Miss Julie'. Her film credits are for 'Ironwood', 'F/X', 'Cotton Club', 'Critical List', 'Wolfen' and 'All That Jazz'. But 'Bird' has been her most challenging film part so far.

Other main parts in the film are fulfilled by Keith David ('Buster'), Sam Wright ('Dizzy Gillespie') and Michael Zelniker ('Red Rodney'), with Damon Whitaker, Forest's younger brother, and again bearing a strong facial resemblance, playing the teenager stage of Parker in his first-ever feature film.

Which leaves me with just something to say about Clint Eastwood's production team. All of them previously tried and trusted by him.

Executive producer David Valdes had worked with Brian Grazer and Francis Coppola before joining CE for 'Pale Rider'—leading on to five more collaborations before 'Bird', on which he had to cope with a host of transitional duties, from storyboarding to pre-release marketing. Jack Green, Director of Photography, had worked as a camera operator on eight Eastwood films before being promoted Director for the recent 'Heartbreak Ridge'.

Designer Edward Carfagno also met up with CE for the first time in a working capacity on 'Pale Rider'. Before that though he was already the gainer of three Academy Awards ('The Bad And The Beautiful', 'Julius Caesar' and 'Ben Hur') as well as being nominated for seven others. Within the context of 'Bird' he has had to cope with sets of New York City timed over three different decades, not least 52nd Street during the early 1940s.

Finally, screenplay writer Joel Oliansky. He is out of Yale Drama School, and, like myself, fell under the spell of Parker after just a single listening. In his case a concert with Jazz At The Philharmonic. After Yale he co-founded the Hartford Stage Company in Connecticut, before moving to Los Angeles in 1964 to work for Ray Stark at Seven Arts. He wrote (and sometimes directed) for ten years at Universal, on shows including 'Kojak', 'Quincy' and 'Cagney And Lacey', gaining Emmies for 'The Senator' in 1971 and 'The Law' in 1975.

All in all, quite a pool of talent under Clint Eastwood's direction.

I once wrote that Charlie Parker was an intrepid musical explorer with a fine sense of harmony as his compass. With a tone rich and bitter, like the taste of an olive. I also happen to believe he was a kind of conscience for modern jazz. Because with his natural gifts and creativity he showed a whole generation musically where next to go. While with his life he showed it where not to go. I look forward to seeing the full film with growing impatience. Given Bird's great talents, and Eastwood's different (and in this case clearly sympathetic) ones, it promises much.

1988

Now proven.

CHAPTER FIFTEEN

AL HAIG

It seems like light years ago (in fact December, 1953) that I had a piece published in *Jazz Journal*, Vol. 6, No. 12 under the heading 'A Case For More Haig'.

At the time Alun Morgan and I were involved in a lonely war trying to press the British majors into issuing modern jazz from a wide variety of smaller American labels, and the pianist Al Haig was symptomatic of many 'key' figures we considered were being neglected. Sure, the record companies had heard of Charlie Parker and Dizzy Gillespie. But who–the–hell was Al Haig; and who was Wardell Gray; and why should anyone want to buy Wardell Gray's tenor-saxophone chases with another obscure player by the name of Dexter Gordon?

It was a pretty depressing time for those who cared about and were keen to collect modern jazz. A few gems did escape on to the market. Kenny Clarke's *Royal Roost*, for instance, with its tremendous trumpet duet between Fats Navarro and Kenny Dorham, one of Bud Powell's best piano solos and our first taste in Britain of Sonny Stitt's saxophone sounds. Also pianist Dodo Marmarosa's *Mellow Mood* and *How High The Moon* with Lucky Thompson, Ray Brown and drummer Jackie Mills. And the odd modernist solo could be heard within Stan Kenton's arrangements. (Kenton's *How High The Moon* was the first time I ever heard Art Pepper, although the disc is better-known for June Christy's vocal.) Generally though we were getting nowhere. In 1952 and '53 my last resort was to pay Carlo Kramer to cut me acetates from his private collection of items I knew were freely available to the British 'big battalions'. It was illegal, of course: the jazz equivalent of Solzhenitsyn's *samizdat* ('material reproduced and circulated in unofficial or clandestine manner'). But the majors didn't want to know us and neither Alun, nor I, nor many other modern jazz fans were prepared to go without the recorded evidence of our personal obsessions.

In fairness, later on in the 'fifties things did improve. But this mainly due to the enthusiasm of the lead-men at two smaller record companies—the aforementioned Carlo Kramer with his Esquire label and David Murray-Sparks at Vogue. Esquire issued an EP of four outstanding performances Al Haig had recorded for Prestige in 1950. The titles were *Stars Fell On Alabama, Liza, Stairway To The Stars* and Al's own *Opus Caprice*. The accompaniment: Tommy Potter, bass, and Roy Haynes on drums. (And incidentally, the sleeve-note was written by a fellow-pianist, Dill Jones.) Vogue then issued a less-impressive 10-inch album which had been set up in New York by yet another pianist, the Frenchman, Henri Renaud. Evidently the session was a rather hurried affair. Al was on edge and at his most introspective. Well-aware that Renaud was also a pianist, he became self-conscious about the purely physical part of his playing and insisted on having a screen between them.

If I was so depressed in the early 'fifties about the lot of certain modern jazzmen, I would have been doubly depressed to know in Haig's case how long that neglect was to last. The end of the 'fifties saw a boom in modern jazz appreciation, but Haig enjoyed none of it; and the 'sixties were bad for jazz generally. Haig made only one record during this decade and at one stage, in desperation, worked down in Miami with a rhumba band.

It wasn't until 1974, and oddly enough in London, that his recording career got under way again. This was under the auspices of Tony Williams of Spotlite Records; of whom more later. Today, considering his place in jazz history, Al is still an underrated piano-player. But at least he is working regularly in New York; and making records. Also he is young enough to respond once he gains the status which is his due. It now seems that the lights are on green for him.

At which point a *curriculum vitae* is needed. If I had to prepare an entry for a Burke's Peerage of Jazz, it would probably begin like this: 'Haig, Allan Warren, 'Al', pianist. Born Newark, New Jersey on July 22, 1924 of Scottish descent. Raised in Nutley, NJ. Classical studies from age nine led to two years of music theory at Oberlin College, Ohio. Plus harp lessons. Some jazz at college. Chief early influence: Teddy Wilson. Also admires Nat 'King' Cole and Mel Powell. In 1942 drafted into U.S. Coast Guard band (playing clarinet and saxophone). Stationed at Ellis Island in New York's harbour, began to frequent the clubs along 52nd Street. Heard the be-bop experimenters out of Minton's Playhouse and became a convert. With own natural talents was quickly accepted into modern jazz groups led by Parker, Gillespie and Oscar Pettiford. One of the first and best of the music's keyboard exponents. Also its finest accompanist.'

A condensed listing would follow of the places and people he worked with through the rest of the 'forties and into the 'fifties.

His first professional gigs were in Boston with Rudy Williams, the former sax-star of The Savoy Sultans. Then in 1944, and just out of the Coast Guard, Al played briefly for clarinettist and leader Jerry Wald. Wald also came from Newark, NJ; his band was a big one with a swing style and a number of be-bop devices grafted on. The pianist doubled up on this job by appearing within a small combo led by the guitarist Tiny Grimes, another peripheral figure in the development of be-bop. But his future lay neither with big bands nor alongside displaced 'thirties artists. Al's true habitat was the unison-ensemble quintets and sextets of those same Minton's pioneers who by the mid-'forties had got themselves organised. In May, 1945 he was with a group which also included Charlie Parker, Dizzy, bassist Curley Russell and Stan Levey on drums. They cut one tremendous session for Guild—although Levey couldn't manage the date and was replaced by 'Big Sid' Catlett, who seemed to be able to cope with every style of jazz, from Louis Armstrong to Bird and Diz. After the quintet had recorded *Hot House, Shaw 'Nuff* and the notorious *Salt Peanuts*, Sarah Vaughan joined the players for her first rendition of *Lover Man*. 'Haig threw out chords like bursts of musical confetti,' Ross Russell, the date's producer, comments in his book, 'Bird Lives!'—'the music seemed to explode from the groove into the listener's ear . . .'

When Dizzy Gillespie organised his big band Al declined to join it. Perhaps he'd sensed (correctly, as it turned out) that once the band travelled below the Mason-Dixon line its much-ballyhooed U.S. tour would end in disaster. Also there was the Jim Crow problem. A white pianist going Deep South with a black band?

Impossible!

But Diz and his management were confident, so Al remained behind and continued to play gigs on 52nd Street. When a considerably-chastened Gillespie arrived back in New York and decided to resurrect his small combo, Haig was happy to rejoin him—together with an ailing Parker, Milt Jackson (vibes), Ray Brown (bass) and Stan Levey (drums). Dizzy's main agent, Billy Shaw, booked the group away across the continent for eight weeks at Billy Berg's jazz bistro in Hollywood. It would be a good engagement, he assured them. They set off by train.

After an enthusiastic opening-night, Berg's was not a success; their weeks there were marred by Parker's addiction, which in the end took him right out of the group. With Lucky Thompson on tenor the remaining musicians cut a session for Dial. Included was a version of Thelonious Monk's *''Round Midnight* containing an early and typical solo by Al. 'Relaxed, thoughtful and beautifully-executed,' I wrote of it in my 1953 piece, 'it reflects much of his melodic charm and propensity towards the pretty themes'. Apart from substituting 'gentler' for 'pretty' I stand by that judgement of his ballad style.

Evenings at Billy Berg's had turned dismal though. Often Bird didn't show at all. Meanwhile Dizzy was still hankering after another big band and their audiences were down to two dozen drinkers per set. By the final week Gillespie could hardly wait to catch a plane East. Haig stayed on briefly to do a few one-nighters with Charlie Barnet; but then he too hurried back towards The Apple. And busy times ahead.

We know he got back to New York in time to make the famous February, '46 session led by Dizzy Gillespie for RCA Victor: the one which produced *52nd Street Theme, Night In Tunisia, Anthropology* and *Ol'Man Re-bop*. Others on the date were Don Byas (tenor), Milt Jackson (vibes) and recorded like a set of jam-jars, Bill De Arango (guitar), Ray Brown (bass) and J.C. Heard (drums). This was a significant session, because it was for a major label: the previously castigated be-boppers were gaining respectability. And Dizzy excelled himself on the day. Since then he has played many longer and occasionally better solos on disc; but I think his contribution to *Anthropology* is his most important early be-bop statement.

Haig's name was greatly enhanced by these Victor sides. He began to be offered work at two different levels. On top, with some of the more commercial names of the period: Coleman Hawkins, Eddie 'Lockjaw' Davis and Ben Webster; then for nine months Jimmy Dorsey's band, where, one suspects, he kept a low profile—neither Dorsey brother being particularly partial to be-bop. Also though he became a firm favourite (and virtually house recording pianist) with a younger, second generation of modernists. This included the main ex-Herman Herdsmen who were beginning to make it on their own: Stan Getz, Zoot Sims, Herbie Steward and Red Rodney. Plus players like Kai Winding, Allen Eager, Jimmy Raney, Tiny Kahn, Bennie Green (the gifted trombonist, not the London broadcaster) and—for the one momentous session of *Stoned* and *Matter And Mind*—Wardell Gray. 1948 was something of a bonanza for these men, despite or perhaps because of another Local 802 union ban. They all recorded prolifically for the small, back-street labels. And, recording quality aside, their performances contain marvellous moments. (I even enjoy the primitive be-bop vocalese by the late Dave Lambert and Buddy Stewart.) Apart from claustrophobic rooms and poor mixer-units Al himself also had to put up with some bad pianos; but his solos still come shining through, and his accompaniments are infallible. No wonder that he was soon to be hired on a permanent basis by the returning genius, Charlie 'Yardbird' Parker.

However, before passing on to this I would just like to insert a note that almost all the 1948 underground material with Getz *et al* has been very carefully collected and remastered by Tony Williams and Haig's discographer Brian Davis on three Spotlite LPs under the headline "Al Haig Meets The Master Saxes'.

I find it difficult to write of Al in 1949 without a couple of personal stories. By the month of the Paris Jazz Fair (May of that year) Charlie Parker had not only pulled himself together as a human being and a musician, but he was leading the definitive unison ensemble be-bop quintet. He had Kenny Dorham on trumpet, Haig on piano, Tommy Potter (bass) and Max Roach (drums).

As for my own young and still developing tastes in jazz, well, the modernists were just names picked up from journals and newspapers. Knowing only the alto-playing of Benny Carter and Johnny Hodges, I was therefore totally unprepared for the impact of Parker! The way the man imposed harmonic changes on a phrase of melody so quickly, the daring intervals he used, his swooping through the octaves, the richness of his improvised ideas and, of course, that special bitter-sweet tone, like the taste of an olive. He was a musical explorer, with the most amazing sense of harmony as his compass. Then too there were crackling solos by Kenny Dorham, already a very mature player; and Al Haig was feeding them exactly the right support chords as if by instinct, filling in with a nimble, delicate tracery of right-hand work.

Charlie Parker was very much an enigma in Paris. I was privileged to spend some time in his company. Off-stage there were times when he communicated, others when he didn't. I was still studying in France, and now a fan, but not trying to interview him, and I guess I got lucky. As anyone who knows Steve Race will agree, he is an understanding and intelligent interviewer; never as spiky one. But instead of having his questions answered Steve was treated to a series of recitations from 'Omar Khayyam'. As I've said, I got lucky. He still refused to discuss his own playing, but he was more than willing to discuss his group. And he insisted that Al Haig was 'the best accompanist I know'. He'd worked with all the important pianists of modern jazz, he told me: Monk, Bud Powell, Dodo Marmarosa, Joe Albany, Duke Jordan and George Wallington. But—and he jabbed a finger in my chest—to have Al backing him was 'an inspiration in itself'.

Back in the States, Parker's health remained more or less stable for the next eighteen months; and Haig was with him for much of this time. He did the Jazz At The Philharmonic tour of 1950 with Bird and was on the Carnegie Hall recording of September 16: although nearly fogbound by a disorganised string section. (Just listen to the way they fall in and ruin his superbly-designed introduction to *I'll Remember April*, alias Gerry Mulligan's *Rocker*.) And already he'd played on the notorious *Visa* and *Passport* sessions: well and truly loused up by the non-playing of trombonist Tommy Turk. Even so, it's interesting that when Parker finally did get his own way with Norman Granz and recorded the greatest, if not quite the last session of his final years (on August 4, 1953), Al Haig was the accompanist he sent for. *Now's The Time* from that session is arguably the performance of its year: by *any* artist. It's just a pity the recording engineer didn't realise he had a jazz classic slipping away under his fingers. The rhythm balance is appalling.

At this time Haig was more in demand than ever. Having made a brilliant contribution to Fats Navarro's last studio recording (*Stop/Go* and *Infatuation* for Prestige), he was now into more than two years as regular pianist with the Stan Getz Quintet, doing freelance sessions, and at last making more records under his own name. The job with Getz could hardly have been an easy one. If anything the tenorman is even more demanding of his pianists than Bird was. Also he had, and still has, an unrivalled memory for the harmonic sequences of both jazz and popular compositions. But Al was perfectly able to keep up with him. (As shown on their 'live' sets from the Storyville Club in Boston. Collected on the double album for Jazz Vogue.)

From the mid-'fifties we begin to lack consistent knowledge of the pianist's activities—a sure sign that the long, lost years for him were about to begin. Already he had cut his great trio and sextet sides for Prestige, plus the solo set for French Vogue and two more which Jerry Newman recorded, one for his own Esoteric label, the other for Period. In December, 1954 we know he replaced Russ Freeman in the Chet Baker Quartet (and he recorded with Baker as late as September, 1958 for Riverside). In between comes the Prestige album with Donald Byrd and Phil Woods ('The Young Bloods', and half-released on 'House Of Byrd'). Recorded near the end of '56, it appears to coincide with the fortnight Al spent in Dizzy Gillespie's World Statesman band. Phil Woods was definitely a member of that band and so was the date's drummer, Charlie Persip. However, Al lost his place with Dizzy due to some confusion concerning his AFM union card. Then after 1958 the curtain descends; and until the 'seventies the neglect of Al Haig's playing is almost total.

Paul Winson, an English scientist seconded to the U.S. and who later got to know Al very well, says it was a full decade of scratching around for every single job. Seeking out restaurants, private parties, even fashion shows; and, of course, sitting in with third and fourth-rate bands. Going anywhere he discovered they needed a piano-player. And the neglect added to his personal problems. Most monumentally when his wife fell down the well-head of their block of flats and the New York police accused Al of her murder. Today he is extremely fastidious; especially about alcohol. He drinks tea and eats cucumber sandwiches. The bad habits of the early modern jazz period took many of its leading exponents many years to shake off. Others didn't make it through.

Near the end of the 'sixties, there was the incident when the pianist had secured and trained himself hard to take part in a concert of classical music. Only days before, he hurt his hand in an ice-cube breaker and the chance was lost.

'It was only after this that things started to pick up,' Paul Winson recalls. 'By the time I got to New York in September, '72, Al had secured the residency at Jimmy Weston's, and happily his playing abilities were unimpaired.' Soon afterwards King Harrison, a Cincinatti businessman and jazz buff, was writing to Tony Williams about the possibility of a fresh start on the recording front.

The written word is no substitute for the human ear when it comes to analysing a jazz artist's style and sound. Especially when the man he is writing about has made a very personal contribution to the history and development of modern jazz.

On behalf of Al Haig, Dill Jones made a good point when he said that Al's style 'is the combination of four of the most sought-after virtues in the field of modern jazz piano—beauty of tone, an advanced harmonic sense, symmetry of phrasing and a completely individual sound.' I particularly like Dill's stressing the fact that the style and the sound are the man, and that these two qualities are interdependent. I'm also grateful to Alun Morgan for his opinion that Haig's work 'seems always to impart a feeling of comparative calm, even at fast tempo; his solos are made up of neatly resolved phrases forming part of an overall idea.' Mister Morgan is indeed right on target here. When Al Haig is improvising, no matter how richly or for how long, there are never any loose ends. His co-ordination of mind with fingers is truly remarkable.

Leading on from this it is easy enough to point to the more superficial features of his keyboard work. One can refer to its nimbleness of notation; and to a combination of subtle swing with a very bright, clear tone. He's always aware of the action of the instrument and he makes an adept, almost sly use of the pedal. (For instance, on ballads he will allow certain chords to reverberate to an extent he never would when the pace is up. This is just a part of his flexible and sophisticated sense of dynamics.) Again, one should perhaps point to his method—especially at speed—of deliberately breaking his own sequence of longish runs in order to insert passing figures and (albeit brief) variations. This goes right back to Art Tatum, and for any second-class pianist is extremely dangerous. With Haig though the continuity never falters.

However, by far the most important thing about Al Haig is that, at a crucial point in the evolution of the modern jazz called be-bop, he provided the music with a viable alternative to the otherwise definitive be-bop piano style of Bud Powell. Moreover, although what he did was purely personal, it was also logical and basically rather clever. (The only other, early alternative was provided by Thelonious Monk, who had, in fact, first inspired Powell, but Monk's influence, pianistically, didn't otherwise begin to be felt until the late 'fifties.)

Powell's playing comes at you like ocean rollers hitting a Pacific or Atlantic beach. (Al told me that the top digits of his right-hand were bent back, he hit the piano so hard!) Even if the phrasing is different, nevertheless his glittering attack is in the same tradition founded by Earl Hines and continued by Billy Kyle. But then—obviously inspired by the style of Bird and Diz, as well as the ideas of Thelonious—Bud established the method of committing all of his improvisations to the right-hand (in this way producing horn-like figures and runs), while giving the chordal support and implied swing to the left. At the same time too, derived from Monk, the separated left-hand harmonic placings were hammered out in the most percussive manner possible and quickly became the model modern style for pianists.

In contrast Haig, who like Dodo Marmarosa could match Powell's fast tempo-playing but not his phenomenal (and ferocious) attack, opted for more interweaving of the hands. When he plays his right-hand still spearheads the improvisation and the main chordal props are still heard from the left. But there are considerable overlaps; so much so that sometimes it is difficult for this listener at least to distinguish which hand is doing what. This is partly because he has ideally balanced the sound-levels coming from under the hands, but also on account of the way he carefully distributes his melodic and even more his harmonic ideas between the two. It allows for great subtlety of phrasing and a kind of tapestry, a weave-and-weft effect. Meanwhile, to complement, there is the quiet of his attack. A quiet which still succeeds in intensity and excitement.

There are lots of precedents in jazz for the creation of a viable alternative: Bix Beiderbecke after Louis Armstrong, Lester Young blowing away from Coleman Hawkins; and with be-bop Lee Konitz after Charlie Parker and Miles Davis following Dizzy. Then, in addition, there is a modest claim that in his brief recording career the late Clyde Hart anticipated one or two of Al Haig's ideas. It doesn't matter. As William Faulkner said: 'What is important is 'Hamlet' and 'Midsummer Night's Dream', not who wrote them, but that *somebody* did . . .' Al Haig has lived to mature his style, is continuing to use it effectively and has succeeded in influencing a whole new generation of pianists. His studied approach to the gradation of touch has been a major influence. Likewise his natural curiosity. As early as 1949 he was quoted as saying: 'I think be-bop is making an important contribution to American music. However, it's not likely to stop here as a basic form— rather it is another milestone along the road of musical progress.' Most of all though, his style led the way to interior harmonic development by modern jazz pianists, notably the ultra-intellectual, Bill Evans.

One other significant aspect of Al's playing stems from something more physical. He has long fingers, but otherwise smallish and rather delicate hands. He cannot span the octave-and-a half (I believe) of Oscar Peterson; and if he doesn't get the right, responsive pianos, then in order to achieve his usual bright sound he often hurts his hands, even splitting the finger-tips. I think this has imposed an additional discipline on his playing, furthering the interior integration of his harmonic style.

Which brings me finally to Al Haig in 1974 and after on disc. His return to regular recording under his own name has coincided with a number of longer residencies in New York City (more recently at the One Fifth Club on Fifth Avenue). He has been able to face the new interest in his career in a relaxed, and perhaps also relieved way, especially in the tackling of recording sessions. His recent recordings are now close to twenty albums, on several different labels and some only available at present in Japan. But they began on January 7, 1974 when Tony Williams of Spotlite recorded Al at Olympic Studios, Barnes, London with Gilbert Rovere on bass and Kenny Clarke, drums. The set is headlined "Invitation" and since then there have been four more sets on the label: 'Special Brew', which teams Al with his ertswhile Stan Getz colleague, guitarist Jimmy Raney; 'Solitaire', all solo performances; 'Stablemates', a quintet date which brings back another neglected player from the 'fifties, trumpeter Jon Eardley, and also teams Al for the first time with the immensely-gifted Art Themen on tenor-saxophone; and finally (again with Themen included) an October, '78 session, 'Expressly Ellington'.

Obviously a piece of writing about Al Haig is not the place to linger over the performances of his fellow-musicians, no matter how much I have enjoyed them. Suffice it to say that all of these collaborations have struck the right sparks, and none more so than with bassist Jamil Nasser. He and Al appear to have developed a very special affinity.

As for Al's own contributions, there is a good deal to be said, but it must be condensed. I have been as guilty as every other writer so far about the earlier stages of his career, dwelling upon his qualities as an accompanist rather than his brilliance as a soloist. The only mitigating circumstances being the scarcity of full-length solos as distinct from insert choruses of solo. With these five Spotlite albums there is no such problem. Al is very much the leader and principal soloist. He is better-recorded than previously, has the use of better pianos and is able to pre-determine the length of his solos. *Invitation*, for example, lasts for seven minutes; while his interpretation of Tadd Dameron's *If You Could See Me Now* on the same record goes to nearly eight. (And incidentally, the latter must rival Bill Evans' Riverside version as being the definitive pianistic performance so far.) In contrast, on the 'Solitaire' record, *Bess You Is My Woman* lasts for only three minutes and eight seconds and sounds just right. Such musical judgement: not one note too many!

Allowing for these increased freedoms, it is not a case of Al's style and sound having changed dramatically over the years, but rather of a gradual refinement. On the one hand he is capable of an involved virtuousity, i.e. *Here's That Rainy Day* on 'Solitaire'; and yet on many of the ballads there is a new austerity. However, it takes a mature mind to know what to leave out. To achieve the art of true simplicity is very difficult indeed.

Two criticisms of his earlier work are also demolished. *Opus Caprice* had led one to believe that he was a gifted, but somewhat reluctant modern jazz composer. But on these recent recordings fresh compositions are beginning to appear: *Linear Motion, Sambalhasa* and *Joanne,* named after his second wife. Plus his *Sawbo City Blues,* which together with *Blues For Alice* demolishes my second criticism. I had always felt that in the 'forties Al (like Bud Powell) was hesitant about following Charlie Parker into the raw, earthier reaches of the blues, preferring instead intricate be-bop themes and the more interesting chord sequences of standard compositions. Now I can say without equivocation that that particular bogey has been laid as well. And he pays generous tributes to his fellow-pianists: Cedar Walton, Billy Strayhorn, Herbie Hancock, Ahmed Jamal, Dave Brubeck, Thelonious (*'Round Midnight* again) and, of course, Duke Ellington.

The temptations to go on and list all the findings of delight are, as the Dark Lord once bragged, legion. There is a deeply-felt sincerity about the thematic statement of the folk-based *Holyland*, a composition by Cedar Walton; then Al kicks off his improvised solo with an obvious quote from *It Don't Mean A Thing If It Ain't Got That Swing.* On Ahmed Jamal's *Lament* there is a daring facsimile of Art Tatum's right-hand runs, but as usual Al gets away with it. And how good he still sounds on a fast be-bop standard like Charlie Parker's *Marmaduke.* On Strayhorn's *Lush Life* (verse included) on the 'Expressly Ellington' album, the atmosphere is deliberately exotic, but there are also more intriguingly subtle tempo changes. Then there are the tracks on the album with Raney where he uses electric piano . . .

But I must stop. I'm simply glad to have Al Haig's music running on a parallel course with my own life again.

Postcript One

Since completing this profile I have had the opportunity to discuss a number of things with Al in person, following a marvellous performance he gave at the University Theatre in Hampstead, organised by David Lund.

Although clearly an immensely shy man, he is at the same time highly articulate. This was the occasion when he gave me a very lucid explanation of how, in their different ways, both Bud Powell and himself obtained their dynamics. 'The ends of Bud's fingers would be literally curled back,' he said. Al's own hands are much more poised over the keyboard. He seems almost to drop the ends of his fingers on the keys: although obviously it is fully controlled.

I also asked him if he came from a musical family. 'No,' he said, 'My father was an engineer.' Upon reflection he added: 'But maybe that's what I am really. An engineer of the piano.'

Postcript Two

Al Haig died, with sudden surprise in November, 1982. I had been talking with him at Burgh House, Hampstead on October 10 of that year. He was 58 and died of a heart attack. I was asked to write his obituary, which I found an unhappy compliment, but it came out as follows . . .

As a man, the real Al Haig, in his last decade he was as elegant as the final form into which his piano style had evolved. Wry, urbane, still introverted but outgoing with his music, fastidious and, above all by this time, supremely self-confident. The trials and tribulations of his earlier career had been shed like last year's leaves from the tree of his genuine keyboard abilities. This was the man of whom, when I was an overawed late teenager in Paris, Charlie Parker had jabbed me in the chest and said, 'Make no mistake about it, he is the best accompanist I know . . .' But in the years after his return to full-time playing Al rarely worked in an accompanying role. Instead he concentrated on a more refined projection of his original solo methods. Methods which, primarily, had indicated how there was a viable alternative to the falling breakers of Bud Powell, and that the devices of be-bop could be harnessed to an interrelation of hands, calmness at fast tempos, a balanced attack and a greater use of the actual mechanism of the piano itself (the pedals and resonance and so on). Certainly without him I think, we would have heard a very different Bill Evans, and his influence over other, later players was more considerable than is generally realised.

His final residency was at the up-market One Fifth Club on New York's Fifth Avenue, he was happy in his second marriage and he usually devoted two or three months of each year to touring abroad. Although, as he told me, he preferred Britain to Continental Europe. He found the audiences more receptive, there were no language problems and he could visit his remaining relatives in Scotland.

I last talked with him over tea and yet more cucumber sandwiches; in between sitting less than three feet away during his remarkable recital and witnessing those long, delicate fingers produce two hours of absolute artistry. I then said to him: 'I don't want to hear anyone else play *You Stepped Out Of A Dream* for a long, long time.' Dry as ever, he murmured, 'Yeah, I thought that one went quite well.' And he showed me his hands again. Three of his fingers had adhesive tape around the tips. He had a good piano that day, but one of the fingers had still split. He also paid me the very great compliment of saying that the pieces I'd written about him for *Jazz Journal* were the most intuitive he'd read. (However, I'd taken the precaution of having him vet them first!)

He seemed fit and well that day, which made the surprise of his death so much more acute. He will be missed. Jazz has many torchbearers, but only a limited number of real pacesetters.

1981-82

CHAPTER SIXTEEN

OTHER ASPECTS OF MILES DAVIS

So much has already been written about this man, including an excellent, straightforward book about his recording career by the English trumpeter Ian Carr. Yet he remains an enigma. Even to the extent of being dubbed by my friend, the late Derek Jewell as 'a lost leader'—having deserted jazz for a musical life in 'pop'/rock fusion.

Well, I have a personal view of Miles which could cause certain eyebrows to be raised by those who no longer like what he does and also those to whom he can do no wrong. But I have been a Miles listener, as well as an observer since 1949 in Paris when he created such surprise by not appearing as a member of the Charlie Parker Quintet (Bird had the accomplished Kenny Dorham with him on trumpet), but instead as part of the Tadd Dameron Quintet, with James Moody alongside him playing saxophone. Each group was playing the classic be-bop unison–ensemble small group style of music. But by this time Miles was known for having been featured on a number of recording sessions with Parker (the Savoys and a Dial session): not always technically adept, but with an immense sensitivity and creative potential. Consequently their sudden separation was quite unexpected. What had gone wrong, either in musical or human relationship terms between the two has never been explained; and Miles is not the most communicative of men, except in his playing, which he gives to the world. So I will not speculate. But it had happened, and they were apart.

At that time in Paris I was an associate fan over the days of the Jazz Fair with Bird. And I never did get to meet Miles. But subsequently I have often thought about their partnership. As well as playing, frequently, their handful of records together. I think they were soul mates musically, except that Miles, with his youth and (then) incomplete technique, although turned on to be-bop, found it difficult to keep up with the sweep of Bird's natural genius. He wasn't the only one. But he went to work on it; on the technique, that is. Developing a control of tone and valve-use on trumpet in a very personal way which would eventually change whole areas of jazz for a considerable time.

All right, in recent years there may have been a few wrong turnings. But these have never, ever involved a *cliché*. He has remained a total musical explorer; and explorations do occasionally take you to an empty island. On the other hand, they can take you to some marvellous places, and most of the things in Miles' career have involved marvellous music-making . . .

Another point to be made about the early Miles Dewey Davis (b. Alton, Illinois in 1926) and which set him somewhat apart from the other be–boppers, all scuffling to make a living, was that he had a degree of financial independence. His father was a well-to-do St. Louis dentist, who not only bought him his first trumpet (at thirteen), but later sent him to New York to study music at Juilliard and made him a regular allowance. Thus, both before and while with Parker he had the time and ease to be working on and refining his technique. For, recognising that he didn't have the blazing assets of Dizzy Gillespie or Fats Navarro, he now chose another direction entirely, leading towards what we have come to know as 'the birth of the cool'. There is a tremendous difference between say, his obviously feeling but hesitant solo on *Embraceable You* with Parker and the sure phrasing and tonal beauty we hear from 1949 onwards.

Which brings me directly to the recordings made under his own name. And I would like to continue by describing in more detail just four of his great milestone recordings.

1) 'Birth Of The Cool'

Titles: Move/Budo/Jeru/Godchild

Personnel: Davis (trumpet), Kai Winding (trombone), Junior Collins (French horn), Bill Barber (tuba), Lee Konitz (alto-saxophone), Gerry Mulligan (baritone-saxophone), Al Haig (piano), Joe Shulman (bass), Max Roach (drums)

January 21, 1949 New York City

Titles: Venus De Milo/Boplicity/Israel/Rouge

Personnel: Davis, J. J. Johnson (trombone), Sandy Siegelstein (French horn), Barber, Konitz, Mulligan, John Lewis (piano), Nelson Boyd (bass), Kenny Clarke (drums)

April 22, 1949 New York City

Titles: Moon Dreams/Deception/Rocker

Personnel: Davis, Johnson, Gunther Schuller (French horn), Barber, Konitz, Mulligan, Lewis, Al McKibbon (bass), Roach

March 9, 1950 New York City All recorded for Capitol

Miles studied particularly hard at Juilliard, in all the music departments, as well as working on his trumpet technique and style, finding time to make appearances and records with Parker, Coleman Hawkins and

Benny Carter; and then he went on the road for five months with the Billy Eckstine band.

In his new trumpet style, although retaining a good deal of intensity, he opted for a radically different tone. Which led to a smaller, tighter sound at fast tempos, usually achieved with mutes; and a stark loneliness when playing ballads. It seemed to confirm his intuitive lyricism though. Also to fit with his improvising across the traditional breaks and bar-lines, a way of allowing his improvised ideas greater continuity. He gives credit to the late Freddie Webster, a trumpeter with the Hines and Lunceford bands, for providing certain clues. Essentially, however, the new style was all his own: and as startling in contrast with the boiling volcanoes of Gillespie and Navarro as Bix Beiderbecke had sounded in deviating from Louis Armstrong. Someone remarked that it was 'like a man walking on blue eggshells'; other musicians called it 'cool'—and so another jazz movement was born.

Miles then began to think in terms of expansion, of an orchestral development. He was aware of certain harmonic affinities with the otherwise more delicate, Bonnard-like palette of the Claude Thornhill orchestra, and so entered into a series of discussions with Thornhill's arrangers, Gil Evans and Gerry Mulligan. The outcome being a nine-piece group which appeared at New York's Royal Roost in September, 1948 and made three historic recording dates in the twelve months following.

The group's instrumentation comprised trumpet, trombone, French horn, tuba, alto- and baritone-saxophones, piano, bass and drums. 'The smallest number of instruments that could get the sound and still express all the harmonies the Thornhill band used.' (Evans) But it was sufficient for a wide range of voicings and orchestral effects. Later Johnny Carisi, who had played trumpet with Thornhill, joined the pool of arrangers. So too did John Lewis, the gifted pianist from Dizzy Gillespie's band, currently working as Ella Fitzgerald's accompanist.

Gil Evans scored the thoughtful and introspective *Moon Dreams*, several accompaniments for the band's projected singer, Kenny Hagood (not heard on the Capitol LP), and finally Miles' composition *Boplicity*. The latter is remarkable for its harmonic subtlety. 'An interpenetration of instrumentation and harmony.' (André Hodeir) Again for the way it guides the shape and structure of what could be a solo invented by Charlie Parker through continual switches of voicing and colour, but still with Miles as lead. Gerry Mulligan, in his own developing linear style, composed and arranged *Jeru, Venus De Milo* and *Rocker,* while making good use of the range of the ensemble (nearly four octaves) and its tonal riches in scoring George Wallington's *Godchild*. 'I write for the people in the band.' (Mulligan to Barry Ulanov) 'I vary the music with their musicianship. The notation actually changes with each guy's time; they won't all read the same notes the same way.' Miles himself wrote and arranged *Deception*, Johnny Carisi contributed *Israel* (an almost Gothically ornate, but otherwise logical blues) and John Lewis composed the more formal *Rouge*, in addition to his arranging Denzil Best's *Move* and Bud Powell's *Budo* (sometimes called *Hallucinations*).

Financially, and also in public, the band was a disaster. Audiences at the Royal Roost were used to all the excitements of Dizzy's big band by this time; moreover in the popularising of be-bop by lesser men. They failed to understand Miles' new concept and he closed after only two weeks, never to appear again with this kind of an ensemble. But gradually, via its records, the band came to have a profound and lasting influence upon modern jazz. Its careful reconciliation of so much that was fresh and stimulating about the be-bop revolution with collective exploration and imaginative scoring represented a point of no return.

As individuals too the associate-members went on to carve out future kingdoms. Miles disappeared to brood upon the subject of a post-Parker Quintet (later to become a Sextet) and then reappeared with the finest small jazz group of the late '50s and 1960s. Lee Konitz, the most featured soloist after Miles, drifted back into his association with Lennie Tristano and perfected the lineaments of his alto-saxophone style. A truer interpretation of the meaning of the word 'cool'. Evans did some commercial arranging and also went down into the streets again; meanwhile letting his tanks fill up for what was to be some of the most staggering jazz orchestration of the next thirty years. Gerry Mulligan took himself and his abilities to California, becoming the leader of a most successful piano-less Quartet there. Carisi had his non-jazz works performed by chamber groups all around the United States. John Lewis organised the Modern Jazz Quartet with Milt Jackson (vibes), Percy Heath (bass) and Kenny Clarke (drums).

'Talent does whatever it wants to do. Genius does only what it can.' (Delacroix)

2) 'Miles Ahead'

Titles: Springsville/The Maid Of Cadiz/The Duke/My Ship/Miles Ahead/Blues For Pablo/New Rhumba/The Meaning Of The Blues/Lament/I Don't Wanna Be Kissed

Davis (flugelhorn), Ernie Royal, Bernie Glow, Louis Mucci, Taft Jordan, Johnny Carisi (trumpets), Frank Rehak, Jimmy Cleveland, Joe Bennett (trombones), Tom Mitchell (bass-trombone), Willie Ruff and Tony Miranda or Jimmy Buffington (French horns), Bill Barber (tuba), Lee Konitz (alto-saxophone), Dank Bank (bass-clarinet), Romeo Penque and Sid Cooper or Eddie Caine (flutes and clarinets), Paul Chambers (bass), Art Taylor (drums), Gil Evans (arranger)

1957 New York City Recorded for CBS

'The mind reels at the intricacy of his (Gil Evans) orchestral and developmental techniques. His scores are so careful, so formally well-constructed, so mindful of tradition that you feel the originals should be preserved under glass in a Florentine museum.' (Bill Mathieu)

'Miles Ahead' is the kind of jazz record that happens only once in a long, long time, like Louis Armstrong's *West End Blues* or Parker's final version of *Now's The Time*. That it occurred within the same twelve months as Ellington's 'Such Sweet Thunder' and 'Jazz Giants '56' is therefore a source of wonder.

Apparently the basic conception for the album was Miles' own; but stemming from the musical association he had formed with Gil Evans in the days of his ill-fated 1948/49 nine-piece band. 'Gil is the one arranger I've ever played who can really notate a thing the way a soloist would blow it.' (Gerry Mulligan) Which was precisely how Miles wanted these new arrangements to be. For he would take the only solos, playing flugelhorn, and in front of the biggest band he had ever worked with: nineteen men in all.

Their various discussions led to a framework by Gil of ten varied themes: each lending itself to becoming a little concerto, but also linked to the one which follows, so that a continuous and overall portrait emerges of Davis the mature soloist. 'He (Miles) confirms what we already knew about him—that he is the most lyrical of modern jazzmen. But whereas the lyricism of Charlie Parker, in his great moments, seemed to want to burst open the gates of delirium, Miles' lyricism tends rather towards a discovery of ecstacy. This is particularly perceptible in slow numbers, where Evans' lyricism is even more closely tied up with Davis's.' (André Hodeir) Meanwhile the flugelhorn gave a rounded edge to his tone.

Hodeir finally stresses the perfection of those written-out passages in which Miles' horn is used to lead the ensemble. But other, equally impressive features come out in Gil's writing for him. A dismissal of the conventional saxophone section, for instance, in favour of one mixing saxophone (one alto) with woodwind. And an obvious delight in having the collective trumpets play fast figures which have the intricacy of early be-bop solos. Then there is a deliberate extending and enriching of the tonal sound, from the rooted depths of the tuba to the tree-tops of the other brasses. Also the juxtaposed time-signatures. In parts of *The Maids Of Cadiz* the bass is in 2/4 while the drums play 4/4, and often through the LP Miles plays 3/4 against the orchestra's 4.

As regards form, texturing and orchestral techniques by Gil I can mention only isolated examples. Again though one becomes aware of deliberate contrasts as well as agreeable links. The brilliant brass outbursts during Johnny Carisi's *Springsville* seem to help emphasize the delicate harmonic effects of the slower *Maids Of Cadiz* which follows. Just as the defined ensembling and Rabelaisian use of the tuba in Brubeck's *The Duke* throw into relief the constantly shifting patterns of Kurt Weill's *My Ship* which follows that. *Miles Ahead* is almost entirely ensembled (behind Miles' lead) and by its spurning of accepted breaks and bar-lines in jazz recalls Gil's earlier *Boplicity* for the 1948/49 band. *Blues For Pablo* is even more unusual, for it develops a creative conflict between the Spanish-type minor theme and a blues theme in the major: the first time this had been attempted in jazz. The short riff of Ahmed Jamal's *New Rhumba* is frequently varied in presentation; nevertheless it reveals Gil's growing interest in brief, strong melodic phrases as the basis for improvisation instead of tricky chord sequences. *The Meaning Of The Blues* is very thoroughly harmonised, and J. J. Johnson's *Lament* features both semi-tone progressions and whole-tone ones. *I Don't Wanna Be Kissed* is a conventional swinger and ends the LP with an Ellington-like flourish.

'I wore my first copy out inside three weeks, so I went round to Miles and said *Give me another copy of that damn record!* Everyone should own it' (Dizzy Gillespie about Miles Ahead)

Subsequent collaborations between Miles and Gil have resulted in a freshly creative approach to George Gershwin's 'Porgy And Bess' score; also 'Sketches Of Spain', which includes a sensitive re-scoring featuring Miles as soloist of the middle movement from Rodrigo's 'Concierto De Aranjuez', originally for guitar and orchestra.

3) 'Kind Of Blue'

Titles: So What/Freddie Freeloader/Blue In Green/All Blues/Flamenco Sketches

Davis (trumpet), Cannonball Adderley (alto-saxophone), John Coltrane (tenor-saxophone), Bill Evans or Wynton Kelly (piano), Paul Chambers (bass), Jimmy Cobb (drums)

Late 1950s New York City Recorded for CBS

I've already stated my belief that the Miles Quintet/Sextet of the late 1950s and into the '60s was the best in small group jazz over that period; and it would have far-reaching effects. However, these didn't really begin to be felt until after 1955 when Miles was suddenly re-discovered by a wider cross-section of musicians and the public. At the Newport Jazz Festival of that year his playing caused a sensation. 'What's all the fuss?' he then asked. 'I always play like that.'

Through the interim period, in comparative seclusion, Miles had gradually 'worked up' his Quintet to a state of preparedness. The overall ideas for it were always intensely his own, but over the early years he was ably abetted by Red Garland, piano, Paul Chambers, bass, and Philly Joe Jones, drums. Plus, of course, John Coltrane on tenor-saxophone. 'Coltrane is the best since Bird.' (Miles to Alun Morgan, 1956)

The first thing to say about this Quintet is that whereas Art Blakey and the 'Hard Bop' musicians re-emphasized the validity of the Parker/Gillespie small groups, Miles sought to *reinterpret* and develop from them. Obviously for him the validity of the actual instrumentation was not yet in doubt. (It would be the later 1960s before he made alterations here.) But the content of the music had to evolve, he decided. And not merely in the transition from so-called 'hot' to 'cool' jazz. It had to evolve in its basic forms.

As early as 1949 Miles had registered his impatience with the four or eight-bar phrases which normally made up a 12-bar or a 32 or even 64-bar theme. He felt that improvised phrases should determine continuity within a solo and not the bar-lines. Then Gil Evans pointed out to him certain advantages (including greater freedom) in a return to melodic sources—as opposed to improvising over the angular chord changes of many bop themes. Which left Miles dissatisfied with the 12 and 32-bar frames themselves, and in turn transformed the musical growth of this Quintet.

This is dramatically illustrated by a record such as 'Kind Of Blue'. The point about *All Blues* and *Flamenco Sketches*, for instance, is that they remain essentially *sketches*. Their composed melodies are intentionally brief and also modal, with just a few, strategically-placed chord changes. Yet herein lies real strength, for the soloists are allowed to develop their improvisation in more elastic, and consequently far richer ways. Obviously with musicians of the calibre of Coltrane, Adderley and Bill Evans on hand the potentiality becomes enormous. It results in jazz of a thoughtful, but at the same time extremely challenging nature. And as for Miles himself, I have never heard him sound so relaxed on disc. He implies so much that he needs to stress very little.

Achieving his escape to a more open-ended, scaler improvising naturally prompted the search after further freedoms. By the late 1960s (and with albums like 'Nefertiti', 'Miles In The Sky' and 'Filles De Kilimanjaro') there is evidence that form itself is being left open—or rather, simply allowed to grow (spontaneously) around a mood, a single motif or even the sounds of the group conceived in layers. While Miles has arrived at a startling leanness in his solos: playing far fewer notes, but investing every one with the maximum significance.

In the meantime, still in the 1950s his Quintet (and Sextet when Adderley joined) set back the cause of 'Hard Bop' and made almost all the younger modernists think again.

4) 'In A Silent Way'

Titles: Shhh/Peaceful/In A Silent Way/It's About That Time

Davis (trumpet), Wayne Shorter (soprano-saxophone), Herbie Hancock, Chick Corea (pianos), Joe Zawinul (piano and organ), John McLaughlin (guitar), Dave Holland (bass), Tony Williams (drums)

1969 New York City Recorded for CBS

'A creative force is always at work within him. His recent albums are pointed in new directions for all who are interested in music. He has incorporated the best of jazz so-called contemporary rock sounds and rhythms, a flair for the long thematic line reminiscent of the 16th century composer, and the technique of the 20th century composer using polyrhythms (many rhythms at once) and polytonalities (different chords played together).' (Frank Glenn)

I still place Miles in the forefront of the jazz *avant-garde*; even if some of his experiments (like 'Bitches Brew') have been decidedly wayward. One must try to take some measure of the man. He is a jazz master in the same sense that Louis Armstrong and Charlie Parker were; that is, not only a supreme stylist on his chosen instrument, but also an influence with wide powers and relativity. And he has remained insatiably curious about all forms of music, while prepared to make use of anything he likes.

His great Quintets and Sextet of the 1950s and early '60s have given way to a more changeable instrumentation. The one he leads on this album, for instance, has Wayne Shorter (a graduate from The Jazz Messengers) playing soprano instead of his usual tenor-saxophone. Shorter had only recently bought his soprano, but immediately Miles heard the sound he wanted to feature it. Then there are not one, but three electric pianos on the record; another effect Miles was the first to introduce into jazz (via his 'Miles In The Sky' and 'Filles De Kilimanjaro' sets). Plus organ and guitar, which had never been heard with his groups before.

The performances too have changed, tending to become longer, with strict control over the levels of sound produced but added freedoms of expression. And there is evidence of an increasingly collectivised improvisation. (Listen to the pianos, organ and bass fit with the other soloists: no more just chords-and-rhythm, but weaving counter-melodies, placing groove-figures and varying the dynamics.) Sometimes there are borrowings from current 'pop' music—especially in Tony Williams' versatile drumming. Also there are passages of typically European beauty. *In A Silent Way* itself—composed by Joe Zawinul—reminds me of Satie in his *Trois Gymnopédies* period with its bare lines and serene atmosphere. (Though Miles fragments the lines somewhat.)

Throughout the LP the leader is forever probing after new ideas, either as trumpeter or overseer. In his own solos there is a preoccupation with time and structuring still; again with variants of feeling, in spite of an increased intensity of tone . . .

After this LP there were periods of illness and consequently musical layoffs. And when he returned to the scene there was more emphasis on fusion music. Which took him into the realm and hearts of the 'pop' young. My last sightings (and hearing) of him were at Nice in '85, when he appeared with a red, electrified trumpet, a roadie who kept changing his sequined jackets and alongside him the mighty saxophone-playing of Bob Berg. He began with half-an-hour of very boring 'pop'/rock fusion and ended the set with more of it, culminating in a startling rendition of *The Marseillaise*. But in between he played a forty-minute sequence of slow, sensuous and sparse melody. Some of the most beautiful trumpet-playing I've ever heard in my life. So, when he is in the mood and has the will to do it he can still turn it all on for me.

1988

CHAPTER SEVENTEEN

BUDDY DE FRANCO

In The Studio With . . .

The great international jazz artists can be absolutely imperturbable. On Tuesday, September 20, 1984 clarinettist Buddy De Franco interrupted a whirlwind tour of the United Kingdom to lay down an album of some of the most stunning solos I've witnessed in thirty years of covering the music scene. Because the recordings were made for the Wave label, and because bassist Peter Ind, who was playing on the sessions, is also the boss of Wave and the Wave studios in the City of London, he—in seeking the ideal sound—had called in the 3-Ms' technicians to go over the heads on the tape-machine. A correct move—but there were a few gremlins, and consequently a delay in the starting time. Buddy was keen to get going—but he understood what was necessary to be done and therefore devoted the rest of the morning to rehearsing; especially the two originals by guitarist Martin Taylor, which were, and now are, fascinating themes but quite intricate. Then, after a lunch-break, Mr De Franco and the other musicians turned it all on as quickly and easily as starting to run a hot-water tap . . .

However, lunch itself was also interesting. I've known Buddy's playing for the whole of my adult life, but this was my first meeting with him—and he's a very good talker as well as being the great clarinettist of modern jazz. Especially when someone prods his memory-bank. I'd said to him how, as a young man, and being in Paris and meeting Charlie Parker I'd been amazed, after all the bad stories about Bird, by the kind and natural way he'd been with me when really I was nothing more than a young fan. Although then I'd seen him give some of the alleged big names in journalism a fairly hard time. 'That was completely typical of Bird,' Buddy said. 'He had his problems, but he could spot the posers a mile off.'

'I was only in awe of two jazz musicians,' he went on. 'Art Tatum and Parker. Though in the end I got to work and record with both of them. (*This Can't Be Love* from the Verve LP with Tatum is a jazz classic: RH) Both of them were *so* strong. Bird was always complimentary towards me. But he still scared me. And he was so unpredictable, forever coming up with surprises. Once, I remember, we were flying back together to New York City. When we got there it was snowing. I was tired, bombed out. But suddenly there's a Salvation Army band playing right outside the terminal and Bird decides he's going to stop and listen to them. I opted out, just took a taxi home. A couple of days later Joe Glaser 'phoned me. Bird had missed a gig—nobody knows where he is. Well, eventually he turned up—minus everything but his underpants. Obviously, he had gotten into some scene and been rolled. However—the next time I played with him, all at once he's incorporating snippets from the Salvation Army band repertoire into his solos!

'Another time we're with some friends out in the country and they've got sixteen rabbits in the cellar that they'd shot. But they know nothing about how to skin them. Bird simply put an apron on, went down and skinned and dressed the lot. What a guy . . .'

Nowadays Buddy lives and works out of Sunnyside, Florida. 'In the end I found the strains and stresses of New York just too much, coming on top of an active touring life. There are times as well when I get tired of hearing myself. So then I rest up until I'm ready to go on. I'm the prisoner of perfectionist strivings—but only for the benefit of the audiences. Who on earth would want to play just for himself? There's got to be some kind of audience response . . .'

Back in the studio everything was ready and Buddy took off on a beautiful, but beaty exploration of Django Reinhardt's *Nuages*. The other musicians present were those on tour with him. Peter Ind on bass is a player whose experience of being with leading Americans goes right back to the 1950s when he lived in New York and was a part of the Lennie Tristano Workshop; also the first Gerry Mulligan Quartet. Tony Lee, the pianist, affects an inscrutable mandarin-like countenance while laying down a seemingly effortless flow of chords and figures, plus very swinging solos. On guitar Martin Taylor has an immense original talent which recently landed an American album contract for him (with Concord). Clearly, too, he has developed a close musical affinity with De Franco and their exchanges of ideas were a highlight of the session. To complete the group, Tony McLennan on drums is from Glasgow, is a favourite of Martin's and works regularly in a trio with him. He has, in addition, played with Art Farmer and James Moody.

After completing *Nuages*, it quite surprised Buddy when I told him that Django had, near the end of his life, also elected to work with a clarinettist, Hubert Rostaing.

Anyway, they were now set to tackle *Angel's Camp*, Martin's original, named after the old West Coast mining camp which is the setting for one of Mark Twain's most famous short stories, 'The Celebrated Jumping Frog Of Calaveras County'. In view of which there is perhaps an intended impressionism about the jumping jazz/rock feel of the theme. But no matter what the tempo nothing ever interferes with the natural clarity of Buddy's sound. He's a considerable expert on the instrument itself as well as an outstanding player. 'I've been with Yamaha's for over ten years now and I get them to do extra work on the clarinets to suit my particular playing and the variations of sound. Not just on the mouthpiece but on the barrel and the bore too.' At the session he alternated between four different mouthpieces—and even at one point changed the bell. And he uses a pullthrough more often than the most conscientious rifleman.

Meanwhile Martin had been laying down some almost brass section-like accompaniment and Peter was really pulling hard on the bottom string to make the root. *Angel's Camp* was recorded in one take.

Don't Be That Way, with its echoes of Goodman, went to two full takes—but with an even better clarinet solo on the second one—which includes a chuckle-dig at Martin Taylor's present domicile with its quote from *Comin' Thru The Rye*. Buddy: 'How do we end this though? I'd like to get something a little more original than just a repeat of the melody. A riff, maybe? Okay.'

Then it's into Martin's other original, *Manhattan Teaparty*, the hardest theme of the collection to master. There is a crash, bang, wallop about going into the swing, with a very intricate notation; and it took several takes and then one edit to get it right. At one point Buddy requested a glass of hemlock. 'My brain's getting scrambled,' he said. 'Help! I want my Mama!' Martin was even more circumspect. 'Let's try to finish it while I still like the tune,' he quipped.

A short break. By now it was six o'clock. 'Can we get fish-'n-chips?' the clarinettist asked. It was, he added, a chance to rest his chops. 'I've a salivary gland not working. Which accelerates one's tiredness.' I was tempted to reply that his enthusiasm had shown no signs of flagging in the studio.

Over the fish-and-chips and with a glass of red wine for me he explained that his first great inspiration had been Artie Shaw. Benny was much to be admired, of course. Shaw though got an extra excitement into his solos, a special brand of attack which really turned me on. Then later I heard Bird and that was what I wanted to play on the clarinet. Actually my first instrument was a mandolin, and later I started playing the alto-sax, but I never truly got on with the instrument.

Returning to the studio he smoked the first of the five cigarettes he permits himself each evening and announced he was fit for the next number: *Theme For Buddy*, a superb fast blues Martin Taylor and Tony Lee had composed over the lunch-break. Martin: 'Buddy, do you want to blow on C minor or B flat minor?' Evidently the latter suited him best, and he proceeded to blow up a real storm of a solo. Another first take.

He next focussed all his care and attention upon *Nobody Else But Me*, the last song Jerome Kern wrote and one of Buddy's longstanding favourites. After the slow clarinet cadenza by way of introduction the group moved into tempo—when suddenly he called a halt. To Tony McLennan he then issued instructions: 'Swing it, Tony, and fill in wherever you sense it's right, but no smashing on the cymbals. I want your swing, sure, but this one has to emerge as a tender song as well.'

Probably the most unusual item on the LP is *The Dark Island*, first popularised as the theme music for a TV thriller, although originally a traditional Scottish piping tune.

'Don't you think we need a nice E major to finish on?' Buddy asked Martin, the only other musician with him on this track. Martin did, and they got it in one take again.

To round things off there were plans to do *We'll Be Together Again* as a further slow ballad, 'but kind of bluesy, right?' However, it didn't go right; so they tried *You Do Something To Me* as a *bossa*—which Martin requested then be dropped because he couldn't get a comfortable approach going. So in the end they opted for *Just Friends* as an ultra-fast samba—and to everyone's approval. They rehearsed it twice; came the take Buddy was truly flying and almost before we'd realised it there was yet another 'hole in one'. Not a bad way to round off the occasion.

Buddy lit a third cigarette and settled down to a very through cleaning of his instrument before the different sections were packed away. He was as imperturbable at the end as at the beginning. But he had clearly enjoyed himself. And he left us with one marvellous crack. 'The bandleader asked the jazz musician: *Do you read music? Not enough,* the jazzman, quick as a flash, replied, *to hang up my playing!*'

1984

Meanwhile Alastair Robertson of Hep Records had been taping the De Franco group 'live' on tour. Four long performances (Love For Sale, Autumn Leaves, What's New *and* Just Friends) *were released as the LP* On Tour—UK *(Hep 2023) and won* Jazz Journal International's *Critics Choice 'Record Of The Year' award.*

CHAPTER EIGHTEEN

SARAH VAUGHAN

Reviewing recently her latest album, 'Brazilian Romance', with as her guest-artist the composer-singer Milton Nascimento, I was reminded, not just of her durability, but her amazing ability, now into her sixties, to tackle an absolutely brand-new area of music (to her), and still come out on top. And not just over the music, but technically too. The tracks were, some of them, recorded long-distance: between the United States and Rio de Janeiro. With overdubbing of vocals at either end. She still came out on top. It's like winning the Ladies at Wimbledon having put all your junior and talented hopefuls to the chop . . .

But then I was reminded of something else. Several years back she herself guested on one track of a 10 CC LP. Within the usual 'pop'-group madness, everything was taking days, even weeks. She was in and out, having completed her business, within an hour.

Some people call her 'Sassy', others 'The Divine One'. I call her simply Sarah Vaughan, the first and still the greatest singer of modern jazz, male or female.

Accepting that all listening is personal, there are for me three supreme living female singers. Beginning with the coloratura soprano Leontyne Price, who has combined Callas' acting abilities with a grand passion and a range and technique which are almost beyond belief. She is also the sexiest singer I've ever heard. In fact, I can hardly bear to play her 'Tosca' without a glass of chilled white wine in hand to keep me calm. I first heard her live in London in the 'fifties, when as a black artist struggling to make it into the major roles, she had taken the part of Bess with the touring company of 'Porgy and Bess' (Cab Calloway played Sportin' Life). I have been her grovelling devotee ever since.

Next comes Peggy Lee (although I don't, like the Trojan Paris, intend to give the golden apple to any one of these three). Miss Peggy Lee first bowled me over as, when a teenager, I heard her stunningly fast rendition of *Lover*. Again I have remained a devotee. And known her personally as a writer about her performances. (I once caught her out by mentioning a single she'd forgotten about, *Where Flamingoes Fly!*)

Then there is Sarah. When I was first getting into an appreciation of modern jazz, of Bird and Diz and Monk, suddenly her voice swanned across to me as if of an instrument, an extension to what all the others were doing. Which, of course, it was. The most instrumentalised, improvisational voice I have ever heard.

People sometimes put me in a corner and demand to know why I prefer her to Ella Fitzgerald. And I always begin my reply by enumerating the very considerable qualities they share. The vocal range, the ability to phrase, the ability to swing, the vast knowledge of standard and jazz repertoire, and so on. But then I add: Sarah has one other quality: the ability to be always able to surprise me. To bring out the unexpected interval or even just a single note which gives her melodic (and harmonic) phrasing a deliberate difference. Ella is absolutely immaculate, and always Ella: note perfect, phrase perfect, swing perfect. Sarah will seize me with something which just doesn't belong in the book.

I can mention, for instance, a single sustained note with which she concludes her interpretation of Kurt Weill's *Speak Low*, recorded 'live' at the London House, Chicago on March 7, 1958; Sarah backed by Ronnell Bright, piano, Richard Davis, bass and Roy Haynes on drums— plus several of the Count Basie band who had stopped by, Thad Jones, Henry Coker and Frank Wess. Having kept her vocal solo deep and throaty and vibrato-laden, she then opts to end on a much higher note. Which you decide she has achieved. But no, she keeps on working with it, and working it higher and higher all the time, with many beautiful bends and passing insertions. When she finally lets go, you gasp—as the audience did that night: yet another of her overt surprises! And, on the same LP, there are quite remarkable moments when she sings the introductory verse to *Thanks For The Memory*. She'd never sung the song before, and was working from a publisher's copy. Twice she gets hung up on a word, the *Parthenon*, but each time and including the third and final introduction she is already *musically* improvising on the melodic line. What a lady!

She was born on March 27, another Aries, in 1924 in Newark, New Jersey and baptised Sarah Lois. Her father was a carpenter, her mother a laundress and the family was religious. Which led to her singing, as a child, at the Mount Zion Baptist Church in Newark. She also took piano lessons (from 1931 to 1939)—with some organ studies on the side. Her breakthrough into jazz came when she won an amateur contest at The Apollo Theatre in New York and was spotted by Billy Eckstine, then himself very much the coming 'star' on the scene and being billed as 'the black Frank Sinatra'. He was the featured vocalist at this time with Earl Hines' band and recommended Sarah to Earl for the job of female singer and also second pianist with the band—with which she made her debut, again at The Apollo, in April, 1943.

'In those days,' Billy said to me, many years later, 'she was the skinniest kid you ever did see. Really thin, you know.' But out of her came this huge, ranged voice: from deep baritone, and even at times reaching to bass-notes, to the high-flying top ones she commands. Plus an already developed and sophisticated harmonic sense. And being with Hines brought her into contact with Charlie Parker and Dizzy Gillespie, which hinged her into the early modern jazz experiments, using her voice like another horn.

When Billy Eckstine formed his own band in 1944, the first real be-bop big band, she went with it, and continued the association with Bird, Diz, Fats Navarro, Dexter Gordon *et al.* Pianist/composer Tadd Dameron wrote *If You Could See Me Now* expressly for her, and with Sarah sitting beside him as he worked on it.

For a couple of months in the Winter of 1945-'46 she worked with John Kirby's Sextet at The Copacabana in New York, to pick up cabaret experience. Otherwise, since leaving the Eckstine band, she has always appeared as a solo artist, either in clubs or touring the international circuit. (Her musical friendship, with Eckstine would be renewed several years later when they made a big 'hit' single together, *Passing Strangers*.)

Both Bird and Dizzy Gillespie had pushed her career on with their praises. There was no other jazz singer who most closely reflected the methods of be-bop, although, of course, her singing was not restricted to their themes, taking in a very large repertoire of standard compositions as well. With such a rich and controlled tone and vibrato it was inevitable that her potential amassing of material would be great. She knows everything about the songs she sings: the chord structures, the melodic possibilities for improvisation, the rhythmic patterns, the whole bit. To which she then adds her own emotionalism and musical imagination.

I think she performs best backed by a trio or a quartet. My own favourite track by her comes from an album she recorded at Ronnie Scott's in London, *Everything Must Change*. And she does change it: halfway through, from a beautiful ballad to a *bossa nova!* (In fact, when I had to do an interview about my own life for LBC and had to choose four favourite pieces of music, after much debate, and after the *Scherzo* from Beethoven's 'Eroica Symphony', because of my separate writings about the Napoleonic period, and then Poulenc's 'Gloria', which was related to a group of religious broadcasts I did, I chose *Everything Must Change* by Sarah and finally Dizzy Gillespie's *Blue & Boogie*.) I also particularly enjoy an album she herself produced (on Pablo) called 'Crazy And Mixed Up', with Roland Hanna, piano, Joe Pass, guitar, Andy Simpkins, bass and Harold Jones on drums. It includes wonderful performances by her of Jerome Kern's *In Love In Vain,* Raymond Scott's *Love Dance* and David Rose's *The Island.*

But she has performed in many orchestral settings as well: conducted by Robert Farnon, Quincy Jones, Michel Legrand, Benny Carter and others. And now she is back in one, albeit a different one, with 'Brazilian Romance'. With arrangements by Dori Caymmi and based on songs by him and Nascimento, Leporace and Sergio Mendes, with her vocal breadth she brings a whole new dimension to the Brazil-jazz tradition first started by Jobim, Gilberto, Charlie Byrd and Stan Getz more than two decades ago.

Last, but not least I have enjoyed her sense of humour. This has often found its way out on to records. After the fluffs and problems which attended the introduction to *Thanks For The Memory* on the London House album, she sings, still based on the song's melody, 'it's the most craziest, upsettin', down-sided recording date I ever made in my life!' (But this was after she had restored order and loveliness to it.) Best of all though was at Nice in 1985, when, tired after a long 'plane delay, she requested a beleaguered George Wein to have a certain olive-tree at Cimiez cut down so she could communicate better to her impatient audience. But then she found the necessary reserves to give a stunning two-hour recital. Yes: what a lady!

1988

CHAPTER NINETEEN

GERRY MULLIGAN

Three Frontier Posts

A letter received just the other day from Art Hodes mentions, among other things, a recent two-week job aboard the *SS Norway* when the Chicago veteran found himself lined up alongside Gerry Mulligan and Clark Terry. 'But we did jam together. And we did enjoy it all,' he adds.

There is much implied in this short, simple statement—but certainly no element of surprise. For in Mulligan's case at least, despite the beautiful care, sculpted symmetry and formalism of his orchestral works, large or small, the fact remains that as a baritone-player he has never missed the opportunity to get in on any decent jam session that becomes possible. The fact that he is the world's leading baritone soloist, making his own, various stylistic contributions to jazz development, has never been allowed to interfere with his curiosity about other musicians and his enjoyment of adventuring with them. Dixieland bands, blues singers, mainstream swingers, early be-boppers, Tristano workshop graduates, big band blowers: all these and more have discovered in him an enthusiastic, if initially unexpected musical colleague. Nor does his natural ego as a creator compel him to dominate the proceedings. He goes into jam sessions on a share-and-share-alike basis. He also loves accompanying other soloists and is one of the finest makers of *obbligati* I've ever heard. Mulligan with Art Hodes and Clark Terry? Yes, it must have been an exciting occasion.

However, the ubiquitousness of Mulligan the player doesn't stop at his accessibility to other jazzmen and other schools of jazz. It has led him into situations where the only common denominator is empathy. And yet, even here, Gerry always manages to sound himself. There is no bending, no straining. He just fits, and suddenly it works. For instance, when he popped up on the Quincy Jones' 'How To Steal A Diamond/Hot Rock' soundtrack he caught me uninformed—but I didn't have to reach for the LP's cover by way of identification. It was unmistakeably his tone, rounded but flexible, his agile phrasing and his inherent swing hooked upon an accompanying bass. And yet the Jones score itself was far from being a conventional one. Ever since, I have come to regard GM in musical terms as a frontiersman. (Minus the Davy Crockett hat, of course. But as sharp as Jim Bowie's knife.)

Consequently, with Jazz Journal International asking me to write a new piece about him I've had the chance to write of his perimeter experiences—occasions when he has taken his own jazz to a musical frontier, looked over at the other side and decided there could be a satisfactory union. I have selected three very different examples: ones referred to in my book 'Gerry Mulligan's Ark', but not examined in detail there because the major space was demanded by the Miles Davis Capitol sessions, his own quartets, Sextets, big bands *et al*; not least his adventures with such giants as Hodges, Ben Webster and Paul Desmond. On the other hand, while peripheral to the Mulligan canon, I should add that I have enjoyed all three of these records immensely, and I still play them a lot. The musicianship and good taste are never in doubt, while each has a clear artistic direction and ultimately succeeds. Plus the aural and foot-tapping evidence that Gerry had thoroughly enjoyed them too.

My first choice had as its original point of departure a labour of love. 'Holliday With Mulligan' (DRG SL5191) was recorded between April 10 and 17, 1961 at Olmstead Studios in New York, though not released as an album until 1980. Mulligan's lengthy emotional involvement with the Oscar-winning actress has been much written-about, if not always accurately. But what the gossip columnists of the time failed to realise was that theirs was also a working relationship. They wrote songs together; and several of a very high quality indeed. Holliday the thinking actress (and only an extremely intelligent woman could have played her dumb blonde in 'Born Yesterday') proved to be a genuinely creative lyricist. Her words were much praised by Anita Loos; and the authoress of 'Gentlemen Prefer Blondes' (James Joyce's favourite comedy) had more of a reputation for throwing brickbats than awarding bouquets. Also, and equally important, Judy seemed able to find the right words to go with Mulligan's naturally flowing melodic ideas. Anyway, following on from this it was mooted that they should record a few of these songs— together with a number of respected, but not overexposed 'standards'. Because apart from her lyrics Holliday was no stranger to singing. One of her biggest successes on Broadway had been in 'The Bells Are Ringing'. Her voice was not strong (it would have to be over-dubbed), but it had a truly sweet quality, and within that sound, on record, her true expressiveness as an actress can be heard at work.

Gerry embarked on the project with the complaisance of MGM Records—who subsequently then failed to release it, despite its being the only example of the Mulligan Concert Jazz Band backing a singer. Well, not quite his regular concert band: because Gerry decided to enrich it with the addition of three French horns. Also he cast the net wide to pull in other arrangers. Ralph Burns, Bill Finegan, Al Cohn and Bob Brookmeyer all joined him for the scoring. Joining him with solo contributions were Brookmeyer (valve-trombone) and Nick Travis or Don Ferrara on trumpets. Gunther Schuller led the French horns.

Longstanding Mulligan *alumni* Bill Crow and Mel Lewis played bass and drums.

Perhaps almost inevitably though, listening to the LP after all these years, my main attention becomes focused upon GM's own contributions. And fascinatedly so. For this is after all his band, his cherished concert ensemble, and although used in an accompanying role, its blend of sounds and precision are flawless. True, he had shared out the arranging, but the overall finished work has the seal of his meticulous rehearsing upon every bar. Not a brass figure, not a stop-chord, not a wirebrush shimmer from Mel Lewis that doesn't sound exactly right.

Then there are his four originals. *What's The Rush,* a ballad, will be known to many collectors from the superb year-before instrumental duet with Johnny Hodges. There is something similarly silky about the approach here—and the bonus of a vintage Bob Brookmeyer solo. *Loving You* is brighter, but with frequent tempo shifts and Judy copes well with the essentially be-bop chording. *It Must Be Christmas* manages to defeat sentimentality in its lyrics and allows Gerry to weave a contrapuntal effect for baritone and orchestra through the central half-chorus. Finally, *Summer's Over* (very poignant, in the minor) is constructed conventionally, AABA, but with a blues feeling through the release.

But where, in addition, the LP has one unique feature, is the use of the baritone-saxophone itself. Consistent solos by Gerry are to be expected. And I've referred already to his skills behind other players or, in this case, a singer. But remember he was laying down his tracks ahead of Judy's, yet he accompanies her every phrase on say, Harold Arlen's *I've Got A Right To Sing The Blues* with uncanny suitability. Clearly they had routined beforehand. Even so, it's no easy thing to do . . .

My second selection originated in Italy: nowadays Mulligan's 'other' home and place of retreat for serious composing. He has a flat in Milan where, for relaxation, and having got to know its manager, he spends hours listening to rehearsals at La Scala. 'Tango Nuevo, Gerry Mulligan/Astor Piazzolla' (Atlantic ATL 50168) was recorded at Mondial Studios, Milan in September and October, 1974. Only one original theme by Gerry is involved here, *Aire De Buenos Aires.* The others are all by Piazzolla: *20 Years On, Close Your Eyes And Listen, Years Of Solitude, Deus Xango, 20 Years After, Reminiscence* and *Summit.* Piazzolla also arranged and conducted the album, as well as being the second featured player, on accordion (or bandoneon as he prefers to call it). The only other soloist, but in a minor capacity, is Angel Pocho Gatti on various keyboards, acoustic and electric. The rest of the orchestra is a large one, of strings, bass and multiple percussion.

The musical content of the album is essentially Latin, albeit Mediterranean rather than Latin-American. It is warm, richly romantic, very varied, rhythmically—and it has to be added that Piazzolla has done a remarkable job on the scoring. For mood and atmosphere it could come straight from the soundtrack of a French or Roman art-film: a Truffaut, a Claude Lelouche or even a Fellini.

What I find particularly interesting though is how little the LP has to do with jazz except when Gerry Mulligan plays, when it becomes nothing but jazz. Amazingly, this is a compromise which works. Which in turn reinforces the argument that a true jazz artist carries the greatness of the music within himself, and ultimately it will out, if need be through his pores. Gerry executes numerous written passages, planned duets with Piazzolla, sustains with the orchestra and so on. Here the jazz content is obvious in his tone, dynamics, accents, stresses and, of course, feeling. In other sections he is freely improvising, and as a jazz master, carrying the rhythmic unit along with him: probing, convoluting melodic variations and harmonic ideas, never once deviating from his own vital, personal musical birthright. But this is not done in the way of moving from lushness into swingtime and out again. The tapestry is much more subtle and sophisticated, a blend of undoubted satisfaction.

Just three illustrations of what I mean: *Close Your Eyes And Listen* is a ballad featuring Piazzolla in the classic European boulevardier tradition. Gerry's continuous counterpoint remains pure jazz in its sinuous lines and changes. Not one moment of clash. Then during *Deus Xango,* against a genuine tango and recurring pedal-point, Gerry places a solo of fragmented melody and *rubato* I doubt if even Sonny Rollins could surpass. For good measure *Reminiscence* declares a theme half-Honneger, half-circus music. Gerry inserts solo passages, first of immense sonority, then of be-bop extravaganza . . .

Third Frontier Post: '2.00 AM Paradise Café. Barry Manilow' (Arista 206 496). This album was recorded at Westlake Studio 'C', Los Angeles in 1984. It therefore represents some of the last session work by bassist, the great George Duvivier—whose musical pedigree took in Nellie Lutcher as well as Bud Powell and the jazz moderns. It was also almost certainly the very last recording made by Shelly Manne on drums. Otherwise the group consisted of Gerry, Mundell Lowe (guitar) and Bill Mays, already by this date the pianist with the Mulligan Quartet. Sarah Vaughan guests on one number, *Blue;* and Mel Tormé on *Big City Blues:* the two tracks without baritone.

When I talked with Gerry towards the end of 1984 he told me how surprised he'd been to be drafted into making the album. But, it seems, Manilow had 'phoned him directly with the request to take part. Evidently the pop idol is a longstanding jazz buff.

All of the musical content is low-key and consequently slow-tempoed. Mulligan plays introductions, *obbligati,* release solos—and sometimes bridges from one song into the next. He sounds relaxed, sonorous almost to the point of a Harry Carney-like vibrato and very delicate in his phrasing. On the surface it is the exuberant jammer tamed. But on careful listening he is still being curious, still exploring. He runs the changes of a type of song previously unfamiliar to him, gently brandishes his finds and again appears perfectly at ease wearing a miner's hat. I regret that he didn't get in on the tracks with Sarah and Tormé, because I don't believe he's ever recorded with these two major voices (although, to go back to his ubiquitousness—any discographer's nightmare—he may well have!)

To conclude, what this and the other two records reveal is GM's determination not to be stereotyped, not to rest on his laurels. He is of an age now to be lionised. He has helped pioneer at least three significant new developments in modern jazz. His place in the Hall of Fame is secure. But we should not forget that he is still very much alive, mentally active and above all energetic. Personally I would like to witness him continuing the series of duets with his living peers. Mulligan with Benny Carter, with Buddy De Franco, with Dizzy (as a variation on his earlier experiments with Miles). I would have liked to own a Mulligan LP with the late Bill Evans. But why not one with Jon Faddis or Bob Berg? Of one thing we can be sure though. The man-musician will never stop trying. I judge him to have an inherent distrust of rocking-chairs.

1986

DIZZY GILLESPIE

SONNY ROLLINS

Clockwise from bottom right:
FREDDIE GREEN, ROY HAYNES,
ARNETT COBB, AL HAIG, &
WARDELL GRAY

LOUIE BELLSON & BUDDY RICH

JOHN HARDEE

COLEMAN HAWKINS

PAUL GONSALVES

STAN GETZ

GIL EVANS

MILT JACKSON, BUDD JOHNSON,
& MAJOR HOLLEY

GERRY MULLIGAN

GARY BURTON

COUNT BASIE & ILLINOIS JACQUET

ORNETTE COLEMAN & CLOWN

SARAH VAUGHAN

PHILLY JOE JONES & BILL EVANS

BUDDY DE FRANCO

MILES DAVIS

CHAPTER TWENTY

ROY HAYNES

A Drummer For All Seasons

I've only ever talked to Roy Haynes once—although, naturally, I've heard him play often enough; and I have a big pile of the records he's made.

It was on a bitterly cold late-Autumn night, I remember. I scrounged a lift up to the USAF base at Lakenheath with Helen and Stanley Dance; then got one back with Max Jones (he had an old, Maigret-style Citroën at the time). It wouldn't have mattered or deterred me from having to hitchhike though—the programme justified the means. Coleman Hawkins; the Illinois Jacquet band with Matthew Gee and Sahib Shihab, newly converted from alto to baritone-saxophone; and finally the Divine One, Sarah Vaughan, backed by one of the greatest rhythm sections in jazz: Jimmy Jones (piano), Joe Benjamin (bass) and—clearly enjoying himself—the remarkable Mister Haynes on drums.

After the performance we talked over plates of Air Force hamburger, and over Scotch. (Coleman Hawkins came over to remind us that 'They make it here, you know'.) I couldn't help thinking how well Roy's appearance and conversation matched his playing. He is a short, compact man who moves very quickly but very neatly. Also an immaculate dresser: sharp and yet subdued. (Years later he was named by *Esquire* as one of the best-dressed men in the States.) As we chatted he was perfectly relaxed—but *exact*, with no scratching of the head to trigger his memory-bank.

'Yes—I was a Boston boy. Born at Roxbury in 1925. No—my first recording wasn't Dizzy's album of Jerome Kern's melodies with strings. I know the one you mean, but I wasn't on those sessions. My first record date was Kai Winding's *Broadway*. My musical background? Oh, a lot of what my drum technique amounts to was picked up as I went along. I'd played a few dates in Boston with Pete Brown. You've heard him, the saxophone player. Also Frankie Newton on trumpet. Well, then I moved to New York in '44 and landed a job with Luis Russell's band. A little bit dreary, but it was a start. I got my real start in modern jazz in 1947 with Lester Young. Stayed with Prez until '49.

'After that . . . yes, I gigged around with Miles, Bud Powell. Then I teamed up with Parker and Al Haig; I was with their quartet from 1950 to '52. I joined 'Sassy' (Sarah) Vaughan late last year.'

There was an obvious precision about the way all of this came out. It wasn't a case of verbal *panache*; there was no boasting. But he sounded confident in his accuracy. He was on top of the facts, just as he is at the drum-kit. He went on to express his admiration for Max Roach, Art Blakey, Shelly Manne, but made it clear that the most important jazz drummer for him has always been Basie's Jo Jones. 'Jo's solo on Basie's *The World Is Mad* was what got me interested in jazz and playing drums.' Also he enthused about a recording session he'd just completed for Swedish Metronome, the first under his own name. He rattled off the titles and personnel (a mixed band of Americans and Swedes).

Finally though—and, it seems, self-revealingly—he began to describe how it was playing behind Sarah Vaughan. 'It's like behind a great jazz trumpet or saxophone, really. She's *so* musical. She can improvise and she'll bend the notes and she'll come out with such surprising things. No wonder though—after all she grew up with Bird and Diz. On the other hand, you've got to have the right control. The pulse and the drive must be there, but the volume of sound has to be right too. Sassy likes me to use sticks on quite a few of the numbers; so I'm learning to concentrate on decibels as well as the beat and the variety of the figures. Because I'm there to accompany, and I hope to stimulate, but you can't intrude over the level of the voice itself.'

He was destined to remain with Sarah Vaughan for five years. By the end of which time he'd become the most *articulate* drummer in jazz. A player who, even at his most dynamic and creative, still manages to be unflappable *and knowing,* the captain of his own ship.

Nowadays, of course, we tend to think of him as one of the busiest drummers around. Always in demand to back this artist or that, going to Japan with Duke Jordan, to Europe with his own Quartet, playing longer stints with Stan Getz or Gary Burton, appearing at Joe Segal's Charlie Parker Month in Chicago, judging as well as playing at the Notre Dame Festival, backing Billy Taylor at New York's Town Hall, and on TV (Merv Griffin's *Soul* and NBC's *Positively Black*), taking his much-praised Hip Ensemble from 1970 into such Eastern coast nightspots as Mikell's Top Of The Gate and The Tin Palace, then flying off to the Colorado Jazz Party; and continuing to fit in innumerable record dates—at least half a dozen of them as leader. He is equally at home with jazz or on commercial sessions. So much so that one wonders if his drums ever see the inside of his own home. (Perhaps, like Joe Morello in his days with Brubeck, he leaves different lots of kit in several strategic places.) And he has proven popular with the younger modernists (Dolphy, Ron Carter, Larry Coryell, Chick Corea) as well as with elder exponents like Sonny Stitt. However, he's a cool cat. He clearly knows when to catch his breath . . .

Naturally, I'm delighted for him. Jazzmen also have to eat. And yet, I've overheard things said, and read a few more. Not just by critics, but by the grunt-and-squeal division of the so-called jazz *avant-garde*. Snide comments about his ubiquitous efficiency, and, tinged with envy, about the amount of bread he must make. Evidently, too, some such similar comments have got to the man himself and deeply upset him. As he complained to LeRoy Jones in a *Down Beat* interview: 'Am I expected to be some kind of nut or something? Seems like they don't dig the guys who make the normal scene. I mean, who make all their gigs and raise families. It's a wild thing.'

In reality though he doesn't need to stay upset. He has a place in the history of jazz already and his 'Who's Who' entry is still being written. Meanwhile his detractors are already on the way out—ignored by the very audiences they themselves chose to ignore.

It has to be made clear that Roy Haynes is one of the four great drummers from the earliest 'classic' period of modern jazz—of the Minton's Playhouse leading into 52nd Street days. And, like the others, or at least two of them, he is still up with the vanguard; still showing some startling playing in his own individual way. (Which includes the best wire-brush recording of all time.) The late Kenny Clarke was the pioneer; Max Roach, Art Blakey and Roy Haynes were the developers. These four ruled the roost in modern jazz drumming (one is tempted to say Royal Roost!) until eventually they were joined by Philly Joe Jones, Elvin Jones and finally Tony Williams. But each of them is distinctively different; each easily identifiable in the style he has consolidated. In Roy's case, it involved taking Kenny Clarke's basic methods and finding out what he could add.

Clarke or 'Klook' had double-handedly overturned the smooth 4/4 beat of the 1930s. Leaving the underlying pulse of the music to the string-bass, he had started phrasing and fitting in with the horns. He did this in what seemed at first a very complex way: accenting, using isolated stick-shots, introducing cross-rhythms and re-evaluating every part of the kit. For instance, he would place a bass-drum beat where previously one might have expected a rim-shot on the side-drum. But also that bass-drum beat would be against the most unlikely beat in the bar. It infuriated some of the old guard, obviously, but it suited the new, jagged, harmonically-dominated melodic lines Parker and Gillespie were playing. Suddenly the Be-bop Revolution was under way.

In an analysis of Roy Haynes' work on record, it strikes me that he has imposed a number of purely personal qualities upon Klook's methods. But also that he has made one extraordinary ecumenical gesture—and justified it.

To deal with the qualities first. Roy can be as fast and fleet as Max Roach and probably moreso than Blakey—while he is less-explosive than either. Because he isn't a particularly heavy drummer. He can be dynamic and he will always swing a group like mad, but he doesn't belong to bomber-command like Roach, and he doesn't pick up and catapult soloists forward as Art Blakey does. On the other hand he has a remarkable degree of *finesse,* a more sophisticated repertoire of ideas—and since his years with Sarah Vaughan—a control of levels of sound second to none. By and large he doesn't take long solos. His improvisation is invariably within the accompaniment. He is neat, he is crisp and soloists respect his knowledge because *they* know he isn't an egocentric player. As Roland Kirk put it: 'I enjoy him so much. He plays so spontaneously and never holds you back from what you want to play. And he does more than just lay down a beat. I can hear him making those drums *talk.'*

As regards the 'ecumenical' move, this is not so easily defined but nevertheless he's pulled it off. There is this overall smoothness to his playing—and to his alone of the leading be-bop drummers. Not a smoothness that is bland, but one that exults. And it seems to me this has come about by his achieving a synthesis between the best of Jo Jones and the originality of Kenny Clarke. Roy is still using Klook's methods, the same accents, the cross-rhythms and so on. At the same time though, there is a special kind of bounce, an inner pulse and a lot of shimmering cymbal-work—all typical of Jo. It's even there on the ballads. That night at Lakenheath I listened to him playing behind Sarah. Close your eyes, I told myself, and this could be Jo Jones accompanying Helen Humes . . .

Roy has contributed to several tremendous recording dates. Most notable from his earlier years is the famous Bud Powell-Fats Navarro Blue Note session of August 7, 1949. It produced four titles which belong to the central clearing-bank of be-bop: *Wail, Bouncing With Bud, 52nd Street Theme* and *Dance Of the Infidels.* Roy was just back from California where his drum-kit had been stolen; all, that is, except for his 17-inch crash cymbal. You wouldn't have guessed though. The rest of the kit might be new, but he still gets a marvellous sound out of it. And how he swings!

From the decades since then and an ever-increasing output my choice is bound to be selective. 'The Blues And The Abstract Truth' for Oliver Nelson; his own 'Out Of The Afternoon' LP for ABC Paramount with Roland Kirk, Tommy Flanagan and Henry Grimes; again his Hip Ensemble albums (on Mainstream); and the Prestige sessions with Eric Dolphy and Ron Carter. On all of these he attains a high plateau of excellence. However, I will conclude by recommending two individual items from two entirely separate LPs where I've found his playing to be quite astonishing. Yes, *astonishing.*

The first is the *I'm Late, I'm Late* track on Stan Getz' 'Focus' LP for Verve. The quotation of the title is from the White Rabbit in Lewis Carroll's 'Alice In Wonderland': hurrying, hurrying and every so often worriedly looking at his watch. Getz and Haynes are the only jazzmen featured, backed by a strong, but European-sounding string section arranged for by Eddie Sauter and conducted by Hershy Kay. Naturally, the tempo is *up,* and the tenor-player weaves one of his most urgently outstanding and inventive improvisations ever. Roy Haynes paces him all the way, but not with a straight beat—rather in the process of a duet. His cymbals are hardly involved. It's ninety-five per cent wire-brushes on skin as he prods, pushes, swings, swerves, inserts pick-up figures and never plays the same thing twice. I have never heard any other brushwork like it, nor do I expect to.

That was recorded in 1961 and issued in Britain on HMV's Verve series with the number CLP 1577. Gary Burton's 'Tennessee Firebird' album happened later on in the 'Sixties when the vibes-master, bassist Steve Swallow and Roy Haynes went on a musical safari to the RCA Victor studios in Nashville. The pundits said it couldn't be done. What! Mixing up jazz musicians with country players? Impossible!

In fact, it turned into a musical bonanza—a one-off, perhaps, but one of the most interesting and enjoyable blends of form so far. The track especially to listen for Roy is *Tennessee Firebird* itself. The finger-pickin' brigade aren't playing jazz. Burton and Haynes aren't playing country. And yet it works. And swings! Which is putting it mildly. It goes like a rocket. It was another challenge and, as usual, Roy just picked up the gauntlet and got on with it. He's like that.

The record number, incidentally, is RCA SF-7992. *If you can find it.*

1982

CHAPTER TWENTY-ONE

SONNY ROLLINS

One gains the impression that once 'in performance' Sonny Rollins actually loathes letting the tenor-saxophone leave his lips. Also that this is an emotion which grows within him as a set goes on. He almost always begins in quiet mood and with spare notational presentation. By the end he has become for the listener a torrid experience. And, one suspects, for himself . . .

At the Royal Festival Hall on April 26, Rollins' own hour of on-stage blowing (as part of the 'End Games' season, a South Bank Centre 'celebration of Late Work') in its turn followed a very good set by the Stan Tracey Big Band. These days, despite (or perhaps again because of) the lingering Thelonious Monk influences, the Tracey musical canon has to be regarded as an integral part of the British jazz establishment. As with Monk, his output sounds harmonically sophisticated still but no longer strange. And since his enlargement to a bigger band (fifteen players) he has reconciled Monkish overtones with his equal enthusiasms for the verve and swing of the Ellington and Basie bands. Not least as a vehicle for his own, intensely personal, especially melodic ideas. On this occasion he gave us his 'Genesis' suite of 1986, a seven-part work symbolic of The Creation. Far from being 'way out', it contrasts warmth and brilliance of attack with a sincere exploration of mood and atmosphere, generally inside a context of regulated pulsation. As well as solo contributions, most notably by Tony Coe, Art Themen, Tracey himself (in the third movement), Guy Barker (whose coruscating trumpet phrases in the Clifford Brown tradition seem to advance on every new hearing) and, best of all I thought on this particular night, altoist Pete King—whom we should never just take for granted.

All in all, I would have liked at least another half-set from the Tracey band, followed by at least two hours of Rollins (a short stretch by the standards of his club appearances). However, the physical practicalities of such an occasion must be considered. A very full house—to judge by the applause—did not go away dissatisfied . . .

Sonny Rollins is an impressive figure as he strides on stage. Tall and powerful, muscular rather than fat and despite nearing sixty still with a full head of jet-black hair; also black glasses. At first he appears to dwarf his tenor-saxophone. Until he puts it to his lips and the big, rich and variable, orginally Coleman Hawkins-inspired sound begins to come through. Then man and instrument are suddenly welded.

145

He was accompanied on this occasion by Clifton Anderson, trombone, Mark Soskin, keyboards (acoustic piano and Rhodes), Jerome Harris, bass-guitar (Bob Cranshaw had been promised on string-bass) and Tommy Campbell, drums. But apart from one trombone solo, two short piano solos and a bass-guitar solo it was a Rollins solo-hour. And it flew by with tantalising compression as one marvelled at the richness and panache of his invention.

He moves around, as if restlessly, as he plays. With his tenor jerking up and down like a yo-yo. But there is nothing jerky about its output. He is one of those jazz masters who can sound intentional while we know he is being spontaneous. Or perhaps it is simply the agility and fertility of his mind while he is being spontaneous. It all adds up to the same thing: that although improvising he is never caught out making a mistake. No matter how much he will fragment and worry the guts out of a theme, getting it into apparently impossibly complicated melodic situations, it always comes out right in the end—until we, the listeners, wonder why we were worried that it might not come out so right in the first place!

He began with several excerpts from a new album he has cut called 'Dancing In The Dark'. The opening, a short, folksy theme of only several bars lent itself to ten minutes of variations; but always coming back to the theme, itself then subtly varied, after each thirty seconds of exploration. *Promise* from the same album is a spare, but sinewy ballad that I have a feeling we could be hearing much more of (in the way that Rollins can never let any good musical material alone for very long).

But I suppose the set really took off when he launched himself into *I'll String Along With You*. For here he began to indulge in that same process of melodic fragmentation which has been a major feature of his matured style over so many years now. Which in turn reminds one that, although an unquestioned master now, he did not have an easy start in jazz. Unlike Bird he did not appear to spring out at us, Minerva-like, fully formed. In fact I have some early titles he cut with Bud Powell and Fats Navarro on which he is definitely heard to be struggling. No, he was one of those players who had to work very hard indeed to fashion his own style, sound and methodology. But the latter, ultimately, and involving his celebrated method of fragmenting melodic lines, has proven itself a major breakthrough in jazz improvising. For he does not simply improvise melodic variations over a given chord sequence. Instead he takes the line itself, breaks it down into as many bits as he can imagine, and then examines each and every bit this way and that as a means towards further recomposition in action. It becomes a fascinating mental exercise just to try and follow him. Because he is still, even in his most outrageous musical conceits, recalling for us the original melodic content. And, of course, at the same time achieving this with immense swing, attack and tonal flexibility.

Another feature in the central area of his *I'll String Along With You* solo was the upsurge of his sense of humour. (Something I, personally, first became aware of years ago when he recorded with the MJQ at Music Inn, 'live' for Atlantic. On that occasion, in equal proportion to John Lewis' striving to be as dignified as possible, so Sonny pushed off in the other direction.) His sense of humour can be exceptionally subtle, but in this instance at the RFH it belched forth in a truly jazz-Rabelaisian fashion, involving rubato, slap-tongued notes and some genuinely guttural effects more closely akin to the Rhythm-and-Blues circuit—although accepted as humour they were fine. They also denoted that, after an initial demonstration of technique and stylism, Mister Rollins was into the business of enjoying himself. Which also means some long distance blowing; and usually includes one of his now-famous unaccompanied cadenza-type solos.

Actualy I did think the latter was coming next. Instead of which it was a short, sharp cadenza leading into *I'll See You Again* done as a vigorous jazz waltz. There was more humour here, but more by way of his having fun melodically with what one thinks of essentially as a 'period' song. Except that Sonny had found it to be a deeper well of satisfaction as well. Even to the extent of making it his unofficial theme-tune.

The *real* cadenza solo followed this. And immediately I was reminded of another night, several years back, when Sonny Rollins played the greatest night of small-group jazz I have ever heard at Ronnie Scott's. On that, very special occasion he was playing with Jack DeJohnette and Rufus Hurley, the latter splendid in kilt and turban and, in addition to his soprano-saxophone, soloing on bagpipes. (He told me later that it was at Kennedy's funeral in Washington and after hearing the Black Watch band he was inspired to become the first jazz bagpipes-player.) Sonny blew for close on four hours that night; and whenever the others took a break he stayed on the bandstand and improvised a cadenza solo. It would vary between ten and fifteen minutes in length—and he never ran out of ideas.

I clocked him at around twelve minutes of the RFH. Twelve minutes of unaccompanied brilliance; and the man clearly would have loved to go on. But it's not just free improvisation. There is both order and form superimposed. And the repertoire of quotations incorporated is clearly the product of an unusually open musical mind: from Offenbach and Friml to Bach and Basie, from Jerome Kern and Gershwin to the Beatles, with many original folk tunes and nursery-rhymes in there too. The most remarkable quote of all was the theme-music from 'The Archers'. Obviously whenever he is over in Britain Sonny listens to a bit of radio and TV. One wonders if now he will be picking up on the music from 'Neighbours', that astonishingly popular 'soap' which manages to make 'DeadEnders' and 'Coronation Street' look like the Royal Shakespeare

Company. Anything, one must assume, can become grist to the mill of his cadenza passages.

But how to follow this I wondered as he reached his reluctant, frenetic conclusion? Within seconds the answer was there. A seam of up-tempo 'Hard Bop' based on the thematic materials of Sonny's long-ago 'Tenor Madness' album with John Coltrane. And after another long blow the tenorman told us what a privilege he considered it had been to work with Trane.

Then there was the second ballad of the evening, *Allyson,* which brought bass-guitarist Jerome Harris into prominence. Again clocking it, I thought this might be final number. Until Sonny plunged back into *I'll See You Again* and an even more impassioned set of variations than previously . . .

Presumably after this latest European tour Sonny will go into a further period of retreat and reassessment. (During one such, rumour has it, he was heard playing his tenor all alone in dead of night on Brooklyn Bridge. The start of his cadenza experiments?) We need not worry though. He always re-emerges more of a jazz master than ever.

1988

CHAPTER TWENTY-TWO

BRITT WOODMAN

The Modesty Flaw

One of the greatest novelists of the 19th century, Henri Beyle, better known as 'Stendhal', used repeatedly to postpone the date at which he hoped to be read: 1835, 1860, 1900 . . . 1935! He was world-weary by this time and growing increasingly ironic; but at least he believed that eventually he would be reassessed and appreciated. How different from today's new-style creator who hates the universe if he isn't an acclaimed millionaire by the age of twenty-two!

One suspects that Beyle's self-centred realism must find connecting echoes in the heads of two or three dozen of the more gifted, dedicated and, above all, hard-working musicians in jazz. *(If they are allowed to be hard-working, that is.)* Unfortunately the apportionment of success, financial or otherwise, in any field, is not necessarily commensurate with the talent involved. There are some of the best jazzmen in their fifties, and some in their sixties, still scratching around to make a living. This, despite their being admired by their contemporaries and by quite a number of discerning fans. Sidney Bechet, of course, was a supreme example of what I'm getting at. When he died he'd become an absolute idol. But it had taken him a long, long time . . .

In writing about Britt Woodman I find there is an additional problem postponing his full measure of appreciation, namely, *Himself.* For it's a plain truth that this trombonist who is so highly-rated by his fellow-players and by knowledgeable listeners throughout the world has never rated himself highly enough. Or rather, he has set his standards at such a level that he punishes himself for never quite reaching them. I know, one can quote Henry David Thoreau here: 'In the long run men hit only what they aim at. Therefore, though they should fail immediately, they had better aim at something high.' Even so, there are limits. The moon? Even astronauts need a helping hand to get up there?

Britt, as I've known for a very long time, is an incredibly warm, beautiful being. But he is diffident and shy. He has lacked (and so lost out on) the natural pushiness which is often, regrettably, a feature of the successful musical life. Also, *he is intensely self-critical.* More so than most other musicians I've ever met. All of which might be totally admirable when put into words like these; but it has resulted in his waiting an age to get the top-grade regular work of which he is capable.

For example, in 1960 when he'd recently left Duke Ellington and was guesting with the Mingus Workshop in NYC, at the justly-praised *MDM* session for Candid his trombone work so impressed the session's supervisor that he was offered a date under his own name. Britt turned it down flat. Said he 'wasn't ready'. His last few months with Duke had been boring. He felt himself stale. So for a while, although he'd enjoyed the *MDM* session, he preferred 'just to keep my own searching going'. Any other player would have jumped at the chance.

I adhere to a longstanding personal opinion that he has been the most interesting and technically versatile jazz trombonist since J. J. Johnson. With only Jimmy Knepper, Bill Watrous and Phil Wilson as his rivals. Reading which will probably cause the man himself to pull a face. At least though, he is now getting more work . . .

When Britt used to play with Duke Ellington, his home address in New York was part of a large apartment on West 158th Street, about five blocks away from the Upper Manhattan Medical Centre. The apartment was owned (and run) by his wife Clara's godmother. It meant Clara could go on tour with him and there was less worry about break-ins. He concentrated on the music; she on the practicalities of their travel. They're now living in New York again, in Brooklyn. But in between there were a number of years in California, and that is where the trombonist hails from originally.

He is an easy man to talk to, because, although shy about his own playing, he is very curious about other people, and his approach to them is one of direct friendliness. People, he says, are more important to him than material possessions. 'It is essential that people communicate. And it works both ways. Allow them to communicate and it adds to your reward. Listen and learn. Human beings are interesting on account of they're so varied.' He might be taken in by certain of them and, in fact, seems only too willing to be. Yet there is something about him. Something that makes one feel it would be hard to pull the wool over his eyes; so maybe better not try.

He was born on June 4, 1920: 'My father owned a large, white-painted bungalow on the outskirts of Los Angeles. He had four sons. I was the third. Life at home was full of love and warmth. Both my father and mother insisted on this. Also, life was full of music. My mother played the piano, and sang and recited poetry at the church. My father, although familiar with several instruments, had chosen to play the trombone. He was a professional musician and worked with the pit orchestra at the Folies Theatre in Los Angeles until 1940. On and off, in the 1940s and 1950s, he then worked with Teddy Buckner.

'People who heard my father play say that similarities exist between his use of the trombone and my use of it. Let me explain, therefore, what he passed on to me. First of all, he taught me the fundamentals of the trombone. The basic slide positions. The breathing. The double-

and triple-tongue effects. Also though, he wanted me to have a distinctive sound and style. He impressed on me the need to be an individual, and he discouraged me from playing smears and slurs like I'd heard the New Orleans musicians do. It was thanks to him that I managed to by-pass the affectations of the tailgate players.

'My younger brother Lawrence (who is now a hairdresser) had not been born when I first became interested in music. At the age of five I was taking piano lessons, along with my two elder brothers, and I had my first trombone lessons. When I was eleven my father formed the Woodman Brothers Orchestra, billed as 'The Biggest Little Band In the World'. Coney, my eldest brother, played piano, banjo and guitar. William Junior played trumpet, alto-saxophone and clarinet. I played trombone, tenor-saxophone and clarinet. Joe Comfort was on bass. George Reed (afterwards with Horace Henderson) was on drums. Later, when my younger brother Lawrence was of age, he beame an added attraction. He played some drums which my father made and he did a tap-dancing act. It seemed that my father wanted all of us to become professional musicians. When we were at grammar school there was less and less time for practice. Most days I was more interested in looking out of the window at the other kids playing than in picking up my instrument. Until eventually I became interested in the trombone for its own sake. After that I spent all my time making music with it.

'In 1938,' Britt continues, 'my father had decided that I should concentrate exclusively on the trombone. For added experience too, he would get me to take his place at the Folies Theatre. Soon I was able to play at sight almost any part they put before me. He obtained the school's permission for me to take the job. I worked at the Theatre for a year.'

1939. 'Yes, then I left school and searched for work as a musician. Sometimes I was successful. I worked with concert orchestras, even with a local symphony orchestra. Sometimes I had no work, and that was when I started sitting in at jam sessions and getting to know the musicians who took part. I had been aware of jazz for several years, of course, and Lawrence Brown's trombone-playing with the Duke Ellington band had initially influenced my own playing. But until 1939 I didn't feel ready for sitting in at sessions with established musicians. As a result of sitting in and being heard at sessions after hours, I was offered work with jazz musicians. Phil Moore used me on several occasions. Also Jimmy Mundy. And I did some 'atmosphere' work in the film studios with Louis Armstrong. At this time I was still concerned with improving my technique as a trombonist. I'd not decided on the way to use this technique to achieve an individual style in jazz—consequently I did not consider working with one particular school of musicians. Not until several years after this, and the advent of The Stars Of Swing, did I seriously consider the question of environment and being with musicians who encouraged one's own development.

'Near the end of 1939, Les Hite, who at that time had one of the finest big bands, decided to tour outside the Los Angeles area. Most of the men with him refused to tour and Hite was compelled to organise a new band. He offered me a place with the trombones. I was anxious to work with this band, in which Lawrence Brown had made his start, and my father agreed to it. While with Les Hite I discovered so much more about jazz and jazz musicians. It was still an impressive band. The trumpets included Walter Williams, later with Hampton, and Paul Campbell. Oscar Bradley was the drummer. T-Bone Walker was singing aggressive blues. I formed many friendships. All the musicians worked hard to develop a kind of brotherhood. I found that a man's opinions were respected by the others, and that all knowledge was shared. It was a unique experience to be part of a big band which played with such a collective feeling.

'In 1940 Les Hite's was one of the five bands engaged to play at the Golden Gate Ballroom in New York City. The others were led by Coleman Hawkins, Teddy Wilson, Claude Hopkins and Harlan Leonard. Listening to the other bands and being introduced to their musicians was an education in itself—one you don't find in books about music. It stabilised my own frequently erratic ideas. At last, after listening to Coleman Hawkins and the others, I understood that to be myself and, even more, to express myself through the trombone was the only way to establish a direct communication with the audience. I realised the time had come to shed the musical influences of my earlier years. It was no good trying to sound like Lawrence Brown. No audience wants an imitation when it can hear the original. My father had been right. I needed to become a complete individual.'

In 1942 Britt was conscripted. He served with the Army until January, 1946. On his return to Los Angeles he became part of The Stars Of Swing. Which he describes as 'the most satisfying jazz workshop group I've ever known'.

'It began,' he recalls, 'after several musicians with almost identical views about living and making music had met and played together at jam sessions. John Anderson, trumpet. Buddy Collette, flute, clarinet and alto-saxophone. Lucky Thompson, tenor-saxophone. Spaulding Givens, piano. Charles Mingus, bass. Oscar Bradley, drums. And myself.

'Each time we played together there would be a lengthy discussion about leadership, and especially about the leader needing to understand his sidemen. We all recognised the importance of the leader with any musical organisation. But we felt that many leaders were resented by their sidemen because they were so thoughtless. Responsible leaders, who looked on their sidemen as individuals and considered their separate feelings, were extremely rare. Then one night we decided to overcome this problem of leadership by forming a jazz unit of our own.

'The Stars Of Swing was a co-operative unit. Each musician in it was leader-conscious but at the same time maintained his feeling of individuality as a sideman. As a result, each idea that a musician put forward was treated with respect by the others and made use of. Charles Mingus, for instance, revealed powers and an unusual concept as a composer which the others encouraged him to develop. Each musician contributed to the whole and had the satisfaction of knowing that his contribution was valued.'

And here is where the modesty flaw creeps in again. One of the Zen texts states: 'Let your neighbours discover you before you make yourself known to them. Modesty is the foundation of all virtues.' But still there are limits. So I am determined to insert the next bit of the story on my man's behalf. *Although rightly now a big name in the history of modern music, without Britt Woodman's intervention Charles Mingus might never have made it at all. Or even got going.*

The facts are these. Mingus started out by wanting to be a trombone-player. Britt was his boyhood pal, but also an objective listener, and told him that he'd never make it on the instrument. Mouth, breathing—everything was wrong. So 'Chas' turned to the 'cello—but went to 'an old jive black teacher who taught him nothin', man!' Eventually Britt couldn't stand the agony of it any longer. He went to his pal's mother, told her her son was wasting his time and her money and why didn't he try the double-bass. Whereupon 'Chas' found his musical feet. But he remained a poor reader of music through to the day he died. He was the only musician Duke Ellington ever sacked (in 1953), following a punch-up with Juan Tizol. However, the argument had started as the result of a sight-reading test Tizol tried out on him. He'd tried the same snag on Britt only to find Britt was a quicker reader than he was!

Anyway, to come back to The Stars Of Swing. The trombonist continues: 'We rehearsed day and night. When we couldn't rehearse, because one of us was working, we'd be composing and arranging for the unit. Once there were enough arrangements, we auditioned for the owner of the Down Beat club, located on Los Angeles' Central Avenue. He accepted us for a two-week engagement at first, but later extended this to six when he saw the audiences responding so well to our music. During the six weeks different agents and club-owners came to hear us. They seemed impressed, but kept asking us if we had a floor-show? Did any of us sing, or did any of us dance while we were playing? Always the same questions. Obviously they wanted the kind of show associated with Lionel Hampton's band.

'Other owners offered us work at less than the Union's scale of pay. We refused, because at the time none of us realised that to maintain an ideal sacrifices sometimes become necessary. The Stars Of Swing disbanded. In the years following I regretted not taking work at less than scale to keep the unit going. Buddy Collette and the others did too. Its potential was so tremendous. Unfortunately, the only recording we did was for an audition. Later on we tried to obtain the recording, but the company had sold out and the master were never found.

'About the music The Stars Of Swings played. It was flexible. It had to be. Often Charles (Mingus) would introduce a composition requiring a different approach to jazz playing. In the main though there was a distinctive style running through all our work. It resulted, I feel, from our having quite similar musical thoughts. The enjoyment of working together, expressing these thoughts, enabled us to feel and interpret each composition in an original *and natural way*. We never had to *discuss* style.'

Britt admits—with no sense of grudge—that the broad outlines of this musical style were exploited at a later date by Charlie Ventura. (He refers to the Ventura group which included Bennie Green, his close friend, on trombone.) The commercial success Ventura and his Bop For The People group enjoyed confirms Britt's belief that The Stars Of Swing, given adequate backing, might and could have been a widely-accepted and powerful force in jazz by the late 1940s.

Also in 1946 he worked with the large experimental orchestra of Boyd Raeburn. 'Lucky Thompson recommended me to Raeburn and I found it a very interesting band. It wasn't a permanently organised band; the musicians were always changing and we did far more rehearsing than actual work. Most of the men enjoyed playing the book at rehearsals. George Handy was arranging and composing for the band, and his unusual style of writing kept everyone alert. The first number the band rehearsed after I joined was *Boyd Meets Stravinsky* and I had an eight-bar solo. Later it was recorded.'

And he worked for three months with Eddie Heywood, when the pianist was leading a sextet which included two trombones. 'This was a good, well-organised group. The repertoire was simple, but arranged very neatly. Eddie did the arranging and this was built around his piano-playing. For the men with him it meant playing well without being extremely serious. When joining the band though, I agreed with Eddie that I would leave if he decided to tour. So when he decided to go back to New York I quit—along with the other trombonist, Henry Coker.'

In 1947 Britt did agree to tour—and spent most of the year working with Lionel Hampton. 'I had no problems with this band,' he recalls. 'I accepted a salary-rate before I joined, and Gladys Hampton knew I'd leave if I didn't get it. I played the book and in solos I insisted on being myself. Gladys didn't try to change me, and when I did leave she promised me a place with the band whenever I wanted one.'

Britt then returned to California and worked there for three years. Studio work, mostly. Jazz music was unpopular with most West Coast audiences over this time. When not working he attended Westlake

College for further music studies. According to him his 'basic' education in music was completed at Westlake. 'I studied harmony, arranging and solfeggio. And I played baritone-horn in the concert group. My main interest was in the solfeggio, which they used for ear-training, and to me this seemed an important part of jazz playing. My trombone teacher was Hy Lammars, and somehow I *felt* his interest in me. He admired my conception of jazz. And he said I had the abilities to play melodies as sweetly and smoothly as Tommy Dorsey. He advised me to use this ability in with my normal style whenever I decided it would suit the purpose.'

In 1950, when his studies at Westlake ceased, Britt was capable of holding down the first trombone position with any symphony orchestra. Which was appropriate, because quite soon he would encounter one of the most demanding books in music. It was in March, 1951 that he joined Duke Ellington's orchestra as the replacement for Lawrence Brown.

One night he was awakened by a persistent ringing of the telephone. It was Duke, calling him long-distance. The band was on its way to Las Vegas, the leader explained, and Lawrence Brown was leaving it at the end of two weeks; Woodman, he continued, had been highly recommended to him for the job and, if they could agree a salary, he should leave for Vegas immediately and understudy Brown during the two weeks.

'It was all so unexpected,' Britt remembers. 'I'd never met Duke, and it came as a surprise that he'd even heard of me. Anyway, we promptly forgot to settle upon a salary there and then. I just packed a bag, cancelled the local work I had lined up and left for the airport.'

In Vegas a further surprise awaited him. At the end of the first night, noting the lack of manuscripts on the stand, he turned to Lawrence Brown and said: 'Thank God I've got a fortnight to learn the book'. 'The Hell with that,' Lawrence retorted. 'I'm taking off in the morning!'

There is a maxim of La Rochefoucauld's: 'The steadiness of the wise man is only the art of keeping his agitations locked within his breast.' Britt agrees he experienced this to the full as he waited for the second night's show to begin. Outwardly he appeared calm, but inwardly he felt sick with worry. Perhaps the attitude of some of the other Ellington musicians had a lot to do with it.

'I felt lonely and insignificant,' he says. 'A kind word from someone would have made all the difference. But the old guard of the band were tough on newcomers. Until a musician had earned their respect he was made to feel an outsider. I realised also that if I failed in my first solo with the band it would be hard afterwards to gain that respect.

'Fortunately though, the show went well for me. I had no difficulty in sight-reading the scraps of parts, for which I had to thank my years of study. And I found the tempos Duke set both stimulated and relaxed me, a rare event in jazz. By the end of the show I'd caught on to some of the subtle and unwritten voicings in the orchestration. When it was over, Duke sent for me and thanked me. He said he liked the way I'd shaped certain passages in the music and that I should continue to do so. I explained that although Lawrence Brown's style had influenced my earlier playing, since then I'd developed a style of my own and I felt I had to reshape Lawrence's parts, including certain lead parts, in order to feel comfortable playing them. Duke absolutely agreed.'

The trombonist re-emphasises his admiration for Ellington both as a man and as a musician.

'He was one of the most understanding persons I've known. Although so deeply involved in making music he still found time to look after the personal welfare of the players. Whenever I had any problems to discuss with him I knew he would listen sympathetically. And he always treated me well financially.' Clara Woodman agrees. 'Duke had a lot of love in him,' she says. 'Travelling with the band I noticed this. He sensed the human side of the musicians working for him. For instance, if he saw a man was feeling lowdown he wouldn't force him to take solos. He preferred a soloist to be ready and eager to play. Once, I remember, Ray Nance was very worried about his wife's health. Now Ray was the band's *Floorshow*: Duke depended on his humour and mimicry a lot at concerts. But when he knew Ray was upset he didn't call on him at all. He respected the man too much to cause him embarrassment.'

After the Las Vegas opening and his confident interpretation of the parts, Britt found the rest of the band accepting him. However, and while they were playing concerts on the West Coast, Duke carried out a further revision of the personnel. He persuaded the three musicians from the Harry James band to join him. Valve-trombonist Juan Tizol had figured prominently in the Ellington band of the 'forties; lead–altoist Willie Smith and drummer Louie Bellson, although established 'name' players, were new to Duke. And soon after returning to New York he revised the trumpet section, bringing in Clark Terry and later Willie Cook. For a time at least, the legendary power of the old guard— particularly in its eccentric social and stage behaviour—had been broken.

Britt expresses the opinion that this Ellington band of 1951/52 was consistently finer than at any other time when he worked with Duke. Two men, he maintains, worked particularly hard: Louie Bellson, whose drumming provided the urgent pulse underneath the ensemble, and, just as much, Willie Smith, who led the saxophones. Smith, of course, was already well-known in jazz as a determined enlivener of saxophone sections. His playing with the Lunceford band had given him a big reputation. He rehearsed and rehearsed the Ellington saxes, and eventually achieved with them a blend of sound and a spirited attack which surprised even Duke himself.

'When the band reached New York,' Britt recalls, 'it seemed like everyone had turned out to hear the new men. Birdland was packed for the opening night, and we suspected some had come to criticise. Nevertheless the show was a tremendous success. At the end people were coming up and saying *What a lot of fire there is in the band's playing!* Count Basie was one who came up.'

Almost the whole of Britt's output on records in the 1950s was made with Duke Ellington. And the *corpus* of this work details the emergence of a very powerful (and original) trombone soloist.

In New York, on May 10, 1951, he recorded with Duke for the first time. Three of the performances for this session contain interesting work by him. *The Hawk Talks,* Louie Bellson's 'hit' composition and arrangement, features meticulous and positive lead playing by him and reveals a new conscience in that department of the Ellington orchestra. *Fancy Dan* contains a solo chorus by him which opens simply and romantically (almost in the style of Lawrence Brown, and Tommy Dorsey), and only in its closing bars changes to a musical attitude typical of Britt, with deliberately elastic phrasing and an easy command of the instrument's upper register. Finally, *Jam With Sam* contains a wholly typical and considerably revealing—albeit brief—solo by him.

What is revealed is, first of all, an ability to create blues improvisation at the bouncing medium tempos which Duke obviously delighted in when arranging for the band. But the improvisation itself is very personal. It is orderly, and at the same time succeeds in being unusually varied for so short a solo. Probably this was achieved because the mental process behind it is so deliberately concise. As Britt explains again: 'I prefer to say what I have to say promptly and directly.' The oblique approach, the elaborate circumlocution of a leisurely mind: these are not for him. 'I refuse to take sixteen bars when the idea can be best expressed in four,' he says. 'I don't consider that I suffered because Duke's arrangements imposed limits on the solos.'

However, to return to my original point, that Britt's solo during *Jam With Sam* is also unusually varied. Although consisting of only three main phrases, it succeeds in touching on many shores. It negotiates difficult musical intervals; it contrasts the smooth with the angular turn of phrase; and, in concluding, it examines once more the trombone's upper register. In addition, it reveals a knowledge of syntax and form. There is an increasing melodic tension throughout, and it appears to be no accident that the drastic climb into the upper register occurs at the end of the solo.

Meanwhile, at another, but still important level in the creative process Britt shows that he has a sure lip and can use tonguing very effectively. Also that he has a well-developed tonal sensibility. The first and longest phrase is played with a pronounced but controlled vibrato (oddly reminiscent of Bill Harris with Woody Herman), and this agrees with the attacking and rhythmic nature of the phrase. The second phrase though is played with a glossier tonal production, and this agrees with a fleeting moment of be-bop melody. Finally, the solo is played with warmth and heart, two qualities badly described in words, but which, at least to the senses of the listener, are instantly identifiable as part of the jazz tradition.

On May 18, 1951, again in New York, Britt recorded with a small unit from the band for Ellington's own Mercer catalogue. All the performances from this session were badly recorded; so badly, in fact, that the delicate two-trombone voicings by Britt and Quentin Jackson during *Britt-And-Butter Blues* are almost lost to the human ear. But the session must not be overlooked. One of the recordings, *Sultry Serenade,* features Britt at length.

The overall plan for this *Sultry* performance is quite straightforward: Britt plays the theme and thirty-two bars of improvisation; Willie Smith plays sixteen bars of improvisation; then Britt plays the concluding sixteen bars and once more ends on a note which is impossibly high for a majority of trombonists.

In the theme chorus he pitches Tyree Glenn's sensuous melody line superbly, and the fat tonal quality he achieves with the trombone is both fitting and impressive. In the improvised chorus, he reveals an extensive knowledge of the jazz developed at Minton's Playhouse in the early 'forties. Certainly with his note values and style of phrasing. (The latter, I should add, is a semi-legato style of phrasing, and appears to be out of Bennie Green rather than the more staccato style of J. J. Johnson.) But his attitude to modern jazz here is a utilitarian one. His be-bop phrasing is effected over an orthodox (1930s-type) rhythmic pattern. For a record made in 1951 this seems unusually prophetic. In the late 1950s we were to witness a rush to link and consolidate modern jazz with its antecedents or, as some prefer to say, its roots. At the time when Britt recorded *Sultry Serenade,* however, such an alliance was severely frowned upon by the ultra-modernists as well as by their enemies.

The sixteen bars Britt plays after Willie Smith's solo are heated and extremely aggressive. Again though, we encounter tonal contrasts. For one phrase he will use a rich and large-sized tone with a heavy vibrato, and for the next he will switch to a small tone which is as smooth as satin. Obviously, his tonal production is determined by his ideas and inherent dramatic purpose. And the swift flexibility he displays when building phrases in the upper register is unbelievable until one hears it. The two solos established a musical pattern for others with Ellington.

The leader did not feature him as a soloist on records for several months after the *Sultry Serenade* session; on the other hand, with the longer *A Tone Parallel To Harlem,* he featured many facets of Britt's exemplary work as a lead trombonist.

Other solos on Ellington records are *Liza* (with a simple, but effective melodic development) and *Ballin' The Blues* in 1953. *One O'Clock Jump* and *Things Ain't What They Used To Be* in 1954. *Theme For Trambean* in 1955. *Stompy Jones, Midriff, Stomp, Look And Listen* and an otherwise untitled blues in 1956. At the Newport Jazz Festival held in the same year he recorded an ironic and humorous solo in the opening movement of Duke's *Festival Suite*. And in the *New Orleans* section of 'A Drum Is A Woman' he played a short fanfare.

But so far I have attributed certain qualities to Britt's playing without first discussing its essential theme or ideal. Perhaps this is a mistake. For without a theme these qualities in themselves have no unity. As an improviser Britt is melodically individual and has developed a flexible and powerful technique with the trombone. Devoid of a unifying purpose though such things would almost certainly be wasted and, moreover, would not justify the claims by other trombonists (including the late Jack Teagarden) that he has been one of the instrument's most exciting players.

What then is the theme or idea which runs through his playing? Well, I believe it emerges at last, maturely, in the two late, great solos he recorded with the Ellington band: *Hank Cinq,* a sonnet used in the musical suite, 'Such Sweet Thunder', and *Princess Blue,* recorded at the 1958 Newport Jazz Festival.

The idea itself is double-edged: one side concerned with the technical flexibility of the trombone, the other with expressing a more complete range of human emotion through the instrument.

About the first side, Britt says 'The trombone as a solo instrument is still looked upon as awkward. Many smaller bands, and usually the ones which concentrate on improvisation are organised without trombones. It is considered less agile than a trumpet or a saxophone. Yet this is a mistaken belief. J. J. Johnson has shown what can be achieved, and I've always worked towards the same end. J. J. can make a series of firm and even notes with a quick and easy use of his slide and tongue. Now, my way is actually quite different to his, based on a more flowing relationship between the notes within a melody line and with a greater emphasis on tonal variation. Even so, our aims are similar. Namely, to work with the trombone alongside trumpets and saxophones and not be looked upon as the poor relation.

'The trombone is capable of elastic and detailed phrasing at speed. And it has a wide musical range. So why ignore these possibilities? While with The Stars Of Swing I discovered it wasn't a problem meeting the challenge of the trumpet and the saxophone in ensemble passages. Since then, I've worked on the assumption that it can meet their challenge with improvised solos as well. I always try to demonstrate its technical flexibility. Only by showing that it can interpret a wide selection of thoughts and ideas can its right to work within a band and to play solos as an equal partner be maintained.'

Hank Cinq, recorded in 1957, is a case in point. (The master belongs to CBS.) The piece was originally conceived as a tribute to Shakespeare's preoccupation with history. Ellington wanted to illustrate how Henry V of England was subject to ups and downs. He composed a solo featuring Britt, therefore, with an ascending and descending effect, and one which stressed certain difficult intervals and tempos to denote the change of pace and the map as a result of war. It was a brief musical sketch, and at the same time Duke had no intention of extracting it from the suite and including it in his normal concert programme. However, it became extremely popular with audiences—mainly due to Britt's solo, which Ellington himself described as a 'lip-shattering performance'.

Hank Cinq is an impressive trombone solo for several reasons. Its internal construction, for instance. Also its short, but perfect form. And its firm dramatic purpose (it was Britt's suggestion that, for concerts, a quick ascent to the upper reaches of the instrument's range would make a more effective ending). Nevertheless, the most immediate and perhaps too the most lasting impact on the listener is because of its musical flexibility. Britt here has covered every aspect of technique. There is tonal flexibility, with the heavy vibrato used for the opening and closing being replaced by an even smoothness in the middle; there is rhythmic flexibility, with the jaunty tempo used for the opening and closing being replaced by an urgent pace in the middle; and there is flexibility in the phrasing, with economic ideas being replaced by more complex ones. The soloist appears quite determined to uncover for himself the possible extremes.

As regards the other side of Britt's ideal, the emotional one, he has this to say: 'The trombone in jazz music has two paths open before it. Either it can base improvisation on purely musical ideas or it can set out to interpret human emotions. J. J. Johnson, who I know and admire, has carried the former method to its most advanced and, I believe, satisfying point. This not to say that he plays without feeling. He plays with tremendous feeling, of course—but he is not concerned essentially with translating *the differences* of human emotion into jazz improvisation. His feeling supports his improvisation, which consists of purely musical ideas. I would not chase J. J. along this path, even assuming I could. I have followed the other path, exploring the subtleties of human emotion, and I'll continue to do so. Ideas based on human emotion are not impossible. In fact, I would say they are comparatively easy for the trombonist, largely because his instrument can be made to sound like the human voice. With other instruments this isn't so easy.

'Ideas which interpret human emotion must take advantage of the trombone's many tonal qualities and of its phrasing. This has been at the back of my mind for many years, and I'm always seeking to develop it. I realise, naturally, that other jazzmen have recognised these possibilities before me. 'Tricky Sam' Nanton, when he was with Ellington, discovered how to effect sadness with the trombone. Vic Dickenson with Basie discovered how to effect humour with it. I am still exploring ways of developing where these two handed over. And trying to uncover the many subtleties of emotion which lie, still untouched, between their extremes. Sadness and humour are only vague terms or ways of describing human emotion, and when sub-divided they have many degrees of meaning. My object is to define these degrees.'

Princess Blue, introduced at Newport in 1958, contains a solo by Britt which ends with a remarkable sustained note (a high D flat). While holding this note he varies the sound of his instrument, first moaning sadly, then introducing a guttural anger. It is an important effect. *Hank Cinq* in contrast uses both simple and sophisticated humour. But the human unity is never strained through these changes. Because the real unity is the man.

Since his 'key' emergence within the Ellington band of the 1950s Britt has worked with Mingus again, with Miles Davis, with Coltrane (the 'Africa/Brass' sessions), Tadd Dameron, Max Roach and with several big bands: those of Quincy Jones, Oliver Nelson, Dizzy Gillespie, Mercer Ellington and Clark Terry. In between, to pay the bills, he played lead trombone in the pit for the show 'Little Me', for ice shows and on a variety of TV jingles. In 1970 he moved back to Los Angeles and worked for Nelson Riddle, Frank DeVol, Quincy Jones, Benny Carter (including two visits to Japan), Gerald Wilson and with the Toshiko-Lew Tabakin orchestra. He also appeared in the Robert De Niro movie 'New York, New York'. And he rehearsed a nine-piece band of his own but couldn't land a recording deal.

Seven years later, disillusioned and with his wife's health suffering, he returned to New York. Since when he has played with Harry Edison, Buddy Tate, Budd Johnson, James Moody, Teddy Wilson, Ray Brown and more recently Benny Goodman. Plus leading on trombone for the Broadway musical 'Sophisticated Lady' based on Duke Ellington themes. All of which looks impressive on paper, but spread over a longish period of time it has included weeks and months without any jobs at all. Trombone Summit at Nice in 1985 was his first overseas jazz festival. And he has not made a recording for a leading label under his own name (although he has made tremendous contributions to other players' sessions: notably Charles Mingus on Candid, Jimmy Hamilton on Prestige/Swingsville and Benny Carter on Pablo.)

Nevertheless, as he says: 'I'm still trying. And I will right through to the end. I want to have people know much more about the beauty of the trombone and somehow this keeps me going. Jazz has been my life and nothing can persuade me to change.'

Robin Sinclair, another friend and Woodman watcher, disagrees that Britt is the soloist on the 1956 Bethlehem Blues *track. He also comes up with the following information. 1) 'He (Britt) didn't play lead with the "Little Me" pit band. Merv Gold played lead, Britt second and Tony Studd bass-trombone. Aaron Bell played bass in the rhythm section. At that time Broadway shows were required to have at least two black musicians in a thirty-piece orchestra; so "Little Me" duly had two, Britt and Aaron Bell. Jimmy Cleveland and Joe Marshall played with "Funny Girl" and Wendell Marshall and George Barrow with "How To Succeed In Business".' 2) 'In discussing the solos, I feel the Seattle* Sultry Serenade *with Duke was sensational and better recorded than the Mercer release. The Seattle version is actually the subject of analysis by Dave Baker in his book on the band and gives a good description of Britt's against-the-grain playing. Which is really his way of going up and down the scale as the slide goes out. Willie Dennis used the same method. Kai Winding and the other modernists didn't play this way.'*

CHAPTER TWENTY-THREE

LOUIE BELLSON

In The Studio With . . .

I was with the remarkable drummer/bandleader in the recording studio on November 1, 1982. The place: PRT No.1, Marble Arch, London. The schedule: one album to be made in the afternoon and evening—six hours of playing-time overall.

I found it a fascinating date from start to finish. And not least because, having been a professional producer for well over twenty years, on this occasion I was there purely and simply as a guest. The album was being produced for Louie by the late Alan Freeman. So that, instead of having to make comments and decisions about the musical outcome, it left me in the position of interested observer—able to sit just behind the trombones and only a few feet from Louie himself; able to pick up on the band's behavioural patterns and repartee as well as enjoying the music as it actually happened.

First observation: that Louie likes to get to a session early. Also, that all the members of this particular band of his are very conscientious about starting on time and then going hard at it. Clearly, certain numbers required longer than others to master; notably a couple which the musicians were blowing after only a rudimentary previous acquaintance. Nevertheless it's a fact that by ten o'clock of that same evening the final bars of the album were being recorded within one minute of the planned ending. And the lips had held firm—despite the often fierce demands of the book.

Although his drum-kit was brought in and largely set up by a road manager, Louie was there to oversee every part of it, continually tightening, moving and adjusting until satisfied that he had a correct alignment—including that of the twinned bass-drums which he first pioneered in big band jazz over the period of *Skin Deep* and *The Hawk Talks* when he played with Duke Ellington. Following this, he would never leave his drum-stool except for playbacks. He drove the band along in its normal concert formation. Any necessary conducting was verbal, never visual. Meanwhile, behind the drummer/leader stood the redoubtable figure of bassist George Duvivier, equipped with headphones and with the comforting words SENSIBLE MUSIC in large lettering on the front of his amplifier. All of the band faced the control room window, with engineer Ray Prickett's twenty-two microphones interspersed like a metal forest, five of them around the drums.

When Alan Freeman signalled he was ready to hear something, Louie—it appeared almost ritualistically—twirled his drumsticks half a dozen times, called the six beats in and, without more ado, I was tapping my foot to *Blues For Freddie,* an original score by Tommy Newsom. I noticed, as the date extended itself, how much Louie smiles when he plays. And in this case right from the start, with the band showing great enthusiasm as well as its pool of talent. The respect for the leadership is such that orders were unnecessary. Points of discussion, yes. But all of these occurred in the friendliest fashion. Like when they prepared to do a second take of *Blues For Freddie.* 'Keep the dirt in there, gang,' Louie reminded everyone. 'Yeah,' one of the saxes quipped, 'we don't want it to sound too LA!''

The current band—and I think Louie's best so far—has five trumpets, four trombones, while the saxes (also five) are required by the book to play a wide variety of doubles, giving the arrangements an extra tonal potential of flutes, soprano, Bb clarinets and bass-clarinet. There is a nucleus of veteran jazzmen: Duvivier, pianist Frank Strazzeri and the trombonist/arranger Hale Rood. Otherwise the personnel is amazingly young. Which in turn reminds one of how in recent years the bands of Woody Herman, Buddy Rich and Louie, apart from being good bands musically, have also been 'blooding' bands—in which capacity they have done an immense service to the future of jazz.

So, with excitement, but at the same time quite steadily, the music moved on. *Put It Right There,* again by Tommy Newsom, *The Drum Squad* by Bob Florence and with a tremendous drum cadenza put into it by Louie. Then just before the interval Hale Rood's *Just For Us*—which, not surprisingly, includes some horrendously difficult parts for the trombones. Despite this, it was nearly a first-take master, with 'only a couple of spiders,' in George Duvivier's words. 'Never mind,' Louie decided. 'We'll do one more take after the break and that should do it.' And, of course, it did. He's a producer's dream in the speed and clarity of his musical decisions—and in his concentration on getting it all together.

Another instance of perfectionism was settled during the break. Frank Strazzeri, an extremely individual pianist, was clearly unhappy about his introduction and second solo chorus during *Put It Right There.* So, with the benefit of multi-track tape, he was able to wipe and then overdub these two passages. 'The notes are okay,' he told me, 'but I just wasn't happy about the feeling.' In all, he had a dozen go's before pronouncing himself satisfied. No matter. When musicians worry like this, it shows how much they care . . .

When we came back the youngsters in the band were busy taking photographs of the recording set-up, or playing pitch-and-toss—or, in the case of lead-trumpet Walt Johnson, doing press-ups. He too is an interesting character. Before joining Louie he'd done five years on tour with Elvis Presley—and was actually on a 'plane bound for Seattle when the news of Elvis' death came through, and the pilot turned back in mid-flight. He's now written a book on how to hit high-notes with comparative ease, and he certainly hits them himself with ease.

I asked Louie if the workload would be any easier for the second session. 'No, not really,' he thought. 'The ballads should be okay, but there are a couple of other roughies. However—I never tell the guys if I think it's hard. They just might start to believe me!'

Just For Us was duly disposed of. But in the first take of *We've Come A Long Way Together* (a Bellson original) there were gremlins in the solo microphone, adding a trace of distortion. At first this seemed very disappointing, and for no one more than Greg Ruvolo who had played a marvellously sensitive flugelhorn solo. Fortunately though the young man kept his nerve as well as his heart, and subsequently created an even better performance than the first time.

The evening's proceedings were completed by *Sing A Song Of Love* featuring lead-alto Matt Catingub and then Catingub's own *Santos* with the brass handclapping against the start. Despite its title, *Song Of Love* in fact goes along at a blistering pace. 'You will page-turn for me, won't you?' Louie asked. I must have gone white. 'But you do read music—' he said. 'Sure,' I replied with a gulp, 'but I'm not used to doing it for one of the world's fastest drummers!' Anyway, it passed off well enough. I didn't louse up the takes—although David Redfern's got a picture of me in which he says I look sufficiently scared . . .

'Check for casualties,' one of the trumpets called out after the last double-*forte* of *Santos;* but this too was okay and then quite suddenly the whole thing was over. The next day Louie could continue his tour with the album safely behind him.

'He's totally unflappable,' I remarked to Hale Rood later over a drink. The trombonist was clutching a big bag of curry powders and chilli to take back with him to the States. 'Well, and that's another reason why the music's so happy,' he told me. 'When they know the skipper won't break under pressure the rest of the crew have security of mind. At least, I like to believe that's how we play.'

1983

CHAPTER TWENTY-FOUR

WYNTON KELLY

Groove Master

What we now refer to as early 'classic' be-bop piano-playing came about through sheer necessity. Following on from the clues and leads given by such radicals as Lester Young and Charlie Christian, when Charlie Parker and Dizzy Gillespie made their great breakthrough in the 1940s it became clear that a new kind of pianistic support was needed. Their revolution was essentially harmonic rather than straightforwardly melodic, and the hitherto perfectly acceptable methods of pianists like Earl Hines and Billy Kyle simply didn't fit.

Clyde Hart (1910-1945) had indicated that other things were possible for jazz pianists. Right-hand figures not dissimilar to what Lester, Bird and Dizzy were saying through their horns. And, of course, Thelonious Monk was already working to extend the frontiers of jazz yet again: with daring intervals, the calculated use of unusual chords and so on. But it was to be a young disciple of Monk's, Earl 'Bud' Powell (1924-1966), who would forge the real be-bop piano style—and who became the greatest piano soloist of the music's earlier years. Bud—to quote from the first edition of Leonard Feather's 'The Encyclopedia Of Jazz'—was 'charged with a fantastic dynamic energy with an incredibly fast flow of ideas'. He had the full mastery of his instrument and played it with a very hard attack. More importantly though, he transferred almost the whole harmonic development of his playing to the left hand, and he made this fit in with the new polyrhythmic ideas coming from drummer Kenny Clarke and, later on, Max Roach. In this way the pianist's right hand was freed for the further flights of his imagination—in other words, the melodic content.

It was a good style both for accompanying and for solos, and the incoming generation of keyboard players were quick to learn from it. However, Bud's peak years were few. His life turned into a series of nervous collapses; his playing deteriorated. Consequently, the mantle of his greatness was shared out between those who understood and could further what he'd set in motion. The new masters of be-bop piano were also very gifted. They were the inheritors, and would keep it going.

Late in 1980 Alun Morgan and I put together a two-LP set for PRT/Pye based on some long unavailable examples of their work, and I supplied the following potted biographies.

'George Wallington (*née* Figlia) was born in Palermo, Sicily in 1924. His father, an opera singer, emigrated to the States a year later and, as well as studying the piano, George was a boyhood friend of Max Roach's. He played with Dizzy Gillespie's first combo at the Onyx Club, NYC in 1944, and subsequently worked with most of the other soloists along 52nd Street: Charlie Parker, Allen Eager, Red Rodney *et al.* He also made something of a reputation as a composer (*Lemon Drop* and *Godchild*), but in recent years has been inactive as a jazz player. Although still tempered by Powell, his own style was much leaner. This wasn't due to any lack of technique. On the contrary, he could play very fast and with great accuracy. But he preferred to display his wares with a more economic selection of notes.

'Allan "Al" Haig was the one pianist to offer a genuine alternative to Powell—and, of course, on record at least, is still very much a force to be reckoned within piano jazz. He has been more of a contemplative perhaps than a frontline fighter—which is especially noticeable within his most recent ballads.

'Irving "Duke" Jordan is also something of a world figure these days—just as likely to be met up with in Japan or Paris as in New York or Phoenix, Arizona. He was born in Brooklyn in 1922, got his first work with Coleman Hawkins and then went on to play with Charlie Parker and Stan Getz. Neglected for many years, he is now a prolific recording artist as well as being the leading composer of the four (*Jordu, Scotch Blues, Forecast, Two Loves* and many other themes). Stylistically he is something of a "halfway house" between Powell and Haig; but this is not said in any detrimental way, because he is a very exciting player to listen to.

'In contrast, Wade Legge was almost pure Powell, and again another exciting pianist to listen to—if anything a trace more blues-inspired than Bud. Wade was born in Huntington, West Virginia in 1934 and both his parents were pianists. Milt Jackson heard him playing in Buffalo in 1952, recommended him to Dizzy Gillespie and that took care of the next two years. Later he worked with the Johnny Richards orchestra and led his own trio. But his death in 1963 meant his recorded output was very small.'

It didn't just end with these, of course. As the years have piled up into decades, so we, the listeners and collectors, have taken possession of the newer modern jazz pianists, several of them very considerable artists indeed. Thelonious Monk came into his own—which in turn metalled the road leading to the freer, percussive Cecil Taylor. While building upon what had been passed to them by Bud Powell and especially Al Haig—and dominating the 1960s and 1970s—there appeared the ultra-sophisticated Bill Evans, the blues-saturated Horace Silver, Herbie Hancock and Chick Corea, McCoy Tyner and finally the anti-pope Keith Jarrett. So . . . with so much other pianistic activity going on, Wynton Kelly (who died in 1971) kind of got forgotten.

Well, not quite. Not by any of those hard-core fans who own any of his comparatively small number of records. But certainly, to the wider audience for jazz—who like the music, but have not so far delved deeply into its past and recent history—he is little-known.

And yet he definitely had the gifts and the status to be called one of the best modern jazz piano-players. The 'status' bit being particularly important because it was largely given to him by fellow-musicians. Including some pretty formidable ones: Dizzy Gillespie, Benny Golson, both the Adderley brothers, Wes Montgomery, Sonny Rollins and Philly Joe Jones. Of even more significance, he was very highly rated by his fellow-pianists.

Bill Evans: 'The first time I heard Wynton was with a trio behind Dinah Washington at Basin Street East, and the trio did a number to start the set . . . *Speak Low*. I did that tune in my first album; it was a result of hearing Wynton play it. He made me like it so much. My impression from listening to Wynton was always that he was a schooled pianist, which I gathered later was not altogether true—but his approach was so strong and so pure, so clear and original. This was more a reflection of how his mind worked than any actual conservatory experience or anything like that. Wynton's playing was in every way thoughtful, and yet everything came out so natural. When I heard him with Dizzy's big band, his whole thing was so joyful, exuberant . . .'

And McCoy Tyner: 'You could distinguish his style from anybody else's because of his very rhythmic approach, his attack on the instrument, the way he phrased notes, and, of course, the way he swung.'

When Alun Morgan and I were putting together our 'Be-bop Keyboard Masters' collection we based it on Prt/Pye's access to the archives of French Vogue. But the one pianist we most regretted not having any material by was Wynton Kelly.

At this point I am being reminded of just how good he was by playing his remarkable solo which kicks off the *Dishwater* track by Al Grey, Lee Morgan and a group from within Dizzy's band of the mid-1950s (on Speciality). And I have just been playing his beautiful accompaniments to Steve Lacy (on Status).

I am also reminded of several other essential things about Wynton quite apart from his music. He was the British Commonwealth's first real donation to New York's modern jazz scene, having been born in Jamaica on December 2, 1931. He was nearly deaf in one ear. And he was an epileptic who liked to drink—which epileptics shouldn't like to do. But perhaps what one remembers him best for—and this *was* to do with music: in the period when he played with Miles Davis he was the only sideman who occasionally up-staged his leader and was allowed to get away with it.

Miles has been one of the most severe musicians to work for. Once, backstage at the Royal Festival Hall, I saw him give his whole group a terrible ticking-off for some minor slip during their previous set. In language which was typically Milesian. However, when Wynton Kelly upstaged him he was totally forgiving. Wynton definitely stole the bouquets from Miles on the Blackhawk sets (two LPs on CBS), and he came very near to stealing them again at the Carnegie Hall concert of 1961 (also on CBS). But there were no tantrums thrown by the leader.

Probably because Miles knew his pianist wasn't being consciously competitive. He just loved to play, and when the atmosphere was right he couldn't resist cutting loose. He was—let's agree—one of the most emotionally imbued (and stimulating) piano-players since Earl Hines, and for sheer drive and excitement a rival to the best, early Bud Powell.

McCoy Tyner again: 'His harmonic colourations were very beautiful. But I think above all it was his ability to swing. John (Coltrane) used to mention that. Miles used to get off the bandstand and just look at Wynton with admiration, because he really held the group together. He was the cohesive factor.' And tenorman Hank Mobley: 'First time we did a record date together—Wynton, Paul Chambers, Art Blakey and me—at rehearsal I had some ideas about a certain kind of groove I wanted. So I said *Hey, Wynton, let's try it like this*. Wynton thought for about a minute and two seconds later he had everything I wanted, understood completely, just that quick: the rhythm, the chords, the feeling . . .' Sometimes after one of Wynton's extra special efforts Miles would shake his head, as much as to say: 'How the hell am I going to follow *that*?'

I would say the term 'groove master' was definitely applicable to Wynton Kelly. He could make nearly anything swing. When I first acquired his double album 'Keep it Moving' (reissued posthumously on Milestone M-47098, but based on the Riverside sessions of 1958/59 which Orrin Keepnews produced), my face fell when I noticed that they'd included *Dark Eyes*. I've always considered the number an absolute *dog*—and one that should be chained up in various Eastern European restaurants where the goulash is as bad as the violin-players. But Wynton transforms it! Sorry to be mixing up metaphors about animals, but he really does make a silk purse out of a sow's ear. And a dazzlingly swinging silk purse . . .

Although a Jamaican, he did most of his growing up in Brooklyn and later for many years lived on the same block as drummer Philly Joe Jones, who became his close friend as well as his playing companion in the Miles Davis combo. 'Wynton was the all-round man,' Philly J.J. stresses. 'He had a certain way of comping (accompanying). A stay-out-of-the-way comping—he's playing and you can hear him, but he'd never get in the way of a soloist.' Many musicians considered him the perfect, sympathetic group player. And singers loved his delicate, unobtrusive sounds behind them. He had a long period of accompanying Dinah Washington.

He also gained the reputation for being a very warm, generous human being. Riverside producer Orrin Keepnews always forgave him for arriving at sessions half-an-hour late, because he then gave so much. 'The most important thing . . . was that he showed up ready to play, knowing what was expected of him, and capable of doing the job swiftly and pretty-near perfectly.' And Philly Joe Jones remembers: 'During his last days, I had just come back from Europe and was working on 12th Street at Avenue A. It was one of those gigs you accept because the people are so appreciative, but the money is never satisfactory—never. I needed a piano-player; so I call Wynton and the first thing I tell him is about the money. And he said: *Listen, Joe, I haven't played with you in so long—it'll be a pleasure!'* So he came over and sat down and fitted right in—you'd think we just came out of rehearsal . . .'

Alcohol was his Achilles' heel—on account of the epilepsy. But although he drank deeply, it was always after, not before a performance. And although his music-making was largely the result of feeling, instinct and haphazardly-acquired knowledge, he was a great connoisseur of pianos. If he landed a bad one on some job or other he knew *exactly* how to go about getting his clear, ringing sound out of it. He usually did his own tuning.

During his forty years of life he played many, many casual gigs—but his regular stays with anyone or any group were few, mainly because he did tend to stay on *and on* when the company suited him. He didn't care overly much about being a leader, although he did have a trio after leaving Miles. (He, bassist Paul Chambers and drummer Jimmy Cobb all left the group at the same time.) Even this trio though was eventually made to fit into a quartet featuring guitarist Wes Montgomery.

Wynton got his first break with Lester Young in the early 'fifties. But for those of us who are his steadfast fans, it was his tenure of the piano stool with the Dizzy Gillespie big band of 1957 which brought him, as its groove master, to our ears and lasting appreciation. Following the Middle and Far Eastern State Department sponsored tour of '56, there were a lot of personnel changes, and Wynton replaced the adequate, but relatively discreet Walter Bishop on piano. Immediately there was a change inside the rhythm section—the band's real 'kitchen'. Before this the band had sounded all brass and saxes. Suddenly now the proper cooking was coming out from the back. And with Wynton giving him the cues, Charlie Persip on drums began to put it all together like he'd never played before.

One can hear the radical changes on 'Dizzy In Greece' (recorded for Verve). Half the tracks were made by the '56 'World Statesman' band and are good. The remainder, made by the '57 one are mind-blowing—and it's Wynton Kelly leading the rhythm section who gives the whole thing lift-off. He plays very economically, but he's still firing the oven. The new, young, headstrong soloists each have their say, and behind them the pianist has to be listened for (the whole session is very poorly recorded). Nevertheless he is crucial. Prodding, pulsing, doing just about all that could be hoped for by way of support. On *Jordu, Birk's Works, That's All, Stablemates, Tangerine* and *Whisper Not.*

Then, when the band played L.A., its main ravers made the date for Speciality (once upon a time issued in Great Britain on London LTZ-U 15121). It has Lee Morgan on trumpet, Al Grey (trombone), Billy Mitchell (tenor), Billy Root (baritone), Wynton, Paul West (bass) and Charlie Persip on drums. With Benny Golson and one Roger Spotts doing the arrangements. The LP was called 'Dizzy Atmosphere' and the opening *Dishwater* track is a modern jazz classic. A blues, taken at breakneck speed, Wynton sets it all up, and after his own marvellous solo continues comping in a totally subjective way. It was also my introduction to the then eighteen-year-old Lee Morgan, and his absolute rapport with Wynton is like a love affair. Or, as Philly Joe Jones once said of the pianist: 'He puts down *flowers* behind a soloist. He never wanted to steal in. He just put together the right things.'

Orrin Keepnews asked tenorman/arranger Benny Golson what it was like working alongside Wynton in the Gillespie band. Specifically referring to his dramatic change from various frigate-like small groups to the full armament of a battle-cruiser. Golson (a very articulate man) is worth quoting in full:

'Well, that difference primarily involves adaptability or flexibility, and this he had. I knew he was able to function effectively with a small group but surprisingly, when he came into the big band, there was no problem. When you have a drummer coming from a small group into a big band he's got to adjust in some way. But Wynton came in as if he'd been doing it right along. And he wasn't just a functional piece of the machine. He kept his identity; yet he was able to add something to the band, not only melodically (which he was known for) but rhythmically. He would set up patterns—never interfering with the arrangement, but he was able to get into the cracks (*like Count Basie?*: R.H.) and he would always be adding something, giving it impetus, more energy. When Wyn left the band, we felt the other piano-players were really more or less scuffling, because we had gotten used to hearing what Wynton used to do in the fifth bar here, the sixteenth bar there and so forth. He would just do these little things and they were gems and over a period of time you just got used to hearing them, and when he left, there was a big gap there and we had to readjust our ears and our minds.

'One thing was that Wynton was one of the great listeners of our times. He would play in such a way that would always complement and add to what was going on at that particular moment. Another thing about him—he could play anything that he had ever *heard* in his life, even if he hadn't played it before. You could just call the tunes: *Hey, Wynton, do you remember this one?* and he'd say, *Yeah, I think I've heard it—what key?* And he's gone; he'd just sit down and play. You know, he had perfect pitch. He could hear any note at any time and tell you what it was. We used to say that he could hear around the corner . . . and anticipate what was coming.'

Not bad for a musician with only one sound ear!

When Wynton joined Miles Davis in 1959 he replaced Bill Evans, over whom the leader had been taking a lot of Crow Jim stick because he was a white player. But Wynton was far from being a sop to the racialists. He made an immediate impact on the group's playing and stayed with it through until 1963. Then there was his own trio and the association with Wes Montgomery (which produced the 'Smokin' At The Half Note' LP on Blue Note). Also too there were stints with soprano-saxist Steve Lacy, with Clark Terry, Dexter Gordon and for several months with ex-Ellingtonian Ray Nance. He died in Toronto on April 13, 1971, of a heart attack following another epileptic seizure.

Above all, he is remembered for the beautiful grooviness of his piano-playing. He had swing, fire, attack, an inbred feeling for the blues (but basic and genuine, not calculatedly 'funky') and a seemingly endless flow of ideas. Listening to his records, there is never a moment when you can't gauge the inner pulse—when you don't tap your foot along with what he's playing. For that alone his work will always command our attention. Meanwhile, among his fellow-professionals *he was loved.*

1983

CHAPTER TWENTY-FIVE

CLEF/VERVE: A COMPANY REPORT

1. THE NORMAN GRANZ YEARS . . .

The Leonard Feather/Ira Gitler 'Encyclopedia Of Jazz In The Sixties' summarises Norman Granz' career as follows:

'Producer; b. Los Angeles, Calif., 8/6/18. Began producing concerts at LA Philharmonic Auditorium in 1944. From the mid-'40s his concerts, in the U.S., and also later overseas, set a pattern for informal jazz stage shows and earned tremendous international popularity. Granz also pioneered the concept of recording "live" at actual performances instead of in recording studios. After his last U.S. tour in '57 he continued to take jazz shows abroad, making his own residence in Switzerland.

'In Jan. 1960 Granz sold his Verve Record Co. to M.G.M. for $2,500,000. Though no longer in the record business he became very active in the importing of various artists to Europe for extended tours, and acted as manager for Ella Fitzgerald, Oscar Peterson and Duke Ellington. Maintaining homes in Paris and Geneva, he returned to the U.S. from time to time, usually to supervise Miss Fitzgerald's recordings and to negotiate tours.'

He also went on to have an apartment in London, a villa on the French Riviera, to become a personal friend of Picasso's and to own several of that modern master's works. He continues to have the most important say at the Antibes Festival, a July rival to the George Wein-run Nice Festival; and in the 1970s he came back into the record industry with his Pablo label. However, what the 'Encyclopedia' does not include, being by its very nature a factual rather than an evaluating book, is that Granz began his life in jazz with only personal enthusiasm and a handful of dollars. This most successful jazz impresario of recent times and singlehanded creator of the music's biggest independent recording organisation started his career as a part-time quotation-clerk on the LA Stock Exchange. Which bored him, so that after 1943 he went to work at M.G.M. Studios as a film editor. But already his enjoyment of and beliefs in mainstream and modern jazz had come together as if with Superglue. And soon he wanted to be further involved.

Still in 1943 he began promoting Monday-night jam sessions at the 331 Club in Los Angeles. He used local musicians, but also, whenever it proved possible, augmented by visiting 'star' sidemen. The format not only grew to be popular, it persuaded Granz to start up his own recording outfit, and to try recording the players under 'live' conditions. For which the 331 Club was clearly too small. So on July 2, 1944 the budding impresario staged a benefit concert at the highbrow Philharmonic Auditorium, got the event broadcast over the Armed Forces Radio Network and the whole future concept of Jazz At The Philharmonic came into being—with the recording empire which grew from its ideas soon to follow. Except for the Benny Goodman Carnegie Hall appearances just before World War II, jazz had never before managed the dramatic leap from small clubs (and often sleazy ones) to the more august concert-platforms of America—and Granz achieved this literally within months. Largely as a result of two things: his own natural energies and determination, and secondly, an additional determination to present the biggest names and most extrovert players currently on the jazz scene all in the same touring package. Exactly how his record company activities then progressed is a different and much more varied, even convoluted story. But there can be no doubt that in the early days Jazz At The Philharmonic was the masthead upon which the most popular jazz names were pinned. Which in turn would allow them to go on and further their more personalised creative ideas.

In subsequent years Norman has taken more than his justified proportion of 'stick' relevant to certain of his promotions and recording policies. Much of it, I believe, based on envy. Because if the occasional JATP outing did generate pandemonium, or a studio concept be ill-conceived or badly recorded, then the balance of creative *largesse* on the other side of the hill was destined to become tremendous. Conversely too, and unlike some of his rival promoters (though not, I'm pleased to report, Gene Norman), Norman from the very beginning always has gone out of his way to pay the musicians he's hired the best possible money for the job, place them in the best possible working environments and to overcome, brushing aside with contempt, any racialist problems. On this last, human rights issue his track record stands second to none in jazz. Overall then, it's not surprising such star performers as Ella Fitzgerald and Dizzy Gillespie have stuck with him as contract artists through the greater part of their respective mature careers.

Also from the outset Norman could be extremely shrewd and tough with other businessmen less scrupulous than himself; without his entrepreneurial abilities ever boomeranging back upon his own collection of great players. He has understood the artists' needs for encouragement and satisfaction as well as good fees and royalties. Oscar Peterson, for instance, even before his association with Granz led to world fame, had a clause inserted in his recording contract which stipulated no release of any material he personally considered substandard. While another, very subtle and 'interior' artist, Lester Young, who did not entirely enjoy the sometimes frenetic atmosphere of a JATP concert, nevertheless stuck with the format because of the more creative opportunities Granz gave him in other directions. (Not least the 'Jazz Giants '56' album; and Lester's last Quartets in reunion with pianist Teddy Wilson.)

Granz once said of a Dizzy Gillespie project that would cost $5000 to set up, a very large budget in those early years: 'It can't possibly make money, but Dizzy wanted to do it. He's happy now.' Another JATP trumpet soloist, Roy Eldridge, later remarked: 'They should make a statue to Norman, and there's no-one else in the business end of this business I would say that about.'

Anyway, of all of them, and much, much more I am now reminded at considerable, fascinating length (876 pages, in fact) by the acquisition of 'The Clef/Verve Labels. A Discography' in two volumes, lovingly, patiently and indeed brilliantly compiled by Michael Ruppli. Not since the late Charles Delaunay commenced a new art-form with his 'Hot Discography' in the 1930s can there have been published a more intriguing book in its own particular genre. And for the whole history of the Granz Clef/Verve years and their aftermath I feel compelled to pronounce it definitive.

Moreover it's ironic, really, that in his years of absolute control before 1960 one of Norman Granz' peculiar eccentricities was an absolute refusal to give out recording dates on his record-sleeves; or to answer individual discographers' queries relating to the matrix numbers at sessions. Allegedly because he hated the idea of his product ever being considered as growing old. (When surely a masterpiece is a masterpiece for all time!) Nevertheless, in subsequent years Michael Ruppli has managed to piece almost everything together. The volumes do not come cheaply. (The Greenwood Press, £74.10 the pair.) But they list every known session, including the unissued ones and alternative takes—and I can't imagine any institution or library devoted to jazz studies being without them.

The Norman Granz period of Clef/Verve began during the Winter of 1943/44 when the aspiring young impresario taped a single session of four titles involving Harry Edison (trumpet), Dexter Gordon (tenor-saxophone), Nat 'King' Cole (piano) and unknown bass and drums, but probably Johnny Miller and Juicy Owens. The titles, like a number of Granz' earliest efforts, were leased to other independent labels, Phoenix in the U.S. and Spotlite in England. Other items would be recorded and then kept under wraps until Norman signed a long-term contract with Irving Green's Mercury label in 1948. In between there would be releases in the U.S. on Philo and Asch.

However, it was the second Granz' recording session which truly changed events in jazz. This occurred 'live' on July 2, 1944—at the inaugural Jazz At The Philharmonic concert in Los Angeles. The evening kicked off with a *C Jam Blues* (never released) featuring Shorty Sherock, Bumps Myers, Joe Thomas, Buddy Cole, Red Callender and Joe Marshall. Then the main proceedings got under way with a set teaming the young J. J. Johnson (so fast and dazzling that many people thought he played a valve- rather than a normal tenor slide-trombone), Illinois Jacquet and Jack McVea (tenor-saxophones), Nat 'King' Cole (piano), Les Paul (with his sensationalised electric-guitar effects), Johnny Miller (bass) and Lester Young's brother Lee (drums). They played *Lester Leaps In, Tea For Two, Blues* and *Body And Soul.* Later in the concert Shorty Sherock, trumpet, replaced J. J. Johnson to jam *I've Found A New Baby* and Nat Cole sang *Sweet Lorraine* (again unissued). Following which Johnson rejoined them to jam a *Bugle Call Rag.*

When these various titles were subsequently released (from 1946 on the Asch label) they sold prodigiously well and brought Granz and what he was doing to a nationwide prominence. Spearheaded, incidentally, by the presence of Illinois Jacquet, who via Lionel Hampton and blowing his notorious 'shriek'-notes and other ear-grabbing effects on tenor had becomes the hottest box-office name in jazz. (Later, when Illinois led his own band, there were times when—on percentage—he would have suitcases stuffed with money at the end of a gig.)

In May and June, 1946 JATP played New York City with equal success; and in the years after this there would be two coast-to-coast tours every year, almost all of which found their way on to disc. The record sales turned into an absolute bonanza—especially after 1948 with the aid of Mercury's marketing and distribution.

Which in turn enabled Granz to expand enormously his other catalogue of studio recordings. The roster of artists included some who never toured with JATP (Bud Powell, Johnny Hodges and Anita O'Day), while to others who did Norman was able to offer long-term contracts: Dizzy Gillespie, Charlie Parker, Lester Young, Flip Phillips, Buddy De Franco and Stan Getz—and of course Illinois Jacquet still. Also there were the celebrated drum battles between Buddy Rich and Gene Krupa.

Then from March, 1950 there began the Oscar Peterson hundreds: sweeping the pianist to immediate success. And Norman had his sights set on yet another, the great Art Tatum. 'If I ever get him under contract, I'll never let him go,' Granz said. Well, in 1953 he did; starting with a marathon session on December 28 when no less than thirty-five titles were recorded.

That same month saw the first Count Basie Dance Session cut, and in the following year 'Stan Getz At The Shrine' with Bob Brookmeyer.

Another characteristic of the Granz years was the impresario's willingness to go along with experimental ideas as well as the bigger commercial names. Thus came about the 'Afro-Cuban Suite' which placed Charlie Parker, Flip Phillips and Buddy Rich within the context of the Machito orchestra and under the composer's baton of Chico O'Farrill; the first magnificent meeting between Dizzy Gillespie and Stan Getz, backed by drummer Max Roach and the Oscar Peterson Trio;

the *Funky Blues* session which brought together the world's three greatest alto-saxophone players, Charlie Parker, Johnny Hodges and Benny Carter; Parker again with a string unit; Stan Getz and J. J. Johnson at the Opera House in Chicago, a truly blistering set; and most ambitious of all, the 'Jazz Scene' album: a collection of contrasting tracks including Ralph Burns' *Introspection,* George Handy's *The Bloos,* Ellington's *Frustration* featuring Harry Carney and Coleman Hawkins' unique set of unaccompanied tenor-saxophone variations entitled *Picasso.*

A writer colleague, Richard Palmer, has pointed out how the Michael Ruppli volumes 'can lead one into sudden serendipities—those that would probably not come to light just by perusing the actual records one at a time.

'My favourite such moment,' he continues, 'concerns August 1, 1955 and centres on Lionel Hampton. On that day Hampton first cut an album with Stan Getz that marked the tenorist's return to the studio—and indeed the ouside world—after his months of incarceration. Both protagonists play extremely well; but Stan's form is, given the circumstances, nothing short of astonishing, chiefly on *Jumpin' At The Woodside,* where he all but wastes the legendary vibist—an experience Hamp would not have greatly cared for! And that last point leads us straight into the day's second date—the famous trio session with Hampton, Buddy Rich and Art Tatum, which is notable for including the only performance I've ever heard where Tatum is upstaged by another musician. It occurs on *Makin' Whoopee,* and the musician is, of course, Hamp. Whether he was still smarting from being 'Getzed', or whether he just got 'on' for some subconscious reason, no one can tell; but to play the two records in tandem, almost as they were recorded, remains a uniquely interesting experience . . .'

My own particular piece of serendipity, after combing the first volume of Ruppli's *magnum opus* is the discovery (many years too late to acquire the records) that in 1954 Granz revived the Artie Shaw Gramercy Five group: with Hank Jones replacing Dodo Marmarosa on piano, Joe Roland (vibes), Tal Farlow (guitar), Tommy Potter (bass) and Irv Kluger (drums). Norman—according to Ruppli—didn't produce this batch of titles (including the intriguingly named *When The Quail Came Back To San Quentin*) but brought them in.

Another unique and major event occurred in 1956 when Ella Fitzgerald joined the Granz recording roster, which since 1953 and the expiry of the Mercury deal had become completely independent and renamed the Clef catalogue. Norman had been Ella's personal manager and concert promoter for a number of years, but had had to wait for the ending of her previous long-term recording contract with American Decca. He coincided her arrival on Clef with another change of name: from Clef to Verve; and set about the series of 'Songbook' albums with her singing devoted to the work of America's greatest popular composers, Gershwin, Cole Porter, Duke Ellington and so on.

Meanwhile too he was expanding his recording activities outside the jazz field. Into cabaret, for instance, and the new humour of Jonathan Winters, Mort Sahl and Shelley Berman. Into spoken word and readings by Evelyn Waugh, Angus Wilson, Dorothy Parker and the prophet of the beat-bums, Jack Kerouac. Even into rock n'roll (Ricky Nelson cut his first records for Verve).

But at the same time, with increased success and further expansion, the pressures upon Norman Granz the human being were mounting. To give him due credit, he didn't crack. But he was forced to delegate. And to reduce the workload somewhat. Although continuing to promote concerts by Ella Fitzgerald and Oscar Peterson, from 1957 he restricted JATP tours to Europe, where he had developed an increasing taste for living and established an acquaintance with Pablo Picasso. And more and more Verve sessions were being handled by secondary producers: Buddy Bregman, Barney Kessel and Russ Garcia. These were the first significant steps towards the impresario's realising one huge final profit-taking after nearly twenty years at the helm.

2. THE CREED TAYLOR YEARS AND AFTER . . .

By 1960, when Norman Granz sold out his Verve holdings to M.G.M., Charlie Parker, Art Tatum and other jazz stars of the Granz era were dead. The label's new owners hired Creed Taylor as chief executive and main record producer. Both they and he indicated that a considerable shake-up was on the way.

Taylor, born in 1929 at Lynchburg, Virginia (otherwise famous as the home of Jack Daniels bourbon) and educated at Duke University, had been associated previously with Bethlehem and ABC-Paramount (where he founded Impulse! specifically as a jazz label). He had a reputation for firm organisation, daring ideas and a willingness to promote younger jazz artists—often towards a more commercial acceptance. Also he was noted for keeping his cool in the face of adversity. Jon Hendricks, the notable singer/composer of jazz vocalese, once told me a remarkable story of how 'Sing A Song Of Basie', perhaps Creed Taylor's biggest-selling production for ABC-Paramount, very nearly didn't come about. Originally the Ray Charles Singers (nothing to do with the blues-singer Ray Charles) had been booked to record Hendricks' set of lyrics to Basie themes. They were a large, smooth and skilful vocal group; but they didn't have the necessary grooviness, and in failing to achieve this they'd used up most of Taylor's budget. 'I though the project was finished,' Hendricks added, 'but Creed didn't give up so easily.' As a result the Lambert, Hendricks and Ross concept of multi-voice overdubbing came into being. Other artists Taylor produced at ABC included Quincy Jones ('This Is How I Feel About Jazz'), Oliver Nelson ('The Blues And The Abstract Truth') and Gil Evans ('Out Of The Cool').

However, while he shared Granz' belief that the best names in jazz should be presented with boldness and a wide distribution, as the incoming man at Verve Taylor was not content just to follow in Norman's footsteps. He didn't care for the Jazz At The Philharmonic format; nor the sometimes rough recording balances, and especially not the scrappy sleeve-notes with their lack of information. Taylor's first act as executive boss, therefore, was to suspend all Verve releases for a period of six months in order to reshape the artists' roster. He then fired many of the JATP veterans; retaining only Dizzy Gillespie, Stan Getz, Ella Fitzgerald, Oscar Peterson and Johnny Hodges. To which he then added his own candidates for stardom—signing up Jimmy Smith, Cal Tjader, Wes Montgomery, Bill Evans, Kenny Burrell and not least Astrud Gilberto and the *bossa nova* experts from Brazil.

Creed Taylor remained at Verve from 1960 to 1967. During which time some of the finest and most successful jazz of its decade appeared on the label. In 1961 the Gillespie big band in concert at Carnegie Hall with arrangements by Lalo Schifrin; followed by Dizzy's tremendous 'Perceptions' LP scored by J. J. Johnson for trumpet and brass ensemble. Oscar Peterson's 'Very Tall' came next: with his trio augmented by vibist Milt Jackson. Then 'Focus', Stan Getz' revolutionary album based on string writing by Eddie Sauter; 'The Individualism Of Gil Evans' LP; Basie's 'L'il Ol' Groovemaker'; Bill Evans' award-winning 'Conversations With Myself', again drawing upon Taylor's penchant for multi-track overdubbing. And, of course, the great commercial single successes: the Getz/Charlie Byrd *One-Note Samba* and the Getz/Gilberto *The Girl From Ipanema*.

But not everything worked out quite so well as these during the Taylor years. He was under constant pressure to record the themes from M.G.M. movies. And in the end he himself fell into the trap of pushing several of his jazz artists too far commercially. As examples of this we have Basie teamed with Arthur Prysock, the excruciating 'Basie's Beatles Bag', the often trite material on Wes Montgomery's 'Goin' Out Of My Head' LP and the later Jimmy Smith sessions which hardly match his earlier efforts for Verve such as *The Cat, A Walk On The Wild Side* and *Who's Afraid Of Virginia Woolf?* All of these records sold well; but listening to them again one realises they were produced towards a chart ('top 100') formula and are less creative in a jazz sense. As with the rest of Creed Taylor's work they are models of good recording technically. Somehow though the spark of enthusiasm is missing. Leaving one often with not much more than a clever gimmick.

It's possible too that by this stage Taylor's own enthusiasm had gone missing. Possibly as a result of his being put upon by 'the men upstairs' to devise ever bigger record-sellers. Certainly when he re-emerged as a producer in the 1970s with his independent CTI and Kudu labels there is evidence that he was seeking to find a middle way between creative jazz and the need to have commercial success; hence, George Benson.

In the aftermath of his departure the management of Verve/M.G.M. grew increasingly faceless—with the production work farmed out to a variety of people: Teddy Reig ('Teddy The Toad', who had supervised 'The Atomic Mr. Basie' for Roulette), Jim Davis, Esmond Edwards, Pete Spargo and Eric Miller. Some good jazz continued to get through. Oliver Nelson's 'Jazzhattton', for instance; also Milton Jackson's album with a string quartet and new work by Phil Woods and the gifted young pianist Monty Alexander. Another pianist, the great Bill Evans was still under contract from the Creed Taylor years and cut his excellent 'Alone' date for the label. While Stan Getz gave it a late jazz flowering with the 'Dynasty' double-album and the wonderful 'Captain Marvel' set. (In fact, as Richard Palmer points out, the latter was Verve's final all-out jazz date, 'a suitably majestic climax to nearly 30 years of endeavour that, all warts admitted, every jazz lover should regard as priceless!)

Otherwise, as the jazz programme was wound down, so there was a new emphasis on folk, commercial blues and rock music. Until, on May 5, 1972 all the M.G.M.-owned record labels were sold to Polydor. Since then reissue programmes have flourished in Europe and Japan, although less so in the United States. On the other hand, even in the States in the 1980s the Verve catalogue has taken on a fresh significance with the promotion of compact discs. Headed by Polygram VP Richard Seidel, we are informed, 'a systematic programme of vault research has begun'; with, it is hinted, the prospect of further recordings after a lapse of many years. Already, it seems, a number of alternative takes by Charlie Parker have been unearthed; and unissued material by Lee Konitz and Kenny Burrell.

Which brings me back, finally to Michael Ruppli's scholarly discography. Did you know, for instance, that on March 17/18, 1958 the revered Negro poet Langston Hughes recited his works on record, backed on the first day by mainstreamers Henry 'Red' Allen, Vic Dickenson and Milton Hinton, then the following day by Mingus, Jimmy Knepper and Horace Parlan? Or that in June, 1960 when Louis Armstrong 'officially' recorded with Bing Crosby in LA under Billy May's direction, they actually overdubbed their voices the following month in New York City? Or indeed that Thad Jones conducted for the last Jimmy Smith Verve sessions (*Blap, Portuguese Soul,* etc) of February, 1973? Such are the delightful dips one can make into Ruppli's accuracy.

Of the unissued material which he lists one would hope that early in seeing the light of day would be the remainder of Stan Getz/ J. J. Johnson at the Opera House, Chicago; the remainder of Kenny Burrell's

'For Charlie and Benny' sessions; two full, never previously issued Stuff Smith dates; Johnny Hodges with Ben Webster and Lalo Schifrin; a whole load of titles by Wynton Kelly and Kenny Burrell; five unissued titles from the Oscar Peterson, Milt Jackson 'Very Tall' sessions; Dizzy with Junior Mance; and most intriguing of all, a Jimmy Smith/Oliver Nelson *Rhapsody In Blue*, cut when they were working over *Who's Afraid Of Virginia Woolf?*

Richard Palmer estimates that Ruppli has listed individual sessions running into five figures, and skimming these two Greenwood Press volumes I have no reason to doubt his accuracy. It has clearly been a monumental task. Richard Palmer, incidentally, mentions finding only three errors. Two concern Oscar Peterson tracks which I haven't heard and, therefore, am not qualified to comment on. The third though I agree with him about. There is no pianist (which Ruppli states is Steve Kuhn) on Stan Getz' 'Focus' LP. But really, after his overall achievement, this is picking fly-shit off the wall.

In conclusion I can only compliment him on his work; and the Greenwood Press for publishing a discographical wonder.

1988

CHAPTER TWENTY-SIX

BILL EVANS

And Two Of His Masterpieces

In the years before his unfortunate, premature and still argued-about death Bill Evans recorded more than fifty albums. I currently possess thirty-two of them; and have heard most of the others. At least six I regard as jazz and pianistic masterpieces. Two I prefer to all the rest.

Memories can crowd in upon one in a claustrophobic way. But I think I first became aware of Bill Evans as a result of the George Russell Smalltet and his 'Jazz Workshop' LP made in 1957 for RCA. The originator of 'the Lydian concept of tonal organisation' had put together a fascinating album. Impossible to describe the Lydian concept in a single sentence, but an important factor is the building of keys by selecting notes in ascending fifths. Thus, the notes in the key of C would be C, G, D, A, E, B and F sharp. In turn this allows the music to be harmonically adventurous without becoming totally atonal or using the 12-tone scale of Arnold Schoenberg. It gives a sense of tonality, of the feeling of a central root in every passage. Such relativities have always been present in music, of course, and what Russell had uncovered of them is immensely important to modern straight composers as well. Meanwhile his jazz output has remained rhythmic, abounds in improvisation and is formally organised without losing emotion. And on the final track of the 'Workshop' LP, *Concerto For Billy The Kid*, George unleashes the piano artistry of Bill Evans, classically trained, a jazz natural, giving us a dazzling display of imagination, attack and sheer technique rarely heard before or since.

The next important stage of Evans' career occurred in the later 1950s and his occupying the piano-stool with the Miles Davis Sextet.

As early as 1949 Miles had registered his impatience with the four- and eight-bar phrases which normally make up a 12- or 32-bar theme. He felt that improvised phrases should determine continuity within a solo and not the bar-lines. Then *Gil* Evans pointed out to him certain advantages (including greater freedom) in a return to melodic sources—as opposed to improvising over the angular chord changes of many be-bop themes, which left Miles dissastisfied with the 12- and 32-bar frames themselves, and in turn transformed the musical growth of his Quintet and later Sextet (the John Coltrane/Cannonball Adderley/Bill Evans group).

This is dramatically illustrated by a record such as 'Kind Of Blue'. The point about tracks such as *All Blues* and *Flamenco Sketches*, for

182

instance, is that they remain essentially *sketches*. Their composed melodies are intentionally brief and also modal, with just a few, strategically-placed chord changes. Yet herein lies real strength, for the soloists are allowed to develop their improvisation in more elastic, and consequently far richer ways. Obviously with musicians of the calibre of Coltrane, Adderley and Bill Evans on hand the potential becomes enormous. It results in jazz of a thoughtful, but at the same time extremely challenging nature. And as for Miles himself, I have never heard him sound so relaxed on disc. He implies so much, that he needs to stress very little.

Achieving his escape to a more open-ended, scalar improvising naturally prompted the search after further freedoms by Bill Evans himself. He was already a master of complex inner harmonies; but as the basis for new melodic inventions, subtly delineated by a Chopin-like gradation of touch. Unfortunately, he did have certain human problems around this time. And his presence caused Miles himself a small amount of trouble. It was a sort of American Mrs McGoldrick incident. Certain people got at Miles and said he had no right featuring a white piano-player in his group. Happily Miles can be delightfully abrasive at such moments. 'I don't care if he's green so long as he plays well,' he retorted. Plus a few choice expletives. He himself had already suffered a beating up by a white cop outside Birdland and collected a reported 100,000 dollars after successfully suing the New York police-department. He has no patience with colour prejudice. Either way. (Witness the presence of Bob Berg, the outstanding alto/tenor-player in his more recent group.)

Nevertheless, Bill did take the hint and made way for Wynton Kelly, born in Jamaica, to take over as Miles' pianist. And although he himself would make further records with guest horn-players, from this point in time until his death he concentrated upon being the leader of a piano/bass/drums trio. He created a duo masterpiece ('Undercurrent') with guitarist Jim Hall for United Artists—which includes another dazzling, up-tempo, Bud Powell-like improvisation based on *My Funny Valentine*; won a Grammy Award for the extremely clever, 3-piano overdubbed 'Conservations With Myself'; transferred successfully to collaboration with a symphony orchestra (playing Granados, J.S. Bach, Scriabin, Fauré, Chopin); and collaborated on what is my favourite Tony Bennett LP (on Fantasy). But I find nothing surprising in the fact that my two chosen masterpiece collections are Bill Evans Trios.

LP: "EVERBODY DIGS BILL EVANS"

Titles: *Minority/Young and Foolish/Lucky to Be Me/Night and Day/Tenderly/Peace Piece/What Is There to Say?/Oleo/Epilogue*

Evans (piano), Sam Jones (bass), Philly Joe Jones (drums)

December, 1958 New York City Recorded for Riverside

'And the fire and the rose are one,' T.S. Eliot wrote as the final line to his 'Four Quartets'. As a description it appears ideally suited to the piano-playing of Bill Evans.

The more I listen to Bill (born in 1929, incidentally) on record, the more I am inclined to believe that he is one of the very few pianists jazz music was always working its way towards. All the earlier streams run through him, together with several classical ones. But he is not merely a composite artist; he is also a *consummate* one, and an individualist in his own right.

If fire is interpreted as a symbol of virility, and the rose of beauty (albeit with some sharp sting), then one can gain an idea of what has become reconciled within a single style. On the one hand there is swing and feeling, an accomplished technique, an often dazzling attack, as well as a sense of humour; while on the other there is delicacy, profound thinking, great harmonic subtlety and the finest gradation of touch ever heard from a jazz pianist. He is as happy with a fast be-bop theme, improvising single-note style with his right-hand over the firm roots of the left, as he is during a quieter, impressionist piece, where there is an interdependence of hands to cope with the richness and variety of his inner harmonies. Above all though, his is essentially a *pianistic* approach—as distinct from the anvil which Thelonious Monk often makes of the keyboard on record. And for this Bill has been rightly regarded as a new pianist's pianist, much as Art Tatum was looked upon by *his* contemporaries.

His long period of classical studies included South Eastern Louisiana College, then the Mannes School of Music in New York; and he spoke of the many hours of finger-exercises in order to develop his sense of touch. He also credited the year with Miles Davis for increasing his confidence. And he implied that, whereas his harmonic thinking drew upon everything he knew about music, some of his melodic phrases (and the interaction of melody with harmony) tended to be inspired by what he had heard certain horn-players do. Especially Miles Davis, with his long lines that include experiment and surprise, contour and form—and intense emotion. (In turn Miles himself, upon Evans' departure from his group, was moved to say: 'I've sure learned a lot from Bill. He plays the piano the way it should be played.')

The scope of 'Everybody Digs' is wide—and again typical of Evans. It includes two fast modern jazz themes, *Minority* by Gigi Gryce and *Oleo,* together with a spirited exploration of Cole Porter's *Night And Day.* There are resurrections of several half-forgotten popular ballads, including *What Is There To Say?,* a particularly good example of the pianist's full sound and magnificent chordal developments. There is an essay in jazz waltz playing, *Tenderly.* and there are two Evans originals:

the 38-second *Epilogue* (which Bill later added to another composition, *Solo—In Memory Of His Father,* circa 1966) and the much longer, quite remarkable *Peace Piece.* The latter has its origins in a piano solo and accompaniment played on Miles Davis' 'Kind Of Blue' LP, but here the concept comes to full fruition. It is basically modal, and unfolds as a series of very beautiful melodic miniatures over a simple rhythmic figure; expressed via an atmosphere which the title suggests. Each of these miniatures (with its supporting harmonies) is complete in itself and the work of a most skilled musical jeweller. However, on closer listening one discovers that in fact they are all related: or rather, that each is inspired by its predecessor, so giving the piece the structure and form of a chain reaction.

LPs: 'SUNDAY NIGHT AT THE VILLAGE VANGUARD' & 'WALTZ FOR DEBBY'

Titles: *Gloria's Step/My Man's Gone Now/Solar/Alice In Wonderland/All Of You/Jade Visions/My Foolish Heart/Waltz For Derby/Detour Ahead/My Romance/Some Other Time/Milestones*
Evans (piano), Scott LaFaro (bass), Paul Motian (drums)
June 25, 1961 New York City Recorded for Riverside

'Everybody Digs' was Bill Evans first solo LP. This later, 'live' session from the Village Vanguard, which produced two LPs, represents a further important aspect of his work.

This is the conscious orchestral development that has gone on from time to time within his trios, especially in the period when Scott LaFaro was the bass-player. It achieved its own *Annus Mirabilis* from late 1960 until mid-1961. Then LaFaro was killed in a car crash. Both albums come from a night only ten before that fatal accident.

One must use the word 'orchestral' guardedly when applying it to a trio. For there are grander connotations which might result in its being misconstrued. But John Lewis has demonstrated with the MJQ how instruments formerly regarded as being of rhythmic value only can become equal partners in a jazz ensemble. Also that an ensemble does not have to be big to be complete; it is simply a question of balance and proportion. The Evans Trio with LaFaro produced evidence of a similar nature.

It grew from regular collaboration and mutual understanding. As Orrin Keepnews, who supervised the session, recalls: 'I was aware of the strong, unusual and richly creative interrelation between them . . . and of the way in which they stimulated, challenged and assisted each other towards the development of an approach they considered far more important and rewarding than the conventional 'lead voice plus two rhythm' of most piano-trio jazz.' From which point they advanced to the stage where everthing they did was ensembled. As Bill was improvising so Scott would be shaping a counter-line, while the drummer kept time, stressed the changes of tempo and delicately filled in gaps. Frequently Scott took over the principal lines of improvisation himself, with Bill or the drums countering. Even theme choruses would be shared: fragmenting and alternating the phrases or—as in *Jade Visions*—making chords jointly.

Naturally all of this required a formidable and imaginative bass-player. (Which Scott certainly was, the most original man on his instrument since Blanton and Mingus.) Also a controlled, thinking drummer in Paul Motian.

Moreover it caused another upheaval within the jazz rhythm section.

In the early days of modern jazz the bass had been the rhythmic pivot, leaving the drums half-free for extra beats, cross-rhythms and a variety of effects. Occasionally a fiercely individual bass-player like Charles Mingus stood out against this and insisted on taking solos. But generally the new drummers hated just a time-keeping role and often dropped out altogether during a bass solo. However, once LaFaro was using the bass almost as flexibly as a guitar, and taking on so much melodically, the responsibility for stated-time was handed right back to the drummer. The latter was still allowed to colour his beat; but mainly he was expected to propel the group and also scale down his level of sound to the needs of the ensemble balance. By the 1970s this quiet revolution had gained ground, resulting in some very intelligent drumming and improved small group teamwork. (Several unsubtle powerhouse drummers went off to nurse their dented egos in the hills.)

After LaFaro Evans found another good bass-player in Eddie Gomez; and occasionally used the mercurial Jack DeJohnette on drums. While just before his own death he was working with another, younger rhythm team: Marc Johnson (bass) and Joe LaBarbera (drums). Two posthumous LPs have been issued by this group on the Musician label which reveal further artistry and a Bill Evans still at the height of his powers.

1987

CHAPTER TWENTY-SEVEN

PHIL WOODS

The Growth Of An Individual

Once upon a time there was a young boy from a good New England family who fell under the spell of the doomed, revolutionary genius of the alto-saxophone, Charlie Parker. Because the boy was quick and intelligent and showed signs of a natural talent his parents encouraged his music studies from an early age. He was the heir to a deceased uncle's alto; later he also acquired a clarinet. And after local teachers had given him a start, he moved from his native Springfield, Massachusetts to New York City where he studied with Lennie Tristano, at the Manhattan School of Music and for four years at Juilliard, where he majored as a clarinettist.

Born in 1931, by his early twenties he was already playing professionally: with Dick Hayman and Charlie Barnet in 1954; also some concerts and recordings with the guiarist Jimmy Raney. But he was under the spell of the great Parker. He felt an absolute conviction that this was the way he should be playing. His adulation even spilled over into his personal affairs. He went to marry Parker's widow and ended up playing Parker's saxophone.

So—he was a very good player and he had Bird's own instrument and he had Bird's musical mannerisms off to perfection. He began to be heard a lot around the East Coast scene, and he thought he was doing well. Until people started to compliment him. They complimented him upon his technique, and on his tone. And then they began to say (sometimes in record reviews) how fantastically like his idol he sounded. *It was truly uncanny!* 'At times you can't tell the difference between the two players,' they said. Whereupon the scales fell from the young man's eyes—and ears. There's only room in jazz for a single Charlie Parker. Like there can never be another Duke, another Louis. Imitations are still by imitators, no matter how good their instrumental ability.

It was from this moment of acute, and no doubt initially painful, realisation that Phil Woods began to develop into the authentic Phil Woods: his own musical man, his identifiable, individual self. It couldn't have been easy, and it didn't happen overnight. But he was determined, hard-working and he let his previously dampened-down imagination come through until it just took over. The result? An ever-increasing acceleration of creative outflow, leading from the basic reassessment to his being in the 1980s the best alto-saxophone soloist around in modern jazz.

187

The first indication that something new and original and exciting was happening in his playing I date from the late 'fifties: the years immediately following his departure from the Dizzy Gillespie big band. There is still much to admire about his occasional choruses on Dizzy's 'World Statesman' and 'Dizzy In Greece' LPs. On *Jessica's Day* and *Night In Tunisia*, for instance, within the overall framework of his solos there occur odd phrases which are brilliant in their concept: standout *tesserae* in the otherwise erratic mosaic of a hectic, ninety-minute, one-and-a-half LP recording session. But of his two main contributions to the date, the brooding ballad (Jerome Kern's) *Yesterdays* and *Groovin' High*, a typical unison-ensemble be-bop quintet setting backed by big band, he still sounds like an adept carbon-copy of the great Yardbird, No—perhaps this is being unkind. There is, in addition, the dynamic elegance of a man who is technically astride all he is doing. But tonally and as regards the phrasing there isn't much original being laid down.

However, the bonus for the alto-player while with Dizzy on tour appears to have been a growing involvement with the band's deputy leader and chief arranger, Quincy Jones.

Over the next few years, in fact until 1961, the two were seldom musically apart for very long, while at times their creative output (together) became quite intense. Woods was a 'key' soloist in Quincy's pick-up groups for recording and then within the ambitions big band which made such a good impression from 1959 onwards, especially in Europe where they toured together on more than one occasion. (It influenced the altoist to spend several years as a French resident on his own behalf.)

There are two albums in particular he made with Jones that I believe herald a whole new improvisational layout to his playing—and obviously his leader must be given some credit for allowing him the necessary freedoms to let it come through. But then, Quincy is noted for his unselfish encouragement of parallel talents.

On the first of these albums, "This Is How I Feel About Jazz" (ABC Paramount) the altoist plays four good solos: on Richard Carpenter's *Walkin'*, the Harold Arlen/Truman Capote song, *A Sleepin' Bee*, Quincy's own *Stockholm Sweetnin'* and again his *Boo's Blues*. What strikes me immediately upon listening to them is that a logical form and organic growth are beginning to be imposed on his improvisations. Also, tonal variety. The consistent Bird-like shrillness of what I'd heard earlier by him has here been replaced by some sharply dramatic contrasts between loud and quiet, but also between deliberate edginess and a rather rounded and mellow sound. His swing is varied too. Before, he always seemed to be pushing hard—early be-bop style—on the first beat of every bar. Now, although there is still this same sense of urgency in places, overall the rhythmic pattern is one of fitting in with the basic grooviness of the arrangement, and if it means laying back in certain bars, then fine, he's in gear to do just that.

Stockholm Sweetin' is deserving of particular praise. Partly because of Quincy's score, which includes an evocative chorus or orchestration for full band based upon Brownie's original improvised solo from the Swedish Metronome session of 1953. But (again) because of Phil Woods' contribution. Instead of—as before on record—darting out brilliantly-conceived, but ultimately butterfly-like ideas in isolation, there is now a definite development from first to last. There is a singing, near-cantabile quality about the way the improvised melodic phrases move over and around the chords. *More importantly though, the phrases adhere.* They sound as if they belong to a correct, well-worked-out sequence of improvised events. Which is, after all, what any good jazz solo should consist of . . .

Anyway—the lines of Phil Woods were becoming more mentally organised affairs. And their initial outflow was more than just promising. It bespoke a stream-of-consciousness playing which would pay the same attention to detail that a writer or painter might spend days correcting to get right. Only jazz of all the art forms can do this. And even then only a select few jazz musicians—the ones we rightly call the jazz masters—are up to it.

On the second LP with Quincy Jones, 'The Birth Of A Band!' (recorded for Mercury), the altoist can be heard in two short, sharp bursts on *Along Came Betty* and *A Change Of Pace,* both arranged by Quincy and both characteristic of Woods' earlier, Parker-dominated style. But on *The Gypsy,* arranged by trombonist Melba Liston, there are again strong signs of the newer Phil Woods moving up into third, if not quite top gear. Particularly in the way he seeks to develop the improvisation as one logical throughway from the first phrase to the last. As a composition *The Gypsy* is far less inspiring a ballad than *Yesterdays,* but his solo takes in what nutrition the chords have to offer and then gives back to us something spectacular. There is some clever play with intervals and also a play on repeats with very subtle differentials. Finally again there is the malleability of tone. He is now letting the ideas and the feeling determine what sounds come out of his instrument. An indication of growling self-confidence about the sound, ideas and feeling.

While still on the subject of Woods in what I've referred to as his Quincy Jones period, a neglected LP is 'Big Brass' issued under trumpeter Benny Bailey's name on Candid. It teams four members of the Jones band, Bailey, Woods, Julius Watkins (French horn) and Les Span (flute and guitar), with a rhythm section comprising Tommy Flanagan, piano, buddy Catlett, bass, and Art Taylor on drums. The scoring is neat, unpretentious, groovy and allows most of the time to the soloists. After Bailey himself, Phil is once more the guy saying some stirring things. On *Alison* by Hale Smith, another ballad, he plays with a stark authority and phrasing and at the same time a grand passion over what is basically a very simple melody line. While on Quincy's *Hard Sock Dance* and Oliver Nelson's *Tipsy* he indulges in lines with quite complicated contours without ever once tripping or failing to resolve an idea. On *Maud's Mood* he also plays bass-clarinet; but the instrument would never become for him a personal obsession as it did with Eric Dolphy.

However, the most dramatic evidence of this, the all-important transitional stage in Phil Woods' development from acolyte to master-musician is, I suggest, contained within the extraordinary 'Thelonious Monk Orchestra At Town Hall' LP of February 28, 1959. Except for the addition of tenorman Charlie Rouse out of Monk's regular Quartet, the selected instrumentation for the concert was the same as Miles Davis' 'Birth Of The Cool' band of 1948/49. With the two variations that Monk's music is even more rewardingly difficult to shine through than the earlier scores by Mulligan, Gil Evans and John Lewis; and that Phil Woods' alto in full, aggressive flight is something far removed from the quiet intellectualism of Lee Konitz. It was hardly a band lacking in solo talent that night. Donald Byrd, trumpet; Eddie Bert, trombone; Pepper Adams, baritone; plus the formidable Thelonious Sphere himself. But Woods' improvisations had everyone leaning forward on their seats—and twenty years or more later still sound the most exciting parts of the album.

Hall Overton arranged the themes for the concert. And the date coincided with what producer Orrin Keepnews has described as 'the dam bursting' in appreciation of Monk's music. He noted at the time: 'I think it was also partly that Monk himself, seeming almost to thrive on public indifference, had been constantly growing as a creative artist until he reached a point where it was literally impossible to ignore him any longer.'

The themes themselves are inherently sophisticated and advanced harmonically, but jaggedly severe from the melodic point of view. Which worried Woods not at all. He leaps into every solo opportunity as if it is the last opportunity he will ever get. But his spirited sallies and the zest of his attack are not those of a wild man just down from the hills. It is quite remarkable how he unscrambles his improvised ideas and makes them fit into continuous lines. With Phil Woods one always has to come back to this question of lines. It was his series of contributions to the highly-demanding album with Monk which persuaded me that he is essentially a melodic player. His grasp of harmonic structure is intuitive, and vivid, but it is the making and continuation (with logical development) of long, very long horizontal lines which has elevated him to the ranks of the jazz masters. His technique? Fantastic! His tone? Marvellously adaptable—including his now accepted 'spitting' notes. But without the melodic content it would all be like the empty rhetoric of our current crop of politicians. Instead of which he keeps us listening—all agog—to how far he can stretch an initial idea and still make it sound interesting.

The contours, too, are very varied. At a certain point they will be involved, ornate, as Gothic as the gargoyles on Notre Dame. Then he'll insert a little bridge phrase: two to four bars at the most—and follow it with a section of elastic, sparsely-noted figures which remind me of the magnificent and deliberate simplicity of Georges Braque or the late cut-outs by Matisse. It might seem odd to be comparing a musician with painters here; but within Phil Woods' lines there is the quality of a man expressing images as automatically right for his materials (the basic themes) as a painter re-interpreting the object of his scrutiny. This is particularly true of Monk's *Friday The 13th*. He kicks off by seeming to run the chord changes as if to demonstrate how fast he can think in harmonic terms. Then suddenly you realise how he is making the changes *work for him* and is, in fact, creating a marvellously melodic solo—at times even pausing to consider what he's just put down before beginning to say it again in an entirely different way!

I'm tempted to write that the Monk LP was his watershed; but perhaps, in view of his previous involvements, *emancipation* is a better description. Certainly from here onwards the altoist has never sounded like anything other than his easily-identifiable self. And that *self* has kept him one of the most active jazz players on the international scene. He must have also remained physically very fit. Once upon a time he was a gaunt, cropped, sharp-suited young man. Now he is more relaxed: longer-haired, heavily moustachioed and favouring plaid jackets and lace-up boots. Otherwise though he continues to jump on jet-planes and keeps up a punishing work-schedule.

To look him up in the Feather /Gitler 'Encyclopaedia Of Jazz' for the 1960s reveals a truly astonishing activity. 'In the Spring of '62 he was a member of the Benny Goodman band that toured the Soviet Union. He was in the band that played *The Lost Continent* with Dizzy Gillespie at the Monterey Jazz Festival in '62. Won the *Down Beat* Critics Poll in 1963 as 'deserving of wider recognition' on clarinet. Busy with recording and TV work in New York, private teaching and a Summer Job as a music director at Ramblerny, a creative arts camp with an extensive jazz department in New Hope, Pennsylvania. As a composer he wrote an extended work, *Rights Of Swing*, recorded in 1960 on Candid. His *Piece For Alto And Piano* and *Three Improvisations* for saxophone quartet were both performed at Town Hall in New York. LPs: "Quintessance" with Q. Jones (on Impulse), "Fantabulous" with Oliver Nelson (Cadet), "Full Nelson" (Verve) and with Joe Morello: "It's About Time" (RCA).'

And in the 1970s: 'Left for Europe, making Paris his home and forming the European Rhythm Machine for clubs, concerts, radio, TV and festivals all over the Continent. In December '72 moved back to

California for ten months, where he led a quarter including pianist Pete Robinson. Returned to East Coast in '73 to live in Philadelphia, playing, writing and teaching. Featured soloist at concerts with Michel Legrand. Played at Montreux, Frankfurt, Molde, Berlin, Paris, Stockholm, Palermo, Nervi, Lisbon, Barcelona, Bologna, Aarhus. Composed ballet for French TV. Also published saxophone method and band arrangements. Polls: Won *Playboy* Musicians' Musician '71; *Down Beat* Critics Poll '70-71; Readers Poll '75. New LPs with own quartet on Muse and Testament. Others with Q. Jones, M. Legrand, Clark Terry.'

On the other hand, the lifelines, no matter how involved or urgent, don't describe the music—only its settings and surrounds. And before leaving the subject of Phil Woods I want to say a few final words on the quality of his *real* lines—the improvised ones.

I've recently been playing quite a lot an album called 'Musique Du Bois' (Muse). It was recorded in New York City in 1974 and, apart from teaming him with a particularly exciting rhythm section (Jaki Byard, piano, Richard Davis, bass and Alan Dawson, drums) from first to last it provides a continuous example of the fertility of his imagination. Having insisted earlier in this piece that Woods is essentially a melody creator (hence his lines' length and flexibility), I must not overlook the source and the sheer volume of spontaneous ideas which have made it all possible. In the even though, in listening to 'Musique Du Bois' it becomes impossible to ignore them.

It doesn't matter how randomly one chooses an individual track: the exotically-paced *Samba Du Bois*; the modal *Willow Weep For Me*, with its antecedents going back to Miles Davis' *All Blues* of 1959; the modern jazz standards *Nefertiti* and *Airegin*; the soundtrack theme, *The Summer Knows*, from 'Summer Of '42'; or, perhaps best of all, a composition the altoist wrote with pianist Gordon Beck, *The Last Page*. The fact remains that the buckets brought up from his private artesian well of the mind are in an inexhaustible chain. Certain jazzmen (Vic Dickenson, for example) do remarkably well with a limited supply of original ideas—which they then vary subtly and present superbly. But with Woods it's a fresh flow of improvisation all along the way. The lines are so extended and still fascinating because there is never a lapse in the thinking; never such a thing as a 'busking' bridge. The line/improvisation (call it what you will) is only ever ended when he judges the other players need to be given their say—or if the performance has gone on long enough anyway. But his own well is merely covered over for the time being when this happens.

Moreover, as on the LP with Monk his lines can cope easily with some terrible obstacle courses and still sound like one melodically continuous thread. (A jazz Theseus? No, better. Woods would not need a score sheet more than once to go into a specific musical labyrinth and take the beat apart!) *The Last Page*, as a good example, has a complicated chord sequence and is also rhythmically complex, not just between ballad-tempo and up, but with shifts from 5/4 to 4/4 time. But its nine minutes of jazz are an unfolding *tour de force* of smooth wonder. Including wondering what will come next but somehow sensing that it's going to be exactly right. Which it invariably is . . .

Hearing *The Last Page* again at several years' remove prompted me to 'phone its co-author Gordon Beck at his Ely retreat. 'With all the hustle and bustle of European festivals and the merry-go-round club circuit, I prefer to live away from the pressures of London,' he explains. Gordon worked with Phil Woods' European Rhythm Machine from 1969 to '72, originally replacing George Gruntz. It was, he adds, the most important breakthrough of his musical career, because it switched him from being a pianist unknown outside the British Isles to being an accepted international traveller. It also coincided with the beginning of his in-depth experiments via the Fender electric piano—greatly encouraged by Woods at the time. 'I found him the ultimate professional,' he says: 'Honest, business-like, but, above all, more dedicated to the further exploration of his instrument's potential than any of the bigger 'name' jazzmen I'd accompanied before that date. He surprised me by the absolute patience of his concern to get things right. He can't accept the possibility of an escape into something second-rate.'

I then read him several sections of what I've written here, but in particular those referring to the apparently effortless flow of ideas which make up the altoist's lines. 'I not only agree with you,' he came back, 'I'd say that's what is almost magical about him. It's inexplicable, really, but it's something he has in common with just a handful of other players—Bill Evans and Herbie Hancock immediately come to mind. He can take either a 'dumb' chord sequence or a truly complicated one and build something great but also easy-sounding over it. Which only goes to prove that you don't have to go on for an hour grunting and squealing through your horn in the quest for something new. What Phil is actually doing is harder, of course—even if he makes it sound easy. But that's the difference between an outstanding musician and those who insist on playing jazz with little or no talent and certainly no real ideas.

'Phil doesn't have to strive to be way out in a ludicrously atonal sense, because he's already ahead of those people.'

1982

CHAPTER TWENTY-EIGHT

CLAUDE BOLLING

Claude Bolling loves to play piano. He no longer needs to. As a composer for films and TV he already owns fame and fortune. But the piano is basically bread and wine to him. And he is now touring the world again at the helm of his Trio: with Pierre-Yves Sorin (bass) and Vincent Cordelette (drums).

At the Barbican Centre on Saturday-night (May 14), he was preceded by a dazzling Didier Lockwood, the violin's heir to Stéphane Grappelli, who in turn was well served by Thierry Eliez, keyboards, Jean-Marc Jeffet, bass-guitar and André Caccerelli on drums.

Both Didier and Claude Bolling appeared under the sponsorship of Eurotunnel ('not long before we hit middle sea') as a part of 'Images De France', a Summer-long celebration at the Barbican of 300 years of French culture embracing the visual arts (painting, photography and Abel Gance's cinematic masterpiece, 'Napoleon'), music and such special events as a complete weekend of Breton folk culture. The music programme varies from a revival of a 300-year-old opera by Marc-Antoine Charpentier ('David & Jonathan') to a celebration of Bizet's birth (a mere 150 years ago), Offenbach's 'Robinson Crusoe', Poulenc's piano music and a recital by the great contemporary flautist, Jean-Pierre Rampal. Plus a single appearance by 74-year-old 'boulevardier'-singer Charles Trenet.

But to return to the initial jazz night.

Ever since his 'Out Of The Blue' album of 1985 with pianist Gordon Beck gained him three gold stars in *Down Beat*, Didier Lockwood has been recognised as a new force in violin jazz, whereas previously he had been known mainly for his electronic work with 'pop' bands (Christian Wader's 1970s neo-romantic rock orchestra and Zao, led by François Cahan). 'Out Of The Blue' represented a major shift of emphasis for him. It was recorded over two days and in one long tape because he 'wanted it to be done in concert conditions to keep the spontaneity of jazz. Synthesisers are great, but—in the long run—the music loses its human quality.'

Didier, now aged thirty-two, still uses an electrified violin, with incorporated multi-tracking. But his overall programme now includes some beautiful classical moments (studying under his father, at sixteen he won first prize at the *conservatoire* in Calais) as well as its guiding umbrella of modern jazz. And his technique and invention, as I've said, are dazzling.

Also dazzling is the acoustic keyboard technique of veteran Claude Bolling. His enthusiasms are undiminished: from his original idol, Earl Hines to Garner, Tatum and Peterson. Note these are all big, two-handed players, which is something very much to Bolling's own taste. He regards the piano as his personal orchestra, to be exploited for its range and flexibility of sound and dynamics over and above its individual notes. His right hand is glittering, his left runs rich and deep. And, not least, he swings like mad. 'La musique de Claude Bolling est à la fois moderne et parodique, efficace et nostalgique.' (*L'Express*)

His programme was more than an hour of pianistic brilliance, except for *Take A Break* (a wire-brush feature by the talented young Vincent Cordelette). It also reflected his personal enjoyments: *Get Happy,* a tribute to Duke Ellington, *I Love You All Madly,* followed by the Duke's own *Sophisticated Lady* and *Dancers In Love,* another tribute, *Ballad To Garner* and not surprisingly the old Hines spectacular, *Boogie-Woogie On The St.-Louis Blues.* Plus Gershwin's *The Man I Love,* his own *Étude In Blue,* some of his film music *(Borsalino)* and finally a fast, and completely fugalised *Just One Of Those Things.*

Actually it was this last solo, and knowing of his strong associations with such classical artists as Pinchas Zukerman, 'cellist Yo-Yo Ma and Jean-Pierre Rampal which set me thinking he came from a fullscale academic background. But not a bit of it. As he told me in an interview before the concert, 'I had a period of lessons as a youngster, but much of what I do on piano has been picked up informally. And it's been the same with my film music. I took some writing lessons with André Hodeir (composer and the author of "Jazz: Its Evolution And Essence": RH). Otherwise though I largely worked out the orchestral parts on my own . . .'

He was born in 1930 at Cannes. His mother came from Bordeaux, but his surname was determined by his grandfather, a Dutchman. He now lives in a cottage at Garches, just west of Paris. When he isn't touring.

He first created a musical stir at the age of fifteen by winning 'Best Piano Player' prize at the annual contests organised by the Hot Club de France. After which his father presented him to the Societé des Auteurs Compositeurs et Editeurs de Musique. He was accepted at their youngest member.

Bach and Mozart became intermingled with jazz inside a growing and increasingly formidable technique. Since when it has been referred to in France as 'jazz-classical crossover' music—with Bolling regarded as its master. Certainly as regards the piano.

At sixteen he formed his own first jazz band, a Dixieland group, and at eighteen cut his first records. But his playing has continued to be eclectic and non-exclusive. As he himself puts it: 'If I'd been born twenty years later, I would surely have been playing some rock music and, in another era, baroque music!'

He went on to compose and write arrangements for many of France's popular singers: an interim stage before his film-work and later classical composing. The films began when director René Clement requested Claude to write and play a small part. Which led on to full-length scores, including the famous 'Borsalino'. Then later collaborations with Marcel Camus, Edouard Molinard, Jean Girault, Herbert Ross, Paul Mazursky and such sound-tracks as 'California Suite' and 'The Awakening'. Together with many TV films. The classical writing would involve pieces for the English Chamber Orchestra. While his 'Suite For Flute' stayed in the record charts for a grand total of 490 weeks . . .

But his piano-stool was never allowed to become the backseat.

A favourite record of mine is the jam session he cut in Paris in 1953 with Lionel Hampton, members of the Hampton band and French tenor-star Alix Combelle: the *Blue Panassié* session. Then in 1956 he formed his big band—a project which was to last for more than twelve years and coincidentally expressed much of his admiration for Duke Ellington (he would also later tour with Ellington). It began as a rehearsal band, but eventually came to include most of the best jazz musicians in Paris, making records and playing some highly successful public engagements. 'All these great players just wanted to be in the band,' Claude recalls. 'They liked the scores and the chance to blow. So we had a ball.'

And he received awards. He is a winner of the Grand Prix du Disque no less than six times. Meanwhile he began to teach at the Rueil-Malmaison Conservatoire and to conduct piano-jazz seminars.

His present Trio has been together for three years and has a fine musical interaction, although naturally spearheaded by the various excitements of the Bolling keyboard. At the end of Didier Lockwood's impressive and revolutionary set, I was left wondering how an older-generation player was going to match it. Halfway through Claude's first number, *Get Happy,* I was left in no doubt. The answer consisted of imagination, technique and a volatile, swinging attack.

Since Grappelli, Django and the early Hot Club days France has made many contributions to international jazz. Claude Bolling belongs with the best of them.

1988

CHAPTER TWENTY-NINE

ORNETTE COLEMAN

Skies Of America

Latterday Ornette Coleman I think of in terms of an astronaut. The kind who spacewalks, but who, although outside the craft, whether feeling free or doing a technical job, still has his air-link to the moving object and, via it, is in firm communication with Planet Earth. It's difficult to image another jazz musician more probing and determinedly revolutionary, but whose personal revolution and freedoms have stayed so determinedly close to *roots.*

He is now a long way from the end of the 1950s and the two albums ('Something Else!' and 'Tomorrow Is The question') within which he broke away from the rigid chord sequences of be-bop and the conventional structures of the 12-bar blues and 32-bar popular song, thus paving the road towards what would be labelled 'free jazz' or 'free-form jazz'. But the essential early ingredients are still there in his playing: those diggings into the soil around the roots of pre-New Orleans, even pre-ragtime music; the fascination for ringshouts and hollers, also the rhythmic bone-beatings of Congo Square; then the escape from fixed tonality as well as chords: leading to an increased 'vocalisation' of instrumental jazz-playing, whereby the song becomes more important than its musical form. All of this remains abundantly present when he solos.

How far he has progressed in other ways though, and especially as a composer, was very fully exposed at the Royal Festival Hall on June 3, '88 when he gave a European premiere of his long 'Skies Of America' backed by his latest group, Prime Time, and the Philharmonia Orchestra under the direction of John Giordano. A thoroughly absorbing work of immense significance, it was in addition the final jazz contribution to the South Bank Centre's *End Games,* a season of late and mature endeavours in various artistic fields. But always in the manner of celebration; not the gloom and doom of Samuel Beckett's famous play.

Ornette was preceded at the concert by the immensely talented, British-born soprano-saxist, Evan Parker, who played an unaccompanied, and, using the technique of 'circular breathing', unpaused solo for twenty-five minutes. It was also unannounced, and therefore unidentifiable.

The programme notes (by John Fordham) referred to 'a fierce, tumultuous and labyrinthine construction', and the solo in question as 'silvery, wriggling, constantly mobile slivers of high-pitched sound jostling with each other over the underpinning of constant drones suggestive of Middle Eastern music.' I found it otherwise. As a reviewer I make it a point of honour never to oppose good musicianship. And especially not musicianship of the high calibre of Evan Parker's. On the other hand, I reserve the right to have my own reservations about *content*.

After the first few dazzling runs I settled back in confident expectation that something truly great was about to unfold. After five minutes though I began to feel decidedly uneasy. The solo was going precisely *nowhere*. After ten minutes my attention began to wander around the stage, looking for an Indian or Arabic basket with a cobra inside. After fifteen minutes I began to do a D. Thatcher, dwelling upon the prospect of an interval gin-and-tonic. A number of the people around me did not weather the full twenty-five.

The point I am making is that a set of notational and tonal and rhythmic exercises do not constitute a public performance. The late John Coltrane, who I believe is one of Evan Parker's main inspirations, also ran a lot of changes and scalar developments and often very fast; but his solos always had a sense of purposeful direction, and of course with the most tremendous dramatic edge. In other words, *they built*.

I look forward to hearing Evan's wonderful skills in another context . . .

In contrast, 'Skies Of America', despite its length (nearly 1 ½ hours) seemed to contain very little waste. Whether one should describe it as a suite is problematical; because it is far more episodic, perhaps *picaresque* even, than the description 'suite' suggests. Again too its actual genesis is interesting. In fact, I am starting to contemplate whether Ornette (b. 1930 at Fort Worth, Texas), apart from his musical talents, has an ongoing preoccupation with the open air; or at least with wide-open spaces, including in this case those going upwards. The word has been put about that when he was younger, and unappreciated, even to the extent of not having any other musicians to play with, he would take his (then) plastic alto-saxophone out into the local desert and blow to the wildlife. Then he had his vital breakthrough—and in a most controversial way, changed modern jazz. Which in turn led not only to worldwide recognition, but, in the light of his new stature, to a number of important writing commissions. As a prophet of the 1960s he was more than prepared to cross the tracks between jazz and classical music, resulting in his string quartet, 'Dedication To Poets And Writers' of 1962 and woodwind quintet, 'Sounds And Forms' of 1965; plus the award of a Guggenheim Fellowship for composition, the first jazz musician to receive one. He was also becoming re-interested in dance and soul music, and in marrying spontaneous ensemble ideas (which he called his 'harmolodic theory') with written symphonic passages.

All of which has managed to find expression in 'Skies Of America', first performed at the Newport Jazz Festival of 1972.

But to return, briefly, to the open air/spatial idea. It's again been put about that during the time he was writing (or still considering) this work, he spent some weeks living amidst a group of American Indians. Which included nights spent lying out under the stars. Which gave him the concept of stars being there to shine upon everywhere and everyone. Which might explain the superb openness of form and feeling 'Skies' has.

For its first performance of 1972 Ornette was leading his then Quartet. For this, latest one at the RFH, his group, Prime Time, has grown into a septet (if you count Ornette himself). He had with him Ken Wessel and Chris Rosenberg, guitars, Al MacDowell and Chris Walker, bass-guitars, Denardo Coleman, a truly dynamic drummer and Badal Roy, who squatted on the floor and played six aligned Indian drums (at least I think they were Indian, because they had the telltale black pitch-spots on the skins). Ornette played one burst of trumpet two-thirds the way through; and one gutsy passage of violin near the end. Otherwise he stayed with the alto-saxophone. But a conventional one. The old, celebrated plastic one appears to have disappeared from the scene.

'Skies' begins with a long symphonic passage where the prevailing influences are Stravinsky (of 'The Rite Of Spring') and Bartok (of the 'Concerto For Orchestra'). and these two hover over the whole of the work's first half (when the orchestra is playing). Later on there are passages of great melodic beauty, where the orchestration is as sparse and open as one finds in Puccini's accompaniments to his operatic arias or in the Debussy setting of Mallarmé's poem, 'L'Après-Midi D'un Faune'. Often here just an oboe suffices to carry the melodic line. At other points though there are *eruptions!* Where the rhythm, carried by Ornette's kit-drummer and percussionist and the orchestra's percussionists, reverts back to the ritualistic primitivism of 'The Rite Of Spring' as well as suggesting the dramatic contrasts of earth and sky, day and night, crisis and peace.

Altogether there are eight basic themes involved, together with additional melodic fragments from earlier Coleman compositions, in total making a musical jigsaw or, if you like, a kaleidoscope but which works wonderfully well.

Against the orchestral opening, Ornette, in a starkly white suit, and Prime Time remained immobile and impassive. But then they too *erupted*, into an earthquake-strength few minutes of free-form jazz where the leader's 'vocalisation' of his alto's potentialities and the shrieking qualities of the most outraged blues singers predominated. From here on he and Prime Time would continue to alternate passages with the orchestra, often over thunderous drumming. Again until two-thirds the way through though—when Ornette surrendered his own solo position to allow each member of the group to improvise in rotation. After this sequence of solos he, his group and the orchestra played largely together, contrasting freedom with scoring, variations against thematic materials and musical contradictions with a triumphant sense of integrated building.

Ornette's music-making is never easy. But that lies in the probing nature of the man himself. His real strength lies in his sincerity, his often naive simplicity and disengagement (in the manner of a Douanier Rousseau), his forceful individualism and, ultimately, his ability to break with convention *and fly,* as a free spirit, as free as air. 'If I'm going to follow a pre-set chord sequence, I may as well write out my whole solo,' he says. But in dispensing with conscious harmony altogether how you replace it becomes of vital importance. 'I began where Charlie Parker stopped,' he continues. 'My melodic approach is based on phrasing, and my phrasing is an extension of how I hear the intervals and pitch of the tune I play. There is no end to pitch. You can play flat in tune and sharp in tune.' And he adds: 'Music is for our feelings. I think jazz should try to express more kinds of feelings than it has up to now.'

So what are we left with? When Ornette is improvising, the melodic phrases have a floating quality—which is why I find them the musical equivalent of taking a walk in space. They are often beautiful, but vary considerably from one another as Ornette seeks to express the minutiae of his own, shifting emotions. To assist with the latter he has pioneered his increased vocalisation of tone: the first jazzman to do so since Bubber Miley and Joe 'Tricky Sam' Nanton within the Ellington band, then Charlie Parker in the early days of be-bop. Eric Dolphy and others are in debt to him for this. Many devices have fallen away like initial-stage rockets from the spacewalker's craft. Pianists because no harmonic support is required. Bar-lines and cadences because his phrases have no predetermined length. Form and structure because his jazz inside 'Skies Of America' is open-ended improvisation in asymmetrical patterns.

However, as I've said, even the spacewalker needs his lifeline and communications channel. Ornette has needed moods, motifs and other launching mechanisms—and for these he has in all sincerity selected from early and pre-jazz roots. Bugle-calls, the New Orleans marching bands, funeral laments, the outcry without the form of the blues, gospel-singing, even the African-derived hollers: all these are echoed at different points in his music, but as new sources of inspiration. Meanwhile, in his written parts he has called upon European sources as well as American.

I regard 'Skies Of America' as the most major achievement of his career.

1988

CHAPTER THIRTY

EDDIE JONES

Bass, Basie And Business

When some years ago I wrote a biography of Count Basie and his orchestra, Eddie Jones naturally had a place in it. He had joined the band in August, 1953 and remained its bass-player until 1962 when he needed an operation for varicose veins. He was heard on all the big recordings of those years, 'A Count Basie Dance Session', 'The Atomic Mr Basie' and especially the 'One More Time' album of 1958/59. This last was composed and arranged by Quincy Jones and includes an Eddie Jones feature: *The Big Walk,* with the microphone wide open on his strings as he takes on a biting brass section but still comes out on top. His huge tone, swing and accurate fingering are ideally demonstrated here.

I talked with Eddie at the Nice Jazz Festival of 1985. He has been a regular at the festival for the past several years, appearing with a variety of frontline soloists from Clark Terry and Al Grey to the Texas Tenors (Illinois Jacquet, Arnett Cobb and Buddy Tate). Also with blues singers, most notably in '84 the formidable Linda Hopkins. I was particularly interested in his work away from Basie, which has been less carefully documented. When I made this point, he immediately suggested meeting up on the beach a couple of mornings later. With a cold beer for me and a cigar for him.

Eddie was born in New York City on March 1, 1929. Not so well-known is that he grew up in Red Bank, New Jersey: actually only two doors away from the Basie family's house there. But it wasn't until he joined the band that the Count realised this fine musician was the same kid who'd once played around the trees outside his earlier home.

Eddie's own family stayed poor during his youth. His father was a chauffeur, and found it difficult to make a decent living. His mother taught school and was very knowledgeable about black history. 'They both struggled hard. And everything they did was for us kids. Which in turn caused us to respond, studying hard, always straining to do our best. My sister qualified as a teacher at University level. My brother later became a manager at IBM.'

His mother in particular encouraged his interest in music alongside his other studies. This involved piano and singing lessons for seven years; then in turn trombone, tuba and euphonium. For one year he became a member of the New Jersey All-State Concert Band, sang with choirs, played for local dances. The switch to double-bass occurred as he

201

attended senior high school—his mother somehow finding the money to buy a good second-hand one.

Meanwhile, as a student, generally it looked as if his future career would be in Science. 'I didn't get a scholarship. But then I worked hard and always got good grades.' Which led on to his gaining a place at Washington University, over these years and probably still today the best black college in the States. 'It meant more sacrifices at home, but my mother considered it necessary I go. So it became a question of studying hard and doing all sorts of other jobs to get extra money for lodging, books, etc. Two summers I worked for the railroad, helping out at the level-crossings—they didn't have automatic gates then. Other summers I played in Atlantic City with a band led by Pee Wee Thomas. Also I remember gigs with Mercer Ellington, Rodney Richards too, and once Erroll Garner.'

Back in Washington he got to know fellow-students and future Basieites Frank Wess on alto and flute and Bill Hughes' trombone. Also he spent two weeks playing opposite Sarah Vaughan. Her backing trio then consisted of Jimmy Jones on piano, Joe Benjamin (bass) and Roy Haynes (drums).

However, it still didn't look as if he'd make music his career, and this seemed to be confirmed when in 1951 he went to teach in Beauford, South Carolina and for a year played scarcely any jazz. 'I taught Music as well as Science, but mostly had to concern myself with the school band and orchestra. This was at the Robert Small High School, Beauford. Smokin' Joe Frazier went there. It was a fantastic idea—all this water and swamp and islands linked up by narrow causeways or bridges. They shot a Jon Voight movie there. The locals spoke a patois and it was as hot as the devil. Really sticky heat.'

After his year was up he returned to Washington D.C. He worked for the Post Office by day and played jazz bass and sang with a trio every night. 'Remember this was before the Social Revolution in the States. There was high unemployment with black people and the Post Office was the only job I could get. Bill Hughes worked there for even longer.

'Then one day Frank Wess 'phoned and said to call Count Basie. He'd obviously put in a strong recommendation for me. So I talked things over with the great man, and then he sent me a ticket. Two weeks later I was playing with the band in Arizona.'

At this point I asked Eddie about his other influences among bass-players. 'Walter Page was definitely the first inspiration as regards jazz bass. He'd been with Basie from the very beginning, and he had that big sound and steady swing within the rhythm section. The bass with Basie was just one instrument, but within his style all parts of the rhythm section were equally important. And the swing and the phrasing were so fine that if you made even the smallest mistake every head would turn.

'Yes, among the more modern bass-players I do have a high regard for Richard Davis. But when you ask me about an all-time favourite on the instrument then it's Ray Brown, Ray Brown, Ray Brown . . .'

Basie's ability to estimate very quickly a man's potential had not gone amiss. Eddie Jones was both a good player and he suited the band's kind of music. As Ernie Wilkins, one of the principal arrangers, wrote to me in 1957: 'He was an eager, but inexperienced kid when he joined us, but he's improved so much so quickly that he's now one of the best bass-players in the business.'

Eddie says: 'When I started with Basie you couldn't call me a professional really. But these guys helped to turn me into one—almost overnight! Freddie Green on guitar was always there, of course, and Gus Johnson was the drummer, an impeccable musician with such a sure swing. Later we had Sonny Payne on drums. He had the flash, the big-occasion solos. But that's show-business and we were in it. Joe Williams brought the same kind of thing into the band. He wasn't just a good singer; he had a commanding presence and he knew how to handle audiences. Anyway, going with Basie became responsible for whatever I am in music.'

He is an impressive figure who enjoys his food as much as his music, and at times appears to cuddle the bass as if holding a pampered child. But this appearance is deceptive. Although he makes playing the instrument look easy, he combines a facile touch with a tremendous drive. While he was working with Basie, he used to swing with Freddie Green as if they had been together for many more years.

Also during his Basie years he made a number of small-group recordings away from the band. Most notably with Joe Newman for Vanguard, with drummer Osie Johnson for Period, the 'Jazz Studio One' album on Decca and one with Kenny Clarke for Savoy (in a group including Henry Coker, Frank Wess and Charlie Fowlkes from the Basie band). On another Savoy LP with the Hank Jones Quintet (Donald Byrd on trumpet) he can be heard soloing during a long jam session track called *An Evening At Poppa Joe's*.

But the endless touring and standing to play aggravated his leg veins until by 1962 he had to drop out and undergo an operation. Which in turn caused him to rethink his future. He wanted to go on enjoying his music and at the same time develop a separate business career.

'After leaving Basie I had a residency in Las Vegas. Tough. Then following the op I tried for other jobs. Some still wouldn't hire blacks. Until my brother told me to go to IBM, where I began to train as a systems engineer. After that I went over to the selling side. In all I stayed with IBM in NYC for nine years.

'I didn't stop playing though. Somehow I never had a weekend without music. And at the same time we were having the Social Revolution in the States. Martin Luther King and others were making it easier for blacks to progress within the big corporations. I got really immersed in data processing. At first it was a struggle. The first two months were a bitch. And meanwhile IBM was changing from its own fight for survival into a billion dollar company. Like from five million to thirty-five million! We sat on the crest of a wave and just went with it. Now people can't do without computers.'

Meanwhile the weekends of music were immensely varied. 'I played trios, duos, even solo. Weddings and other client music, I found, paid better than clubs. But I did work at one very hip club, The Tenement. Herbie Hancock was in the room upstairs. Also I played Gilbert & Sullivan, Brahms, Betthoven. I joined the Village Light Opera and still do a couple of things with them each year.

'Then I decided to try and become a millionaire. I went with Jim Ling of LTV, who had one of the biggest defence contracts in the US. For 'planes, data processing, computer technology generally. I got to be Director of Operations. Until recession when the money ran out. Following which I became VP of Systems with Apex Computer Services. A grand title but it didn't make me a millionaire!

'Never mind. I'm happy in my present job. I'm Director of Operations and a VP with Commercial General (CIGNA) of Hartford, Connecticut. It's mainly insurance in a very big way, but I'm still on the computer side—with responsibility for three hundred people.

'In the interim I'd often played with Thad Jones and Mel Lewis at the Village Vanguard. But what I mainly do now is devote my entire month's holiday to playing at the various summer jazz festivals. This year, for instance, I've appeared at The Hague, at Molde in Norway, and I'm going to Japan with the Texas Tenors. George Wein has booked me five times for the Nice Grande Parade du Jazz. Working with lots of different players: Clark Terry, Buddy Tate, The Count's Men, Doc Cheatham. It all makes for a real fun vacation.

Other seasons he has his own group every Saturday night at a supper club in Hartford. 'They're not well-known players, but I find them really stimulating to play with. Don De Palma, piano, Matt Ericsson, vibes, and a terrific drummer, Larry Denatale. His wife sings with us too. We feature mainstream and bebop. And we've got our own special sound. But that's what jazz is all about. You get where you are because you're different. You work hard and get out of the music what you put into it. It's always been the same, whether you're called Count Basie or are just starting out.'

I noticed his cigar had become a mere stub. And I was feeling thirsty again. However, there was one final question I wanted to put to him. Which concerned the actual bass he plays—a magnificent instrument by any standards. He smiled. 'Yes, it once belonged to my teacher at college. He was a Hungarian called Desno Namethe Borath and he played 'cello and bass with the Cleveland Symphony Orchestra. It's a great bass to play. It's my fingers on the strings, but the sound is its own answer.'

1987

CHAPTER THIRTY-ONE

GARY BURTON

In a recent radio interview (I won't say who the interviewer was) I was suddenly put on the spot by being asked which, in my opinion, are Gary Burton's best recordings. Being a broadcaster since the 1950s, it was one of the only two occasions when I nearly 'dried'. (The other was years before, in St. Ives, when I was taken to meet the poet W. S. 'Sidney' Graham to discuss his book, 'The Nightfishing'. He was in hospital, doing his own kind of 'drying'. He grasped my hand, and said, *Hello, Raymond—have you had any good orgasms lately?*) But in Burton's case there are many riches. I got out of it by saying I'd enjoyed all of his work I'd heard. Which was true. But I left the studio with a small sense of resentment. Which in turn set me thinking. Which are my favourite recordings by this so gifted jazz artist? Aside from the experiences when I've heard him under 'live' conditions.

I decided they go all the way back to when I first heard him, on a Stan Getz/João Gilberto album, recorded in concert at Carnegie Hall on October 9, 1964 . . .

Gary Burton is the third important vibraphone, or vibraharp, musician to come into jazz history (the fourth, if one counts the early pioneering work of Red Norvo), and on the evidence so far the most sophisticated player of the instrument. Lionel Hampton, behind his leaping-about kind of showmanship, combines sound technique with great drive. While Milt Jackson has demonstrated an all-round musicality both inside and outside the Modern Jazz Quartet. But Burton has successfully carried his qualities of playing into whole new areas that jazz had not ventured into before. 'More than ever, the modern musician is aware of the relationships between different kinds of music. Experimenting with mixtures of music is just one of the effects that modern technology, communication and cultural exchange have had on art forms.' (Burton)

He was born in Anderson, Indiana in 1943 and started playing at the age of six, but only piano. Which he later took lessons on at high school, then some formal studies in music theory and composition. But in his later gravitation to the vibes he was entirely self-taught, and a natural, revolutionary force. He made his professional debut in Nashville, Tennessee in 1960. Then took a group of his own to South America in 1962. But his first big break came in 1963 when he joined pianist George Shearing, whose quintets have had a tradition of featuring vibes going back to 1949 with margie Hyams and his first 'hit' record,

September In The Rain. Burton stayed with George for a year, then joined
Stan Getz and stayed with him until 1966. As well as Carnegie Hall
he also played at the White House and on the soundtracks of two films:
'The Hanged Man' and 'Get Yourself A College Girl'. Meanwhile, in
1964 George Shearing had recorded an album, 'Out Of The Woods',
based entirely on Burton themes.

But probably the best introduction to Gary's work would still be
two or three of the numbers he recorded with Getz: *Grandfather's Waltz,*
Duke Ellington's *Tonight I Shall Sleep* and *Stan's Blues.* On these he plays
with a smaller sound than his gifted predecessors, but also with a more
oblique harmonic sense. Even when just playing chords behind the Getz
tenor his choice of them is apt to be surprising. Otherwise too he seems
already well-endowed with a jazzman's basic swing and improvising
abilities.

However, when I frist heard him 'live' (at Ronnie Scott's, London)
in the later 1960s he was experimenting a good deal with time. And
his technique had progressed to a point where, when he used four
mallets, not only were the chords freshly adventurous, but with the
two inner mallets he was setting up cross-rhythmic effects. On a second
visit he was borrowing extensively from the current 'pop' idiom, then
reshaping and building up these comparatively simple sources into viable
materials for the jazz soloist. Also by this date he had gone back to
Nashville to make the impressive 'Tennessee Firebird' LP, the first real
attempt by jazz and Country-and-Western musicians to explore their
respective fields together.

Asked about personal influences, he named the pianist Bill Evans,
for interior harmonisation, rather than any other vibes-player. (In fact,
he has been sharply critical of a number of his contemporaries on the
instrument.)

In 1967 he formed his own Quartet with Larry Coryell, guitar, Steve
Swallow, bass, and Bobby Moses, drums. And made his first
overwhelmingly satisfactory jazz album: 'Lofty Fake Anagram'.
Listening to it again, and to such Burton originals as *June 15, 1967, Lines,
The Beach* and *Good Citizen Swallow,* what I find truly remarkable is the
way it progresses on collective lines, via what I can only describe as
'ensembled freedoms'. The interest in other musical soils and cultures
is still present, while the solos by Gary and guitarist Larry Coryell are
often astonishing in what they venture to suggest. Clearly, the album
is also telling us there is much more to come from Burton yet. And
in whatever form it should be intensely stimulating. Because, apart from
his purely musical abilities we can trust his flair and integrity . . .

Bobby Moses would remain with him over years, and the gifted bass-
player Steve Swallow has been with him almost permanently ever since.
But Gary himself has often opted to take time off to work as an educator.
Notably as a staff-member at the Berklee School of Music, but also as

a peripatetic teacher at many universities across the United States. He has a compulsion within him to encourage the upcoming talents of the young. So his solo concerts and other public appearances tend to be in and around the college curriculum. Wherein he frequently presents his Quartet in a lecture, seminar, 'live' concert format. In addition to writing books of instruction: 'Jazz Vibes', 'Solo Book' and 'Four-Mallet Studies'.

Nevertheless, he somehow manages to tour the world. Japan, Australia, England (many times, where apart from liking it, he also likes working with Gordon Beck) and the East European countries, including Russia. And, of course, he continues to record. Sometimes with other name-artists: Stéphane Grappelli, Chick Corea, Keith Jarrett and Carla Bley. Mostly though still under his own name.

He won a Grammy award for his very fine solo album, 'Alone At Last' on Atlantic. But for me, and standing by my original point that I've liked everything by him I've heard, three records rise above even his own high standards.

First, 'In The Public Interest' recorded in 1973 in New York and issued by Polydor. Gary Burton had first met the Rhodesian-born, now London-based composer/arranger Mike Gibbs in 1960 at the Berklee School, and quickly established a musical affinity. Gibbs then wrote a number of themes for the Burton Quartet, including *Family Joy, Oh Boy,* which reappears in a big band orchestration on this particular album. For this was the first time Burton had appeared on record with so large a group. A trumpets, trombones and saxophones band, but with the additions of two bass-trombones, tuba, 'cello, guitar, percussion as well as drums, and Steve Swallow playing bass-guitar.

There is an architectural quality about the style of Gibbs' big band writing. Not that it isn't fluid and doesn't swing, but he does seem to create ensembles like buildings; which the will-o'-the-wisp Burton then either enters or weaves his way around. The only other featured soloists are Mike Brecker, tenor-saxophone, and Steve Swallow. Gibbs has used one or two of his earlier composed pieces and gone to an enlargement of orchestration with them. For instance, *Four Or Less,* No. 4 in a set of pieces written for a Canterbury Cathedral concert in 1970. It had gone into the repertoire of the Burton Quartet, simply because Gary liked playing it. Here it is done with the full band, but with, apart from Gary's vibes, a strong 'cello melodic line. *Dance: Blue* are two pieces originally written for Graham Jones' ballet 'Totems'. Gary acts the part of the dancer (or perhaps magician of his instrument) against the lean, magnificent backdrop of the ensemble.

Mike Gibbs says of *To Lady Mac(beth): In Memory,* which opens Side Two: 'who caused me such hardship in my schooldays, and which memory I recalled in writing some music for the Shakespeare birthday celebrations at Soutwark Cathedral in '73.' He doesn't elaborate on what the hardships were. (I realise, I was damn lucky at college. I got 'Julius Caesar' in the fourth form; it was then selected as the matriculation play, which gave me two full years on it and eased the examination problems considerably!) Gibbs portrait of *Lady Mac,* with Burton's vibes very resonant, is appropriately chilling—and totally different from Duke Ellington's (in 'Such Sweet Thunder'), who believed she 'had a little ragtime in her soul'. But after the exuberant *Family Joy, Oh Boy,* and the peaceful/turbulent collision of *In The Public Interest,* he returns, as the finale to his writing, to *Lady Mac: In Sympathy,* a more tender sighting of the same lady's problems and which allows Gary to exploit his own lyricism.

Of the album overall, Burton himself wrote: 'I feel that the ideal for us is the opportunity for the player to feel as if he is part–composer, and for the writer to be an improviser with the orchestra. With the openness of Mike's unique orchestration techniques there is room for all of this and more. For me as a soloist, this collection of music has been the best opportunity I've ever had to strive for the ultimate. That's the best you can have it.'

He should have added a cautionary 'so far'. But then he didn't know that he would be playing a recorded concert with Chick Corea at Zürich, Switzerland in October, 1979 . . .

My other two choices were both recorded and issued by ECM of Munich.

'Works' is a limited–edition record consisting of various tracks made between 1972 and 1975 and in a wide variety of places: Fayville, Massachusettes, Oslo, Ludwigsburg and Hamburg. Naturally, therefore, the personnels alter too. Including not only Steve Swallow and Bobby Moses, but sometimes Pat Metheny or Mike Goodrick on guitar, Ralph Towner on classical guitar and Chick Corea, piano. Sometimes it is a six–piece group, often just a duo (*Matchbook* with Towner, *Chelsea Bells* and *Domino Biscuit* with Swallow) and on one track, contrarily called *Brotherhood,* Gary plays alone.

But, despite the disparity of sources, what I get from this particular disc is a series of windows opening inwards, with consequent glimpses on the musical core of the man. The tracks have been skilfully collated from other records in such a way that they offer the most interior, introspective side of GB I've yet heard. And they prove that, with all his phenomenal vibes technique, and his swing, he is at the same time one of the most cerebral of jazz musicians, whose developed physical manifestations are channels for a hyperactive imagination. He uses as his basic palette a lot of different themes: Carla Bley's *Olhos De Gato* and *Vox Humana,* Mike Gibbs' *Tunnel Of Love* and *Three* (the latter accompanied by the NDR-Symphony Orchestra of Hamburg, with Gibbs conducting), Chick Corea's *Desert Air* and Keith Jarrett's *Coral.* (Steve Swallow wrote *Chelsea Bells* and *Domino Biscuit.*) But he then, like a master-painter, mixes everything on the palette, so that what comes out, in the end, in musical terms, is the equivalent of a long thought-out, structural landscape by Cézanne. It is an album of mental glory . . .

My final selection is an accidental masterpiece. Accidental, because no musical artist going into a concert can possibly predict that he will be giving one of the greatest of his life, or then be fortunate enough to have it recorded.

Burton had recorded with Chick Corea before, of course. The Oslo album of 1972 from which *Desert Air* came. The album was called 'Crystal Silence', and *Crystal Silence* is the 'key' track on this, the last of my choices, which is a double-album. I repeat though: there can be few 'live' concerts which have reached such a high level of creativity as the Zürich one of 1979 does—*and been caught!*

Corea slightly predominates early on, with his composition *Senor Mouse* and then the tribute solo, *Bud Powell* (although there is a fast and dazzling duet between them in the course of the former, with Burton's four-mallet technique almost beyond the normal listening ears). *Bud Powell* is pure be-bop, as its name implies; and Gary lays back here, except for playing 'unison ensemble' style during the thematic statements and a brief, agile solo which follows. But through the twelve-minute *Crystal Silence,* which opens Side Two, he plays with genius (and I do not use the word lightly). The most inspired and beautiful vibraphone-playing I have ever heard. Complex, deeply thinking, using the far-frontier resonances of the instrument as well as the struck notes, his improvised ideas come out, not just like crystal, but individually dropped musical diamonds: each phrase cut with many facets. Corea solos first, then paces Burton's solo—which again troubles the time-signatures. Moving, even of the spirit, I think Burton plays the *ultimate* in vibes sensitivity within the context of his balladic approach. And I go back to this solo a lot. Partly with admiration for its sheer musicality; but also because at difficult or dangerous times in my own life, I find it calms the agitations of the soul. Which in turn is a reminder of something Paul Tortelier once said to me: 'Music is, after all, not just serenity or excitement, but a service to humanity as well.'

1988

CHAPTER THIRTY-TWO

GORDON BECK

An Interview

The British Isles, coming later to jazz music, have since produced a remarkably good crop of gifted and original piano-players. But all too often this has meant that they, the pianists, have had to exile their talents in order to gain a truer form of recognition. George Shearing, a boy accordionist grown into a mature keyboard stylist, emigrated to the United States soon after World War II—and promptly topped even the 'pop' charts with his otherwise all-American quintet recording of *September In The Rain.* In the next decade other British pianists followed him across the Atlantic: Ralph Sharon, Ronnie Ball, Derek Smith and the late Dill Jones.

Came the 1960s and the new, innovative keyboard sounds were being made by Stan Tracey. I remember being a record producer with the Ted Heath band when he replaced Frank Horrox as its pianist, doubling on vibes. Eyebrows were raised, because here was a stylist directly influenced by Thelonious Monk at a time when Monk himself was only just beginning to gain public acceptance after a long struggle. However, sanity fortunately prevailed and Stan Traccy did win his case, not merely over the right to pay sincere homage to Thelonious, but also to bring through his own individuality with vehicles as different as the 'Under Milk Wood' suite and later the fine octet which toured with Gil Evans in February, 1978. Moreover he proved his case while remaining British-based. And this has been the trend ever since. Eddie Thompson went to the States, but returned. Other, all-season players (I am thinking in particular of Brian Lemon and Tony Lee) have proven especially adept at working with visiting American soloists. Plus, from the 1970s on we have had the three outstanding Johns: Taylor, Horler and Pearce, all of whom work in or outwards from London.

The situation with Gordon Beck is different again though. Not just because he stands somewhat apart from the others in his individuality as a jazz pianist but because he is British-based (albeit far from the rat-race at Ely) and yet has gained greater recognition abroad—in the U.S.A. and Europe—than in his own country. In fact, in the States, subsequent to his tours and recordings with Phil Woods, Helen Merrill *et al,* he is regarded (with justification, in my opinion) as the most important British jazz pianist since Shearing who, ironically, and although now so different, in style at least, was Gordon's first inspiration. As if to compound this internationalised stature his recording contract over the past several years has been with a French company. While, when I visited the Nîmes Festival in 1985, I found that his name on the posters outside the Roman arena there had been given the same-size billing as Miles Davis, the Count Basie Orchestra and even Ray Charles. On the other hand, where music is concerned sight cannot compete with the human ear. And so I prefer to fall back upon a tape dating from August 26, 1971 which he made at Château Vallon; with Gerry Mulligan, Ron Mattewson on bass and Daniel Humair, drums.

It happens to be a bootleg tape, but no less revealing for being so. Within other writings about Mulligan I have pointed out his being one of the most ubiquitous of jazzmen. Truly a musician for all of the seasons. At the same time though I can personally testify to how fastidious he is about his accompanying rhythm sections. He simply cannot be fooled. Therefore, what I find so significant about these Château Vallon tracks (*There Will Never Be Another You, The Shadow Of Your Smile, Line For Lyons, Get Out Of Town* and *Major Minor*) is the way the baritone-saxist, one of the great jazz masters, treats his piano colleague as an equal. Not just in the allocated solo spaces, but in the mutual respect and shared excitements which clearly come across when listening to their performances. It confirms my own persuasion that GB has been one of our finest jazz exports over a longish period.

But now, having made this, what might seem an extravagant claim on behalf of his playing, I must do my best to say *why*.

Well, for one thing there is the sheer scope and daring of his inventions. Obviously other pianists also possess a considerable amount of technique, plus the ability to swing and to project their improvised ideas. But in addition, and within the bounds of a style I've grown to know well, he never fails to come up with something in the improvisation which surprises me. Having once worked as his record producer, and heard him on countless different occasions, I can say that I've never once heard him put in a *cliché* or a phrase purely to be smart.

A complementary reason for throwing so many roses around his work is that I find him among the most orchestral of piano soloists. Not floridly so in the Oscar Peterson manner, but exploring every possible potentiality the instrument has to offer him. All the dynamics, the sounds, reverberation, use of pedals, the whole bit. In this respect, even at his most probing (and/or provacative) he stays firmly in the main tradition of jazz piano. Because it links him right back to Earl Hines. And in between to Tatum and more recently Bill Evans, Herbie Hancock and Keith Jarrett. It also makes for particularly satisfying listening. To be able to enjoy the full as well as the lean . . .

Like Shearing, he was born in Battersea, on September 16, 1938 (not, as the Feather/Gitler 'Encyclopedia Of Jazz In The Seventies' states, 1936) and, between the ages of fourteen and sixteen, undertook three years of very concentrated formal piano studies. But, as he explains, 'Over this period I came almost to hate music. Largely because of the regimented practising. I grew up mostly in South Harrow and I'd be stuck at the keyboard while my friends were all out enjoying themselves. I'd known little about the classics before this and not much more about popular music or jazz. I do remember picking up a smattering of boogie-woogie and being hauled up to play it in front of my class at grammar school. But although the music came easily to me, I'm afraid the constant need to practise had turned it into a near-total bore.'

RH: Was there then one single event which changed your attitude, as it were a 'striking down' of Gordon Beck like Saul/Paul on the road to Damascus?

'There was, yes. After leaving grammar school, at seventeen I began an engineering apprenticeship and started to enjoy music again over the radio. Then I heard, and was bowled over by, George Shearing. His early quintets. I could only half-understand it, of course. And I still had no thoughts of ever becoming a professional musician. Yet I recognised this had something a lot different going for it, and at last my curiosity about jazz was genuinely aroused. In classical studies I'd got to 7th grade of an LRAM in a very short time . . . without being excited in quite the same way.'

RH: Even so, I always hear in your matured playing a classical gradation of touch.

'Yes. Also, in retrospect I no longer put down those early years of training. I'm much more aware of them now than I ever could be at the time. Influences can go underground inside you and then re-surface when the moment is right. Another thing, relevant to touch. It was one of the first qualities I came to admire about Bill Evans. Naturally I marvel at *all* his great qualities. But touch is a vital ingedient of his intensely individual style. Much later, when I got on to the international circuit myself, and our paths crossed, it was one of the elements in piano-playing we most frequently discussed.'

RH: Again, you make much use of the instrument's physical features, the pedals, resonances and so on.

'Another aspect of the classical legacy, I believe. Mind you, we're only talking about the acoustic piano here, not the various electrified keyboards. And moreover much depends on your getting a high standard instrument to actually play. Some of the ones you have to put up with on tour or in certain clubs don't really allow you any scope for a full exploitation of what should be there.'

RH: In writing about any jazz musician, I'm convinced, it's important to get at those aspects of a man which lie behind, but relate to, his playing. I'd hazard a guess, therefore, that you were also good at mathematics while at school. Which in turn affected the next part of your career.

'Certainly maths were important to my apprenticeship. In fact, you see, I was training to become a design draughtsman—with the further aim of going into the aircraft industry.'

RH: With as a sideline the beginnings of your longstanding fascination with cars! (*GB is not a frustrated Grand Prix driver. His passion lies in acquiring and then rebuilding cars, both their engines and the bodywork. He has owned many vehicles over the years, but the one he would never part with is 'Beige Bird', a 1965 3.4 litre Mk 2 Jaguar. Hence the inspiration for his composition* The Beige Bird Beckons *on the French Connection 1 LP.*) 'Yes again. It has gone on ever since I had my first car at seventeen—and not even legally entitled to drive it. That was a 1935, straight-eight, side-valve Packard. The Al Capone car. I just wish to God I had that car now. It was a fantastic experience. Not for speed, but for the controlled, pent-up power.'

RH: I find a definite connection here with your keyboard-playing. Because much as I've enjoyed your ballad performances, the tone, touch, delicacy and so on, I know how much you really love to fly when you're improvising.

'I agree there is a connection. Which in turn links up with another ambition, probably never to be realised, that I have my own Tiger Moth or some such 'plane. I did begin to take flying lessons, but had to abandon them when I joined Phil Woods. Where it connects with the piano, and jazz improvisation, is in going for the challenge of the unknown, reaching out for something without being fully aware of what the outcome might be. The high-flying aspect you speak of reminds me of forming that first Trio in the 'sixties (*leading up to the 'Experiments With Pops' LP: RH*) and finding in Tony Oxley, who at the time I regarded as *the* drummer, who played *the drums,* an ideal stablemate. Likewise Jeff Clyne on bass. The music we were aiming for encompassed the already-established structured jazz, the composition, rhythm and so on, with an attempt to cross the barrier and greet some other people who were into unstructured playing, Trevor Watts, Evan Parker and a few others who I think called what they did European Contemporary Improvised Music. The interest for us, the Trio, at that time was to attempt the bridge, to win the excitements of the new probing without losing sight and sound of the roots we were brought up on.

'But to conclude on the car business, or if you like, those design thrusts of my nature, they act as a therapy too. I only truly enjoy driving at night now. Most other people have to go to bed sometime, so where I live the roads belong to myself then. But working on and rebuilding a car can be a great release, of energy, the desire for coming close to perfection. Again, for a long time I've believed that music is a part of life, rather than the other way round. And I've witnessed a number of fellow-musicians desperately come to grief through having no foil in their lives, no other release.'

RH: Can I now draw you back to the chronology? Your work in the aircraft industry took you to Canada.

'Which geographically drew me a lot closer to jazz music. I spent two and half years in Canada, in Toronto, beginning in 1960. Within a fortnight I ran slap into a mountain called Oscar Peterson at a club called The Brown Derby. And I met lots more local musicians at the famous George's Spaghetti House—which, incidentally, is still going strong. Kenny Wheeler went over and played there recently. Anyway, from this point on I began to do some playing. I was 21 and it was pretty abysmal. But everyone has to start somewhere.'

RH: And did you head right away towards a modern be-bop style? The purpose of asking this is because I also know you as a fine blues player, with all the earthier elements there.

'No, it didn't happen that way. I came back to England to get married. It didn't last, but that's another story. So I began to gig in a semi-pro way, at a little place called the Club Octave: but playing in the old, apprentice-days style. And that was where I first bumped into Pete King. Something happened then. I was trying to live an almost impossible life. I was married, trying to work with an engineering development company, going to Pete King's house at Tolworth, not getting home until four or five in the morning, then going off to work again. Absolutely impossible. But I can honestly say this. Being in physical contact with Pete, playing with him, actually unlocked the door for me to what this music is all about. His was the door leading to Charlie Parker, Dizzy Gillespie, Bud Powell, all the modern jazz pioneers, and through knowing him, I don't claim *consciously* to begin with, but I do now in retrospect, the engineering job, the other distractions, well, they just went out of the window. By 1963 I was a full-time musician and playing the new jazz.'

RH: What were your first professional jobs?

'The first professional job was a dream. It was with Tony Crombie, at the Metropole Hôtel in Monte Carlo. At that time Tony had a contract with the Danziger Brothers, the film producers, and they made a series called 'The Man From Interpol'. Tony wanted a holiday, so they made him work for it by playing three hours every evening to the diners of Monaco. I didn't mind. It was two months with the season going at full pace. And then Don Byas came down from Copenhagen to play at a club just below the Metropole. My first chance to sit in with an American 'star' musician. And what a musician! Some teacher too. I remember him telling me: always play the diminished chord before the minor seventh. It took me some while for this lesson to sink in, but I got there in the end. Don was a master jazzman, he knew how the notes ran, and now, when I teach in Summer schools it's one of the things I always pass on to students who want to play our kind of music.'

RH: Moving on in time now. In fact, to 1967. We first met due to my having been commissioned to produce a piano album called 'Doctor Doolittle Loves Jazz', based on the Bricusse film themes. I discussed the project with Laurie Holloway, and he said I ought to hear you before making the final choice of player. Which was how the LP came about—with yourself, Kenny Baldock on bass and Jackie Dougan, drums. Plus all your arrangements.

'Oh, yes, of course. That was a very good period. I mean, I had commercial work. I was MD for Susan Maugham and others. But with plenty of time for jazz. Also my name was becoming known in the studio world, which underpinned the financial side. Question most of the guys who were around then and they'll tell you that the 'sixties was one of the very best decades to be playing.'

RH: But with 'Doctor Doolittle' you had to convert some highly unlikely material into a jazz format.

'It was a good challenge. With 'Doolittle' and the follow-up album, 'Half A Sixpence', I think we managed to stay a little less contrived than say, the André Previn 'My Fair Lady' or Billy Taylor's 'My Fair Lady' which I heard somewhere later. I don't claim that our albums were or are better, simply that they contain a few more surprises—which really came about because we took rather more chances.'

RH: Later, when we made the 'Experiments With Pops' LP, by way of contrast we were able to choose from the whole field of 'pop' composition going on around us.

'Well, I don't think, *I know* that record of 'Experiments' is the one which always sets a standard for me. Since then I've done lots of different things, used different ideas, used electric keyboards, made use of improved studio techniques and so on. But 'Experiments' has to stand as the album to be measured against.'

RH: It set certain rules for you, you mean?

'Yes. I can remember coming to your place to hear the final mixes and being knocked out by it all. The pace and excitement of *These Boots Are Made For Walkin'*, for instance, the opening track. I haven't felt as excited over a playback since. Not even with 'French Connection 1'. And d'you know, to this day, everywhere I go in the world 'Experiments' is always mentioned. And *why is it not available anymore? (The master tapes of* 'Experiments With Pops, *originally issued on Major-Minor, are now the property of Thorn-Emi. They also feature the earliest recorded jazz solos by guitarist John McLaughlin.)*

RH: Also over this period you had the settled Gordon Beck Trio. You've already mentioned Tony Oxley. But in addition you had a considerable bass-player in Jeff Clyne. A player, like you, who extracts a near-classical tone from his chosen instrument.

'Another thing about Jeff with the Trio was his innate sense of space. He could provide all the bottom of that group and yet leave it uncluttered, that is, in linear terms. We were breaking new ground and Jeff contributed a lot to it.'

RH: Still, with your Trio and 'Experiments', you were playing fast and loose with time signatures on certain tracks in a way that no one else in this country was doing then.

'Ah, well that goes back to Tony Oxley again. Over that period I equate him with the young English pianist I have such a high regard for today, Django Bates. Tony struck me as one of the most original musicians who suddenly arrived. And I'll always remember the day, no the night when he telephoned me from Sheffield and said he was available. Because his time was so fantastic, so right, you could play fast and loose and still come out on the one. It was so exhilarating! We'd do such unbelievably complicated passages, based on structural music, and he'd add to it all in a purely musical way. He'd play to the melody of a song as if he was my *alter ego*. But this has been the way with all the best artists I've ever played with. I've learned from them, matured in their working presence. Phil Woods, Sonny Rollins, Lena Horne, Gerry Mulligan, Joe Henderson, Venuti and Grappelli, Helen Merrill. When you're alongside giants all you can do is learn.'

RH: Just to conclude on 'Experiments With Pops', there was something special about it. We all went into the studio with crazy enthusiasm. Adrian Kerridge got a marvellous balance with very little screening—and you had the piano sounding exactly as you'd hoped.

'I think too that I'd reached the stage of being more aware of recording possibilities. And of not being overawed by the sense of occasion. It was a question of getting on with the music-making—and simply enjoying making something new!'

RH: So, back to the chronology. You kept the Trio, or a trio together for quite a few years.

'Yes, although naturally there were personnel changes. But the first Trio continued until 1968/69, when Ron Matthewson joined us on bass. Which leads on to Phil Woods and his European Rhythm Machine. We backed him for a whole month at Ronnie Scott's—and this obviously planted the idea in his mind that I might be okay for his group. (The Washing-Machine, we called it!) Which, well, I don't have to elaborate on it too much, had become an international unit. When he offered me the job it took me a millionth of a second to say 'yes'. Also I must add here: that I was truly devastated by the experience of working with Phil. I mean, he didn't come across then as a megastar like say, Dizzy or Sonny Rollins. It was simply a question of his total musicianship. And near-perfection in that post-Be-bop style on alto he's made so conspicuously his own. He just knocked me sideways. So three and a half years of magic went by.'

RH: Was it heavy to begin with?

'The first three months or so were. After that I became less overwhelmed. It helped too having previously played alongside drummer Daniel Humair with Bobby Jaspar. Then I began to compose for the group. I wrote one very long piece, *The Executive Suite,* in four sections with links of improvisation, motifs and so on. And it was heartening to discover Phil responding to the opening up of such an area in music. I feel we 'took off': with a genuine group development and not just one great soloist backed by an adequate rhythm section. After this I wrote a lot of music for us. Right up until Phil decided to leave Paris and settle in America again. By which time we'd been through a quartet partnership no amount of money could buy.'

RH: So. After Phil Woods, Gyroscope: your own group again, a quartet, and with you wailing on electric keyboards. Had you picked up on electric instruments while with the Rhythm Machine?

'I had, but should point out that, like a lot of players, I changed to electric because of the many rotten acoustic pianos I was faced with while touring. The inadequacies of an electric piano make it a cul-de-sac. The road to nowhere. But often in clubs it was the only answer, albeit a temporary one. Happily, since getting known on the international circuit has meant more concerts and festivals, where the pianos are generally of a higher standard. I helped develop a portable Hohner electric to begin with. Which they never thanked me for. Then I switched to a Fender. It's useful for creating certain sound effects. But none of the electrics have contributed anything to the art of piano-playing.'

RH: I've sometimes heard Gyroscope described as a jazz-rock fusion. Which I believe is completely wrong. In fact it was a progressive jazz group. As, I think, Steps Ahead is now.

'Well, it definitely wasn't intended as a jazz-rock thing! What it began as was an attempt to fuse bits of all kinds of music with jazz and so cross a number of barriers yet again. I don't think the Latin American parts always came off—one has to be realistic here. But it often made up for its various shortcomings by being exciting in its projection of the music. The closest we ever got to be playing *true* Brazilian rhythms was like the distance between here and the moon. But that doesn't stop one wanting to try. And otherwise it was a good band, in its musicianship. We enjoyed it, and it lasted for two years.'

RH: Around this time you were putting out solo recordings as well. But on cassette—and by subscription, through the post.

'It was a time when no one in this country wanted to know about recording native jazz. Also before I had the contract in Paris. So I began with a collection called 'All In The Morning', recorded in Milan with Ron (Matthewsen) and Daniel Humair. We got a fee and tape rights for outside Italy. Naturally, I couldn't afford my own record company, but I tried the cassette idea, by mail order, and it did quite well: here and on the Continent. Capital Radio were especially helpful in promoting it. It only folded because I was getting no time for playing!'

RH: And Gyroscope itself, the group, was wound up in 1975.

'After which I might have got swallowed up in the more abysmal aspects of studio work. Some of it could be okay. I did the Morecombe & Wise shows, which were hilarious. And it meant earning well. But then I had to reach an important decision: this or playing jazz—with fortunately the latter winning out. There'd been some horrible 'pop' recordings too: with 16-year-old Liverpudlian girls one never heard of again, that sort of thing. I was glad to take a financial cut and see the back of it all. As it turned out though, being with Phil had done my name an awful lot of good in Europe and in the States. Most importantly, perhaps, with other leading jazz musicians. Gary Burton asked for me. Sonny Rollins. I got to play with Milt Jackson. Then with Helen Merrill, Didier Lockwood and so on—which brings us pretty well up to date. On our latest Helen Merrill LP the featured guest soloists are Steve Lacy and Stéphane Grappelli. That's where my career has presently arrived.'

RH: And the future?

'Well, I'm not twenty-five anymore. I feel mature as a pianist now, and so I want that piano-playing to go more into specific projects. For instance, this year Alan Holdsworth asked me to go to California and Japan with him. A continuation of playing together in the early '80s with Sun Bird, the French musicians. So that was me having to drop into his world, just as before he'd dropped into mine. I mean they, his band, don't have anything written down—so I had to *learn* everything they were doing. But their being such fantastic musicians made it all worthwhile.

'I hope too to be able to continue with singers as well as instrumentalists. Helen Merrill is an ongoing project. At the same time I still enjoy a good blues bash. Which was sparked off by accompanying Jimmy Witherspoon at The Bull's Head years ago. While one of the most enjoyable two weeks I've ever done was with Carrie Smith at Ronnie's, when everyone in the club, even the seasoned drinkers, got up and danced! When I haven't enjoyed it though is with someone like Dakota Staton. Then the show becomes a brilliant carbon-copy each and every night. Sorry Dakota!

'However, the composition continues to absorb me as well. It used to be a case of writing isolated pieces. *Mallet Man* for Gary Burton. And *The Day When The World Comes Alive* for Cleo Laine. But within the last year I've been commissioned by the Arts Council to write for the Cambridge Festival, another suite which I based on a local folk theme, *The May Song*. Again it comes back to projects. I love space you see. And the quiet of composing. Travelling is becoming the worst part of music now. The joy has gone. Except for trains. I hate the back of every 747. So time off to compose becomes a wonderful break, not a chore.

I'm less interested in arranging. It can be tedious. But the creativity of composition is something else. I wouldn't want to lose that. One must learn to apportion one's energies.'

On three contemporary pianists . . .

RH: In the course of our discussions you have referred to three modern jazz pianists who have been more important to you than all others: Bill Evans, Keith Jarrett and Herbie Hancock. A fascinating trio, not least because if, as I believe, Bill is now revered as a kind of Pope of the instrument, then Keith Jarrett has to be regarded as the anti-Pope, a schismatic of Avignon. Yet they both have an amazing, different relevance not only to our present, but also to the future of jazz. Of course I'm interested in your views about all three.

'Well, before, there was for me Shearing, a father-figure. Then the overwhelming impact of Tatum. And one other pianist I've loved on the sidelines: Horace Parlan. Oh, I had a week, a lovely week, when we were making the second "Piano Conclave" album in the Jazzland Studios in the sub-basement of the Sheraton Hotel in Munich. And who's working in the club down the road but Horace Parlan! So every night, after working it, it was straight down there listening to him. *The Music,* he makes real music . . .

'However, back to the Big Three. Mm, Pope and anti-Pope? I think I see what you're getting at. You see, for me, Bill has what is the closest I've heard in jazz to a classical technique. Plus these incredible inner harmonies which only he seems to be able to pull off. Except for Gary Burton on quite a different instrument. Keith, in contrast, is an oddity. He has a technical ability which is beyond anybody. Keith to me is the modern-day version of Art Tatum. But there are many elements, many levels, aren't there? You can talk about a genius. You can talk about all sorts of things. For me Bill is a genius . . . while Herbie Hancock is *The Master.* Now, by that I mean, like Miles (Davis) he's moved the music on in logical steps. With Herbie, with each stage, the music is so shatteringly different. Bill came along. He didn't do that. What he did, for me, was the same kind of thing that Charlie Parker did: *he changed the whole way of rhythmic playing!* Okay, by his influence. He met people. He *integrated* rhythm sections, with the bass and drums becoming of equal importance within the trio set-up. Okay, so you could say it was only coincidence that he met Scott LaFaro and Paul (Motian), but I think Bill's music influenced them as well, more than even they thought at the time. I don't know for sure, of course. But what is sure? *No rhythmic playing was ever the same again,* that much I know. It was like Jo Jones throwing his cymbal across the bloody dancefloor. It was never the same again.

RH: Whereas with Herbie?

'He's gone from one logical phase to the next phase, progressing, and mastering every technological new thing that has come along. You know, we are living in the age of rapidly advancing technology—and whatever Herbie touches, he picks it up in no time at all . . . and does it better than anybody. In fact, and this sounds like nit-picking, he does it even better than Chick Corea, and let's face it, Chick Corea is himself fantastic. Everything Herbie does is so incredibly beautiful, a total entity. Now Keith Jarrett I've called an oddity. He's like the mad genius. You never know what he's going to do. You can't pigeonhole him. He's got a technique that nobody in the world's got.

RH: He's also the one pianist you shouldn't ever mention to Oscar Peterson. Because he's the one pianist who can pull in a bigger crowd!

'I'll probably be hauled over the coals for saying this. I wouldn't detract for one moment what Oscar Peterson stands for. He stands for the black, swinging, rhythmic music. But I've got to be honest with you, that he hasn't said anything new to me in twenty years, and so with *me,* personally, he doesn't rate with Bill, Herbie, Keith—or for that matter John Taylor. He's a swinger, one of the greatest swingers—but there's more to jazz piano-playing than just that. I mean, you've only got to listen to this kid Django Bates in our own country. The invention he's got. His pianistic technique is remarkable, I don't know where the hell he's found it from. He seems to have just *appeared.* No one has the answer to the eternal question: what is genius? But to finish off, and going back to my three greats, Keith has explored his own road, becoming very interior, very fully absorbed. Herbie is the Lord of All he surveys. And as for Bill, well, I think that even now the world doesn't realise how great Bill Evans was.

1986

CHAPTER THIRTY-THREE

RAY SWINFIELD

And The Artist/Producer Axis

For some time I have been urged to write about the role of the record producer in his relationship with leading musicians under studio conditions, but been reluctant to oblige because in an earlier book, 'The Music Goes Round And Round, A Cool Look At The Record Industry' (*Quartet Books*, 1980) I felt I'd already said sufficient on the subject, albeit in a wide arc from the late Sir Thomas Beecham and 'cellist Paul Tortelier to other personal involvements—Ted Heath, Mel Tormé, Sammy Davis Jr, Anthony Newley *et al*. Also with some actors, including Sir John Gielgud and Ian Richardson, and certain playwrights, most notably Alun Owen and Alan Bennett.

However, just recently I've been working as producer for an album featuring the Australian flautist and multi-saxist Ray Swinfield—which has, in retrospect, set my mental processes going again on the subject of record making. When, for instance, in 1983 I wrote about Louie Bellson's sessions in London, and later the ones with Buddy De Franco, I was present purely *as a writer*—sitting amidst the musicians, able to be objective, but detached; free to look at and listen to, with no responsibility except to my own words and the need to be truthful. Suddenly, by contrast, in the making of the Swinfield LP I was back in what musicians often refer to as 'the driving seat'—although personally I prefer to call it a co-pilot's seat, since in working with an artist of his calibre I put forward (and at times strongly) my own suggestions, but would never then think of proceeding without his approval. 'You're the producer,' a musician will often say. 'And you're the player,' is my inevitable reply. 'Only you can do the playing. I'll put in my own ideas how it should be collected and kept, but I don't want to collect thin air. If you're not happy over the sound or direction then you're not going to relax and play anything like your best . . .'

In 'The Music Goes Round And Round' I said that while making a record its producer is normally entitled to have the first word and also the last one. (Since he will have to direct the course of the sessions and at the same time look after the budget.) In between these two points though he *must* remain totally flexible, with his intelligence open to everyone else's ideas and abilities. He should, assuming he is genuinely professional, listen to each and every other suggestion, thinking of how it can benefit the overall product, or, if unsuitable, harm it. In fact, this parallels the artist's own creativity; especially in the case of jazz musicians,

222

because while the improvising soloist becomes, in effect, a composer in action, so the producer is mentally editing what is happening and selecting towards the whole eventual performance. It often means split-second decisions, but if you're not up to these then it's a question of looking for another job. There are two things guaranteed to undermine an artist's confidence within the context of a recording session. One is the producer who opens his mouth and immediately displays a lack of knowledge; the other is a producer who dithers.

Another bad feature of certain producers is when they themselves are actually frustrated performers. I have witnessed this lead to, first of all, envy, then abrasiveness and finally to a total breakdown of good personal relations with the artist. Make no mistake here—a principal feature of record production is keeping the artist contented, helping him overcome nerves, self-doubts and similarly any quirks of temperament. Each artist is an individual and, allowing that his talent is worthwhile, needs to be handled with tact, diplomacy and, above all, sound advice from the other side of the control-room window. Plus efficient direction. All the finest artists are anxious to have direction. It can be light or firm, sensitive or exacting, depending on the occasion, but it has to come from someone they respect and know is looking after both the music and their own best interests. I've always stressed how I like working with artists who begin by showing nerves (which can then be calmed), because this also shows they care about their work and about getting it right. And usually the better the performer the more he or she requires encouragement and reassurance. I've often quoted the great Orson Welles on this particular subject: 'Of course the most gifted people want direction. Also, they're the only ones you *can* direct. With the second-raters you just wheel them on and let them do what they can.'

Anyway, it therefore becomes very important for a producer to get to know as much as possible about the artist *before* the occasion of a session. This is partly in order that an easy working relationship can be established between them, but in addition so that the producer is fully aware of what to expect from an artist and how much he can ask of him. This is doubly necessary when the concept for an album is new, and especially again if the subject is jazz. For instance, one might easily imagine that with certain groups like say, the Modern Jazz Quartet or Art Blakey's Messengers, the instrumental formula is so established that the pattern of a session will fall into place automatically. Not a bit of it. There are nearly always fresh compositions and arrangements coming into the picture and/or, as in Blakey's case, new faces appearing within the group. The wise producer, as a result, will do a lot of work in advance of the sessions—and such preparations should include learning everything he can about his musicians: what they have to offer, in which direction they're facing and again what makes each of them tick . . .

It's my intention, as this piece develops, to try to illustrate the different aspects of record production in the stages as they occurred while making the Ray Swinfield LP. With such a method one is dealing with something specific and now achieved, but still sufficiently recent for the memory-bank to remain unclouded. Every recording is different, of course, but in record production other things remain constant.

So I'll begin by writing about the man, endeavouring to unravel the facts I knew about him before we got down to discussing the new LP, which is in reality his third as a principal soloists and group-leader.

I'd made his acquaintance over a number of years during which his actual talents as a jazz player were, as far as I was concerned, largely hearsay. By this I mean that he'd often turned up at commercial sessions I was responsible for on the initiative of my contractor, Charlie Katz. Consequently, I was aware he had obvious skills as a flautist and, if need be, could double on the different saxophones and clarinet. But the orchestrations we were recording then didn't call for any jazz; moreover, as I discovered later, his natural gifts in this area were generally restricted to impromptu jamming and with no fixed group of players.

Then chance, as so often happens, became a part of it. In 1980 I went to a local jazz night organised by Bill McGuffie's Niner Club, heard the new Swinfield Quartet (or the Argenta Ora as it's now called) and was so greatly impressed I determined to canvass every record company I knew until I had a go-ahead to record him for it. The result of which was 'Rain Curtain' (an album Terry Brown took for the Piccadilly label) with his group as it then consisted—i.e. Ray himself on flutes, alto-saxophone and clarinet (sometimes electrified), John Pearce, keyboards, John Aué, bass-guitar and Art Morgan, drums and percussion. Chris Laurence played acoustic bass on several tracks and Dick Abell played electric guitar on others.

The recordings were all made in PRT/Pye's No. 1 studio at Marble Arch and the recording engineer was Terry Evennett. I had worked with the latter on numerous occasions already, and this too was important because he knew my methods of approach and had been carefully briefed beforehand as to what was required in the way of sound and set-up. Producers shouldn't have to tinker with faders or the setting of levels, etc. on record dates, nor with the placing of microphones. But they need to know how the desk and recording systems function, and to be able to explain to their engineer in detail what they are seeking in order for the music to fulfil itself. Also, of course, if they want the session to start and finish on time! Then at least there should be no cause for gloomy faces or expensive post-mortems.

I'd alerted Terry to the several (and sometimes complicated) 'overdubs' I'd persuaded Ray to include. These were not in any sense a gimmick, but there to develop the compositional materials and to showcase his multi-instrumental activities. Happily, they all worked—and in particular the improvised alto solo he plays against his original solo track on *Italian Village*. It really does make a logical use of stereo. The editing and remixing of this and the other Swinfield originals then became a matter of care and patience. But I noticed how difficult Ray found it to be physically present when we were working on them—on *Thinking On It, Hughie, Dulcinea, Rain Curtain* and *Caroline*. The first half-hour or so of a mixing session sounds like absolute chaos if you're not used to it—while the producer and his engineer are checking out each individual track and how to enhance it with equalisation and echo. Consequently, if the artist is there at this stage he has to hear his performances seeming to be broken apart before they finally come together. It can be a touch traumatic therefore, and usually the producer has to explain that in reality everything's on course and will be well in the end.

The 'Rain Curtain' LP received very favourable notices, but for reasons beyond our control I didn't work as the producer for Ray's second LP, 'The Winged Cliff' (on the Merlin label) and which includes his six-part 'Sydney Suite', a work sponsored by the Arts Council. Although I did agree to write the sleeve-notes for it. With 'Rain Curtain' I hadn't wanted to 'say' anything on the sleeve. It could have been misinterpreted as the producer merely wanting to advertise his own work, so I asked my friend and earliest writing partner Alun Morgan to take care of this department. But I did devote much time to the preparation of the sleeve, even down to selecting the photography and sorting out the copyright details. One must see these aspects of a record through. After all, what's the point in everyone knocking themselves out to get the sound of the music right only for the final product to be issued inside a shoddy cover?

However, to return briefly to 'The Winged Cliff'. It was recorded at CBS Studios, but this time taken direct to ¼-inch stereo, with no overdubs or remixes. I like the album; in particular, the autobiographical impressionism of his 'Sydney' themes. And so I was able to be quite sincere in praising it on the sleeve. As I said, 'In my life I have been a writer and a record producer; and a few other things. If I'd been a flautist and a jazz composer I would like to have been credited with these Sydney sketches.'

Meanwhile though, I'd been getting into further discussions with Ray which would lead not only to his statements in the next part of this chapter, but eventually to the making of his third LP, 'Angel Eyes' for Peter Ind's Wave Label . . .

Any personal file on Ray Swinfield has to begin with the fact that he was born in Sydney, Australia on December 14, 1939. Also, that he is, as far as is known, the first musician in his family. Since then he has crossed the intercontinental boundaries and settled in England, and it's been here that he has played the greater part of his jazz. Moreover, like many musicians, he has used his playing skills to make a living in the recording and TV studios while allowing the jazz part of him to develop in an entirely free and spontaneous way.

I think I will let my actual assessment of him for 'The Winged Cliff' collection stand. That he is the best player of jazz flute in Europe—and that I've yet to hear any U.S. flautist who is better. The fact that in addition he plays very fine alto-saxophone and clarinet is a bonus, and his work on these instruments must not be underrated. But I put the flute foremost, partly because it is still something of a Cinderella instrument in jazz, and because with it he has set new, high standards which I personally, even after working with him a lot, have found truly outstanding. 'Also,' I concluded, 'how he plays is not mere technical dexterity—although his technique is considerable and based on much formal training—but he has the gift of jazz *within him*, in his mind, his framework and above all his soul. He has the ability to swing naturally and then to improvise from his memory-bank of standards and other compositions, including his own. This is the ability which is denied to otherwise very gifted classical players who are not born to jazz . . .'

However, we are concerned now with the alliance of an artist and his producer and how much a producer should endeavour to learn about the musician he is recording. First of all, get to know the man, then study the musician in him. And three areas really matter here: his background, his subsequent career and, most important of all, his current musical attitudes. Know and understand these things, and you are well on the way to streetlighting his work.

As regards the background and career of Ray Swinfield I have a good deal on tape. 'Tell me about how you got going in Australia,' I asked him. 'I mean at the very beginning of your music . . .'

'Well, I started when I was nine years' old on the fife. I was coached by a Mr. Roberts. Then I joined a Police Boys Club, which is similar to English Boys Clubs. I was in the fife-and-drums band, and we played at the opening of fêtes, etc. So they decided that if you were okay on fife you should have some clarinet lessons. I had them with one Serjeant Bowers—and the club provided the instrument on loan.

'Next I was bought a saxophone by my grandfather. (*RH*: You mean Hughie, of your composition of that name?) Yes, that's right. By which time I was thirteen, maybe fourteen. I liked a wide variety of music, but I can remember buying two records as a result of the clarient. One was an album of Benny Goodman's 'Session For Six' with *Easy Does It,* and the other was a 10-inch LP on Verve by Buddy De Franco. I liked the Goodman one a lot, but I thought the De Franco was too advanced for me and so I took it back to the shop. Later I went back to the shop and bought it again! You see, Benny was playing straightforward music which I immediately understood; Buddy De Franco was playing be-bop, which was a bit much for me to begin with . . .

'My tutor for the clarinet and saxophone was now Neville Thomas, a prominent Sydney musician. Later I went to the Sydney Conservatory of Music, which nowadays has a big jazz tutorial section, but in my time I was there to learn music theory. I had lessons in this from the Australian Ray Hanson.'

RH: This, I realise, is a difficult question. But how and when did you realise you had the ability to improvise—which is so vital in a jazz sense but which other trained, and even distinguished players can't do?

'Oh, I think it depends on your interests. For example, some classical players *can* improvise, but they wouldn't do so in the way a jazz musician does. I mean cadenzas in classical music can be given the feeling of improvisation. In my case, if I had a good melody line then I soon wanted to discover new ways of feeling it and using it.'

RH: Were your earliest endeavours to improvise sparked off by classical pieces—and the desire to explore further the melodic lines of, say, Ravel?

'No. It began when a group of other young musicians in Sydney would come around to the house and we'd play over various things. It was all pretty amateurish, of course—and fortunately there weren't any other listeners! But we were trying things and learning.

'My big influences at this time? Well, they mixed. I was a great fan of the late Freddie Gardner. We had his records with the Peter Yorke Orchestra out in Australia.'

RH: Really? Now, that is interesting, because as a boy I used to devote my Sunday afternoons to the Peter Yorke broadcasts. I thought it was a marvellous orchestra, with lots of strings but also featuring jazz soloists—Freddie Gardner, Laddie Busby and so on. And Charlie Katz booked the men—which eventually is how you and I came to meet.

'Yes. Charlie Katz had a considerable influence on music in London. He was the busiest contractor for such a long time. I owe a big part of my start in England to him.

'When I arrived here, by this time I was regarded principally as a flautist. But in fact, after the fife, I hadn't seriously concentrated on the flute as my, if you like, lead instrument until I was eighteen, nineteen. In my middle teens it was always the clarinet and the saxophones.'

RH: Do you join in the consensus of opinion that the clarinet is the hardest of the reed instruments to play?

'Yes. To a moderate standard, that is. However, if you're talking about virtuoso standards, then it's difficult on all of them.'

RH: Sorry! I'll try to put the point in a different way. Buddy De Franco told me recently that he first of all experimented with an alto-saxophone but couldn't get on with it. And neither Benny Goodman nor Artie Shaw did anything to push their ideas through a saxophone. Now you've flown in the face of the storm and on your new album you've featured the whole family of reeds, clarinet and all the saxophones.

'Yes, but that's as a colour—they're purely for support. This is the first album I've done which has been entirely concerned with the flute.'

RH: The next question is probably also a difficult one. But what made you opt for a position in European jazz rather than going directly to the United States?

'Originally I was going off to work in Canada as a kind of stepping-stone into the States. Then I decided to come to London instead. I'd been encouraged to travel abroad by several Australian musicians: Errol Buddle of the Australian Jazz Quintet, Don Burrows, of course, Don Harper the jazz violinist and another musician, Ron Falson, who is well-known to your colleague Alun Morgan for his recordings with Pat Caplice. Ron is a great jazz trumpet-player, somewhere between Bobby Hackett and Clifford Brown, if you can imagine that. He's also a very inventive jazz composer—one of the best, in my opinion. Don Harper gave me some names to look up in London, including Roy Willox, who proved to be a big help when I did come.'

Then naturally there was a long period of consolidation. Of playing in all sorts of combinations before eventually Ray formed the Argenta Ora. He had to live, and he had to mix with lots of other musicians before finding out what he wanted to do in the way of a more personal expression . . .

RH: But with your present group you can travel the world now and justify a position on any billing.

'Well, I think it's a strong unit, and at the same time I get a lot of enjoyment out of working with the other musicians. John Pearce is a tremendous pianist and arranger. Dave Green on bass is well-known for his work with Humphrey Lyttleton, but for instance, he's also been booked to appear with George Coleman. And Allan Ganley, who's on drums with us now, is one of the best musicians I know—he has drive, he plays so cleanly and he too is a fine writer.

'If I can just say something more about John Pearce though. He's a great accompanist as well as being such a good soloist. He never locks one in but he suggests things subtly and then never gets in the way.

RH: Can jazz players actually think their way into each other's brains? After all, the creativity between the best players does happen with split-second accuracy.

'It's certainly what we aim for. But it's not simply down to ability. It's a musical feeling between players . . .'

I asked Ray at this point about how important *ego* is within his work. For ego is too often confused with big-headedness. In my own view, it is a compulsion towards self-expression if one has something burninghly obvious to say. In other words, ego can become the very *need* to communicate. And I think it also means determination. He agreed with this.

We talked then about admirations and influences. Predictably, these are also many and varied, as befits a man who has elected to play jazz but is equally capable of playing the flute in a symphonic situation. But at the same time, he is very specific. For example: 'In the Mahler 5th Symphony it's the *Adagietto* I most like to hear. In Mozart's Clarinet Concerto the middle movement. Of Beethoven's Symphonies the 5th and the 9th. Out of all Ravel, it's 'Daphnis And Chloe', with Stravinsky 'The Rite Of Spring'. However, his mental cataloguing is equally good. In stating his admiration for the Elgar Cello Concerto he reminded me that it was Opus 85, in E Minor. 'I like most of Shostakovich, the symphonies especially—and one work that not too many people know about: Benedetto Marcello's Concerto For Oboe, Strings and Continuo, in C Minor. Again it's the slow movement—and by the Dutch school of oboe-players. I'm thinking now of Hans Meijers.

'As regards favourites on my own instruments, well, I'd say Eric Dolphy, Johnny Mince, Tony Coe, Stan Getz and Bob Berg. Also in jazz the sheer versatility of such players as Ron Carter, Mike Brecker and now Wynton Marsalis. Nothing wrong with versatility though. After all, Eric Dolphy, before he became one of the heroes of modern jazz, had once recorded with Fats Domino. Another European musician who has been an influence on me is Ronnie Ross. I like the way his solos flow along.'

Finally, I went into the area of how his own compositions seem to be a logical extension of the way he plays the flute and his other instruments. I might just as well have opened up Pandora's box. His themes are very melodic, as I've said, but their contours suggest the kind of ideas he is, in the spirit of adventure, apt to improvise. *Italian Village,* I said, really related as clearly to the alto-saxophone as, by way of contrast, *Thinking On It* and *Rain Curtain* lent themselves more closely to the flute as a solo instrument.

'They didn't evolve through the instruments in the sense of writing down what I was playing on them. I think they happened because of all I know about the instruments and what they can do. Their styles, their technical make-up and so on. And too there are the effects of where I've been, whether Sydney, Italy, the Tropics. And remember, although *Rain Curtain* is essentially a flute solo, it was you who then persuaded me to put in the jungle bits on alto-sax!'

RH: All right! It just seemed to fit at the time, to me as a producer at least. But this apart, there is a strain of romantic impressionism in you I find, both in your work as a soloist and as a composer. And I'm no longer prepared to believe, as some present figures writing about music do, that romance is outdated. If it is, then I have to dislike Chopin, and I refuse to! If the combination of melodic playing with technique is going to be dubbed romantic, then I'm a romantic. Because if Chopin was a great melodic composer, he was also the greatest piano soloist of his day. But can I just go back to jazz on this point? All the greats, Armstrong, Charlie Parker, Eric Dolphy: they made up melodies. They also explored the outer spaces of their instruments . . . and they kept on trying.

'Yes, I believe that preparation of instruments and pieces is of the utmost importance. You've written about the amount of work Buddy De Franco has done on his clarinets. That's right, and that goes a long way towards explaining why, over and above his basic inventiveness, when you hear Buddy play it's instantly recognisable. A lot of players have their instruments adjusted in some way to suit them better. Sometimes this is obvious, as with the basses of Scott La Faro, etc. I've had all my flutes adjusted in action and modified by Albert Cooper. My alto and clarinet have been altered by Bill Wrathall. These two men are master craftsmen. On the other side are the ones to beware of. I once had a favourite flute worked over on an ill-advised venture by someone who fitted in an electronic bug. His workmanship was excellent. Unfortunately, he knew nothing whatsoever about the flute. To cut a long story short, it took me about seven years to find an equally good flute!

'And can I just say something more? While I do believe in a selection of opinions about music generally, I think that a lot of what is said comes totally from cloud cuckoo-land. I mean, I remember a person of some influence once saying to me he only liked jazz musicians who came 'up from the farm'—i.e. rough and unpractised. Rubbish! Of course, all good jazz players work on their instruments as much as possible, and if it's not possible because of the circumstances of travel like, say, the busiest of flautists, Rampal, then they have to forego practice. But not for long. These sort of statements by people who don't themeselves play the instruments do jazz a great deal of harm. It makes for the image of the happy blower, who is not to be taken seriously. And, of course, any musician who is serious is saddened by such statements by misguided 'twits'—especially if they have gained some sort of position of influence . . .'

So, to the actual recording of 'Angel Eyes', the third Ray Swinfield album.

The sessions took place in the Autumn of '83 at Peter Ind's Wave Studios, Hoxton Square—which is just on the edge of the City of London and previously part of Jack the Ripper's manor. Earlier negotiations with Peter had settled that the album would be released on his Wave label, and it made sense to use his studio facilities as well. Given the individual skills and experience of the Swinfield Argenta Ora I wasn't anticipating any great difficulties at the original playing sessions. But some of the overdubs we had planned were fairly complicated and therefore extra time needed to be allowed for the remixes. The balance-engineer was to be Mike Brown; he I already knew from several albums made at the PRT/Pye Studios. Also he has had experience as a cutting-engineer, which is an additional asset.

If the recording had been a standard or 'pop' one featuring a singer or singers, then the preparation for the sessions would have differed quite a lot. There would have been the question of choosing a suitable arranger, of sorting out the best keys for the voice/voices, of which instruments could sound most appropriate within the accompaniment, where exactly to use them and so on. With the Argenta Ora being a self-contained and regularly working group, and including its own main arranger in John Pearce, this didn't arise. On the other hand, there had to be a major discussion about which themes to use, and then further discussions on how precisely to utilise them.

Even with a self-motivated unit creating jazz it remains important from the producer's point of view to have relevant variations and contrasts *inside* the programme of music. A typical 'disco' LP can have the same tempo throughout its entire length and still fulfil its purpose. A jazz album will be listened to far more carefully—and often far more critically. Consequently, in most, if not all, cases one has to plan for tempo changes, the stress of light and shade, good dynamics, etc and with themes chosen accordingly. Other considerations come into it, of course. The themes must serve as a genuine basis for improvisation; equally, they have to act as a kind of airframe containing the soloists' separate sophisticated mental processes and natural capabilities.

In addition, with this particular Swinfield album we had decided well beforehand that of his personal contributions we were to keep the flute-playing uppermost.

I made only one specific suggestion to Ray about themes and that was *If You Could See Me Now*, the ballad Tadd Dameron wrote originally for Sarah Vaughan (and actually in her presence). It has beautiful intrinsic qualities, but has been somewhat neglected, and I felt it would lend itself well to a first exploration via the flute; plus, as well it ought to, being highly suitable for the piano. Then I discovered that Ray had started working it over within the group anyway! Also, we both coincidentally seemed to want to tackle Chick Corea's *Bud Powell*—although I take no credit for what was later grafted on to it, except maybe technically. Otherwise all the suggestions came from his side, and I was happy with his reasons for selecting them. We needed another ballad, and I knew he was anxious to do *Angel Eyes* on alto-flute. Meanwhile another Chick Corea composition, *500 Miles High*, promised to yield up all kinds of fascinating ideas; like-wise Roland Kirk's *Serenade To A Cuckoo*. And both the leader and John Pearce were each to contribute one original.

It was nearly time for Ray to go back to the drawing-board, so to speak, and work on the arrangements with John. But two other important matters were settled at this stage. The first concerned the approximate timings of the performances. We had to allow a reasonable amount of solo space in individual numbers, but not overload the LP with so much playing-time that it couldn't be mastered and put on disc with a reasonable listening level.

The amount of level going on an unmixed multi-track tape presents less of a problem. It's when you start cutting and the side-time is running towards thirty minutes that the troubles start. The longer the side the tighter the grooves are pushed together. Amazing things can still be done. Once, when I produced a first-ever recording of Sir Arthur Sullivan's 'The Zoo', in the interests of a definitive completeness I insisted on going to nearly thirty-seven minutes per side. And the music involved large forces: ten soloists, forty-six chorus, the Royal Philharmonic Orchestra *and sound effects*—the latter bought from Regents Park Zoological Gardens. We managed it, but my reputation in the Decca cutting-rooms took a nosedive and three master acetates went down in the processing bath before a suitable pressing was eventually made.

Naturally, new developments in the industry introduce increased possibilities—and now we have the advent of digital recording and CD (compact disc) which offer important breakthroughs within the timescale. Generally though, let's just say it can be dangerous to go on too long. Because on top of the technical difficulties there's the further risk of boring the listener.

As a result, with the Argenta Ora we allocated approximate timings and agreed that for one theme, *500 Miles High,* the margin ought to be more generous. A decision which proved to be correct, because while its development promised to be quite ambitious, it did become in our ultimate evaluations the only conceivable track with which to close the LP.

The other important thing to be resolved before the sessions was a working headline—which in fact turned out to be the final one: 'Angel Eyes'. We'd had several ideas of what would constitute a good cover design, and the sooner we could brief the designer, Tim Motion, the better—since he'd been booked to take the pictures as well.

Tim is a favourite photographer of mine at sessions. He's able, is extremely quick to grasp what the producer has in mind and then never afterwards gets in the way. Probably because he's musical himself. Certain other photographers I've met ought never again to be allowed even near a recording studio. Because they don't understand and in any case are utterly selfish, they become a nuisance to the producer and a distraction to the musicians. Not so with Mister Motion, who can come in, light the place and then get his close-ups and/or longer shots with the subtle tread of a cat-burglar . . .

Over the next few weeks the real responsibility rested with Ray and John Pearce as they pushed on with the arrangements—and then with the rehearsing. But I had regular reports on how the different ideas were shaping up, and they checked with me that a number of effects would be possible technically. Also Ray hinted darkly that John had got into something with his arrangement of *500 Miles High* which was frightening them both!

During this period too the remaining themes were confirmed: *The Best Thing For You Would Be Me* and finally *Montevideo*, which, not surprisingly, has an SA feeling as well as long association with pianist Cedar Walton, a favourite player of John's—as indeed he was of the late, and considerably fastidious Al Haig. Meanwhile Ray's original had further associations with his native Sydney and now existed under the title *Flood Street Dolly*. John Pearce couldn't come up with an identity tag for his. (In the end it was named *Back From Tomorrow*.)

I left my talk-through meeting with engineer Mike Brown until quite close to the time of the sessions. This was partly because I wanted to have the maximum information available, but equally on account of the fact that any busy recording engineer has to cope with a wide miscellany of music often within the space of a single week, and he can't be thinking of everything all at the same time. Far better to brief just a day or two before the sessions, so he can retain that knowledge in the face of other commitments.

Apart from giving him the basic instrumentation I wanted to outline what I'd visualised for the stereo layout. Which was to have the solo flute centre with the bass, the keyboards just off-centre, and I wanted stereo drums to emphasise the spread. No problem over this last request since we were planning to use up to six separate microphones, all of them directional, on the different parts of Allan Ganley's kit. Any further musical activity—i.e. Ray's overdubbed parts—would then take place on the left and right extremes of the stereo (the one exception to this I'll come to in a later paragraph). Finally I double-checked that the studio Steinway would be tuned on the morning of each session . . .

It would be pointless to go over everything exactly as it happened at the sessions themselves. Musically the greater part of it can be picked up far more effectively (and quickly) than from my words by listening to the album itself. But to sketch in a few essential background details might still prove interesting to anyone who comes to know and, one hopes, to enjoy what is encapsulated there.

Physically the musicians were positioned as close to each other as possible while at the same time allowing for good separation (without the latter there's no point in having a multi-track recording involving remixes). And they all needed a clear view of Ray for his cues on tempo-changes, etc. Headphones were also available, containing an approximate mix if they wanted them. No artificial reverberation (echo) was applied to their sounds at this stage. You can always put it on later—and experiment with it—but if it goes on at the session then you can't later take it off.

I find it's always the best idea at the beginning of an album—and especially a jazz album—to let the musicians play a number they feel, not so much over-confident about, but one they are relaxed with. This is while you're working with the engineer on the basic balance and until you're ready for a serious 'take'. Then the chances are you'll be able to collect the right performance fairly quickly and everyone will be happy. Moreover, with this much under their belts, it usually happens that they'll then want to tackle the harder numbers and get them out of the way. So we started with *The Best Thing For You Would Be Me*, which is fast and involves some fairly agile phrasing, but otherwise is rhythmically quite straightforward. Once accepted, the guys were ready for *500 Miles High* and the taxing nature of John Pearce's ambitions.

Chick Corea's composition has a very mysterious, almost futuristic atmosphere through its quieter passages, combined with great technical dexterity when there are abrupt switches of tempo for its second theme and improvised parts. The mysterious element would be enhanced later by a judicious use of echo, but the initial tracks required the utmost togetherness between Ray and John during these slow sections which are nearly all rubato. Ray needed to watch John's fingers moving at certain points. It was a musical knife-edge in fact, although fortunately, in the end, I believe it comes off outstandingly well. He was naturally playing flute here; however, for the up-tempo second theme, and then for his solo, he switches to piccolo.

But the most difficult part of all was yet to come, because after the piccolo and piano solos John had then painstakingly transcribed Chick Corea's original freely improvised solo for the flute and piano to play in unison—again at a lightning tempo. For anyone who knows the fullness and intricacy of a Corea piano solo I don't need to stress that this required much determination on John's part as well as much playing expertise. Still, they did it and the duet choruses are now a vital part of the track.

And so everything was developing from initial hopes towards overall reality. I should explain that all of the featured solos were put down over Allan's and Dave Green's rhythmic patterns *in* the studio. The overdubs (Ray's) are important as supports and/or colouring but peripheral to the main group feeling and, when in tempo, the beat.

Two of the overdubs require special mention though. Behind the alto-flute solo which is the central feature on *Angel Eyes* there is a very delicate addition to the mood made by Ray using three clarinets. While on *Bud Powell* both the introduction and coda are enlivened by his creating a big band section sound of five saxophones. The idea for this had occurred to him because Corea's theme has overtly be-bop phrasing and therefore lends itself to the kind of saxophone style Woody Herman's arrangers began to feature from the mid-1940s onwards.

'But you haven't got a baritone!' I said to my artist while we were discussing this. 'Actually I have,' he replied—completely demolishing any potential objection. 'It once belonged to Phil Goody. I've had it tucked away for years.' Well, nothing ventured, I thought—and so it came to pass. Ray gradually built up the whole saxophone section over five separate tracks: lead alto, second alto, the two tenors and baritone— which was then spread out across the entire stereo spectrum. It gives the opening and closing of *Bud Powell* an additional (and appropriate) impact, I find, out of which the subsequent flute solo then sails forth to explore the melody line and chords.

It also made for a tricky internal balance later, but who cares? If everyone has done their job well, then the listener only hears the satisfactory result. Which is as it should be. When a record collector pays out real money he shouldn't be made a shoulder to cry on because of any problems which went before this. When I read about certain 'pop' stars taking ninety hours in the studio to make their next single—and in addition seeming proud of it—then, to quote Henry Miller 'I want to reach for my revolver.' Pride in self-indulgence is not the overture to a creditable career . . .

The minutiae of a multi-track remix is the stuff of another piece of writing. I've merely concerned myself thus far with one man's approach towards jazz record production and some specific examples of what can, and often does, occur.

1984

CHAPTER THIRTY-FOUR

JOHNNY O'NEAL

Every once in a while, in every art form, there arrives on the scene a great natural primitive whose originality and talent then appear all the more startling because of the clear absence of a formal background—or, in a few cases, of even the most basic lessons. In painting, for instance, one has the well-known example of Le Douanier Rousseau: the French Customs Officer who waited to retire on his modest pension before creating the exotic jungle oils which so impressed the young Picasso and Braque. Or perhaps still more so Paul Gauguin: a stockbroker and Sunday afternoon amateur until the age of thirty-six, when suddenly he threw up everything to go to the South Seas, living in dire straits but painting undoubted masterpieces.

Jazz music, on account of its need for improvisation and individuality in style has been comparatively rich in great primitives. Louis Armstrong couldn't afford lessons and went on to become the first soloist of genius jazz had ever known. Meanwhile Art Tatum was prevented by blindness from having much in the way of academic training. Nevertheless what lay inside him, musically and towards technique, caused him to be much admired by Rachmaninov as well as Fats Waller. And he is still the most admired jazz pianist today, years after his death and by every other keyboard player of importance.

However—as jazz has developed and in certain ways become more sophisticated, so more emphasis has come to be placed upon set studies and the campus life. Nothing wrong with this. A jazz player must have the ability within him; and if he decides then to study formally as well, or comes up through the college system—well, fine.

Even so, the occasional great natural primitive can still make out, and one such is Johnny O'Neal. I now learn, for instance, that he had only six months of paid-up lessons; but this doesn't prevent me thinking he is one of the most exciting young piano soloists I've heard since the vintage years which all at once, or so it seems, gave us Bill Evans, McCoy Tyner, Keith Jarrett and then Herbie Hancock and Chick Corea.

I encountered him to begin with at the Nice Jazz Festival of '82. But although clearly impressed by what I heard on the staged sets he was locked into the 'Hard Bop' formula of Art Blakey's Messengers and, therefore, his solos tended to come in short bursts. The real revelation to me concerning his talents occurred one afternoon at Valentino's, a wine bar along the Promenade Des Anglais where musicians like to go

236

and jam. John played for just a few of us all afternoon, completely unaccompanied. And played with something like the effortless flow and freedom of ideas that Tatum used to display so easily. What impressed me even more though—he seemed to have the entire history of jazz there in his mind and his hands. He was still only in his twenties, but he had blues and barrelhouse and Jelly Roll Morton and Waller and then some of Tatum and Bud Powell and McCoy Tyner and Herbie Hancock—in fact, the whole lot on parade. Plus a seemingly inexhaustible memory for compositions and popular standards. I think each of us privileged to catch him that afternoon realised that here was one of those every-so-often players of genuine significance.

Anyway, in 1984, and after the release of his first, long-delayed solo LP on Concord, George Wein got him back for the Nice Festival and this time placed him in a wider variety of musical settings. Johnny sat in with Al Grey, Georgie Auld, 'Sweets' Edison, Oliver Jackson, Phil Wilson, Joe Newman, Buddy Tate, George Duvivier, Benny Carter, J. J. Johnson and Dizzy Gillespie. As well as playing a couple of late solo recitals and one duet programme with Judy Carmichael.

I started talking with him again, and it became less of a surprise that he has such a grasp and knowledge of earlier jazz piano. Because his father, also a John O'Neal, was a long-time blues pianist and singer who at one time played with the Erskine Hawkins band. 'But he wasn't getting that much out of music. Maybe ten or fifteen dollars for an all-night gig if he was lucky. Still, there was always some blues and jazz around the house. And from about eight, everything I heard I found I could memorise easily.

'I was born on October 10, 1956 in Detroit—and that's always stayed my town when I'm not touring. I began to tackle the piano seriously from the age of thirteen. First time I ever played in public was gospel-style at the local Baptist Church. But at home I liked to play blues and standard songs. I only did about six months of formal piano studies. And all those difficult chord changes and things—well, they came to me naturally. Before I joined Blakey, as an example, I merely played over some of his tapes and I knew right away how to play with his band!

'I became truly serious about jazz from about '76. Before that it would be more 'pop' jobs I'd get. I remember in 1974 in Birmingham, Alabama—a sax-player there, David Amoril, got me the spot in a local piano bar. I'd play the top 40 numbers in the pop charts and they paid me a hundred-and-fifty dollars a week and I lived at the YMCA. I felt really rich, and I was still only eighteen! So then they fired me—said my playing was encouraging too many blacks to come into the bar . . .'

He scuffled for a while. Until one day a crooner-type singer offered him two weeks as an accompanist in St. Louis at the Riverfront Inn. 'I stayed there one-and-a-half years. Until '76, when I told you about becoming really serious about jazz. It all began as a sort of comedy.

Late one Saturday evening I wandered into this joint where a group called the Kenny Gooch Quartet was playing and asked if I could sit in. Well, I got wiped out by the parts they shoved in front of me. I was booed off the stage. I cried. It was the worst night of my life. But at least I recognised there was a lot more to good jazz playing than I'd believed. If I wanted to improvise effectively and then invent my own ideas, I had to get to know these old-timers a lot better—Jelly Roll, Fats, the great Earl Hines. As well as listening carefully to the more modern players—Monk, Bud Powell, Al Haig, Red Garland with 'Trane, Wynton Kelly with Miles Davis and then McCoy Tyner with 'Trane. Until about 1980 I left Art Tatum alone though. I'd get confused by so much genius all in one man. So I studied him bit by bit—but cautiously.

'Back in Detroit both my parents and all the gospel people were surprised at how determined I'd become to make it as a professional musician. I was lucky to have such understanding parents. My father wasn't well-off, but he went out and bought me a really good piano. Then he said I'd have to master it properly—or eat it! And he paid for my six months or so of lessons: with Mr. Benny Jones at three dollars a time . . . he never asked me to do a paper-round or anything like that. But he was delighted when Mr. Jones reported back that I could absorb more than a half-hour's lesson in five minutes!'

Johnny disclosed too that he could adapt to almost any musical occasion, from a disco gig to a cowboy hop—but that his real ambitions now lay within modern jazz. And, I can confirm now also—via a powerful and rapidly developing style of his own. It's certainly distinctive, this O'Neal piano-style—both eclectic, rich with historical allusions and effects, but at the same time highly individual, in which individuality can come at you sometimes just like a shower of sparks. It's also an 'orchestral' piano-style, full and strong like Oscar Peterson's as distinct from the more delicate traceries of, say, Bill Evans. But always tremendously swinging. And when he hits hard, then it's as if one moment you're listening normally and then the next you're bouncing back off the wall . . .

I asked Johnny when the first professional breakthrough came. 'That was in '77 when I joined Benny Carew. You probably know about him in any case. He was a drummer, aged about sixty-five then, and his group sounded a little like the Nat Cole Trio used to do. He played at the Hilton Inn, Kalamazoo and other places in upstate Michigan: billed as Benny Carew And His Fabulous Two'. He taught me so much. I stayed with him for a year and he became another musical father. He taught me the importance of good melodies. Tunes like *Fools Rush In*. I had to combat a variety of bad or indifferent pianos, but we always had great melodies! Buddy also showed me when to add and substract musically. He made me listen to Hank Jones on how to accompany singers. It got better and better with him. In the end I was concentrating on melodies as much as Benny was. And he was a really swinging drummer to have behind one. He reminded me a lot of Ed Thigpen. Just played good time, no solos. And if I did anything wrong, so he'd stop and help me put it right.

'I think my love of singers grew up through being with Benny Carew. I'd begin to pick up the lyrics as well, and realise how much they help determine the feeling of a song.'

And then? 'In 1978 I'd go into Chicago quite a bit. Or Toledo. To a joint where Art Tatum had once played. That was where I got to play on his piano, and I met an old schoolfriend of his, Harry Gregory. Harry thought I was good; so he'd fill me in on some of the famous and lesser-known Tatum stories. I landed a job in Toledo. It was a straight commercial job with a group led by Clifford Murphy, the bassist. But then one week I read in a jazz magazine that the great Ray Brown was going to be playing in Chicago with Ernestine Anderson. It was only thirty miles away. I knew I had to go over and hear them there. Oh, man, THAT NIGHT! I was so nervous that by the time I asked Ray if I could sit in with his group, well, he was starting to pack up. So I decided to ruin my chances and run through a couple of solos anyway. Whereupon the amazing Mr. Brown decided to unpack and play alongside with me. Yes, Ray Brown!

'And at the end he was even more amazing. He said: *How'd you feel about making a record with me: but under your own name—and then go on tour with Milt Jackson?* I couldn't believe I was hearing right. But that's Ray Brown for you. If he says he's gonna do something, he will.

'The record was with Carl Jefferson for Concord. I believe you now have it, Ray. Ray (Brown) played bass with me and we had Frank Severino on drums. Great tunes too: *It Could Happen To You, They Say It's Wonderful, If I Should Lose You, Sometimes I'm Happy, Just The Way You Are.* Ray Brown contributed *Devastation Blues* and I wrote *Joan's Gospel Blues.* Carl headlined the LP 'Coming Out'. But that was in October, '79—and he didn't put it out for nearly six years! It was only when I played the Concord Festival with Art Blakey and got a standing ovation that he decided to issue it.

'Anyway, also Ray Brown put me at Milt Jackson, and I joined him in Milwaukee. I was scared again, naturally, but we hit it off as human beings and, of course, it was top exposure. We played all the major clubs. Sam Jones was on bass part of the time. In Boston we backed Lena Horne. Altogether I stayed with Milt for two years and I'd been promised a European tour. But then the MJQ was reunited and I had to go back to freelancing.

'Happily, it was in worthwhile clubs though. I especially enjoyed 'E.J.'s' in Atlanta. And the last time there, it was for three months—with great guests passing through, like 'Jaws', Milt, Urbie Green, Scott

Hamilton, 'Sweets', Nat Adderley. Then in '81 Clark Terry was booked. I told him that next year, '82, I wanted to try my luck in New York City. He gave me his telephone number.

'So when I got there I did give him a bell and asked if he knew of any piano gigs going. He said: yes, he needed me that night for his own group at The Blue Note. And there I was! Then on Saturday night Art Blakey drops by. Suddenly, right in the middle of one of my solos this great big hand grabs me by the shoulder. It's Blakey, and in that gruff voice of his he says: *I want you in my band. Next week, okay?* He really scared me, you know? But sure enough, next week I was with the Jazz Messengers in Washington. Which is how that Summer I was at the Nice Jazz Festival when we first met . . .'

Also that summer Johnny recorded with the Messengers. In Holland for the Timeless label, and Art included one of his themes, *Tropical Breeze.* It was Ray Brown again who had pushed his getting the job with Blakey. He told Art: 'In ten years he'll get as big as Peterson!'

So, Art Blakey proved to be the best kind of leader one can possibly have. 'Musically, it's like he's throwing you out into the middle of the ocean without a liferaft! The group has its style and the soloists have theirs. He lets you be what you're best at. But he certainly knows how to pick the right men for his particular group. And he really studies and watches his guys. He encouraged me to write. One gig in Washington and already he'd agreed to record *Tropical Breeze.*

'Now, thanks to Art and other good friends like Ray Brown, at long last I'm getting the kind of work I like to do. I'm working on a new solo LP for George Wein. I think it's planned to be called 'Reflections Of Youth'. And I even get to do a little singing on it!'

It should be an album well worth waiting for; because of Mr. O'Neal's individual pianistic abilities there can be no possible doubts.

Coda: He never did get around to telling me where his surname came from!

1985

CHAPTER THIRTY-FIVE

RICHARD DAVIS

1. THE EARLY YEARS

I have a fascination for numerals; Arabic, Roman, the binary code *et al*. And for none more than the number seven. Especially when it appears on the printed page as 7. One can't be sure whether it originated with the Old Norse *sjau* or the Sanskrit *saptá,* but whenever I see it reproduced as 7 it strikes me as looking like an old Camargue fisherman bent over with rheumatism. *Or* the way a master bass-player surrounds his instrument. So let me use this numeral as an excuse to list my most-favoured jazz bassists. Not in any sense to detract from many other fine players (especially the Basie ones, Walter Page and Eddie Jones, or the veteran Milt Hinton). But my overall 7 would still have to be, in chronological order: Wellman Braud, Jimmy Blanton, Ray Brown, Charles Mingus, Scott LaFaro, Ron Carter and finally, Richard Davis.

Wellman Braud, the man from New Orleans, took his big, broad tone and sure fingering into the Duke Ellington band of the late 1920s and gave that group its first swinging rhythm section. Then, again with Ellington, at the end of the 1930s and over a few short years came the great Blanton, who revolutionised the jazz bass and turned it into a real solo vehicle. With the advent of be-bop Ray Brown took over the story. A very gifted technician, he refined and matured modern jazz bass-playing as the contemporary of Mingus who was simultaneously pushing the instrument into new areas of emotive fire and aggressive composition. In turn Scott LaFaro introduced a further element of interior intellectualism to the bass, most notably during his period of duets with Bill Evans, whose keyboard artistry was equally rich with harmonic qualities. But LaFaro died young, done over in a car-crash just days after making his finest records with Evans, the rightly valued Village Vanguard sets of 1961.

Which brings me now to Carter and Davis; the two latest master bassists in my personal chain. I make no claims for the abilities of one over the other. But they have developed in very different directions; and in these directions both men have proved considerable. One thing they do have in common is that both became very important to Eric Dolphy. Even here though their work was noticeably different.

Since his period with Dolphy (1960-1), and then Miles Davis (the mid-'60s), Ron Carter has moved into other fields of research. Into fusion music, eletrification and sometimes using a piccolo-bass. He is also his own record producer and has worked with 'cellos. He remains a magnificent straight swinger (e.g. his participation in V.S.O.P. with Herbie Hancock and Freddie Hubbard). But there is a plurality in his approach, as in his experimentation.

In contrast, Richard Davis, my subject from this point on, has brought certain classic qualities both backwards and forwards into modern jazz. I do not use the word 'classic' lightly. For he has the richest symphonic training and practical background of any jazz bassist so far. And he has brought these same qualities into his improvised music-making. Apart from a natural talent and the necessary schooling, his classical credentials are daunting. Not only work with the New York Philharmonic and at least eight other symphony orchestras. But under the batons of almost all of the big name conductors: Igor Stravinsky, Tauno Hannaikainen, Leopold Stokowski, Leonard Berstein, George Szell and Pierre Boulez.

As a result, the origins of several characteristics within his playing become obvious. The pure tone, rounded when required, but otherwise boldly flexible. Likewise the exceptionally clean fingering. And also a great skill when using a bow. But one feature of his playing is decidedly non-classical, namely, his actual stance. When I first saw him 'live' (in the 1970s, at Ronnie Scott's, with the Thad Jones, Mel lewis band), he had his leg thrust unusually far foward, with the bass laid back along it—and consequently well back over his body; so that at times his fingers worked upon it as if over a guitar. It reminded me somewhat of Paul Tortelier's special spike for the 'cello: again allowing him to hold the instrument well back, almost into himself. Since then though I have seen Richard alter his stance to suit the occasion . . .

However, to bring such classical qualities into jazz does not make a jazz master. For in themselves these are still matters of technique, and technique alone, albeit superb, is not enough for the alternative music. The reason why Richard Davis makes the conversion work is by an amazingly emotional attitude to jazz combined with a truly vivid imagination. As regards the former, when he has the feeling for a piece or a group, and the force wells up from within him, then I can think of no other bass-player of recent years who is more driving (the frequently broken rhythms and lightning tempo switches notwithstanding). Nor have I heard one more moving playing a ballad. Meanwhile his imagination is the twinned cylinder. I can only describe it as sheer inventiveness. With never a *cliché*; as full of surprises as Sarah Vaughan's singing; and a breadth of improvisation which not only allows him to turn lines of solo or accompaniment into tapestries, but also to jump the confines of style and still be unmistakably Richard Davis. He can play Mainstream, he can play the Be-bop Revolution, he can play straight, free, fusion, all the labels—and then back Barbra Steisand. *The only thing he can't do on bass is ever be taken for granted.*

Richard Davis was born an Aries on April 15, 1930 in Chicago, Illinois. And from an early age he grew towards manhood with, unswervingly, two great passions. One clearly was for music. The other had to do with horses. As regards the latter, he is a fine rider and has showed in many Dressage and Jumper Hunter competitions. But it didn't just end with riding. It was everything connected with horses. So that by 1977, when he left West 87th in Manhattan, NY to become a professor at Wisconsin, with its wide open spaces, his over-whelming ambition was to breed a thoroughbred. When I met up with him at the Nice *Grande Parade Du Jazz* in 1984 (he was there with J. J. Johnson) the dream was about to be realised. The mare he owned was with foal. However, he has not gone on to horse-trade or to enter the racing business. 'One profession is enough,' he says.

To return to music though. At his grade school (Francis E. Willard) and high (Jean Baptist Point Dusable) he didn't experiment with other instruments before going towards the bass.

But he also learned quickly to read music and study its theory. By which time his course in life was set. He moved on to, in turn, the music departments of Vandercook College, De Paul University, Roosevelt University, the City College of Chicago and finally, the Manhattan School of Music. (Ron Carter, 7 years his junior, earned an MM degree at the Manhattan School in 1961. Davis, because other events intervened, left just 6 hours short of his own MM.)

But perhaps his most important bass training was happening outside these distinguished academies. His Director of Music at Jean Baptist, Walter H. Dyett, was a teacher of many instruments, who recognised Richard's talent and subsequently gave him much advice and encouragement. Which led on to his own studying privately for 10 years with no less than Rudolf Fahsbender, the world-famous contra bassist with the Chicago Symphony Orchestra. And to a further period of studies in New York under David Walter, contra bass with the New York City Ballet.

Also too he had been listening to jazz. The first 'key' influences here were Duke Ellington and his band. Because by the later 1940s, though still in his 'teens, he had caught up with the Ellington records featuring Jimmy Blanton. Especially the Ellington/Blanton piano-bass duets, *Pitter Panther Patter, Mr J.B. Blues* and so on. Plus *Jack The Bear* with the full Ellington band. Suddenly a whole new area of bass potential was opened up before him. (In this writer's opinion Richard's bass duets with Eric Dolphy have been the finest with another jazz instrument since the Ellington/Blanton's. While what I heard him do underneath the Thad Jones, Mel Lewis ensemble was a further revelation . . .) At the same time he was also digesting what had and was still happening with the Be-bop Revolution. What had been opened up by Dizzy, Parker and in particular the reachings and experimental freedoms suggested by Thelonious Monk.

Another important factor in his development was escaping the ghetto situation. His immediate family were middle-class. His father had a restaurant business (which for a period in the 1950s Richard helped manage). His education was never in jeopardy. He had a precocious talent which was soon spotted. He made many public appearances with the Yough Orchestra of Greater Chicago (1946-48) and then the Chicago Civic Orchestra and the Sinfoniettas of both De Paul and Roosevelt Universities from approximately 1948 until 1954. At the same time playing with a local dance band led by Eddie King, but under the aegis of his bass teacher Walter H. Dyett. Another bass-player he had heard by this date and come to admire was Oscar Pettiford.

But his real spillover into jazz professionally occurred from 1953 when, while still only twenty-three, he became involved with one Fritz Jones, better known to us as Ahmad Jamal. Jamal, originally from Pittsburgh, had had a combo called the Three Strings at the Blue Note in Chicago before in 1952 turning itself into the Ahmad Jamal Trio and going on to play at The Embers in New York, the sophisticated nightclub for so long dominated by pianist Joe Bushkin. Jamal achieved some national prominence from this (' . . . he is unbelievably subtle': John Hammond), but eventually elected to go back to his home base in Chicago. Richard joined him in 1953 and stayed with the Trio for a year, playing most of the leading Chicago clubs.

But his own turn for national prominence began in 1954 when he became the other half of the Don Shirley Duo. (It was also, incidentally, the first time he appeared on my own listening horizons. I'd just started work on the staff of Decca Records and from early 1955 we issued their Cadence LPs.) Don Shirley was another amazing phenomenon of a musician. Born at Kingston, Jamaica in 1927 into a learned family of doctors and musicians, he was invited (at age 9!) to study under the famed Mittolovski at Leningrad Conservatoire. He then progressed, not only to develop a prodigious piano technique, but also to gain a BA, MA and Ph.D in psychology at Harvard, as well as a degree in Liturgical Art at Catholic University. Meanwhile, into the 1950s, he was being encouraged by his pianistic admirers (including George Shearing, Duke Ellington and Nat 'King' Cole) to enter more fully into the jazz world. Which led to the formation of his Duo with Davis. For in order to complement his talents he needed a bass-player of quite extraordinary ability. I'll never forget the first impact those Cadence LPs made on me. It occurs only once every few years in jazz, but this was decidedly one of the occasions. Their playing wasn't just advanced technically; it had a genuine emotional excitement as well.

But forget for a moment my outsider's impressions. Because the most distinguished personage to be impressed by them was Igor Stravinsky himself. After listening to them with rapt attention he was heard to murmur, 'They have the virtuosity of Gods!' Stravinsky was soon to embark upon the conducting of a new complete cycle of his works for CBS—and into the '60s Davis was now booked into the project, in itself a considerable achievement because black musicians, no matter how good, were only just beginning to gain places in such musical scenarios. But Stravinsky was a big and powerful-enough name to state his own terms.

Richard remained with Shirley until near the end of 1956. By which time he was widely known and much in demand. He played on a TV show with Benny Goodman. And then undertook a tour of Europe as part of the rhythm section backing Sarah Vaughan. His versatility seemed to know no bounds (he would later record, for instance, and most satisfactorily, within a Dixieland set-up led by cornetist/trumpeter Bobby Hackett). Or as pianist, composer, the Haitian Andrew Hill, who would later record with him for Blue Note, put it: 'He (Richard) . . . can do anything you demand of him. He works with a lot of technique but his technique doesn't overpower the imagination.' He concludes, 'he is for me simply the greatest bass-player in existence.' In preparing an entry on Richard for the 'Encyclopedia Of Jazz', writer Ira Gitler put it another way. 'Although he has departed from the tradition of four-beat accompaniment, Davis places more emphasis on rhythmic implication, a strong tone and blues emotion than do many modern bassists.'

He now entered into a bewildering range of musical activities. But in 1961 came the next crucial stage in his jazz career. One night going home on the subway from a gig, he was approached by a young man of slender build and gentle expression with a goatee beard. Upon confirming Richard's name, he introduced himself. It was Eric Dolphy.

Richard has helped me considerably with my book 'The Importance Of Being Eric Dolphy'. And there can be no disguising his still intense feelings on the subject. 'Eric was *pure*,' he stresses. 'I . . . grew to love him as a friend as well as respecting and admiring his musicianship. He . . . was the most angelic individual I have ever met. To be in his presence, socially and musically, was indeed a benefit to anyone fortunate enough to know him.'

By the end of that fateful subway journey he had agreed to become a part of the then in-the-process-of-formation Eric Dolphy, Booker Little Quintet.

2. THE MIDDLE YEARS

As a sub-title 'The Middle Years' suggests that there is a third portion still to be written. Which, of course, there is, but fortunately not yet. Because in his 'fifties Richard Davis is at the height of his technical and creative powers, very active and, above all, continuously enthusiastic about his music. I can confirm this after witnessing his 1984 appearances in Europe with J. J. Johnson, and from recordings received since then, the most recent being 'Eric Dolphy & Booker Little Remembered Live At Sweet Basil'. No living bass-player is more impressive and only one or two are his peers.

Following their chance but fortuitous subway meeting, Richard joined Eric Dolphy in time to play the justly-celebrated 'Eric Dolphy—Booker Little' week at New York's Five Spot Café in July, 1961—although six months too late to be on their Newport Rebels tracks of 1960, when Little's *Cliff Walk* was recorded, with Peck Morrison on bass.

The Five Spot week is now a quarter of a century away from us, and both of its co-leaders are dead. But everyone who attended has attested to its importance and great promise. And one night, July 16, was set aside for recording: resulting in three separate Prestige LPs (reissued as a boxed-set in 1974 with as its title, 'The Great Concert Of Eric Dolphy').

Prior to Dolphy the Five Spot already had its own share of legends. Situated in NY's East Village, it began to operate a jazz policy from 1956. It had housed the famed Thelonious Monk Quartet of 1957 with John Coltrane, and booked the East Coast debut of Ornette Coleman (1959). As well as featuring such earlier giants as Lester Young and Coleman Hawkins (the latter having recorded in the club with Randy Weston as his pianist). But all who heard the Dolphy—Little Quintet there agree it was, in jazz parlance, 'somethin' else'. And most nights there were as many musicians as fans and casual drinkers in the audience.

Multi-instrumentalist Dolphy had by this time come into his full magnetic inheritance as a soloist. While in Booker Little, a trumpeter aged only twenty-three, he had found a most gifted frontline partner. Little, from Memphis, Tennessee, began to form a reputation in 1958 when he played with Max Roach. He then took part in Eric Dolphy's 'Far Cry' sessions of 1960 and on Coltrane's 'Africa/Brass' LP of the following year, recorded only weeks before the Five Spot stint. Originally a graduate of the Dizzy, Navarro, Clifford Brown school of jazz trumpet, with a 'hot', stinging tone and crackling ideas, he was, in the months prior to his death, sharing in Dolphy's probes and reaching towards something new. He *Cliff Walk* with the Newport Rebels is a remarkable example of how to play in *legato* style against an otherwise blistering up-tempo. Again, as he told Robert Levin of *Metronome,* 'I can't think in the terms of wrong notes—in fact I don't hear any notes as being wrong. It's a matter of knowing how to integrate the notes and how to resolve them. Often more emotion can be expressed by the notes that are played flat.'

The Quintet at the Five Spot was completed by Mal Waldron, piano, and Eddie Blackwell, drums. Richard Davis' role in the group was never to be straightforward. He had to generate a maximum, but variegated swing while allowing drummer Blackwell his own particular freedoms; at the same time underpinning the two frontline players' totally unpremeditated phrasings and sound departures, and finally integrating what amounted to an ongoing bass adventure with their twisting and turning lines. So superbly does he succeed in all three of these departments that there are times when it becomes hard to recognise this as improvised music, with only skeletal themes and roots.

Being 'live' and with such individual forces present, the takes are, and are to be expected, long ones: in matrix order *Status Seeking, God Bless The Child* (an unaccompanied Dolphy bass-clarinet solo), *Aggression, Like Someone In Love, Fire Waltz, Bee Vamp, The Prophet, Number Eight (Potsa Lotsa)* and *Booker's Waltz*. But they have a marvellous flow, as if the group had been cooking together for many months and not just a matter of weeks, or in Richard's case, days.

During the next month (August, '61) Dolphy and Little cut a number of titles for Impulse under Max Roach's leadership, but the bass-player for these was a different Davis, Art. And Little's own brief musical race was now almost run. He died that same Autumn of uraemia.

Richard Davis' friendship and working involvement with Dolphy continued into 1964, the year of Eric's death, and concluding with the 'Out To Lunch' LP (Blue Note), probably *the* new jazz masterpiece album of that year, possibly even of its decade. In between their partnership took in recordings with John Lewis (*Tillamook Two, Another Encounter*), the enormous Orchestra U.S.A. conducted by Gunther Schuller, most of 'The Individualism Of Gil Evans' LP and the Sextet of Orchestra U.S.A. (Nick Travis, Mike Zwerin, Dolphy, John Lewis, Richard and Connie Kay) playing *Alabama Song, Havana Song* and *As You Make Your Bed*. Plus a number of tracks made in 1963 again under Eric's name. Several of these (for Douglas International) include Woody Shaw, trumpet, Clifford Jordan, tenor-saxophone and Bobby Hutcherson, vibes: *Burning Spear, Music Matador,* Fats Waller's *Jitterbug Waltz* and the much-praised *Iron Man*. But for me the real gems for these sessions are the three titles cut by just Dolphy and Davis in tandem. Not since the original revolutionary Duke Ellington/Jimmy Blanton duets have I heard the jazz bass used so imaginatively with another single instrument. They play *Alone Together* (which was Richard's suggestion), *Come Sunday* from Ellington's 'Black, Brown And Beige' and Jaki Byard's 'Ode To Charlie Parker'. But 'play' is altogether too tame a word for what ensues. It's like listening to one mind playing counterpoint with itself. *Alone Together* is so uncannily integrated that it could be Dolphy, given the technical ability, overdubbing the bass part, or Richard, again given the technical ability, picking up and overdubbing the clarinet. But *no!*: that's too pat an explanation as well. It's the product of two absolute jazz masters striking sparks off one another, being excited by the fire following on and as a result raising their individual inventiveness to dizzying heights, albeit with much musical gentleness as their starting point.

The 'Out To Lunch' LP of February, 1964 was Eric Dolphy's greatest single studio recording. All of the composing was his, he was at the summit of his known technical powers and within the context of his various solos, on all three of his main instruments, he gives us some very clear guidelines of where his personal, improvisational revolution was heading. The musicians with him for this occasion where Freddie Hubbard, trumpet, Bobby Hutcherson, vibes, Richard Davis and Tony Williams on drums. I've written at length about the album in my book, 'The Importance Of Being Eric Dolphy'; and most of what I have written need not concern us here. But one of its significant features which does involve Richard Davis was Dolphy's conscious decision to include vibes and not use a piano. For this immediately opened up the rhythm section to Richard in a whole new direction. He no longer had to weave in and around the piano's complementary chords, but could distribute his lines as a central bridge between the frontline instruments and Williams' freestyle drumming. Such is the advanced pattern of his thinking that in many passages he appears to be running lines which act as parallel duets between what Dolphy and Hubbard are blowing up-front and the creative bombast of Williams coming from behind. But figure through all he most certainly does. And yet the basic, elastic swing is never in doubt.

'Out To Lunch' was Eric Dolphy's final studio recording in the United States as a leader, but the following month (on March 21, 1964), just before he left for the terminal trip to Europe, both he and Richard Davis took part in another session for Blue Note: this time under the leadership of pianist Andrew Hill. Kenny Dorham was on trumpet, Joe Henderson, tenor and Tony Williams again on drums. The titles were *Refuge, New Monastery, Spectrum, Flight 19* and *Dedication*.

Richard, not yet knowing that his immensely productive teaming with Eric Dolphy was over, now entered a fullscale whirl of playing activity. Everyone, it seemed, had heard of his great flexibility and inventiveness, and demanded his services. Over the next decade his recording roster alone reads like a music industry's *Who's Who,* 'pop' as well as jazz. Barbra Streisand, Ben Sidran, Ben Webster, Bo Diddley, Booker Ervin, Bruce Springsteen, Carly Simon, Charles Lloyd, Chick Corea, Dave Brubeck, Earl Hines, Bobby Hackett, Edie Gormé, Frank Sinatra, James Taylor, Frank Foster, Jimmy Smith, Janis Ian, John Lennon, Milt Jackson, Paul Simon, Laura Nyro, Sammy Davis Jr, Stan Getz, J. J. Johnson, Van Morrison, Manhattan Transfer. Which is something like one third of the tally.

Meanwhile his travels took him to Europe, Russia, Brazil, Puerto Rica, Cuba, the West Indies, Japan, Hong Kong and Israel.

Then there were the TV accompaniments: to Antia O'Day, Streisand again, Bob Hope, Bobby Hackett again, Jack Benny, Lena Horne, Liza Minelli and Tony Bennett. Plus 500 or so TV jingles.

And not least there was the area of his own leadership. No less than twelve albums for Muse: 'Muses For Richard Davis', 'With Understanding', 'As One', 'Fancy Free', 'Song For Wounded Knee', 'Dealin'', 'Epistrophy & Now's The Time', 'Heavy Sounds' (co-leading with Elvin Jones), 'Divine Gemini' (with Walt Dickerson), 'Harvest', 'Way Out West' and a duo collection with Larry Levy. With a good sprinkling of Davis original compositions upon them, all published via his own company Sympatico: *Joshua, Step Across That Line, Pitter Pat, Half Pass, A Third Away, Agnewistic, Mr Nixon & General Thieu, The Rise & Fall Of Tricky Dick, Song For Wounded Knee, Watergate, ITT & Allende, What'd You Say?, Dealin', Julie Rag Doll, Blues For Now* and *Fuge'n*. A quick backward glance over this last listing will confirm that Richard is not exactly a Republican hawk!

I'm not going to try to fool anybody that I've heard all of this recorded output. But three albums in my personal collection do get themselves played fairly regularly. And not surprisingly for their bass content.

To take them in chronological order, 'Dialogue' is another Blue Note LP from 1965 which brought back together Freddie Hubbard, Bobby Hutcherson and Richard from the 'Out To Lunch' session, adding Sam Rivers (tenor-saxophone and flute), Andrew Hill (piano) and with Joe Chambers replacing Tony Williams on drums. Hutcherson is named as leader, but the composing is shared between Hill and Chambers, who opt for further freedoms beyond those of 'Lunch'. The standout track for Davis is Chambers' *Idle While*, where the bassist, apart from his own fine solo, has a hand in developing and shaping all the other players' lines.

Next (and still with Blue Note) I pick their 'Consummation' album of 1970 by the Thad Jones, Mel Lewis Orchestra. This is for me the best record this stellar rehearsal band ever made, and a 'key' element in its usccess is Thad's discovery (in his 'forties) of his possessing real abilities as a composer and arranger. He had dabbled (certainly no more) in scoring jazz towards the end of his featured years with Basie. But it was an urgent need to have a basic book and to fashion an identifiable ensemble style for his own group which finally unlocked the revolving doors of his imagination. Every written note on 'Consummation' is by him. Compositions with memorable lines, a pronounced pulsation (even during the slowest of ballads) and an ideally textured orchestration which circles and defends the soloists with an array of strongly fortified places. It places much responsibility on the bass—and all the tracks, *Dedication, It Only Happens Every Time, Tiptoe, A Child Is Born, Us* and so on, are as much a showcase for Richard Davis as for any other member of the group. He can be heard here at his most swinging; also how well he can adapt to a wide variety of soloists: Thad himself (who opens the album alone except for Richard's bowing), Marvin Stamm, Eddie

Daniels, Billy Harper and Roland Hanna. The central plank of *Tiptoe* is a scored duet for bass and ensemble.

Thirdly, and dating from 1974, there is the Phil Woods' 'Musique Du Bois' LP on Muse, with Woods on alto, Jaki Byard, piano, Richard Davis and Alan Dawson, drums. Again, I have written about this session elsewhere, in a profile of Woods himself. But I can never play it without marvelling at the quality of the bass-work—and the ease with which Richard can switch from a big band environment to the different vigours of a quartet.

Also dating from the 1970s there have been his increased activities as a teacher. As the winner of the *Down Beat* Critic's Poll on bass from 1967 to 1974, and the same magazine's Reader's Poll from '67 to '72, plus the ASCAP award for 9 years in a row, he was at the top of his particular instrument's tree as regards both national and international attention. Add his own classical background, his work for Stravinsky (*Pulcinella, The Soldier's Tale*) and Gunther Schuller (*Suite* from the opera 'The Invitation') and Milton Babbitt (*All Set*), and it's not surprising that the music institutions should have become interested in his work.

American universities have come in for a lot of stick over recent years. William Saroyan: 'Yeah, creative writing courses are very important for people who are never going to be able to write.' Cyril Connolly: 'Factories of thesis-grinding about poor James Joyce.' And, most recently, and perhaps even more damaging, Gore Vidal in *The Hacks Of Academe* chapter of his book 'Matters Of Fact And Of Fiction', the argument that complicated modern novels such as Professor John Barth's 'Giles Goat-Boy' are now being written for the purpose of being 'taught' on campus rather than actually read for their own merits or even (horror, horror!) plain *enjoyment.* Yes, much as I admire 'Ulysses', clearly 'Finnegans Wake' and such deliberately-difficult works as Nabokov's 'Pale Fire' and that ultimate cult-book, John Barth's 'The Sotweed Factor', have much to answer for. Happily, however, such erudite practices do not so far appear to have infected the music departments of American universities and colleges. I know of no other country in the world (not even the Soviet Union with its famous ballet and opera schools) where music is better founded or more varied and comprehensive.

Richard Davis has become a prominent member of this academic community of musical authorities. Often this has involved one-off clinics as a bass-teacher/lecturer. He has played in Paris, at the Pompidou Centre, at the University of Texas and many other institutions, as well as being elected to a wide variety of musical bodies and writing an instructional booklet, 'Writing On Chords'. But since 1977 his main positon has been as Professor Of Music at the School of Music, University of Wisconsin, Madison. Where he teaches bass, jazz history and combo improvisation. Plus passing on his love of Tchaikovsky (especially the *4th Symphony*), Beethoven (the *9th*), all of Richard Strauss and lots more. Between times, as well as riding, he does his best to be a good family man. With four offspring and two grandchildren: Robert Davis is 30, Richard Gregg Davis 23, Joshua 14 and Persia Lee just 6. His other consuming interest is in Nichiren Shoshu Buddhism. 'Its philosophy is for me the greatest and if practised correctly will change your life.'

However, the jazz part of him has not been neglected by these other demands. When I corresponded with him towards the end of 1987 he was already readying for another John Coltrane-inspired tour with McCoy Tyner and Elvin Jones. And into the 1980s he has been heard in the public company of saxist David Murray and drummer Joe Chambers ('A Special Thanksgiving Event' at Carlos 1 on New York's Sixth Avenue, December, '86), guitarist A. Spencer Barefield, pianist Ben Sidran (a fairly regular duo-teaming), flautist Barbara London (with trombonist Phil Wilson turning another duo into a trio) and Van Morrison. But a more significant group over the past couple of years has been his own intermittent one, Richard Davis & Friends: an all-star quintet which has a lot in common with his cherished Eric Dolphy/Booker Little memories. Its personnel has altered, depending on availability. To begin with he had Jon Faddis on trumpet, Ricky Ford, tenor-saxophone, Kenny Barron, piano and Freddie Waits on drums. More recent though the unit has moved even closer to the Dolphy/Little grouping with the inclusion of Mal Waldron, piano, and Eddie Blackwell, drums; plus the two young ex-Blakey Messengers' players, Terence Blanchard, trumpet and Donald Harrison, reeds. This quintet appeared most successfully at New York's fashionable Sweet Basil at the end of 1986, playing much of the Dolphy/Little book. And some of their performances have now appeared on record as 'Eric Dolphy & Booker Little Remembered' (Paddle Wheel, manufactured in Japan). The album features three long performances: based on Dolphy's *The Prophet* and *Booker's Waltz* and Little's *Aggression*. Further releases from the Sweet Basil digital tapings are promised.

'I've never seen interest in Eric Dolphy diminish,' Richard emphasises. 'To me interest has always been there. But then I'm into Dolphy's music. He had such a beautiful statement to make.'

Of his own continuing playing he says, 'You can learn your instrument through any form of art. Some people have never studied classical repertoire and can play better than someone who has—and vice versa. But the point is, you have to know your instrument. How to get around it.

'Teaching has me search. Every day I feel I learn about what I can do. It depends on the standards you set yourself.'

He doesn't necessarily reach for the spotlight. 'The frontline players are, relatively speaking, more appealing. You expect to hear the melody from them, not from the bass. But when you make a cake, you can't do it on one ingredient. It's like that in music. You have to have all the ingredients. You have to have the whole band. Hopefully, when you go to hear a band, you go to listen to the whole thing.'

Meanwhile as trumpeter Blanchard puts it, 'When you have someone like Richard Davis behind you it's like finding yourself in a lifeboat in the middle of the ocean.'

1988

CHAPTER THIRTY-SIX

JOHN COLTRANE

A Love Supreme

A script for BFBS: written & presented by RH.
Music: Impulse 8001—Side 1, Band 1 *Acknowledgement* (fade after 1 min. 30 secs).
Voice: A love supreme. From drugs and alcohol dependence to God. Such is my theme in this edition of 'Reflections'.

The late John Coltrane has been one of the greatest and most influential tenor-saxophone players in the history of the Afro-American music we call jazz. A giant of technique and, in musical terms, a dazzling, continually questing and probing mind. Also, because so much of his art was spontaneous and improvised, a composer in action. A player of natural talent who then added knowledge and so proceeded to creation and the Hall of Fame.

But this was all achieved intially against a background of years of human error and weakness. Until, that is, he moved from the traps and snares of a self-destructive addiction, to God. Or rather, not moved to, but rediscovered Him. For Coltrane had grown up in a household where God was treated with reverence and love. And it was only when life took him out into the harder realities of the modern world that he succumbed to its temptations.

First though, a brief note about his lifelines. He was born John William Coltrane in Hamlet, North Carolina on September 23, 1926. He died on July 17, 1967 in Huntington, Long Island. When still a small child he was exposed to the religious music of the South's African-American churches. Both his grandfathers were ministers of the African Methodist Episcopal Zion Church. These Baptists and Methodists were the first to accept large numbers of blacks into their churches, and because of the participatory nature of these two denominations it was in keeping with what the African called his ORISHAS.

Trane saw the movement between minister and congregation, and from this he saw the cycle of the breath of life. He also felt the power of the musical spiritual. Religion for him would always be an outgoing as well as an introspective thing. And, of course, as time went on he developed the abilities to make it outgoing. To make a gift of it, via his music, to others.

He gained his first instrument, a clarinet, at the age of twelve. From which the spell of jazz music was on him as well, never to lift. Creation, and the striving towards perfection became obsessive. Even to within weeks of his death. Throughout his public career he practised every day from nine in the morning until four in the afternoon. With just a short break then, if there was an evening performance. Often he would play variations on the same theme for two hours without pausing.

A major event occurred in 1939 with the death of his father, and his mother's moving to Philadelphia. From the black ghetto there came his professional launch, first on the Rhythm-and-Blues circuit with Earl Bostic's band. By the mid-1950s, playing with Miles Davis, he had become the most admired tenor-saxophone soloist in jazz. Which in turn led to the formation of his own group.

But life in the ghetto and on the road had taken its toll. Prejudice. Rejection. Struggle. By the mid-1950s he was both famous and heavily addicted. The critic Nat Hentoff recalls seeing him in Sheridan Square, in Greenwich Village, around this time. 'He looked awful. Raggedy, vacant. Junk, said a musician with me. He's been hooked a while. *But,* Hentoff added, *he's got a bottle of wine in his hand?* Yeah, that too, the musician said.

Then, suddenly, in 1957 John Coltrane stopped using both. He did it by himself, during a huge spiritual and musical ascent . . . he got himself clean and he stayed clean. Now, to me, that's real power.

Certain non-believers have claimed that he stopped because someone went up to him and told him he wasn't playing so well. Rubbish! He had what was for him the equivalent of a Pauline shock. Only it happened in New York City and not on the road to Damascus. Whereupon he switched from a materialistic high point to a spiritual high point.

As he himself put it, 'During the year 1957, I experienced, by the grace of God, a spiritual awakening which was to lead me to a richer, fuller, more productive life. At that time, in gratitude, I humbly asked to be given the means and privilege to make others happy through music. I feel this has been granted through His grace. ALL PRAISE TO GOD.'

His letter goes on, 'Thankfully, now and again through the unerring and merciful hand of God, I do perceive and have been duly re-informed of His Omnipotence, and of our need for and dependence on Him. At this time I would like to tell you that NO MATTER WHAT . . . IT IS WITH GOD. HE IS GRACIOUS AND MERCIFUL. HIS WAY IS IN LOVE, THROUGH WHICH WE ALL ARE. IT IS TRULY: A LOVE SUPREME.

When John died in 1967 it was from liver disease, a deadly throwback to his drugs and alcohol period. But this was after recording his marvellous suite called 'A Love Supreme'. As he describes it, 'This album is a humble offering to Him. An attempt to say THANK YOU GOD, through our work, even as we do in our hearts and with our tongues. May He help and strengthen all men in every good endeavour.'

To conclude, I want to play for you the beautiful *Psalm* which ends the suite. So, John Coltrane (tenor-saxophone), McCoy Tyner (piano), Jimmy Garrison (bass), Elvin Jones (drums): A Love Supreme.

Music: Impulse 8001—Side 2, final Band *Psalm* (fade after 2 mins. 05 secs).

1987

CODA

There is a story, it could be apocryphal, but if not then no doubt considerably polished up in the retelling, that during a lean year of his long career Jo Jones, the first great Count Basie drummer (or 'The Wind' as younger, fellow-drummer Don Lamond has called him), drove a New York bus. One night he was passing Birdland, and noticing from the billposters outside that one of his favourite groups was appearing there, promptly pulled his bus into the kerb and, forgetting all about his payload of passengers, went down into the club to listen . . .

False or true, I like this story. Not just because it amuses me, but because it fits with the total absorption all the great jazzmen have. Something I have found with very few of the classical musicians I've worked with. Absorption and dedication. For jazz is not just a music; for the majority of its exponents it becomes a way of life. And, at the same time, a life-force.

The Colonnade, Isle Of Wight, 1989

Introduction to Discography

The discography is laid out as follows, the LP title and/or artist as quoted in the text, followed by the record company and issue number. In some cases I have added a few selections of my own.

The record numbers are usually the original issue and any good specialist record dealer should be able to advise on the availability of any recording from the information supplied. In addition, many of the LP's are available on tape cassette and compact disc.

Tony Middleton, London, January 1989

Sidney Bechet:

The complete Sidney Bechet	Vol. 1/2 (1932–1941)	RCA NL89760 (2)
The complete Sidney Bechet	Vol. 3/4 (1941)	RCA NL89759 (2)
The complete Sidney Bechet	Vol. 5 (1941–1943)	RCA 89751 (2)
Mezzrow (Bechet Groups—King Jazz)	Vol. 1 Storyville	SLP 6004
	Vol. 2 Storyville	SLP 6005
	Vol. 3 Storyville	SLP 6006
	Vol. 4 Storyville	SLP 6007
	Vol. 5 Storyville	SLP 4115
Bechet—Spanier Big Four	Swaggie	S1392
The complete Blue Note recordings of Sidney Bechet	Mosaic	MRS110

Noble Sissle featuring Tommy Ladnier and Sidney Bechet
Classic Jazz Masters   CJM22

The complete Jelly Roll Morton	Vol. 7/8 (1930–1940)	RCA NL89748 (2)
Clarence Williams Blue Five	1923–1925	Rhapsody RHA 6031

Sidney Bechet avec Claude Luter et son orchestra
Vogue LP060/061

Art Hodes:

The complete Art Hodes Blue Note sessions	Mosaic 5-114
Art Hodes and his Hi-Fivers	Mercury MG20185
Albert Nicholas Quartet	Delmark DL207
Barney Bigard - Bucket's got a hole in it	Delmark DS211
Art Hodes - Someone to watch over me	Muse 5252
Art Hodes - Southside memories	Sackville 3032
The authentic Art Hodes with Doc Cheatham and Carrie Smith	Parkwood 106
Kenny Davern - Hot three	Jazzology J-167

Budd Johnson:

The Indispensable Earl Hines	Vol. 1/2	
	(1939–1940)	RCA NL89764 (2)
Rushing/Hines - Blues and things		Vouge 500076
Gil Evans - Out of the cool		Impulse AS4
Earl Hines live at the Village Vanguard		CBS 462401.1
Blues à la mode - Budd Johnson Quintet/Sextet		Affinity AFF169
(also features Charlie Shavers - see chapter 4)		
Ben Webster and associates		Verve MGV 8318
Hawkins, Webster, Eldridge		
The Old Dude and the Fundance Kid		Uptown UP27-19

Charlie Shavers:

The John Kirby Sextet	Vol. 1 (1939)	CBS 450167.1
The John Kirby Sextet	Vol. 2 (1939/1940)	CBS 450183.1
The John Kirby Sextet	Vol. 3. (1940/1941)	CBS 450184.1
Lionel Hampton All Stars -		
Stardust		Jasmine JASM 1044
Jam Session - Funky Blues		Verve 2-2508
Session at Riverside		Capitol T761
Charlie Shavers and his Orchestra		Capitol ST1883
Charlie Shavers (with strings)		Bethlehem BCP5002
Charlie Shavers live from Chicago (1962)		Spotlite SPJ154

Art Tatum:

Art Tatum - Pure Genius	Affinity AFF118
Art Tatum - The Complete Capitol Recordings	Affinity AFF190
Art Tatum - 20th Century Piano Genius	Emarcy 826129.1
The Art Tatum Solo Masterpieces	
(13 LP box set)	Pablo 2625703
The Tatum Group Masterpieces	
(8 LP box set)	Pablo 2625706

(the above Pablo sets also issued as single LP's)

Ben Webster:

The Indispensable Duke		
Ellington	Vols. 5/6 (1940)	RCA NL89750 (2)
The Indispensable Duke	Vols. 7/8	RCA NL89274 (2)
Ellington	(1940/41)	
The Indispensable Duke		
Ellington and Small Groups	Vols. 9/10	
	(1940/46)	RCA NL8958(2)
Art Tatum/Ben Webster		
Quartet	—	Pablo 2310737

(also included in The Tatum group masterpieces set)

Freddie Green:

Brother John Sellers—	VanguardVRS8005
Joe Newman − All I Wanna	
* do is swing*	RCA LPM1118
A Buck Clayton Jam Session	Columbia CL548
* (re-issued in Spain − 1988 − Fresh Sound Records FSR626)*	
Count Basie Recordings 1937-1984	
(Columbia, Decca, RCA, Verve, Roulette, Pablo)	
Jazz Giants '56	Verve MGV8146
Memories ad-lib − Basie/Williams	Roulette S/R52021

Arnett Cobb:

Lionel Hampton − Leapin' with Lionel	Affinity AFS1000
Arnett Cobb − The	
Complete Apollo Sessions	Vogue 500116
Arnett Cobb − Blow Arnett Blow	Prestige PR7151
Cobb, Tate, Hawkins − Very Saxy!	Prestige PR7167
Red Garland − Sizzlin'	Moodsville LP14
Arnett Cobb − Party time	Prestige PR7165
Arnett Cobb − Arnett is back	Progressive PRO7037
Illinois Jacquet with Milt Buckner	JRC 11433
Arnett Cobb live at Sandy's	Muse MR5236
Arnett Cobb Quartet	
* — with Milt Buckner*	Black and Blue 33052

George Gershwin:

Piano solos from "Tiptoes"	Monmouth
	Evergreen MES7037
Lady be good	World Records SH124
Early piano rolls (1918/20)/	
* Porgy and Bess rehearsals and more*	Mark 56 Records 667
The song is . . . Gershwin	ASV Living Era AJA5048
Royal Philharmonic "Gershwin Gold"	ASV Digital RPO5008
Lee Wiley sings songs of	
* Gershwin and Porter*	Audiophile AP1
Ella Fitzgerald Sings the George and	
* Ira Gershwin Songbook*	Verve 2615063 (5 LP's)

Mel Powell:

Benny Goodman	Vol. 2	CBS460829.1
(The Earl; Clarinet a la King)		
Benny Goodman	Vol. 3	CBS461100.1
(Clarinade; Darktown Strutters Ball; Mission to Moscow)		
Glenn Miller's Uptown Hall Gang		CBS63052
Glenn Miller's Uptown Hall Gang		CBS63130
Benny Goodman – The Small Groups		Swaggie S1364
Mel Powell Trio – Borderline		Vanguard VRS8501
Mel Powell Trio – Thiamagig		Vanguard VRS8502

Jimmy Blanton:

Duke Ellington and his Orchestra –
The Blanton/Webster Band (4 LP Box set)   RCA 5659-1-RB

Duke Ellington:

Record Companies and Recording Periods

RCA (France) 24 LP's – *The Works of Duke Ellington*

CBS (France) 14 double LP's – *The Complete Works of Duke Ellington*

Musicraft (mid forties)

Columbia/CBS (late forties to early sixties)

Capitol (1953/55)

Reprise (sixties – some reissued on Discovery)

Pablo (Seventies)

Also endless transcriptions, radio broadcasts and film soundtracks have been issued.

1956

Jazz Giants '56	Verve MGV8146
Concert by the sea	CBS451042
Dizzie Gillespie World Statesman	Verve MGV8174
Brilliant Corners	Riverside R226
Such sweet thunder	CBS84405

Gil Evans:

Out of the Cool	Impulse AS4
Porgy and Bess (with Miles Davis)	CBS32188
Gil Evans plays Jimi Hendrix	RCA CPLI-0677
Farewell (live at Sweet Basil 1986)	Electric Bird K28P6486

Dizzy Gillespie:

Dizzie Gillespie World Statesman		Verve MGV8174
Dizzie Gillespie	Vol. 1/2	
	(1946-1949)	RCA42408
Dizzie Gillespie reunion		
Big Band	(1968)	MPS15207

Clint Eastwood and Bird:

Bird — original sound-track recordings	CBS461002-1

Al Haig:

First sessions (Fats Navarro, Al Haig Trio)		Prestige PR2408
Dizzy Gillespie — In the beginning		Prestige PR24030
Dizzy Gillespie	Vol. 1/2	
	(1946-1949)	RCA PM42408
Al Haig meets the master Saxes—Vol. 1		Spotlite SPJ139
Al Haig meets the master Saxes—Vol. 2		Spotlite SPJ140
Al Haig meets the master Saxes—Vol. 3		Spotlite SPJ143
The Verve Years 1950-1951		Verve VE2-2512
Charlie Parker Quintet		Verve MGV8005
Stan Getz at Storyville—Vol. 1		Vouge 500079
Stan Getz at Storyville—Vol. 2		Vouge 500107
Phil Woods Quintet		Prestige LP7046
Invitation		Spotlite SPJ AH4
Special Brew		Spotlite SPJ LP8
Solitaire		Spotlite SPJ LP14
Stablemates		Spotlite SPJ LP11
Expressly Ellington		Spotlite SPJ LP20

Miles Davis:

Birth of the cool	Capitol CAPS1024
Miles Ahead	CBS 460606.1
Kind of blue	CBS 460603.1
In a silent way	CBS 450982.1
Bitches brew	CBS 460602.1

Buddy DeFranco:

Art Tatum – Buddy DeFranco	Pablo 2310736
On Tour – UK	HEP 2023

Sarah Vaughn:

Live at the London House	Mercury MG20383
Live at Ronnie Scott's	Pye N103
Crazy and mixed up	Pablo 2312137
Brazilian romance	CBS 460156.1
Passing Strangers	Mercury 6641868

Gerry Mulligan:

Holliday with Mulligan	DRG SL5191
Tango Nuevo	Atlantic ATL51068
2.00 am Paradise Café	Arista 206496

Roy Haynes:

Trombone by Three (Kai Winding)	Prestige LP7023
Sarah Vaughan Live at the London House	Mercury MG2038
The Amazing Bud Powell – Vol. 1	Blue Note BLP1503
The Amazing Bud Powell – Vol. 2	Blue Note BLP1504
Blues and the Abstract Truth	Impulse AS5
Eric Dolphy – Out There	New Jazz NJLP8252
Eric Dolphy/Booker Little – Far Cry	New Jazz NJLP8270
Out of the Afternoon	Impulse AS23
Hip Ensemble	Mainstream 313
Stan Getz – Focus	Verve MGV SG.8415
Tennessee Firebird	RCA LSP3719

Sonny Rollins:

Stan Tracey – Genesis	—	Steam SJ102
Tenor Madness	—	Prestige 7047
Dancing in the Dark	—	Milestone 9155 (1988)

Britt Woodman:

The Complete Duke Ellington 1947-1952	CBS 66607
Billy Strayhorn's All Stars (The Coronets)	Mercer LP1005
The Great Big Bands Vol. 1, Duke Ellington	Capitol T20808
Ellington '55	Capitol T521
Ellington Showcase	Capitol T679
Historically Speaking – The Duke	Bethlehem BCP60
Ellington at Newport	Columbia CL934
A Drum is a Woman	Columbia CL951
Such Sweet Thunder	Columbia CL1033
Newport 1958	Columbia CL1245
Charles Mingus – Mingus	Candid 9021
Jimmy Hamilton All Stars	Swingsville SVLP2022
Benny Carter Live and Well in Japan	Pablo 12308216
Britt Woodman in L.A.	Falcon FJP100

Louis Bellson:

Louis Bellson Big Band – The London Gig	Pablo 2130880

Wynton Kelly:

Dizzy Atmosphere	Speciality LP5001
Steve Lacy – Soprano Today	Prestige PR7125
Miles Davis Live at the Black Hawk, Vol. 1	Columbia CS8469
Miles Davis Live at the Black Hawk, Vol. 2	Columbia CS8470
Miles Davis at Carnegie Hall	Columbia CS8612
Hank Mobley – Soul Station	Blue Note BST84031
Wynton Kelly – Action	Riverside RLP12-254
Wynton Kelly – Kelly Blue	Riverside RLP12-298
Dizzy in Greece	Verve MV8174
Smokin' at the Half Note	Verve V68633

Verve

Books:

The Clef/Verve Labels by Michel Ruppli
Vol. 1 The Norman Granz Era   –   368 pages
Vol. 2 The MGM Era   –   894 pages

Published by Greenwood Press,
Hardback – set of two.

Bill Evans:

George Russell Jazz Workshop	RCA LPM 1372
Kind Of Blue	CBS 460603.1
Undercurrent	United Artists UAJS1500
Everybody Digs Bill Evans	Riverside RSLP1129
Sunday Night At The Village Vanguard	Riverside RSLP9371
Waltz For Debbie	Riverside RSLP 9399
Conversations With Myself	Verve VG-8526
The Tony Bennett Bill Evans Album	Fantasy F9489
The Paris Concert, Edition One	Electra E0164
The Paris Concert, Edition Two	Electra 960311.1

Phil Woods:

Dizzy Gillespie World Statesman	Verve MV8174
Dizzy In Greece	Verve MV8017
This Is How I Feel About Jazz	ABC Paramount ABC14
The Birth Of A Band	Mercury SP60129
Benny Bailey Big Brass	Candid CS9011
Monk At Town Hall	Riverside RSLP1138
Musique Du Bois	Muse MR5037
Phil Woods Little Big Band	Concord CJ361 (1988)

Claude Bolling:

Lionel Hampton Complete 1953 Paris Sessions	Vogue VJD532
Bolling Plays Ellington, Vol. 1	CBS FM42474
Bolling Plays Ellington, Vol. 2	CBS FM42476

Ornette Coleman:

Something Else	Contemporary S7551
Tomorrow Is The Question	Contemporary S7569
At Town Hall 1962	ESP 1006
The Music Of Ornette Coleman	RCA LPM2982
Skies Of America	Columbia KC31562
Virgin Beauty	Portrait PRT461193.1

Eddie Jones:

The Complete Basie Dance Sessions	Verve/Polydor 2632068
The Atomic Mr Basie	Roulette S/R52003
Basie — One More Time	Roulette S/R52024
Joe Newman And His Band	Vanguard VRS8007
Osie Johnson — Period	Reissue — Jazztone J1234
Jazz Studio 1	Decca DL8058
Kenny Clarke	Savoy MG12006
Hank Jones Quintet	Savoy MG12037

Gary Burton:

Getz/Gilberto — 2	Verve V6-8623
Tennessee Firebird	RCA LSP3719
Out Of The Woods	Capitol ST2273
Lofty Fake Anagram	RCA LSP3901
Alone At Last	Atlantic S1598
In The Public Interest	Polydor 2383252
Works	ECM 823267-1
Crystal Silence	ECM 1182/83

Gordon Beck:

Doctor Doolittle Loves Jazz	Major Minor SMLP8
Half A Sixpence	Major Minor SMLP22
Experiments With Pops	Major Minor SMLP21
Phil Woods And His European Rhythm Machine At The Frankfurt Jazz Festival	Atlantic 90531.1
Gyroscope	Morgan MJ1
Didier Lockwood — New World	MPS 68237
Phil Woods — Chromatic Banana	Affinity AFF84
The French Connection	OWL11
Helen Merrill and Gordon Beck — No Tears, No Goodbyes	OWL38
Helen Merrill Music Makers (with Grappelli, Lacey)	OWL44

Ray Swinfield:

Rain Curtain	Piccadilly N132
The Winged Cliff	Merlin MRF82401
Angel Eyes	Wave 23

Johnny O'Neal:

Coming Out	Concord CJ228
Jazz Messengers – Oh-By The Way	Timeless SJP165
Johnny O'Neal Live At Bakers	Parkwood 105

Richard Davis:

Don Shirley Duo	Cadence LP1001
Eric Dolphy/Booker Little At The Five Spot, Vol. 1	New Jazz NJLP8260
Eric Dolphy/Booker Little At The Five Spot, Vol. 2	Prestige PR7294
Eric Dolphy/Booker Little At The Five Spot, Vol. 3	Prestige PR7334
John Lewis Orchestra	Atlantic SD1425
Orchestra U.S.A.	Colpix 448
The Individualism Of Gil Evans	Verve V6-8555
Sextet Of Orchestra U.S.A.	RCA LSP3498
Eric Dolphy	Douglas International DLP6002/3
Out To Lunch	Blue Note BST84163
Andrew Hill	Blue Note BST84167
Dialogue	Blue Note BST 84198
Consummation	Blue Note BST84346
Musique du Bois	Muse MR5037

John Coltrane:

Music: Impulse 8001 – Side 2, Final Band
Psalm: (fade after 2 mins. 05 secs)

JOHN COLTRANE